Issues in World Politics

Issues in World Politics

Dr. Anand Prakash

RANDOM

RANDOM PUBLICATIONS

NEW DELHI (INDIA)

Issues in World Politics

ISBN 978-93-5111-655-4

Published in 2015 in India by

RANDOM PUBLICATIONS

4376-A/4B, Gali Murari Lal, Ansari Road
New Delhi-110 002
Phone : +9111-43580356, 011-23289044, 011-43142548
e-mail: sales@randompublications.com,
info@randompublications.com, randomexports@gmail.com

Reprinted 2022

Type Setting by : Friends Media, Delhi-110089
Digitally Printed at : Replika Press Pvt. Ltd.

Preface

Our world is united and fragmented. Common links and challenges bind the international community together, while political phenomena are increasingly driven by regional dynamics and by conflicting national perspectives on security, wealth and identity. Globalization is still on the move along with processes of regional integration and the proliferation of new states. Military power is still concentrated at the state level, but is also becoming available to non-state actors. Technologies and information spread globally, and are variously transformed into forces for cooperation and conflict.

The two-year taught Master (Laurea Magistralis) in World Politics and International Relations is designed to help you analyse the major issues arising out of these processes. Whether you are aiming at a career in national or international public services, in non-governmental organizations or in the private sector, you need a multidisciplinary approach to grasp the key issues. How are foreign policy and domestic policy related? Is regime change necessarily inconsistent with political stability? Under what conditions can power be tamed in contemporary international relations? To answer these questions, you need expertise in political science. Are contemporary international relations more or less conflict-driven than in the past? How, exactly, did the current international system arise? How did we get from Statecraft to "Globecraft"? To address contemporary challenges you need expertise in contemporary history. Is international law just a set of formal rules, or does it impact on the content of international relations? How are human rights promoted or enforced internationally? Are Mercosur and Nafta comparable to the European Union? To answer questions like these, you need regional and international expertise not only in politics but also in law.

Globalization of world politics, better known as Political Globalization works for the betterment of the existing political relationships among different nation-states across the globe. In fact, Globalization of world politics has an important role to play in maintaining sound and healthy relation among worldwide countries, to preserve international peace and harmony. The concept of Political Globalization leads to the creation of a world government which works for the normalization of the existing interactions among countries on political levels. This in a way helps in maintaining the political balance on international levels. Political Globalization also guarantees the rights rising out of Economic and Social Globalization. Political Globalization has indeed a vital role to play, as far as inter-state and inter-continental political relationships are concerned. It helps in making powerful and developed nations like the United States of America to consolidate its strengths and position on military and economic grounds. As far as the developing and weaker states are concerned, Political Globalization makes them subordinates to the American powers, either deliberately through mutual approvals and alliances, or forcefully through threats. In fact, the growing popularity of Political Globalization has given birth to some sort of imperialism in the past, which can be traced through an entire dynasty of forms.

Amidst recent developments in the field of world politics is 'terrorism'. In the name of suppressing terrorism power is polarising time and again and various power nexuses are emerging. Apparently, with the collapse of Soviet Union, world politics has become unipolar revolving around the U.S.A. Recent Iraq War has shown America's ambitions and nefarious designs to dominate the world proving itself the sole super power.

The World Health Organization (WHO) reports more than 14,400 confirmed or suspected cases of Ebola, mostly in the countries of Guinea, Liberia, and Sierra Leone, as of Nov. 11, 2014. More than 5,100 people have died in the largest Ebola outbreak ever recorded. A person infected with Ebola virus will typically develop a fever, headache, joint and muscle pain, a sore throat, and intense muscle weakness. These symptoms start suddenly, between two and 21 days after becoming infected.

Perspectives on World Politics have been essential reading for students of international relations. Its focus on three competing perspectives provides a clear and coherent organisation of the divergent conceptual tools used to study world politics.

I would like to thank my team for standing beside me throughout my career and writing this book. My special thanks go to "Random Publications" who have published the book.

– Dr. Anand Prakash

Contents

1

The Globalization of World Politics

DEMOCRATIC GLOBALIZATION

Democratic globalization is a social movement towards an institutional system of global democracy that would give world citizens a say in world organizations.This would, in their view, bypass nation-states, corporate oligopolies, ideological NGOs, cults and mafias. One of its most prolific proponents is the British political thinker David Held. In the last decade he published a dozen books regarding the spread of democracy from territorially defined nation states to a system of global governance that encapsulates the entire world.

These proponents state that democratic globalization's purpose is to:

- Expand globalization and make people closer and more united;
- Have it reach all fields of activity and knowledge, not only the governmental one, but also the economic, since the economic one is crucial to develop the well-being of world citizens; and
- Give world citizens democratic access and a say in those global activities.

Supporters of the democratic globalization movement draw a distinction between their movement and the one most popularly known as the 'anti-globalization' movement, claiming that their movement avoids ideological agenda about economics and social matters.

Democratic globalization supporters state that the choice of political orientations should be left to the world citizens, via their participation in world democratic institutions. Some proponents in the "anti-globalization movement".

Do not necessarily disagree with this position. For example, George Monbiot, normally associated with the anti-globalization movement (who prefers the term Global Justice Movement) in his work *Age of Consent* has proposed similar democratic reforms of most major global institutions, suggesting direct democratic elections of such bodies, and suggests a form of "world government."

BACKGROUND

Democratic globalization supports the extension of political democratization to economic and financial globalization. It is based upon an idea that free international transactions benefit the global society as a whole. They believe in financially open economies, where the government and central bank must be transparent in order to retain the confidence of the markets, since transparency spells doom for autocratic regimes. They promote democracy that makes leaders more accountable to the citizenry through the removal of restrictions on such transactions.

SOCIAL MOVEMENTS

The democratic globalization movement started to get public attention when New York Times reported its demonstration to contest a World Trade Organization (WTO) in Seattle, Washington, November 1999. This gathering was to criticize unfair trade and undemocratic globalization of the WTO, World Bank, World Economic Forum (WEF), the International Monetary Fund. Its primary tactics were public rallies, street theater and civil disobedience.

Democratic globalization, proponents claim, would be reached by creating democratic global institutions and changing international organizations (which are currentlyintergovernmental institutions controlled by the nation-states), into global ones controlled by world citizens. The movement suggests to do it gradually by building a limited number of democratic global institutions in charge of a few crucial fields of common interest. Its long term goal is that these institutions federate later into a full-fledged democratic world government.

DEMOCRATIC MUNDIALIZATION

Mundialization is the name of one of the movements aiming at democratic globalization.

Democratic globalization is the concept of an institutional system of global democracy that would give world citizens a say in world organizations. This would, in the view of its proponents, bypass nation-states, corporate entities, Non-governmental organizations (NGOs), etc. For some, democratic mundialization is a variant of democratic globalization stressing the need for the direct election of world leaders and members of global institutions by citizens worldwide. For others, it is just another name for democratic globalization.

PURPOSE

Proponents state that democratic globalization's purpose is to:

- Expand mundialization in a different way from economic globalization and "make people closer, more united and protected"; (because of a variety of opinions and proposals it is still unclear what this would mean in practice and how it could be realized).

- Have it reach all fields of activity and knowledge, not only the economic one, even if that one is crucial to develop the well-being of world citizens. This implies some intervention not only in the economic and political life of the individual but also in their access to culture and education.
- Give world citizens democratic access (*e.g.*, presidential voting for United Nations Secretary-General by citizens and direct election of members of a United Nations Parliamentary Assembly) and a say in those global activities.

Global democracy

Thus, it supports the International Campaign for the Establishment of a United Nations Parliamentary Assembly, that would allow for participation of member nations' legislators and, eventually, direct election of United Nations (UN) parliament members by citizens worldwide.

DIFFERENCE TO ANTI-GLOBALIZATION

Some supporters of the democratic globalization movement draw a distinction between their movement and the one most popularly known as the 'anti-globalization' movement, claiming that their movement avoids ideological agenda about economics and social matters although, in practice, it is often difficult to distinguish between the two camps. Democratic globalization supporters state that the choice of political orientations should be left to the world citizens, via their participation in world democratic institutions and direct vote for world presidents.

Some supporters of the "anti-globalization movement" do not necessarily disagree with this position. For example, George Monbiot, normally associated with the anti-globalization movement (who prefers the term Global Justice Movement) in his work *Age of Consent* has proposed similar democratic reforms of most major global institutions, suggesting direct democratic elections of such bodies by citizens, and suggests a form of "federal world government".

PROCEDURE

Democratic globalization, proponents claim, would be reached by creating democratic global institutions and changing international organizations (which are currently intergovernmental institutions controlled by the nation-states), into global ones controlled by voting by the citizens. The movement suggests to do it gradually by building a limited number of democratic global institutions in charge of a few crucial fields of common interest. Its long term goal is that these institutions federate later into a full-fledgeddemocratic world government.

They propose the creation of world services for citizens, like world civil protection and prevention (from natural hazards) services.

PROPONENTS

The concept of democratic globalization has supporters from all fields. Many of the campaigns and initiatives for global democracy, such as the UNPA campaign, list quotes by and names of their supporters on their web sites.

Academics

Some of the most prolific proponents are the British political thinker David Held and the Italian political theorist Daniele Archibugi. In the last decade they published several books regarding the spread of democracy from territorially defined nation states to a system of global governance that encapsulates the entire planet. Richard Falk has developed the idea from an international law perspective, Ulrich Beck from a sociological approach and Jürgen Habermas has elaborate the normative principles.

GLOBALIZATION PROMOTE DEMOCRACY

An enduring tenet of the post-Cold War era is that globalization can be a catalyst for democratization. In one formulation, when democratic ideals sweep (or even trickle) across borders into authoritarian states, globalization makes democratization inevitable. Proponents of this view point to the contagion of democratic transitions in the world over the past quarter-century and to the ability of technology to penetrate the most closed societies. Even the Orwellian North Korean government, they point out, has gone gingerly online, though the country's broader population has no electronic access to the outside world.

But these broad trends cannot yet confirm a strong and direct connection between globalization and democratization. The evidence is mixed and will continue to be so for some time. For every society in which a "people's power" revolution is helped along by international cheering squads and satellite television, another is daily becoming more cosmopolitan while adhering to traditional (and often authoritarian) practices.

The city-state of Singapore, rated as "most global" on the A.T. Kearny/ Foreign Policy magazine Globalization Index in terms of cross-border contact between people, has remained resolutely semi-authoritarian for the past 30 years and shows few signs of greater democratization. Moreover, while entire regions, particularly in the former Eastern bloc, embraced economic globalization and more open political processes at the onset of the 1990s, by the end of the decade many new democracies were faltering under the weight of globalization, whether because of unfavorable economic trends or greater transnational crime. It may not yet be possible to make a final judgement about the connection between globalization and democracy, but a closer look will clarify where globalization has helped democratization, where it has inhibited movement toward greater openness, and, assuming an increased pace of globalization, what the greater flows of people and ideas will mean for the world's governments and societies in the years ahead.

TOWARD INTERNATIONAL NORMS OF DEMOCRACY

Perhaps the most tangible evidence of globalization's impact on democratization has been the infusion of democratic norms, and the principles of human rights that support them, into many international and regional institutions. The principle of accountability for human rights abuse is increasingly unfettered by national borders, as the 1998 arrest of former Chilean President Augusto Pinochet in London demonstrated. The ad hoc United Nations war crimes tribunal that was convened for the former Yugoslavia in the early 1990s was extended to Rwanda in the middle of the decade, presaging a broader move toward international justice. In the coming decade, the establishment of an International Criminal Court will be a watershed in that move.

Democratic principles are also reshaping regional institutions. The European Union, originally an economic community, now requires democratic government as a precondition for membership and promotes democracy in its collective foreign policy.

The Organization of American States, once a diplomatic forum for both democratic and nondemocratic governments, now works actively to restore democracy when it is imperiled in member states. The Organization of African Unity, also a traditional diplomatic group, is attempting to forge a regional human rights code modeled after the Helsinki process in Europe.

But the process has its limits. Regional groups adopt codes of democratic practice where a quorum of democracies already exists or where the largest and most economically powerful states are democratic. In these cases, the weight of the democratic majority (and the benefits of membership in the club) are sometimes sufficient to help persuade nondemocratic states to liberalize. But the trend halts abruptly where the political spectrum includes an equal number of democratic and non-democratic states or where authoritarian regimes are predominant. In Asia, for example, the diversity of political regimes has largely kept democracy and human rights off the table in the Asian-Pacific Economic Cooperation (APEC) group and the Association of Southeast Asian Nations (ASEAN).

A more encouraging but more low-level trend has been the growth of transnational non-governmental organizations devoted to promoting democracy and protecting human rights. These groups, which usually originate and are headquartered in Western nations, establish beachheads (and nurture local counterparts) in authoritarian nations, although they are seldom able to operate there without significant restrictions. Thus, in regions where authoritarian trends remain strong?most notably in Asia and the Middle East?the only networks dedicated to spreading democratic values and strengthening human rights are non-governmental. For the foreseeable future, the best chance of building intergovernmental democracy and human rights regimes in these regions will be in a gradual crossover process, as NGO networks pull government officials into "track two" (mixed government and NGO) dialogues and other informal exercises.

THE INSTRUMENTAL EFFECTS OF GLOBALIZATION

In regions lacking a widespread and overt commitment to democracy, Western policymakers and non-governmental groups trying to promote greater political liberalization have placed their faith in the indirect effects of globalization. In this view, globalization offers a bait and switch. An authoritarian government agrees to a global regime to gain benefits of one sort (usually economic) but is forced to accept the political consequences (greater popular pressure for democracy) that follow. Policies crafted in accord with this theory focus on two aspects of globalization?international trade liberalization and telecommunications. Not surprisingly, the theory also supports two cherished American beliefs: that open markets and democracy are the inspiration and consequence of one another and that the march of technology cannot be stopped.

Thus, for more than a decade successive U.S. administrations have claimed that broadly maintaining trade with China, and specifically encouraging China's entry into the World Trade Organization, would provide a back-door route to political reform. Adhering to WTO rules would require the regime in Beijing to provide more transparent and accountable government and would strengthen the concept of the rule of law, two fundamentals in modern democratic systems. In addition, foreign telecommunications companies would gain parity with government companies in China, spreading their technology and loosening the regime's control over contact between China and the outside world, as well as among Chinese citizens themselves.

The logic, compelling in the long run, has short-term limits. In countries with enduring authoritarian regimes, leaders are more likely to accede to legal reform for pragmatic reasons?to improve economic conditions through increased international trade?so long as the reforms are not viewed by the populace as ideological capitulation.

Leaders may also consider reforms pertaining to international trade to be easier to contain, because the initial focus is on commercial codes that primarily affect foreign business. Although it is possible to cordon off domestic populations in the early stages of such reform, the consequences of trade liberalization and marketization eventually require the regime to adopt a broader approach. But economic liberalization can also exacerbate problems that seem to outpace legal reform efforts and even encourage popular support for authoritarian or semi-authoritarian government. Russia's entry into the international economy has, in the minds of many Russians, worsened official corruption and economic crime. As long as these trends are perceived to be stronger than (even impervious to) reform, citizens are likely to tolerate less than democratic rule as a short-term solution.

Moreover, some of the economic powers poised to enter international trade regimes, most notably China, could themselves affect the rules governing those regimes. Thus far, global trade rules have largely been written by Western democracies, whose combined economic power has placed aspiring entrants in the role of supplicants. But the entry of more "mixed" economic powers?governments committed to market reform but not necessarily to Western-style democracy?may change these institutions. At the least, the link between trade preferences and transparent processes may weaken slightly, as may support for overt political conditionality linked to trade, in the mode of the European Union. At worst, global trade institutions could be rent with bloc behaviour, not unlike that sometimes seen in the United Nations.

TECHNOLOGY AND POLITICAL OPENNESS

Technology's impact on democratization is likely to be more immediate, although not sufficient in itself to effect political change. Weak economies, along with government resistance, have contained the spread of technology in many Middle Eastern and some Asian states and will for the near future. But technology's advent has added a new dimension to the prospects for political change. The most dramatic episodes of popular resistance against authoritarian regimes in the past decade have featured prominent roles for technology. In Tiananmen Square in 1989, Chinese demonstrators communicated with one another and the outside world by fax. In Bangkok in 1992, Thai professionals, dubbed "mobile phone mobs," coordinated antimilitary demonstrations with student leaders and one another by cellular phone. In Indonesia in 1998, anti-Suharto resistance was largely directed via the Internet.

But for all these moments of high political drama, technology's greatest promise in promoting political openness lies in the everyday intercourse of civil and political life. In authoritarian societies, the Internet differs from print and electronic media, because no government-dominated media exist for the regime to use as a counterweight. From its inception, the Internet has been a freer form of communication than any other, at least for those able to obtain it.

Modernizing authoritarian states often wish to expand the use of technology for economic development but also to keep citizens from using it for political purposes. Doing both, however, is increasingly difficult. China's ambitious plan to build a national computerized information infrastructure has spurred domestic telecommunications industry growth of 30-50 percent a year since 1989. At the same time the government registers all Internet users, is investing in technology to monitor and filter cyber communications, and regulates acceptable topics for online discussion. But Chinese Internet users have learned how to circumvent many of these restrictions using proxy servers, a sign that technology can usually outmaneuver attempts to control it. Today China's 17 million Internet users are a small fraction of the nation's population. But their number is increasing rapidly?growing 75 percent from 1997 to 1998 and then tripling in 1999. More important, political discourse in China has expanded despite state attempts to censor and prevent it. In the medium run, the effects of government efforts to control the Internet will depend in part on whether China can maintain brisk economic growth. If it does, Internet growth is likely to overwhelm attempts to control it. In the long run, the prognosis is favorable. In countries where technology is growing, control of global media may alternate between government and society, but the advantage will usually go to society in the end.

DOWNSIDES FOR DEMOCRACY

But globalization can also hand authoritarian regimes an edge. Regimes that accede to economic reforms most often allow openings they are confident they can control. If the immediate impact is favorable?an improved economy, greater access to modern technology and goods?the regime's popular legitimacy may be strengthened by the perception that it has delivered (or at least permitted) the improvements. Ironically, globalization can thus extend the longevity of the regime, at least in the short run.

Conversely, bad economic times that are attributed, correctly or not, to globalization can also give authoritarian leaders a boost. When disillusionment with economic reform sets in, Western policymakers' insistence on the link between reform and democratization can be used to authoritarian advantage. In the Asian economic crisis of 1997?98, Vietnam and Laos, which had begun very modest political reforms to accompany marketization, jettisoned these political moves when their trade with the countries hit hardest by the crisis declined. The failure of some of the region's fastest-growing economies?those linked most closely to the West?was taken as a warning of the dangers of globalization. Hard-liners eclipsed reformers in the early post-crisis years or replaced them altogether in the political structure.

Globalization has also helped sustain authoritarian regimes by feeding nationalism in some non-Western states. During the Asian economic crisis, anti-Western sentiments flared even in countries well on the road to democracy, such as Thailand, when catastrophic drops in currency values were popularly attributed to manipulation by Western traders. In more authoritarian countries such as Malaysia, leaders turned this new nationalism to their advantage by salting their political platforms with anti-Western (and anti-globalization) rhetoric and portraying themselves as national champions.

Technology too has fed the nationalist backlash against globalization. Democracy promoters have long heralded the "CNN effect," in which television brings world events into the living rooms of people whose leaders would prefer to block such coverage. In Thailand in 1992, when the military government banned reports of Bangkok street demonstrations on government-owned television stations, coverage of the events (and the military crackdown on demonstrators) was transmitted to citizens through satellite television, creating a galvanizing force for resistance. In recent years, authoritarian regimes have used television to their own advantage. In 1999, satellite TV brought NATO's bombing of the Chinese embassy in Belgrade into the homes of urban Chinese, who were quick to respond with public protests. During that same incident nationalists also made use of the Internet. At the height of the protests, Chinese hackers broke into the web site of the U.S. embassy in Beijing, in an eerie modern-day parallel to the 1900 Boxer Rebellion.

NEW "GLOBAL" ELITES?

Perhaps the most important impact of globalization on political reform, and one of the most difficult to foretell, will be the way it shapes new political and social classes, particularly in authoritarian countries. In recent decades social scientists have theorized that globalization?in particular its ability to improve economic conditions through trade?will help create new middle classes that will, in turn, increase pressure for democratic reform. There is some truth to this generalization, but it downplays the role of elites in political change. However strong popular pressure for democracy might be, a democratic transition usually requires the approval, overt or tacit, of a significant segment of the ruling order. The key question is not whether globalization can help serve up larger street crowds demanding change, but whether it can change the very nature of elite groups.

Signs are emerging that globalization may be doing just that, with mixed effects for democratization. In countries (whether authoritarian or democratic) that emphasize modernization and economic growth based in part on foreign trade and investment, two developments are reshaping elite political culture. The first is the rise of technocrats, particularly those trained in global economics, in government and politics. In China, for example, technocrats are gradually assuming greater responsibility in the bureaucratic structure.The Communist Party of China has even begun to recruit them to enhance its own legitimacy. Technocrats are not, of course, automatically democratic reformers, but their influence can help make government more accountable and transparent, helping to lay the groundwork for a more democratic system.

A more noteworthy trend is the rise of new commercial elites in the power structures of many authoritarian and democratizing societies. Many made their fortunes in modern commercial sectors that benefited greatly from globalization. Seeking influence wherever they can find it, these new elites often pack the parliaments in countries where the executive branch had traditionally enjoyed exclusive control. In applying new communications techniques (and portions of their fortunes) to connect with voters, they have inspired a modern push for grassroots politics. Although generally considered reformers, they may also epitomize globalization's lack of regulation. As these new elites have assumed power, indictments for political corruption have increased.

A REALISTIC APPRAISAL

Clearly, globalization is not a political panacea. At best a long-term ally in promoting democracy, it provides no automatic solutions. The sanguine correlations offered by some policymakers in the early post-Cold War years?particularly regarding the link between increased trade and democratization?should be Re-examined. Although the advanced democracies can prime the pump of globalization, they should not expect to control the outcome or to realize immediate results. Indeed, the more enduring aspects of globalization may take at least a generation to realize. Until then, policymakers should be as ready to recognize globalization's costs to democratization as they are to laud its benefits.

GLOBALIZATION SPREAD DEMOCRACY AROUND THE WORLD?

Globalization is a complex and controversial process. It has changed the world in many ways and has brought several countries together. However, as well as bringing countries together in some ways, it has also driven them apart. One of the most controversial changes it has made is to the political culture of many countries around the world. Many scholars such as David Held would agree that democracy is commonly being regarded as the best form of government. However, is globalization solely responsible for the spread of democracy around the world?

The concept of democracy is derived from the Ancient Greek term *d•mokratía* which means "rule of the people" and it defines "a form of government in which the supreme power is vested in the people and exercised directly by them or by their elected agents under a free electoral system." (Dictionary.com Unabridged. Random House n.d.). This form of government, however, has become increasingly popular since the demise of communism in the late 1980's. Hence it is widely regarded that "*Democracy is a cornerstone of human dignity and the good society. A public should shape its own destiny, even if some might doubt the wisdom of certain of democratic decisions taken. A society that is not striving after democracy tends to be a less worthy and also more dangerous place.*" (Scholte 2005).

Parallelly, globalization has also become an increasingly popular process that countries are opening themselves too. The concept was created in the late 1800's by American entrepreneur Charles Russell, but was only popularized in the 1960's by economists and social scientists. Pro-globalists would argue it is inevitable for countries to open themselves up to globalization. There are too many benefits and the ones that do not, become isolated from the rest of the world. Hence, this essay will examine if globalization has led these countries to opt for a democratic form of government and if so, what the reasons were behind it.

Many scholars such as Jens Bartelson would agree with the idea that globalization poses a threat to the democratic state instead of aiding its expansion. It is believed that it undermines the essential requirements of state autonomy, patriotism and national identity. For this reason, one could argue that political globalization could be a contradiction in terms. One of the anti-globalist theories is that globalization is causing the decline of the nation state, as governments no longer have control over their economy, their trade and their borders. Nation states may have in the past been in complete control of their markets, exchange rates and capital.

Now, trans-national companies are becoming increasingly imperative to the economy, and the state is becoming obsolete. This supports the argument that globalization is reducing the power of democracy and the state, resulting in hollow democracy. Sceptics believe that while globalization promotes opportunity for growth and increase in wealth, it has also increased the socio-economic disparity between people, making nations less democratic and progressively more ruled by the wealthy multi nationals. This means that "governments now try and compete for foreign capital and design their policies to please global investors and firms, who may not act in the best interest of, nor be held accountable to, the voters. It follows that the level of democracy declines.". Also, scholars such as Peter Drucker argue that globalization cripples even more those who are less fortunate, as previously stated. Companies who are unable to compete with multi nationals on an international scale lose from more economic openness. The results of this loss cause a weakening in the country's democracy.

The unfortunate losers in the globalization battle thus, tend to seek support and unity with their identities, usually based on religion or ethnicity. This encourages the prosperous economic winners to maintain their edge over the poorer and reduce their competition. These actions intensify social inequality and undermine the progress democracy has made. This inequality, however, is not only carried out on a national scale. Even in the international community, globalization has increased the cleavage between the developed countries from the north and the developing countries from the south. In international organizations such as the United Nations it is commonly witnessed that the elite wealthy countries always have the final say in conflicts or important issues that are discussed, which ends up swaying the domestic politics of less developed countries to their favour.

Another argument made by many such as O'Donnell is that in order for a stable and functioning democracy to work, the concept of citizenship and participation must be active and embedded in the population. Globalization has transformed the common citizen into an individual who is more willing to pursue its own economic interest than to be concerned with the content of public policy.

As observed, there are many reasons as to how globalization has weakened democracy around the world. However, like any controversial issue, it is important to evaluate the two sides of the argument to fully comprehend the implications of the statement. For this reason, there are several claims of notable scholars that defend the idea that globalization has spread democracy around the world.

According to Schumpeter's *Capitalism, Socialism and Democracy* globalization has helped promote economic development which has augmented the number of educated and well trained citizens, which has resulted, contrastingly to previous statements, in a decrease in economic inequality. This illustrates the freedom and development of the people in allowing them to prosper from the benefits of globalization.

As previously stated, globalization has increased the power of multinationals. However, differently to what has been stated, international businesses demand an increase in democracy. In order for businesses to grow, peace and stability must be entrenched in all potential investment countries. Subsequently, as democratic countries scarcely ever fight with each other, there is an increase in the demand for a democratic form of government. As economic links among states expand, authoritarian countries experience an increase in pressure from trans-national companies for political liberalization. These authoritarian states, as a result of globalization have fewer incentives to cling to power or proceed with their radical policies. Globalization encourages authoritarian states to decentralize power as they hand over their control to make progress for the market, which is fundamentally democratic. This concept of allowing the economy to fluctuate is known as laissez-faire, a French expression meaning "let it be" which allows industries to be free from state involvement in restrictions such as taxes and state monopolies.

Many other advantages of globalization also help promote democracy. The reduction in information and travelling costs mean that people have access to a lot more information not only from their government but from all over the world. This means democracies can now promote their values and ideals to autocratic countries a lot more freely, as autocracies have diminishing control over information. Other advantages of globalization reducing borders is that is strengthens the distribution of democratic values over borders. The more democracies border non-democratic countries, the more the chances that country has of becoming democratic.

In addition, with the increase in the demand for human rights and humanitarian interventions in countries which abuse power, democracy is progressively becoming the only alternative to autocratic regimes. As the preponderance of states withholds democratic values, it is expected that any other state that is non-democratic is in violation of human rights as they are not allowing their citizens to voice their opinion and have a say in the way their government is run. Hence, interventions have contributed to the democratization of numerous countries such asIraqand several other countries in Sub-Saharan Africa. Currently, international organizations such as the IMF and the World Bank have reformed numerous of these authoritarian countries so that they become potential investment opportunities for multi-nationals, and this is only due to the result of the expansion of globalization to such nations.

This, however, is one of the main causes of rising military conflict and tensions amongst nations in the international community. Many sceptics and especially countries with alternative values believe that the process of globalization has pressured them into becoming liberal democracies and believing in western capitalist values. Since the beginning of the cold war, there has always been a great tension between the western democracies and the rest of the world. Now, the few countries that do not withhold western values feel threatened and ever more forced into opening their economies and becoming a democratic system.

Globalization encourages democratic institutions which promote democracy. As the global market relies on capitalist democratic values, it is inevitable that organizations that reinforce these values are rewarded meaning they can expand into countries with other forms of government and promote these ideals. Hence, the increase involvement of INGO's and other businesses furthers the transparency and liability of institutions that reduce state intervention, all which facilitate democracy. "*Western policymakers and non-governmental groups trying to promote greater political liberalization have placed their faith in the indirect effects of globalization. An authoritarian government agrees to a global regime to gain benefits of one sort but is forced to accept the political consequences that follow.*"

In conclusion, the question of globalization and the spread of democracy is a complex one. On one hand, it may be considered a threat to democracy as it is believed that it undermines the essential requirements of state autonomy, of patriotism and of national identity. Many argue that globalization is the sole reason for the decline of the nation state, as governments do not have control over their economy, their trade and their borders anymore. Now, trans-national companies are becoming increasingly imperative to the economy, and the state is becoming obsolete. Even though globalization has many advantages and one of them is the opportunity for economic growth both at an individual and a national level.

This means that governments now try and compete for foreign capital and design their policies to please global investors and firms, which results in them not necessarily acting in the best interest of its citizens and this disregards its primary purpose. Many people, however, cannot benefit from the advantages of globalization. Small companies who are unable to compete with multi nationals on an international scale lose from more economic openness. The results of this loss cause a weakening in the country's democracy. Hence, globalization has transformed the common citizen into an individual who is much more willing to pursue its own economic interest than to be concerned with the content of public policy. On the other hand, however, globalization has expanded greatly the values of the democratic state. According to Schumpeter globalization has helped promote economic development which has increasedd the number of educated and well trained citizens, which has resulted, in a decrease in economic inequality. Also, international businesses demand an increase in democracy. In order for businesses to prosper, peace and stability must be established in all potential investment countries.

As economic links among states expand, authoritarian countries experience an increase in pressure from trans-national companies for political liberalization. Globalization encourages authoritarian states to decentralize power as they hand over their control to make progress for the market, which is essentially democratic. Another proof that globalization has expanded democracy is through the reduction in information and travelling costs.

People have access to a lot more information not only from their government but from around the globe. This means democracies can promote their values and ideals to autocratic countries, as autocracies have less and less control over information. It is because of these and other reasons like globalization encouraging democratic institutions and INGO's which promote democracy, that democracy had expanded so drastically over the past decades. Hence, if one were to analyze carefully how globalization had reduced democracy and how it has expanded it, one could safely affirm that even though it has somewhat decreased the power of the nation state, on the whole, the process has in fact spread democracy around the world.

GLOBALIZATION AND INTERNATIONALIZATION

DEFINING GLOBALIZATION

One of the terms that is used by everyone regardless they are businessmen, politicians or academicians and whose meaning and nature are not settled is the term "globalization". The origin of the word globalization is "*global*". The word *global* may take different meanings in different languages. The most common meaning however is the 3D geometric figure. According to Meydan Larousse the term global means "*undertaken entirely*". This is the meaning attributed to the word global by Western languages. Besides, the term means "*homogeneity*" in French. Hence the term means both "*entirety*" and "*homogeneity*".

There are different ideas on the first usage of the term globalization with its contemporary meaning. Although the origin of the term with its contemporary meaning goes back to 17th century, the term grounds to the term "*global village*" used by Canadian sociology professor Marshall McLuhan in 1960 in his book titled "Explorations in Communication". According to some other claims, the term *globalization* was first used in 1980s in the prestigious American colleges of Harvard, Stanford and Columbia and popularized by these environments. Another claim is that fist formations and forecasts of globalization were written by American entrepreneur-minister Charles Taze Russell with the term *"corporate giants"* in 1897.

The book of Ronald Robertson called "Globalization" has brought in theoretical content to the term. The term which had not been used in 1980s even by academic environments, was started to be used increasingly as a key term in the explanations of the theories of social change in 1990s.

The American Defence Institute defines globalization as "fast and continuous inter-border flow of goods, services, capital (or money), technology, ideas, information, cultures and nations".

According to the Institute, through globalization an unprecedented integration among economies is occurring, an information reform is being experienced, and markets, corporations, organizations and governance are becoming more international.As can be seen from the definition, the term globalization covers many concepts. The term cannot be assessed solely as either political or economic process, or worldwide spanning of production or capital flows. Globalization covers a process that encompasses the whole aforementioned dimensions.

Therefore, the term globalization can be given different meanings by different people. It can be interpreted differently due to the different dimensions of the terms such as time/location, its dimensions, cause/result cycles and its perspectives. Hence the term can be used in different meanings by different people. Besides there are academic studies on which meaning is the term used. In one of such studies it is proposed that the term should be differentiated according to the disciplines.

In this study the term globalization that has wide, complex and contradicting effects is tried to be analyzed mainly with its economic dimension also with some references to cultural, social, political and historical facets.

The study intends to help young people that must interpret globalization correctly in order to shape their career paths and prepare themselves to the working life. This obligation necessitates cogitation on globalization and internationalization for young in order to shape their future. While economic, social and political developments in various countries easily affect firms, economic and national policies, employment markets and individual enterprises, the employment opportunities have crossed the frontiers.

Understanding Globalization: Behind the Curtain

Today labour and capital flows among countries and corporations with an unprecedented pace and amount. Therefore capital flows, production and service activities, commercial and technological developments attain international character. Billions of dollars can be transferred with only one "click". In this framework the dimensions and the domain of the competition that enterprises face change inevitably, enterprises become international, production and service activities, and international horizontal integrations increase. Multi-National Companies (MNC) and foreign direct investment (FDI) become more effective on individual economies. Now national frontiers disappear or at least lose its former rigidity and world head for an economic, political and cultural integrity.

There are historical origins of this process of chance and transformation and this process can be traced back to the first eras of mankind. On the other hand a common belief, that globalization has accelerated after some specific developments, prevails and the globalization process can be divided into stages according to these developments.

As the result of these developments and stages trade increases in the world and this increase bears economic, social, political and cultural effects. While trade furnishes the spanning of goods and services all over the world, it also generates the spanning of cultures, their interactions and competitions. At this point worldwide branding, pop stars, similar TV programmes are the examples to be thought of. While economic activities affect cultures, sometimes cultures may shape economic activities. Furthermore MNCs and FDI flows arise when trade is insufficient or inefficient. This alternation first affects the global economy and then the whole human values and causes different structures to arise as a result of new formations.

Historical Background

One of the most fashionable concepts of today, globalization, is in fact not a product of 20th century. Trade is international since the flint stone trade of Neanderthal human and globalization is a subject of history since first ages. It existed when the Silk Road started in China and reached to the frontier of the Persian Empire and enlarged towards the Roman Empire and during the Roman Empire, the Persian Empire and the Dynasty of China. Another example is the Golden Age of Islam: Early global economy created by Muslim merchants and explorers that ended up with the globalization of crops, commerce, knowledge and technology in the Old World-wide and the times that more integration was achieved along the Silk Road during the Mongol Empire.

With the accession of Portuguese and Spanish Empires to every corner of the world in the 16th and 17th centuries after they had reached India, global integration continued through the enlargement of European trade. During their dynasties Roman and Ottoman Empires developed "world systems" consistent with their hegemony in the "discovered" world and Pax Romana and Pax Ottoman constituted examples of globalization that "effects and compasses the whole world" in 19th century with the Pax Britannica known as the world order developed by Britain. The development in the automation network with the Industrial Revolution accelerated the globalization process. Two significant world wars and then the competition between the United States of America

(USA) and the Union of Soviet Socialist Republics (USSR) carried humanity into a very dangerous point. Consequently, the reality that instead of "power" "norm" should operate in order to alleviate the tension between these two blocs loomed large.

The idea of the Conference on Security and Co-Operation in Europe (CSCE) was the originating point of the appearance of this norm. With the Final Act adopted at the Helsinki Conference which is the first step of the conference and hence second wave of globalization a general agreement on the subjects of security, economy, trade, energy and humanity between the two blocs was achieved. Thereafter, Summits of Belgrade 1977-78, Madrid 1980-83, Vienna 1986-89 and Paris 1990 were held.

New rings were added with the Summits of Copenhagen 1990, Moscow Meeting on Human Dimension 1991, Prague-Vienna Confidence Building Measures 1992 and Helsinki. Finally significant contributions were done to the formation of a smoother world in 200s in the "democracy and human rights" framework with the come up of "full respect for human rights" as a consequence of Lisbon 1996 and Istanbul 1999 Summits of the Organization for Security and Co-Operation in Europe (OSCE).

In the USSR the Perestroika reforms were accepted by Gorbachev in 1985 which means the restructuring of the planned economy in order to modify it. Partial liberalization of the world of business was aimed. In this process Glasnost aimed to decrease the level of corruption in the public sector through openness and transparency. This background today resting in the dusty pages of history books in fact constitutes the infrastructure of immense contemporary changes.

Stages

Continuing globalization process may be divided into many stages encompassing colonization, slave trade, church constructions abroad, inventions in the high-capacity transportation, industrialization, highway constructions among provinces and countries, electrical and electronic infrastructure. On the other hand Robertson claims that globalization which is thought to be peculiar to present day is in fact a process began before the modernity and capitalism and divides this process into five stages and suggests that the last stage started in 1960 is full of ambiguities. A commonly accepted division divides the globalization process into three stages.

First Stage (1490): Started with the overseas discoveries of the West. The discoveries were followed by the establishment of colonial empires.

Second Stage (1890): Second extension of the West started after 1870 and institutionalized in 1890s. The utilized technology after the industrial revolution generated high imbalances between the West and the rest of the world. This difference was resulted with the deployment of Western countries into the markets of countries that had not experienced the industrial revolution and exploitation of the resources in these countries. A merciless competition that curtails profit rates started. This competition previously had remained at the firm level as the land and resources abounded but later on as the free lands become scarce it raised to the national level. Increased competition resulted in conflicts and the First World War.

Table. Stages of Globalization

Stages	**First Stage1490**	**Second Stage1890**	**Third Stage1990**
Impulse	Nautical developments	Industrialization and its requirements	Multi-National Companies in 1970s, Communication Reform in 1980s, Disappearance of Competitors of the West in 1990s
Process	Profit and then military occupation	Evangelists, then explorers, then companies and finally occupation	Cultural-Ideological effect, therefore countrywide spontaneous effect
Medium	To get the God's religion to the pagans	Burden of the white man, humane mission , racialist theories	Highest level of civilization, governance of international community, "invisible hand" of the market, globalization: for everyone's interest
Political Structure	*Empires and Colonization*	*Nation States*	*Regional and Economic Integrations*
Result	*Colonialism*	*Imperialism*	*Globalization*

The world changed in many respects after the First and Second World Wars. Almost all the ordinary balances collapsed and a new formation in the world started. First, balances that collapsed and changed were the former economic powers and political authorities connected to these powers. The empires and monarchies and their colonies which are the power source and scattered into various continents diffused one by one through declarations of independence. When economic and political balances changed, social and cultural values and balances disappeared, the newly gaps were closed by new balances. One of them was USA and the other was USSR. Thereby two poles and two blocs formed in the world. But during the Second World War major changes occurred. When the vast part of Europe was ruined, industrial economy in USA experienced a huge growth. Third Stage (1990): In the first two stages instable balances aroused. The number of independent states increased, conflicts increased and accelerated. Identity conflicts reached to peak in the underdeveloped countries.

The national markets of the West were insufficient; markets were desired to expand in order to encompass the whole world. In this process there were no competitors against the West like the ones in 1490 and 1890 stages because the third stage both was the factor that engendered the collapse of Soviet Bloc and the West was left alone to conquer the world as a result of this collapse. The third stage was more powerful, widespread and faster than the first two stages because of the hegemony of MNCs on the world economy started in 1970s, communication revolution created by putting technological inventions of the West like optical cable, communication satellites, computers, internet in 1980s and disappearance of power balances with the dissolution of the USSR and Europe's turning up as the only focus of power again in 1990s. Therefore globalization has become a process that can not be reversed and it should be accorded and strategies should be developed against the process.

Increasing Trade as a Vehicle

World trade volume of $380 billion in 1950 has increased to $21.2 trillion in 2005. The reasons of such a high increase in the world trade can be listed as the decrease in tariffs, trade agreements signed among countries and regions, regional integrations, developments in and cheapening in communication and transportation technologies, the mass and just-in-time production and the standardization of the tradable goods, convergence of human needs and the creation of new needs for humankind that can be denoted as "New World Order" or "Reganomics".

Table. Trade in Goods

Billion $		1995	1996	1997	1998	1999	2000	2001	2002	2003	2004	2005
World	Export	5,163.5	5,401.3	5,589.2	5,498.9	5,709.5	6,452.5	6,185.6	6,485.7	7,578.3	9,203.1	10,431.2
	Import	5,283.9	5,545.1	5,738.1	5,681.4	5,919.6	6,724.0	6,481.1	6,739.8	7,856.6	9,555.6	10,783.4
Germany	Export	523.5	524.6	512.9	543.8	543.5	551.8	571.6	615.8	751.6	909.9	969.9
	Import	463.9	459.1	445.7	471.5	474.0	497.2	486.1	490.3	604.6	715.7	773.8
Czech Republic	Export	21.3	22.2	22.4	25.9	26.6	29.1	33.3	38.5	48.7	69.0	78.2
	Import	25.1	27.8	27.1	28.3	28.5	32.0	36.3	40.7	51.7	70.0	76.7
Lithuania	Export	2.7	3.4	3.9	3.7	3.0	3.8	4.6	5.5	7.2	9.3	11.8
	Import	3.7	4.6	5.6	5.8	4.8	5.5	6.4	7.7	9.8	12.4	15.5
Turkey	Export	21.6	23.2	26.3	27.0	26.6	27.8	31.3	36.1	47.3	63.2	73.4
	Import	35.7	43.6	48.6	45.9	40.7	54.5	41.4	51.6	69.3	97.5	116.6
USA	Export	584.7	625.1	689.2	682.1	695.8	781.9	729.1	693.1	724.8	818.8	904.4
	Import	770.9	822.0	899.0	944.4	1,059.4	1,259.3	1,179.2	1,200.2	1,303.1	1,525.5	1,732.3

While this increase in the world trade makes the consumption of goods and services of the home country possible in other countries, it also creates the diffusion of the consumption patterns, culture, social life and life expectancies of the home country into the whole world. The striking point in this process is that although all the countries make certain amounts of export, their effects on the world differ as their shares in total exports vary. Should the world export figures are examined, the hegemony of the USA prevails, except for 2004 and 2005. Therefore it is not a coincidence that the process of globalization in which trade increases is denoted at the same time as Americanization. If the ratios of world trade volume to the world income in 1999 (46.63 per cent) and in 2005 (53.84 per cent) are compared, it is seen that even in this short time span the world trade increases faster than the world income and therefore the international trade and globalization are important. The increased ratio of trade increases the effects on the world and creates positive and negative ideas on the subject.

Multinational Companies as a Transporter: Theories of MNCs and FDI

MNCs are the companies that make FDI and produce value added in more than one country and own this process. These companies may prefer to produce where the product will be marketed instead of producing in the home country and export it. If this preference is analyzed at country or the source of investment points of view instead of firm viewpoint, one encounters with the subject of FDI.

The Organization for Economic Co-Operation and Development (OECD) and the International Monetary Fund (IMF) have reached a common definition of FDI with their collective studies. Accordingly FDI means the international investment in s foreign country done by a resident company in one economy with the intention of the creation of long-lasting business relation.

Theories of MNCs

MNC has become a concept of that concerns the business world with the establishment of the so called first MNC, Dutch-East India Company in the 17th century. The company was the first that allocates the risk as international trade has considerable risks and allows collective ownership through share issuing that is the impulse of globalization.

The modern MNCs were formed mainly in Europe, particularly in Belgium (Cockeril), Germany (Bayer), Switzerland (Nestle), France (Michelin) and UK (Lever) in the 19th century and applied FDI strategies in order to overcome the difficulties in exports resulted from tariffs. The aim of MNC is to get capital where it is cheapest and produce where they get the highest rate of return.

Today the number of MNCs and their efficiencies in the world increase parallel with the globalization process. The number of such companies is more than 37,000 as of 2000 in the world. The number of branches or agencies of MNCs' in different countries has reached to 450,000. Therefore theories of MNCs have been developed. The most significant ones of these theories are the location and internationalization theories.

Location Theory

According to the location theory the location of the production is determined by the resources. The determining factors of the location choice are the cost of transportation and trade barriers. If the transportation costs are high then the production is located in the country or region where the product will be marketed. Another reason of such relocation is the high tariff rates that the host country applies.

Internationalization Theory

According to the internationalization theory the reason why production is done by only one company instead of many in various locations is that it is more profitable to produce with one company. In the explanation of the advantage of internationalization the first approach of the internationalization of MNCs emphasizes the importance of technology transfer. Technology transfer may come across with some difficulties. It is difficult for a potential buyer to appraise the actual value of knowledge. Besides knowledge can not be packed and sold. The intellectual property rights are also difficult to secure. Therefore for a MNC the establishment of a new enterprise in a foreign country is more profitable than the sale of technology to another company.

The second approach intensifies on vertical integration. For example under the assumption that both companies are monopolies, the price of input used by first company and produced by second company is tried to be lowered and increased by the first and second companies respectively. Therefore a dispute between these two companies will exist. Moreover some coordination problems may occur because of the demand and supply imbalances between two companies. Volatile prices constitute high risks for both companies. In case of a vertical integration of these two companies the problems will disappear or be relieved.

Theories of FDI

FDI started to be analyzed as it partly substitutes and represents trade and because of its effects on the home and host countries. These analyses have resulted with theories; these theories have diversified and evolved according to the flows, theories of economics and the effects they generate. Main stream of the FDI theories with imperfect competition encompasses Product Life Cycle Theory, Internationalization Theory and Eclectic Paradigm. Besides these main stream theories there are also instrumental theories. Although any of these theories is sufficient by itself in explaining all the FDI flows, each of them has considerable contribution in the explanation of FDI flows.

Product Life Cycle Theory

Theory explains international production that the traditional Nco-Classical trade theory does not. Theory becomes important in the literature with Vernon's paper "International investment and international trade in the product cycle" in 1966.

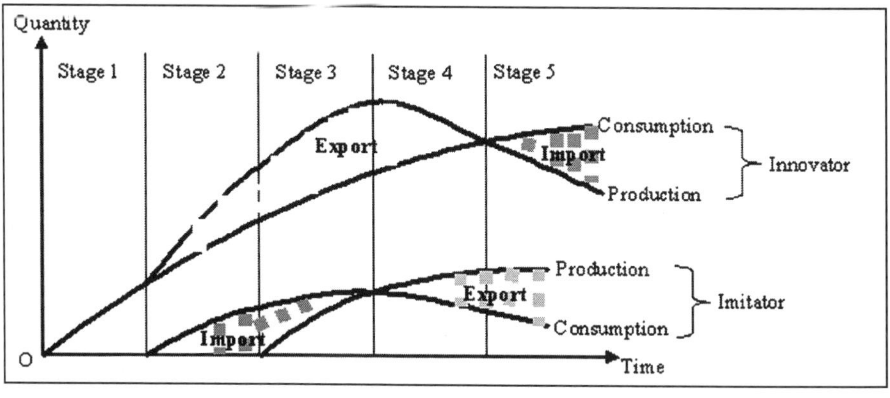

Fig. Product Life Cycle Theory

According to the theory, an innovation occurs in the unsatisfied markets where per capita income and purchasing power are high because the sale of high priced product that contains the innovation and therefore the research and development (R and D) costs is easier in such markets. Furthermore in such markets the communication between producers and consumers is advanced. Therefore the markets with the ease of taking feedbacks which is important for the process of product standardization are proper as the location of production initially.

After the product started to be produced in such a market, the demand for the product increases and the product get standardized. The increased standardization does not stop the product differentiation process, in the contrary the increased competition boosts specialization (*i.e.* the shift to the production of table radios, automobile radios and mobile radios from the radio production).

Increased production affects the choice of production location. As the product standardizes the production also standardize and the need for elasticity decreases while the cost of production becomes important. Increased importance of cost connotes the question of whether to move the production into low-cost locations or not. This choice is done through the comparison of the costs in the host country and home country together with the transportation cost to the host country.

Consequently production shifts from the high-cost home country to the relatively low-cost developing country. In the beginning the home country produces and markets the product only domestically and therefore she starts to export and finally relocates its production into foreign countries. At the final step most of her production relocates and she may even become a net importer.

Although the product cycle theory has crucial contributions for the explanation of FDI flows, it can not be used for the resource-seeking FDI. Besides the theory is also criticized as it becomes weaker in the short-life-cycle cases, it loses importance in contemporary economic structure as most of the innovations are done by MNCs, and it overrates the ambiguity and costs of overseas production.

Internalization Theory

Internalization theory tries to explain whether MNCs use leasing or licensing methods for the sale of their products abroad or they produce abroad through FDI by themselves. In other words it answers the question why a company prefers FDI instead of producing in the home country and then exporting it.

The theory is based on the study of Buckley and Casson in 1976. According to the theory firms maximize their profits in an imperfect competition environment. In this process if

- Transportation costs are high, there are trade barriers,
- There is the problem of inadequate foreign market information,

- There is information asymmetries between sellers and buyers,
- There are transaction cost-increasing conditions, the firm chooses internalization and make FDI.

Thus firms may avoid delays, bargaining and customer ambiguities, and take the opportunities of the minimization of governmental regulations' adverse effects through transfer pricing and price differentiation between different markets.

OLI Paradigm (Eclectic Paradigm)

The theory has the most extensive scope among FDI theories. Dunning has created the theory by combining many former studies (eclectic).

According to Dunning production of a firm in a foreign country depends on these three conditions:

1. Firm should have tangible and intangible assets and skills so that can compete with the domestic firms of the host country who have national knowledge and experience.
2. For a firm through an advantage taken from the host country it should be more profitable to produce in the host country than to produce in the home country and export it.
3. Making FDI should be more profitable than selling, leasing or licensing the skills.

These conditions which are called OLI by Dunning are the ownership (O), location (L) and internalization (I) advantages respectively.

The ownership advantage can be achieved through privileged ownership of some income bearing properties (patent, trade secrets or trademarks) and governance of separate but related activities from one head firm (economies of scale and synergy, diffusion of geographical risk and cross-country arbitrage).

The location advantages are those caused by the superiority of production method in the host country, high transportation costs, cheap labour, and proximity to the consumers, local image and the foreign governments' trade applications.

Internalization advantage means the advantage that is caused by the imperfect competition.

Although the theory is much broader than the others, it is also criticized. First criticism is the decreased significance of the variables as they are immense. The variables are correlated with others. Another criticism is that the theory is static and can not explain the paths and processes of firms in the internalization process. Some blames the theory as entirely micro economic and even claims that it has no difference with the theory of internalization.

Other Theories

Although these theories are not as popular as the main stream theories, they have significant contributions in the development of main stream theories.

Caves Economies: According to Caves, if a firm wants to invest horizontally (the production of the same product in another location) its property should prevail the advantage of domestic firms in the host country resulting from being resident and the firm should decide that FDI is more profitable than either export or licensing.

Caves believes that the following factors are important in the decision stage of FDI:

- Product differentiation (is formed with subjective alterations by little physical modifications, branding, advertisement, marketing strategies and differences in the complementary products; and maintained by property rights and high cost barriers against physical imitation).
- Oligopolistic market structure
- Organizational skills
- Transportation costs and tariffs
- R and D activities
- The FDI decision in vertical foreign investment (the production in which each part of a product may be produced in different locations and finally assembled) is made after the determination of optimal vertical integration level.

Oligopolistic Reaction Theory: According to the Oligopolistic Reaction Theory of Knickerbocker, one firm invests in one country in order to increase its market share. Immediately thereafter the other rival oligopolistic firms invest in that country in order not to lose their market shares. This kind of investment is also known as "Follow-the-leader". Besides as firms avoid ambiguities and risks, they wait for an investment of a leader firm before themselves and its consequences and then they invest. This constitutes the reasoning of follow-the-leader theory. Hymer and Kindleberger's Theory: The most important contribution of Hymer's doctoral dissertation -completed in 1960- to the theory of FDI is that it explains why MNCs transfer intermediate goods such as knowledge and technology among countries.

Hymer separates two types of the division of labour. He states that the division of labour among firms is controlled by markets and therefore is the subject of international trade theory and the intra-firm division of labour is controlled by the entrepreneurs.

Hymer and his instructor Kindleberger rather focus on firm-specific factors. Foreign firms have superiority such as the ability to find cheap capital, marketing experience, privileged entry permits for some markets, patented or non-tradable technology, managerial efficiencies and economies of scale. Hymer and Kindleberger can not explain precisely why a firm having these advantages tends to make FDI instead of export or leasing. Therefore the theory remains only as a guideline to other theories. On the other hand all the studies following Hymer's dissertation are constructed upon Hymer's ideas.

Multi Faces of Globalization

Economic globalization can be characterized with four main streams. These are:

- Flows of goods and services,
- Flows of labour/people,
- Capital flows and
- Technology flows.

Even the economic effects of globalization are extensive. The properties of the process in terms of economies are as follows:

1. Changing consumption habits and behaviours favoring the pace of consumption,
2. The changing scale from national to international in the production, distribution, consumption and marketing of resources,
3. Developments in information and communication technologies (ICT),
4. Utilizing the high-technology in the production of goods and services,
5. The death of two bloc (socialism-liberalism) world after the collapse of the USSR,
6. Global changes,
7. The formation of elastic, dynamic, flexible and rapid environments and markets,
8. Rapid development in technology; digitalization of trade and economy,
9. Increased competition,
10. The increase in the "unknown",
11. Increased R and D activities, innovation, economic dynamism, technological innovations,
12. Important changes in human resources and
13. Trade liberalization.

The major effects of globalization are tried to be examined under the titles of death of distance, end of the nation state, hegemony of R and D, cultural erosion and glocalization.

Death of Distance

In the history one of the most important barriers against trade was the distance. It may constitute a barrier against the transportation of goods safely, on time, securely and with acceptable prices. The trade of goods and services has become feasible with technological developments and trade agreements that decrease or eliminate tariffs.

In this process the decreases in the prices of overseas transportation by 50 per cent, airline transportation by 80 per cent, transatlantic phone calls by 99 per cent have the key role. Thanks to this process a module printed in Germany can be sent anywhere in the world in less than two days. Furthermore online broadcasting eliminates this two day-lag.

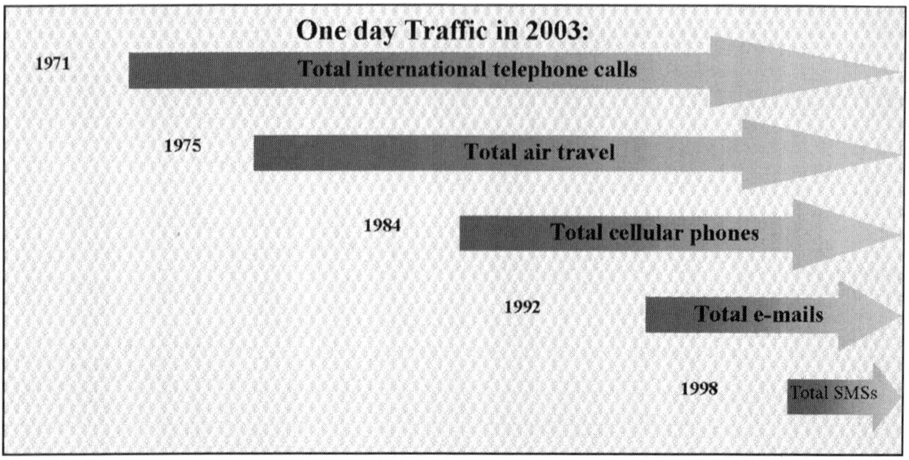

Fig. Comparison of Economic Activities with 2003

The international phone calls of the whole year of 1971 is made in just one day in 2003. Similarly air travels of 1975, cellular phone calls of 1984, e-mails of 1992 and cellular phone SMSs of 1998 are done in just one day in 2003.

On the other hand another medium that causes the death of distance is the diffusion of production into the whole world. Currently, through FDI, MNCs have diffused their productions to many countries. Hence a Japan car can be produced in Turkey. This in turn means the break up of production of that car in Japan and exportation to Turkey.

End of the Nation State

Although debate on the effects of globalization on nation-state has been continuing since 1970s, foresights about the future of nation-state may differ. For example, some accepting the presence of economic globalization claims that nation-state will survive in current structural form. Articulation of "concurrency of differences" to globalization by Robertson does not mean the negligence of modern roots of globalization because concepts such as nation-state, individual, universality are the components of the field of globalization and survive with interaction. For example, Robertson's interpretation on the nation-state which is an important element of modern era is that there is no reason to claim that the organized society and particularly the state are about to disappear. On the contrary, as the development of modern nation-state depends on inter-state relations, the definition of state becomes more evident in the globalization process. In other words, globalization increases the local awareness and solidifies "auto-awareness" instead of eliminating nation-state.

On the other hand, under the conditions of cold war period while ideological and political polarization between two parties let developing countries to develop with the demolition of the Berlin Wall the international ideological combat has ceased and the dependency of these countries on developed Western countries has increased. This, in turn, is more efficient on the countries that have high external debt such as Turkey and mostly limits the functions of nation-state in the area of economy. Therefore a nation-state that could not realize economic growth faces with the problems on income-distribution, social state, technologic innovation, basic needs of the society such as education/nutrition/health, and democracy. In short, nation-state loses its basic function and its function of national integrity runs a risk. In this framework it is obliged to embrace and support the economic policy of globalization.

The structures such as European Union (EU) aim to solve the economic and political problems nation-states that discarding part of their hegemony face. In this framework both the disappearance of nation-states and the sustenance of their existence in an evolved form can be claimed.

Hegemony of R and D

Investment on knowledge forms the basics of innovativeness and technologic development. This investment that can be measured through R and D, software and education expenditures is increasing in most OECD countries. Today developing countries have significant R and D expenditures. For example, in 2005 China with an average annual growth of 18 per cent between 2000 and 2005 is third after the USA and Japan in terms of R and D expenditure.

Table. Total R and D Spending as a Percentage of GDP

	1981	1985	1990	1993	1995	1997	1999	2000	2001	2002	2003	2004	2005
USA	2.34	2.75	2.65	2.52	2.51	2.58	2.66	2.74	2.76	2.66	2.66	2.58	2.62
Germany	2.35	2.60	2.61	2.28	2.19	2.24	2.40	2.45	2.46	2.49	2.52	2.49	2.46
Czech Rep.	---	---	---	1.14	0.95	1.08	1.14	1.21	1.20	1.20	1.25	1.26	1.42
China	---	---	---	0.70	0.57	0.64	0.76	0.90	0.95	1.07	1.13	1.23	1.34
Japan	2.14	2.58	2.81	2.65	2.71	2.87	3.02	3.04	3.12	3.17	3.20	3.17	3.33
Turkey	---	---	0.32	0.44	0.38	0.49	0.63	0.64	0.72	0.66	0.61	0.67	---

It can be seen from Table above that developed countries have high R and D / Gross Domestic Product (GDP) ratios. All countries that aim development should increase R and D investments. Countries that attain this increase can grow fast. It can be seen that today economic activities depend on factors of production such as information, computer, knowledge, network and intelligence and that can be attained through R and D or that eases R and D.

The result of R and D investment is reflected in the number of patents. They are positively related. This positive relationship can easily be followed from realizations. Another point is the severe relationship between inventions and transformation of these inventions into economic activities. The invention of Tetra Pak in Sweden, turbo by SAAB, dialysis, dynamite, cooker and fridge and their transformations into economic activities are good examples for this relationship.

Table. Transformation in Technology

	1700 - 1900	1900 - 2000	2000 - ...
Economics	Agriculture	Manufacture	Information
Technology	Plow	Machine	Computer
Output	Food	Good	Information
Resource	Land	Capital	Knowledge
Unit	Family	Company	Network
Energy	Muscle	Fossil Fuels	Brain
Competition	Local	National	Global
Education: ***Demand** ***Focus**	Primitive Minimal "What?"	Procedures Remarkable "How?"	Thought Continuity "Why?"

Today R and D has entered a new phase and started to globalize. Increasing R and D costs as a result of increased elasticity in cross-border R and D projects, strengthening of intellectual property rights or the taxation of R and D activities, and important policy changes support this tendency. In the 1995-2005 period the number of scientific publications that are jointly written in the international platform tripled.

The ratio of cross-border cooperation in total world-wide inventions doubled (from 4 per cent in 1991-3 to 7 per cent in 2001-3). From the beginning of 1990s the ratio of the inventions that have cross-border property in total inventions has increased to 16 per cent from 11 per cent. The internalization process in the field of research is supported by MNCs final investment models. Much more than 16 per cent of the total industrial R and D expenditures in OECD region in 2004 (it was 12 per cent in 1993) is constituted by R and D done by domestic and foreign affiliates moreover, in most countries the affiliates under the control of foreign investment has more R and D intensities than the domestic firms.

Although per capita R and D expenditures differ widely among countries, all are increasing. An important reflection of this increase can be seen in the number of R and D personnel.

CULTURAL EROSION

The globalization process supplies two distinct culture presences simultaneously. The first of them is to reach to upper limit of "particular culture". This upper limit is the globe. All heterogeneous cultures dissolve in the prevailing culture that covers the whole world. Second presence is related to the "tightening of cultures". Different cultures flow side by side without any organizational principle. Field of culture that includes more and more cultural movement and complexity constitutes the second stage of the globalization of culture. Therefore there are important discrepancies on the effects of globalization on culture.

Some intellectuals like John Meyer and Daniel Bell believe that globalization brings integration. Cultural globalization indicates common shape of local cultures. The concept used to define this situation is "McDonaldization". The term means the resemblance of life styles, cultural symbols and behaviours. For example, people from Germany to India, Singapore to Brazil watch the same series (Dallas), wear the same brand (Levi's) and smoke the same cigarette (Marlboro). Marshall McLuhan through "global village" conceptualization and Ohmae through "cross-border civilization" definition designate the formation of global culture.

This resemblance certainly does not indicate that local cultures are dependent on global culture. Local cultures have the possibilities to interpret the global and redefine it in their authentic characteristics framework. In this framework a lot of philosophers ranging from Giddens to Friedman, from Robertson to Cox refuse that globalization will combine all societies under a single economic, politic and cultural unit (cultural integration). Anthony Smith declares that "global culture" is problematic. According to him "global culture" is impossible as the term "culture" refers to a plural fact.

If internet, satellite and mobile communication systems and the fact that the committee of Olympics has more members than the United Nations (UN) are taken into consideration, it can be said that cultural globalization diffuses faster than economic globalization. This process causes both the dissolve of local cultures in the global culture and the contributions of local cultures in the global culture. While the corruption of local culture by global culture occurs very easily and spontaneously through technology, communication and interaction, the protection of local cultures and the contribution of it to global culture is a process that should need endeavor and that should be managed.

GLOCALIZATION

The term glocalization is produced with the combination of the terms global and local. The term means "the creation of goods and services that are customized to supply global markets but consistent with local values.

The fact that the terms glocalization and globalization are related to each other is accepted by many authors. For example when Ronald Robertson defines globalization as "the simultaneity of the universality of resolution and the resolution of universality" he actually highlights the simultaneity of globalization and glocalization.

The problem of simultaneous globalization of the local and localization of the global can be denoted as dual-process of macro-localization (globalization of a local value) and micro-globalization (localization of a global value).

Key features of glocalization are as follows:

1. Variety is in the basis of social life.
2. Glocalization does not eliminate all differences.
3. History and culture causes differences in all groups.

4. Glocalization ceases the fear that globalization will wipe all the differences out.
5. Glocalization does not promise a world without any conflict or tension; instead it makes a more historical view of the complex structure.

In this framework, glocalization that means the modification of globalization according to local conditions differentiate globalization from Westernization, Americanization and even McDonaldization. Now globalization evolves itself in order to include local values.

IMPACTS

As globalization compasses a large scope and process, it has considerable effects while some effects can be seen in daily life; some has large-scale-deep effects.

VISIBLE IMPACTS

One important result of globalization is the acceleration of changes of eras. It is denoted that human being having a history of more than one million years on earth took the first step to civilization with the settlement on land and therefore with the beginning of agricultural culture in 10,000 BC. The invention of writing in 4,000 BC has accelerated the development of human being. The widespread use of press in 14th century and the Reformation and the Renaissance movements followed by industrial revolution in the late 17th century have caused human being to develop but in the mid-20th century the concept of era starts to alter and pick up pace. The 1970s are called space era as a result of stepping on the Moon in 1969; 1980s are called communication era as a result of developments in communication through satellites; 1990s are called knowledge era-knowledge society as a result of the increased importance of knowledge and 2000s are called information era.

In the information era, human being using computers can reach all new information online.

The fact that 65 per cent of the world trade volume in the beginning of 2000s is made online reveals the significance of this new concept.

Information Tachnologies and Technology Flows

Technologic development – developments in the production of goods and services, marketing and supply techniques (including firm organizational structures) takes place in the core of human progress and development. Technologic development at the national level occurs through invention and innovation, adaptation and modification of pre-existing technologies, and diffusion of technologies among firms, individuals and public sector.

Statistical indicators can be confined in three major groups: scientific invention and innovation, diffusion of pre-existing technologies and benefiting new technologies. Another indicator is the measure of how much countries are exposed to foreign technologies. Measuring technology directly is difficult because it has no physical and easily countable presence such as pencils or automobiles. Contrary to services it has no well-defined price that allows measurement and summation either. Instead, it is embedded in products, intermediates, and processes. Consequently the studies trying to measure technology should use indirect techniques such as level of education, number of scientists and engineers, R and D expenditures and personnel, diffusion of technology, indicators of innovation (number of patents issued), ratio of high-tech activities in manufacturing value-added and exports, and national innovative capacity.

If technologic diffusion in the world is examined under these three major groups of indicators, for the first group -scientific invention and innovation- scientific and technologic articles, patent and intellectual properties, and income from licensing statistics can be used. When analyzed, it is seen that these variables are related to income. According to 2003 data number of articles and patents per 1 million people in high-income countries are 83 and 36 times higher than those in low-income countries respectively. As of 2004 low-income countries' income from intellectual properties and licensing is almost zero.

Under the second group -utilizing older technologies- the statistics of per capita electricity consumption, phone lines per 100 people, phone call fees, highway and railway densities and airline usage can be used. When analyzed, although income has no effect on these statistics, culture and capacity has crucial implications on the usage of these variables. High-income countries consume 26 times more electricity (in 2004); have 18 times more phone lines and use it 20.7 times cheaper (in 2004); have 3.25 times more intense railways (in 2005); have 4.8 times more agricultural machines and tractors (in 2003); use airlines 60 times more (in 2004) than low-income countries.

Third group is the utilization of new technologies. Under this group statistics of internet users, broad-band internet users, personal computer ownership, mobile phone ownership per 1000 people and internet band capacity can be used. When these statistics are analyzed, it is seen that income has direct effect as this kind of development is less costly and more elastic than older technologies necessitating infrastructure investments. High-income countries have 12 times more internet users (in 2005); 163 times more broad-band internet users (in 2005); have 53 times more personal computers (in 2004) and have 19 times more mobile phones (in 2004) than low-income countries per 1000 people.

The relative efficiency of goods and services that an economy can produce with certain amount of labour and capital is called total factor productivity (TFP). In general, TFP is interpreted as the measure of production technology and its rate of growth as the measure of technical progress. International TFP comparisons reveal high productivity differences between high, and low and middle-income countries in the production of goods and services. As of 2005 average TFP in low-income countries is only 5 per cent of the productivity in the USA. While this gap closes in low and lower-middle-income countries, upper-middle-income countries can only maintain their position against high-income countries. In the light of these indicators diffusion of technology has the following features:

- Although technologic levels of countries depend on their income levels, the nature of this relationship may differ according to the scope of technology analyzed.
- Although the level of technology is in the tendency to increase with income, the levels of technologies among countries converge.
- The level of technology may differ widely within the country.
- In the last decade the technology gap between middle and high-income countries narrowed.
- On average technology improved faster in low-income countries.
- The diffusion of technology between countries gets pace.
- As a consequence, the most important feature of the level of technology is the diffusion pace of technology within a country.

Labour Hyper-Mobility and Global Distribution of Labour

As an unprecedented number of people move, migration is one of the most important variables that set the conditions of globalization in the beginning of 21st century. In today's mobile world there are many global tendencies effecting migration and its management. These are:

- Demographic tendencies,
- Economic differences between developed and developing countries,
- Trade liberalization necessitating more mobile labour force, in other words globalization,
- Communication network integrating all parts of the world,
- International migration.

In the world as of 2005, 192 million people (49.6 per cent of whom are women) live somewhere outside their place of birth. Between 1965 and 1990 the number of international migrants increased by 45 million –an annual growth rate of 2.1 per cent. In 2006 the growth rate is 2.9 per cent. The remittances of these migrants are estimated to be over $276 billion worldwide in 2006 whose $206 billion flow to developing countries. There are roughly 30-40 million illegal migrants constituting 15-20 per cent of migrant stock in the world. In recent years, migration may shift according to the centers of attractions for labour migration.

As of 2005 the country that has the largest immigrant stock is the USA with 38.1 million immigrants. Russia and Germany follow her with 12.1 and 10.1 millions respectively. The countries that have the largest emigrant stocks are China, India and the Philippines with 35, 20 and 7 million emigrants respectively.

Table. Migration Statistics, 2005

	# of Immigrants (Million People)	The Ratio of Immigrants to the Population of the Region
Europe	64.1	8.8
Asia	53.3	1.4
North America	44.5	13.5
Africa	17.1	1.9
Latin America	6.7	1.2
Oceania	5.0	15.2

In some regions in the world, the level of migrant stock shrinks:

- Although the level of Asian migrants reached 43.8 million in 2000 from its 28.1 million level in 1970, the share of Asia in the world migrant stock decreased to 25 per cent from 34.5 per cent in this period.
- Africa too experienced a decrease in international migrant share: from 12 per cent in 1970 to 9 per cent in 2000.
- The same holds for Latin America and the Caribbean's (from 7.1 per cent to 3.4 per cent); Europe (from 22.9 per cent to 18.7 per cent) and the Oceania (from 3.7 per cent to 3.3 per cent).
- Between 1970 and 2000, only North America and the former USSR have achieved increases in their migrant shares (from 15.9 per cent to 23.3 per cent and from 3.8 per cent to 16.8 per cent respectively). The reason of the increase in the USSR is not the increase in the number of migrants, but the re-determination of the borders of the country.

International stock of migrants concentrates in relatively low number of countries. 75 per cent of international migrants are living in 12 per cent of all the countries. In order to determine which one is most global among labour force, trade and capital flows one can examine the shares of these variables in the world labour force stock, production volume and total capital. As of 2004, while migration constitutes only 3 per cent of total labour force stock, international trade constitutes roughly 13 per cent of production and capital flows constitute 15-20 per cent of total capital on average. Therefore the statistics reflect less global labour force than trade or capital.

DEEP IMPACTS

In the last five decades a triad structure prevailed and in one end of this structure is the pluralist economies based on market economy, and socialist states attached to planned economy on the other end. Third structure is composed of the former colonies of mostly the West – the developing countries. These countries have socio-economic, political and cultural differences. However the dissolution of the USSR in 1990s facilitated a unipolar world based on market economy and democracy instead of bipolar world. All these political and ideological developments increased the popularity of the concept of globalization and increased its pace and deepened its effects.

Economic Issues

Globalization affects economies profoundly. It has strong effects on economic issues such as income, income distribution, capital formation, enterprises, production, competition and information flows. This part aims to identify these effects.

Income, Income Distribution and Poverty

In order to see the income differences between countries there is even no need for statistics. One watching TV can easily recognize that when Angola suffers famines football players in other countries may earn millions of dollars. In the world 3 million people die due to HIV, therefore 15 million children lose their parent or parents each year, at least 1.6 billion people live under unhealthy conditions, each year half a million women lose their life during pregnancy or birth. On the other hand it is estimated that there are 94,970 people whose financial assets exceed $30 million as of 2006 and their total financial assets worth more than $13.1 trillion, there are 9.5 million people whose financial assets exceed $1 million and their total financial assets worth more than $37.2 trillion.

As of 2008 countries having per capita income of $905 or less are called low-income; those having per capita income between $906 and $3,595 are called lower-middle-income; those having per capita income between $3,596 and $11,115 are called upper-middle-income and those having per capita income of $11,116 or higher are called high-income countries. Accordingly among 210 countries with populations higher than 30,000 53 countries are low-income, 55 countries are lower-middle-income, 41 countries are upper-middle-income and 61 countries are high-income countries. In the year 2006 Norway had the highest nominal income of $66,530 and Burundi had the lowest -$100. In that year the average income in the world was $7,439. If these income figures are re-calculated according to purchasing power parities in order to eliminate price level differences among countries, as of 2008, the wealthiest individuals live in the USA with an average income of $44,260 and the poorest live in Burundi with $710.

The world average is $10,218. If the income realizations are analyzed it can be seen that even in industrialized countries the average incomes were about $6,200 as of 1976. In other words, it is certain that the world has attained considerable income growth since then.

Income growth rates differ among countries, so the income distribution. The studies on global income distribution are divided into two – those finding divergence and those finding convergence. In an example finding divergence, the income gap between African countries and western countries (the USA, Canada, Australia and New Zealand) was found to be 1 to 2.6 in 1820; 1 to 12 in 1980 and 1 to 20 in 1998. On the contrary there are also scientific studies finding convergence. The reason of such a division may be different conceptualization of income (nominal exchange rates or income customized by purchasing power parity), different measurement techniques (extreme values vs. Gini coefficient) and different data sources. Each measurement has its own advantages and disadvantages, so all of them may be evaluated as correct.

The reason of the deterioration of the world income distribution may be:

- Higher growth rates in the OECD countries,
- Higher population growth in developing countries,
- Low output growth in rural China and India and in Africa,
- Increasing output and income differences between urban and rural parts of China and India –deterioration of income distribution within large countries,
- Variation in the terms of trade in favour of developed countries (the price of industrial and technologic goods that developed countries export increases faster than the price of goods and services that developing countries export).

Differences in income levels are apparent in statistics. Countries may assign poverty threshold according to some norms. Besides, some international measurements are assigned for international comparisons. The best known of these is the ration of those who must live with less than $1 daily (absolute poverty) or +2 (poverty) to the population. These ratios are 70.8 per cent and 92.4 per cent respectively in Nigeria as of 2003. On the contrary the ratios are below 2 per cent and 20 per cent respectively in most countries.

Although income distribution worsens among countries, poverty reduces. Today people get rid of absolute poverty but become poorer against developed countries have high income growths. This in turn causes the shrink of middle-class and resolution between rich and poor.

Capital, Finance, FDI and MNCs

Scale and scope of the financial globalization before 1914 is really impressive. More than 60 government securities and shares of firms from almost whole continent and sectors were traded in European Stock Exchanges. London was undoubtedly the financial centre of the world but Berlin and Paris challenged her.

During 30 years of classical gold-standard there were no restrictions on financial flows and cross-border financial flows reached incredible levels. Between 1880 and 1914 Britain exported 4 to 5 per cent of her GDP on average. European countries following the footsteps of Britain started to export capital in the last quarter of 19th century and in the 20th century the USA merged into the first global capital market boom as a capital exporter.

A similar boom in international finance has been experienced 30 years after the collapse of Bretton-Woods system that introduces fixed exchange rates and restrictions on capital account. Till the end of 1980s liberalization of capital flows has widened into developing countries. Global financial markets built up in 1990s. Nowadays financial globalization is a word that is used in daily life.

In 2006 foreign direct capital constituted half of net capital flows into developing countries. FDI inflows in 2006 increased by 38 per cent and reached \$1.31 trillion (second highest score after \$1.41 trillion in 2000). This increase, although in different scales, has been experienced in three regions, namely developed, developing and Southeast Europe and the Commonwealth of Independent States (CIS) countries. FDI inflows to developed countries increased by 45 per cent and reached \$857 billion.

FDI stock increases each year as FDI inflows increase with the globalization process. While FDI stock in 1990 is estimated to be \$1.78 trillion, as of the end of 2006 this figure is estimated to be \$12 trillion.

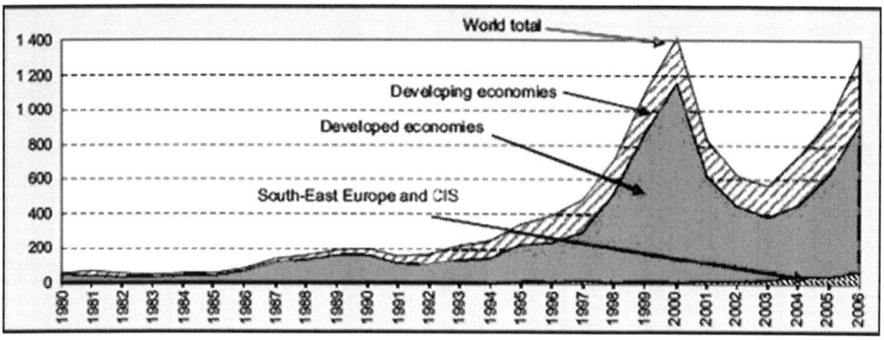

Fig. FDI Inflows

The largest 5 non-financial MNCs of the world are General Electric (USA), Vodafone Group (United Kingdom), General Motors (USA), British Petroleum Company PLC (United Kingdom) and Royal Dutch/Shell Group (United Kingdom and Netherlands).

In the first 100 MNCs there are 12 German, 2 Hong Kong, 2 Korean, 1 Mexican, 1 Malaysian and 1 Singapore enterprises but no enterprises from Turkey, Czech Republic or Lithuania. MNC that has investments in highest number of countries is the German Deutsche Post AG with investments in 103 countries.

As of 2004 there are 2,129; 9,225 and 42,753 foreign MNC affiliates in Turkey, Germany and China respectively. These affiliates create employment of 2.28 million and 24 million in Germany and China. On the contrary Germany has 22,997 affiliates all over the world. The total employment in the world that is created by foreign MNC affiliates is 21.52, 25.10 and 72.63 million in 1982, 1990 and 2006 respectively. The other side of the coin regarding employment is that MNCs' foreign investments instead of domestic investments export employment. For example Germany creates an employment of 4.61 million abroad through her MNCs. That means Germany loses an employment of 2.33 million due to MNC type of production. This figure is 3.5 million in the USA and 3.71 million in Japan. While governments of the countries that make FDI take precautions against capital outflow, host countries attracting FDI use this capital in order to solve their unemployment problems.

The highest bilateral FDI relationships in the world are between United Kingdom- USA, Hong Kong-China, USA-United Kingdom, Japan-USA and Germany-USA (first country is the investor and second is the host country and ranking is done according to FDI inflows). The FDI stock in these countries is $1.13 trillion in 2005.

Lastly, countries may be ranked according to their FDI performances and potentials. Accordingly, China, Czech Republic, Lithuania, Hong Kong and United Kingdom have both high performance and potential; Germany, Turkey, Japan and USA have high potentials but low performances. Countries that have low potentials and performances are generally those from Africa.

Production and Competitiveness

In recent years, global economy transformed with the elimination of obstacles against floes of goods, services, capital and labour and with the acceleration of technologic and scientific development. While the decreases in transportation and communication lowered the importance of location and promote enterprises to move their activities to low-cost locations, technologic developments create new business opportunities. This makes governments more sensitive in creating more business friendly environments and enhancing national competitiveness.

Table. Global Competitiveness Indices

Rank of Country	2005	2006	2007 / 2008
Germany	6	8	5
Czech Republic	29	29	33
Lithuania	34	40	38
Turkey	71	59	53
Singapore	5	5	7
Korea	19	24	11
China	48	54	34

International competitiveness is a concept that is related to marketing. If countries compete in marketing their products, then production bears a sense. If the goods and services that the country produces can not compete, the country's production would have no-sense and she would prefer importation instead of domestic production. National competitiveness is measured by the "Global Competitiveness Index" of the World Economic Forum (WEF).

Table. Income Statistics

Billion $		2001	2002	2003	2004	2005	2006
World	GNP	32,030	32,131	35,013	40,373	45,222	48,482
USA	GNP	9,930	10,145	10,927	12,059	12,913	13,446
Germany	GNP	1,978	1,899	2,115	2,545	2,876	3,018
Czech Rep.	GNP	588	613	746	940	1,141	1,295
Lithuania	GNP	11	13	15	19	24	27
Turkey	GNP	166	174	198	269	342	394
China	GNP	1,273	1,407	1,631	1,928	2,273	2,642
$		**2001**	**2002**	**2003**	**2004**	**2005**	**2006**
World	GNP Per Capita	5,216	5,168	5,563	6,338	7,016	7,439
USA	GNP Per Capita	34,800	35,180	37,570	41,060	43,560	44,970
Germany	GNP Per Capita	24,020	23,020	25,620	30,840	30,870	36,620
Czech Rep.	GNP Per Capita	5,750	6,010	7,310	9,210	11,150	12,680
Lithuania	GNP Per Capita	3,270	3,630	4,330	5,560	6,910	7,870
Turkey	GNP Per Capita	2,420	2,510	2,800	3,780	4,750	5,400
China	GNP Per Capita	1,000	1,100	1,270	1,500	1,740	2,010

The narrow shifts in terms of ranking. What is important is the persistent tendency. These tendencies of increase or decrease in not persistent and after a threshold it may transform into narrow shifts. For example the first five ranks are pooled by 7-8 countries. The countries at lower ranks may achieve large shifts. These countries are those which utilize the globalization of production, technology and knowledge. Singapore, Korea, Hong Kong and Taiwan are of good examples. Malaysia and China follow them. Although she is behind these countries, Turkey is a promising country with her upward climb.

In the era of rapid globalization countries have incomes as much as they can compete. The world income continuously increase but the shares that individual countries get vary. Therefore gaps between countries in terms of income and per capita income appear. Globalization gives countries that can integrate to world economy the chance to increase their income, but on the other hand intensifies competition and make integration to world economy more difficult.

Globalization of Knowledge

As the openness of economies increases, more people and firms take part in the process of un-marketed connection intensification that includes knowledge and integration of knowledge, culture, ideology and technology flows.

The globalization of knowledge may differ according to economy and sectors. There are four layers in the globalization of knowledge. These are:

1. *Local industrial specializations serving the world and specific-skill based activities:* This title includes the most developed and location-specific activities of developed economies.

a. *The winner gets all the goods and services:* There are some functions that are fulfilled by globally known individuals or those who supply different services and are well-known in the sectors such as financial services, media, sports, science and medicine. The activities that are fulfilled by those individuals can be transferred into international markets with low costs. This can be done by disclosure of consumers about the activity and its features or by adaptation of consumption patterns such that these products will be demanded.

b. *Export oriented specialized industrial cluster:* Such specializations have increased in the last 25 years. Each country has some goods and services that she is good at due to her advantages attained by scale, resource based relative advantage, skill and know-how embedded in institutions. These types of activities are more important than they were as they locate in clusters and permanent technologic learning processes.

In both cases knowledge does not globalize. Knowledge is anchored where it is generated and its replication is impossible. Therefore this kind of production results in specialization and trade.

2. *Globalization through displacement (Global product chains):* It is the shift of non-location-dependent production to the low-labour-cost regions through FDI or licensing. In this case knowledge flow occurs from home country to host country.
3. *Non-tradables or quasi-tradables serving locally:* Some products can not be traded as they are specific to regions. Therefore production is run where the consumption will take place. In other words production depends on location. In such conditions production is done in the market under globally-known brands. That is to say the mixture of global and local (glocalization) prevails. As MNCs standardized all the production processes flows of knowledge, particularly globalization of knowledge and ideas, appear in intangible assets.
4. *Debatable markets in manufacturing and service sectors:* It is the production of standardized product such as durables, capital goods and other intermediate goods. As standardized products are produced with codified knowledge in general, the globalization of knowledge is pretty high. In such conditions economies of scale and vertical integrations may occur.

In all types of production it is possible to talk about globalization. It is possible to talk about globalization even in the first layer that is the most closed one to the globalization of knowledge through spill-over effect and reverse-engineering. Development in the knowledge and communication techniques, the globalization of production and the intensification of competition trigger globalization of knowledge. The global knowledge in turn increases competition and therefore productivity.

Environmental Issues

Global environmental concerns have arisen with the recognition of the facts that ecologic processes are not restricted to national boundaries, environmental problems have cross-border effects (eco-systems and water basins that sustain life exceed national boundaries; air pollution diffuses all continents and oceans and there is only one atmosphere which yields protection against climate-preservation and harmful UV rays) and these problems have global effects, *i.e.* the disaster of Chernobyl effected many countries ranging from Bulgaria to Canada. In this framework, the concept for the ability that people should think and behave global bears a new dimension of global responsibility –not just for universal resources, but also for global justice.

Therefore the connections between environment and globalization should be re-examined and taken into consideration. The negligence of these connections means misinterpretation of the dimensions and the nature of globalization and the loss of most important opportunities that may be beneficial for the solutions of hardest environmental problems that humankind faces.

The fact that the world economy globalizes with the integration of national economies into international economy causes some pressures on global environment and natural resources; this in turn makes the sustainability of environment difficult and proves the dependency of human on environment. A global economy may bear global externalities and may worsen global inequality.

The global nature of environment bears the necessity of global management of environment and in fact causes the infrastructure formation of international treaties and institutions and the growth of these.

While the importance of the relationship between globalization and environment is explicit, the level of knowledge on how these two dynamics interact with each other is low. The literature on globalization and environment is uncertain (debating only the generalities); myopic (focused only on trade-related connections) and/or partial (focused only on the effects of globalization on environment, but not the reverse).

However, the relationship between environment and globalization is bidirectional. Like globalization has effects on environment, environment also has effects on globalization. In this framework five striking interactions of the environment-globalization relationship are as follows:

1. Rapid increase in global economic activities and the increase in demand for crucial and limited natural resources may affect the process of continuous increase of economic wealth negatively. Some studies revealing that the productive capacity of nature is exceeded by 25-30 per cent or the fact that annually 2.5 million people lose

their life because of environmental problems involving air pollution, unhealthy water and low quality of health services in the Asia-Pacific region highlight the significance of the situation.

2. Interrelated processes of globalization and environmental deterioration form new threats for already insecure world. They affect the fragility of eco-systems and societies, at least the most fragile ones. The poorest societies face the highest risk. For example, even the adverse effect of climate changes excluded, the number of people that will be adversely affected from water shortage is expected to reach 5 billion in 2025 from its current level of 1.7 billion.
3. Newly prosperous and the established wealthy should learn about the limitations of the ecological space where they live in and should behave consistent with the needs and rights of the people who are not that much lucky. In this context, the "workshop" metaphor (production in developing countries like China and consumption in wealthy regions like Europe and North America) seriously requires placing the "workshop" within a supply chain that is (a) really global in nature, and (b) not just an economic supply chain but an environmental one.
4. Consumption – both in the North and the South – not only determines global environment, but also the future of globalization.
5. Concerns on global markets and global environment will mix each other and become more interdependent.

Most challenging environmental problems the world faces today are caused by developed or developing countries that are industrialized or industrializing. In 1990 the USA and China emitted 4,818.3 and 2,398.9 metric tones of carbon dioxide (CO_2) respectively. They emitted 6,045.8 and 5,007.1 metric tones of CO_2 respectively in 2004.

Therefore in this period USA's CO_2 emission increased by 20 per cent while China's emission increased by more than 100 per cent. Between 1990 and 2004 world CO_2 emission increased by 2 per cent on average annually while the rate of increase in developing countries is 5.7 per cent and in OECD countries it is 1.3 per cent. It is possible to say that as a result of globalization the shift of production into developing countries cause this difference. On the other hand more than half of the total of CO_2 is emitted by a few developed countries. Therefore one of the important movements against environmental problems (particularly against global warming), Kyoto Protocol which was signed in 1997 in Japan and have 174 member countries has not been signed yet by the mostly industrialized country, the USA. 19 countries including Turkey have not announced their positions.

Finally, although there are organs that determine the problems in the system caused by environment and globalization, the endeavor of these organs are divided and lacks coordination and consistency. Efforts and instruments for the holistic processing of the "system" either missing or poorly exploited.

Social Issues

As of 2006 total world population is 6.52 billion. China and India have the highest populations with 1.31 billion and 1.11 billion. Like income, population is not distributed evenly in the world. While 6,728 people live in Hong Kong per km2 and 6,376 people in Singapore, only 2 people live in Mongolia and Namibia, and 3 people in Australia.

The level of education which can be qualified as infrastructure in the way of development may differ greatly among countries. While countries like Latvia and Lithuania have a literacy rate of 100 per cent, the rate is only 24 per cent in Mali. Another indicator for education is the rate of primary school completion. In some countries this rate may be 100 per cent or higher (because of the education of people outside the assigned age group) but as of 2005 it is only 23 per cent in the Republic of Central Africa.

When the data of 1991 and 2005 are compared an improvement in the rate of primary completion can be seen easily. The largest increase was experienced in Venezuela with an increase from 43 per cent to 92 per cent. The differences in the level of education are closely related to the investments of these countries into education. While in some countries expenditure on education to GDP ratios are below 1 per cent (Indonesia, 0.9 per cent), some countries have a ratio above 10 per cent (Botswana, 10.7 per cent).

Developing countries increase the share of education expenditure in public expenditure. Therefore developing and developed countries converge in terms of education.

Today there is no gender discrimination in the primary and secondary education. As of 2005, the Republic of Central Africa has the worst ratio of 60 per cent (the rate of female students to male students), but she experienced a significant development from the ratio of 40 per cent in 1991.

The life expectancy at birth differs among countries according to these countries' health, environmental, cultural and wealth levels. For example, as of 2005 life expectancy for males is 39 and 38 for females in Zambia. At the other end is Hong Kong with life expectancy of 79 and 85 for males and females respectively. When the mortality rate under the age of 5 (per 1000 people) is analyzed it is seen that the world average decreased from 95 in 1991 to 75 in 2005. The worst statistics for infant mortality are experienced unfortunately in developing countries such as Sierra Leone, Nigeria, the republic of Central Africa and Mali. Even in these countries the mortality rates improve. In this improvement, assistance by various health and aid institutions to the developing countries and globalization of knowledge and health services has significant contributions.

When the health expenditure per capita statistics are analyzed it is seen that there is 400 fold gap between the highest (USA with $6,096) and the lowest (the Republic of Congo with $15) expenditures as of 2004. This huge gap creates differences even in the rates of infant vaccination against tuberculosis and measles (only 40 per cent and 23 per cent of infants were vaccinated against tuberculosis and measles in Chad in 2005). A similar view prevails in the health services and improved water source utilization. Although 100 per cent of people in developed countries benefit from these services, the rates in developing countries are about 10 per cent and 50 per cent respectively. What is satisfactory is that these ratios are improving.

THE DEBATE

When all the benefits and costs of globalization are taken into consideration, for some it is a process that should be supported while for others it should be avoided. In this part advocate and opponent institutions and ideas are analyzed.

ADVOCATES OF GLOBALIZATION: NEO-LIBERAL VIEW

Established in Sweden as a non-profit organization World Economic Forum (WEF) is independent and international which was first designed by a group of businessmen in January 1971 with the leadership of European Commission and European Industrial Associations. It was founded as European Management Forum in Geneva, Sweden. However, the collapse of Bretton Woods fixed exchange rate system in 1973 and the Arab-Israel enlarged the focus of these meetings from management to economic and social issues and political leaders were invited to Davos in January 1974. European Management Forum changed its name as World Economic Forum in 1987 and tried to enlarge its vision in order to solve international conflicts.

Organization endeavors for a worldwide governance system which is based on not only the rules but also on values. Its motto is "entrepreneurship in the global public interest". Its members (1000 largest firms that have global activities, rank among top companies within their industry and/or country and have a leading role in shaping the future of their industry and/or region and 200 relatively small firms from developing countries) believe that without economic development, social development is infeasible and vice versa.

The organization's vision has 3 dimensions. These are:

- To be the most important organization that forms and strengthen leader global communities,
- To be the creative force that shape global, regional and industrial strategies,
- To be a catalyst in the choices of communities which have global attempts for the development of the world.

Members get advantage as they recognize and affect two new developments:

- The key problems of the world can not be solved by governments, business or civil society alone and
- Strategic foresights in a world characterized as complex, fragile and synchronized can not be achieved passively. These foresights can be achieved through continuous interaction with partners and those who are best informed in their fields of study.

Therefore in order to realize its mission the WEF formed an integrated value chain through the inclusion of world leaders into the communities, inspiring them with strategic foresights and evoking them with initiatives.

Another globalization advocate is the Washington Consensus which was initiated in 1989 by John Williamson in order to support the countries that had experienced crisis through Washington D.C. based institutions such as the IMF, the World Bank (WB) and the US Department of Treasury and that comprises of ten special economic policy recommendations (fiscal policy discipline, redistribution of public expenditures, tax reform, marked-determined interest rate, competitive exchange rate, trade liberalization, FDI inflow liberalization, privatization, elimination of restrictive terms and the protection of property rights) that are taught to be a "standard" reform package.

Since its initiation, the concept "Washington Consensus" has attained a second meaning that is sometimes called neo-liberalism or market fundamentalism where markets have bigger roles while governments have limited roles. Especially with this second and broader formulation Washington Consensus has been the target of individuals and groups' tough criticisms seeing it as the way to open less developed countries to MNCs and the investments of their owners in the first world economies.

These criticisms often refer to 1999-2002 Argentina economic crises where they think the policies of Washington Consensus are defective because Argentina applied most of the policies recommended by the Consensus.

Many trade liberalization critics like Noam Chomsky, Susan George and Naomi Klein denote the Washington Consensus as the gate of exploitation of the labour markets of under-developed countries by the firms of developed countries. The decreases in the tariffs and trade restrictions let the free movement of goods according to market among countries, but because of tight visa applications labour does not move freely. This creates an economic climate that goods are produced in under developed countries with low labour cost and then exported to prosperous first world economies with high mark-ups taken by MNCs. Criticisms claim that the workers in the third world economies are poor; although they take higher wages than the ones before trade liberalization, these wages are melting with inflation. While the owners of MNCs get richer, the workers in the first world economies become unemployed.

Some criticisms or all of them are denied by the advocates of Washington Consensus as a result of some realizations. For example the inflation rates are at its lowest level in recent years. Workers of the factories established by foreign capital earn more and have better working conditions than those working in domestic firms. In most countries of Latin America the economic growth is at its highest levels and the debt services are at its lowest level relative to the economy. Despite these macroeconomic developments, poverty and inequality are high in Latin America. Nearly 2 people out of 3 have daily incomes below $2. Again one third of the population lacks electricity and sanitation and presumably 10 million children suffer from malnutrition.

OPPONENTS OF GLOBALIZATION: ANTI-GLOBALIST MOVEMENT

In his speech at the University of Houston the Nobel Prize winner Rigoberta Manchu said "Globalization –the intensification of capital and particularly communication systems- affect the life of not only the indigenous but also the poor people. When one talks about free trade, he/she does not talk about small and medium sized commercial sectors but rather huge monopolies.

Anti-globalists focus not on the figures like GDP that are announced by the WB and its derivatives but on the indices like Happy Planet Index calculated by New Economics Foundation. This index focuses on interrelated vital consequences like social resolution, death of democracy, fast and extensive deterioration of environment, spread of new diseases, increasing poverty and alienation.

The organization that is at the position of the representative of anti-globalist movement is the World Social Forum (WSF).

WSF is a meeting arranged by the members of anti-globalization or alter-globalization movement annually in order to coordinate world campaigns, share and refine organizing strategies, and to inform each other about movements around the world and their issues. Its motto is "Another world is possible". It tends to meet in January when its "great capitalist rival", the WEF is meeting in Davos, Switzerland.

WSF has encouraged the organizing of many regional social forums, *i.e.* European, Asian and Mediterranean Social Forums, and many local and national social forums such as Turkish, Liverpool and Boston Social Forums.

WSF defines itself and its mission in its charter of principles. According to the charter the Forum is and open platform to everyone who contributes to the exchange of ideas, proposals, experiences and inter-linkages for effective action in a democratic environment. It is universal. It refuses the process of globalization that serves the interests of MNCs. It aims to unite world non-governmental organizations but it is not a representative of such organizations. No one is authorized with the representation of the Forum. The organizations that attend Forum meetings can freely declare their ideas. The Forum has a plural structure and open to differences provided that they respect the principles of the Forum; it is an organization that does not have religious, statist, military or biased dimensions. The Forum contradicts all repressive economies, views of development and history and the usage of these as a repression factor by governments. It also contradicts the racist, sexist and environment pollutant effects of capitalist globalization. It encourages national and international linkages among organizations and social movements in order to ease the achievement of its goals. It allows local to global movements by its participants.

Besides WSF, there are other anti-globalist organizations. Their globalization oppositions vary in terms of scale and content. The major of these movements are:

International Forum on Globalization (IFG): It is an establishment constituted by activists, economists, scholars and researchers that analyses and criticizes the cultural, social, politic and environmental effects of economic globalization and runs north-south research and is instructive. It was established in 1994. The most important criticism of the organization is the lack of criticism for "free trade" and "neo-liberalism" or the institutions and treaties such as World Trade Organization (WTO), IMF and North Atlantic Free Trade Agreement (NAFTA).

IFG encourages more equal, democratic and ecologic economies that can be alternative to neo-liberalism or to globalization. In its alternative search, the Forum highlights living democracy, supporting local, ecologic sustainability, joint heritage, diversity, human rights, business and life, food security, equity and precaution principle. Besides, the Forum claims that the institutions of globalization, IMF, WTO and WB are under legitimacy crisis.

People's Global Action (PGA): It is an organization formed by anti-global movements from all continents in February 1998 in Geneva. The movement defines itself as anti-capitalist beyond neo-liberal opponent. Movement defines itself as an opponent of the hegemony of capitalism, imperialism, discrimination, racism and transnational capital in the documents of rules, manifesto and organizational principles. In this framework, the movement has a more radical attitude than other organizations.

CorpWatch (CW): The organization was first established in 1996 under the name of Transnational Resource and Action Center (TRAC) and then in March 2001 took the name, CorpWatch. The organization drew attention with the analyses of poor working conditions of Nike in Vietnam and Enron before its crash, and firms that make profit from wars. Organization defines itself as globalization opponent in the subjects of human rights, social justice, environmental sustainability, peace, negative economic realizations, corporate transparency and accountability.

Friends of the Earth (FE): The organization which was established in 1971 mostly deals with environmental problems. Organization has some targets about climate change, recycling, energy-saving houses, organic agriculture and the protection of nature. Organization runs with the ideas of "there is tomorrow", "everyone gets a fair share" and "change the rules for a better economy". In this framework, the organization opposes enterprises and globalization in case they affect environment negatively.

THEORIES OF INTERNATIONAL TRADE

International trade deals with good, service and payment flows among countries and the policies that regulate these flows and their national wealth effects. In short, international trade deals with physical good exchange among countries and the problems arisen from these transactions; international finance deals with the policies that regulate foreign trade markets, balance of payments and imbalances in the payments. Theory of international trade can be accepted as the expansion of the theory of economics so that it covers particular problems arisen from international trade.

The theory of international trade academically was firstly discussed by Adam Smith and his famous book shortly known as Wealth of Nations in 1776. Smith explained classical trade theory and showed that trade is profitable for both sides trading. The win-win character depicted by Smith contradicts the then prevailing view.

The prevailing view until Smith's theory was Mercantilism. According to Mercantilist perception "wealth of nations" is measured with precious metals, gold and silver, and with productive capacity countries have. Therefore each nation desires the highest amount of gold and perceives export as beneficial but imports (except imports of raw materials) as harmful. Therefore trade is a win-lose game. While exporters gain, importers lose. Hence the win-win perception of Smith's absolute advantage is of great importance.

SMITH AND RICARDO: CLASSICAL VIEW

The first scientific steps of the theory of international trade were taken by Adam Smith (1776, The Wealth of Nations: An Enquiry into the Nature and Causes) and David Ricardo (1817, On the Principles of Political Economy and Taxation). They have some assumptions in doing so. They are:

- *Real sector and monetary changes are independent of each other (neutrality of money).*
- *All the prices (and foreign exchange rates) are elastic and determined under perfect competition.*
- *The amount of the factors of production is constant and all the factors are fully utilized (full-employment).*
- *Factors of production are mobile within countries but immobile among countries.*
- *Level of technology (therefore production functions) is same within a country but may vary among countries.*
- *Consumer tastes are constant and international trade does not affect tastes.*
- *The distribution of income is constant.*
- *There are no trade barriers in terms of transportation, knowledge and communication.*

Smith think that total wealth of the world is not constant, foreign trade can increase the wealth of both parties –not just one- therefore the wealth of world through the productivity increase of world recourses by division of labour and specialization and with the help of assumptions tries to explain international trade with absolute advantage theory. Smith claims that a country that can produce more output with one unit of labour has an absolute advantage in that good. For example, if Turkey it will be beneficial for both parties that Germany specializes in steel production and Turkey in wheat production and trade with each other because Germany produces 1 unit of wheat with a cost of 2.5 units of steel. However, Turkey can produce 1 unit of wheat with a cost of only 0.5 unit of steel. Therefore an international trade with a price of 1 unit of wheat=1.5 units of steel will be profitable for both parties.

On the other hand Ricardo claims that absolute advantage theory constrains international trade, it can not explain the trade when one country has absolute advantages in the production of both goods; instead he developed comparative advantage theory. Accordingly, if Turkey can produce only 10 units of steel or 40 units of wheat with one unit of labour while Germany can produce 50 units of steel or wheat, Smith claims that Germany has absolute advantage in the production of both goods and there won't be trade, but Ricardo claims that even in this case trade will be beneficial for both parties. Germany can produce 1 unit of wheat with a cost 1 unit of steel. On the other hand Turkey produces 1 unit of wheat with a cost of 0.25 unit of steel, that is to say Turkey can produce wheat with a comparatively lower cost. In such a case an international trade with a price of 1 unit of wheat=0.6 unit of steel will be profitable for both parties.

Classical trade theory has been criticized because of its simplifying assumptions. Although they are aware of the factors of production except labour, namely capital and natural classical economists choose to perceive natural resources as endowment and capital as accumulated labour. Therefore classical trade theory is based on labour theory of value and excludes other factors of production. Another criticism is that classical trade theory covers supply-side analysis but not the demand-side. Besides it lacks technologic developments, mobility of the factors of production, product differentiation and imperfect competition that contemporary theories cover.

NEO-CLASSICAL THEORIES OF TRADE

Neo-classical economists by using the concept of "opportunity cost" instead of labour theory value that contains other factors together with labour have revised the model of Ricardo. According to this theory production is the result of all the factors used together. Therefore, cost which is the reverse of productivity is the sum of resources used to produce 1 unit of good and is calculated by adding up all the monetary values of factors used. Opportunity cost of a good is the amount of the foregone production of other good for the increase in the first good by 1 unit. Accepting that more than one factor involve in the production process it becomes impossible to make a comparison in terms of individual factor productivities between countries because when all the factors are used in the production simultaneously, it is impossible to measure the productivity of one factor by abstracting it from other factors. Production is the result of collective contributions of all the factors used. Therefore individual factor productivities can not be measured but the collective productivity of them. As a result, with the opportunity cost analysis it is shown that international specializations can not be determined with the comparison of individual factor productivities. In neo-classical framework the comparison is done by production cost. The theory adds up a pricing such as 1 unit of wheat=□30 and 1 unit of steel=□10 behind the final figure of 1 unit of wheat=3 units of steel and then reaches to opportunity cost.

Neo-classical trade theory analyzes production capacities and opportunity costs through transformation curves and demand conditions through indifference curves. On the other hand neo-classical trade theory can not explain different domestic prices among countries. This defect has been debugged by the contributions of Heckscher and Ohlin, Heckscher-Ohlin Theory. According to the theory a country has comparative advantage in the production of the good that necessitates the factor that the country has abundantly. From Heckscher-Ohlin model which is also known as Factor Endowment Theory the theories of Factor Price Equalization, Income Distribution and Rybczynski have been derived.

Factor price equalization theory claims that free trade reveals the same results with the factor markets that equalize the factor prices under perfect international factor mobility even with imperfect factor mobility. Firstly, Heckscher claims that factor prices equate with free trade then Ohlin revised absolute equality as a tendency towards equality and finally Samuelson analytically proved factor price equalization through free trade.

Stolper and Samuelson by contradicting the Ricardo's most widely-accepted idea for more than a century "free trade is beneficial and protectionism is harmful for all in the country" introduced the foreign trade-related income distribution theory. According to the theory, free trade is beneficial for the factor used intensively in the export sectors and protectionism is beneficial for the factors used in import-substitution sectors. In other words, although an economy suffers from protectionism, people working in the import-substitution sector benefit it. In sum, free trade is beneficial for the abundant factor of the country and protectionism for the scarce factor.

Rybczynski theory, which is derived from Heckscher-Ohlin theory and analyzes the production results of the changes in factor supply, betrays that in a two-good, two-factor and full-employment model when the supply of a factor increases, the production of the good that necessitates this factor intensively increases and the production of the other good that necessitates the other factor intensively decreases because of factor transfers between the sectors. Although neo-classical trade theory introduces opportunity cost to the theory and there are the theories of Heckscher-Ohlin, Stolper-Samuelson and Rybczynski that complement the theory, it has been criticized because of its deficiencies. The most important of these criticisms is the Leontief Paradox.

Leontief developed the input-output table technique in order to test factor endowment theory and by forming "representative commodity bales" he analyzed 1947 foreign trade data of USA. However, he found the result that the USA which was the most capital intensive country in the world exports labour-intensive goods and imports capital-intensive goods. This result is named as Leontief Paradox and caused the birth of a new literature.

ALTERNATIVES

As a result of the debates on factor endowment that are created by Leontief Paradox, new theories have been produced since 1960s in order to explain international trade.

Skilled-Labour Theory: Authors like Keesing and Kenen point that most part of the international trade between industrialized countries can be explained by the differences in skilled-labour. According to the theory, countries that are abounding in vocational or skilled-labour in some specific sectors mostly specialize in the production of goods that require these features. On the other hand, countries that have unskilled labour abundantly have advantages in the production of goods that requires unskilled labour.

Technology-Gap Theory: The theory that emphasizes the imitation process was suggested by Posner in 1961. According to the theory the countries that invent a new good or production process become the first exporter of that good. In the course of time after technology transfers, imitation or the end of property rights the good is produced by other countries and because of low labour costs and natural resource advantages these countries produce with lower costs than the innovator country. In this way the good starts to be exported by less-developed countries. The innovator country imports it as she can not compete with these countries. Best example for the case is that once the number 1 exporter of textile, United Kingdom is now a net exporter of textiles.

Product Life Cycle Theory: Theory which emphasizes standardization process was developed by Vernon in 1966 and is a generalized and enhanced version of the technology-gap theory. As mentioned in the theories of FDI part, it has 5 stages and the innovator country that invents a new product and standardizes it becomes a net importer at the end of fifth stage. In other words, product life cycle theory tires to explain dynamic comparative advantage for the new product and production process instead of the static comparative advantage explanation of Heckscher-Ohlin model. *Preference Similarity Theory:* The hypothesis that is developed by Swedish economist Linder in 1961 deals with the trade of non-homogenous industrial goods. According to this view the trade of goods depends not on the production costs but on the similarity of taste and preferences, that is to say on demand conditions. The basic factor that determines the taste and preferences is relative income level.

According to Linder, firms in a country produce the goods that are demanded by the majority of public and have a large market. As firms produce in order to cover domestic demand they get experience and efficiency in the production of that good; later on these goods are exported to the countries that have similar taste and preferences or more broadly to the countries that have close income levels. On the other hand the demand of low or high income individuals who have different taste and preferences are supplied with importation from the countries that have similar taste with them. According to this view which is also known as "Over-lapping demands" the trade of industrial goods will be intensive among those countries that have similar preferences and income levels.

The Linder's theory has not been supported much because it can not explain the trade of industrial goods that do not have domestic market or in other words that are produced only for export.

Theory of Economies of Scale: In some goods average production cost depends on the scale or volume of the production. If average costs decrease with the scale of production, there is decreasing costs and increasing returns to scale. In the factor endowment theory the assumption of constant returns to scale prevails. In case of increasing returns because of economies of scale, profitable trade arises even when both parties are identical in every aspect. This is another type of trade that Heckscher-Ohlin theory can not explain.

Economies of scale, besides the cost advantage of large enterprises over small ones, cause the formation of imperfect competition.

Monopolistic Competition Theory: In real life, especially the industrial goods are not homogenous contrary to the assumption in factor endowment theory because goods are different in terms of components, usage, outlook or at least brands.

World trade is traditionally thought as the exchange of goods that are produced by non-similar or completely different sectors. However, currently the majority of trade occurs between the differentiated goods of the same sector. This is called intra-industry trade (bi-directional trade). Monopolistic competition theory explains the case of bi-directional trade of industrial goods through economies of scale.

The idea of utilizing economies of scale forces firms to produce one or a few kinds of goods instead of various kinds or types of goods. In fact, the cause of this is the possibility of substitution among differentiated goods and the effort of firms to decrease costs for international competition. As production intensifies on few kinds or type specialization follows, more efficient machines are used and economies of scale is exploited. Thereby countries become exporters of that product and import other types of the good from other countries.

NEW TRADE THEORIES

The theories that are called new trade theories are in fact the alternative theories themselves. New trade theories are those that internalize the concepts of scale, network, innovation and global competition.

Costs of a firm may be decreased by two ways. As the scale of production increases per unit fixed cost will decrease and the decrease in variable costs will boost it (internal scale economies); as the scale of the sector where a firm operates, the costs of that firm will decrease and the chance of it to find skilled-labour that enables quality inputs and exchange of experiences will increase (external scale economies).

Firms can avoid the factor endowment constraint of the country through innovation. Technologic progress and facilitator effect of R and D firms on innovation have converter effects on factor endowment, because knowledge has been included among the factors of production.

Networking enables firms to internalize the experiences attained through knowledge exchange, fast experiences, learning by looking and learning by doing.

The global competitiveness of firms depends not only on national factor endowment or the structure of the firm, but to a larger spectrum of variables that are mentioned in the Porter's diamond such as factor conditions, demand conditions, related and collateral sectors and the strategies, structures and competitiveness of firms.

REGULATING GLOBALIZATION AND INTERNATIONALIZATION

The acceleration of globalization in the post-2nd World War period is the result of the plans of economists, businessmen and politicians that recognized the negative effects of protectionism and poor international economic integration. The effects of these people resulted in the Conference of Bretton Woods and the foundation of various institutions aiming the promotion of growth and the management of negative effects and the globalization process. These institutions are the International Bank for Reconstruction and Development (World Bank-WB) and the IMF. Thereafter General Agreement on Trade and Tariffs (GATT) was signed in order to eliminate the barriers for international trade. In the Uruguay Round (1984-1995) the WTO was established for the solution of commercial disputes and for the construction of a standard platform for trade. Besides many bi- or multi-lateral trade treaties such as the Maastricht Treaty and the NAFTA has been signed whose aims are to decrease tariffs and eliminate trade barriers.

There are certain factors that accelerate and widen the domain of globalization. These are:

1. Huge international organizations that desire to affect and if possible control the politic developments in the world; *e.g.* the United Nations,

2. International pacts – large scale treaties covering many countries; *e.g.* the North Atlantic Treaty Organization (NATO),
3. Transnational economic associations that are large scaled and have many members; *e.g.* the European Union, the North American Association, the Black Sea Economic Cooperation,
4. MNCs that operate in more than one country and are business, manufacture and trade centers, banks and corporations,
5. Certain socio-politic movements that are called international trends and affect almost continents, countries and people deeply; *e.g.* ethnic nationalism, fundamentalism, feminism, ecologic movements.

With the light of these developments and factors, the international organizations and integrations have emerged. These institutions and agreements are crucial as they manage or direct the process of globalization.

INTERNATIONAL ORGANIZATIONS

At the national level the stabilizing institutions are social and financial safety nets. At the international level they are the WTO, the IMF, the Basel Committee of Banking Supervisors, the WB, the OECD and others.

International Monetary Fund - IMF

The IMF is an international organization of 185 member countries. It was established in 1944 to promote international monetary cooperation, exchange stability, and orderly exchange arrangements; to foster economic growth and high levels of employment; and to provide temporary financial assistance to countries to help ease balance of payments adjustment which in turn means the regulation of globalization at individual country level.

Some countries view globalization as a process that is beneficial—a key to future world economic development—and also inevitable and irreversible. Others regard it with hostility, even fear, believing that it increases inequality within and between nations, threatens employment and living standards and thwarts social progress.

Globalization offers extensive opportunities for truly worldwide development but it is not progressing evenly. Some countries are becoming integrated into the global economy more quickly than others. Countries that have been able to integrate are seeing faster growth and reduced poverty. Outward-oriented policies brought dynamism and greater prosperity to much of East Asia, transforming it from one of the poorest areas of the world 40 years ago. And as living standards rose, it became possible to make progress on democracy and economic issues such as the environment and work standards. Therefore, according to IMF, encouraging this trend, not reversing it, is the best course for promoting growth, development and poverty reduction.

On the other hand, the crises in the emerging markets in the 1990s have made it quite evident that the opportunities of globalization do not come without risks—risks arising from volatile capital movements and the risks of social, economic, and environmental degradation created by poverty. This is not a reason to reverse direction, but for all concerned to embrace policy changes to build strong economies and a stronger world financial system that will produce more rapid growth and ensure that poverty is reduced. In this framework the IMF advises individual countries to apply the following policy recommendations in order to manage the process efficiently and benefit it:

- Macroeconomic stability to create the right conditions for investment and saving,
- Outward oriented policies to promote efficiency through increased trade and investment,
- Structural reform to encourage domestic competition,
- Strong institutions and an effective government to foster good governance,
- Education, training, and research and development to promote productivity,
- External debt management to ensure adequate resources for sustainable development.

The IMF's control and regulation process involves surveillance (through visits to gather information, discussions with government and central bank officials and annual reports), financial assistance (through Poverty Reduction and Growth Facility, Exogenous Shocks Facility, Stand-by Agreements, Extended Fund Facility, Supplemental Reserve Facility, Compensatory Financing Facility and Emergency Assistance) and technical assistance (through staff missions of limited duration sent from headquarters, or the placement of experts and/or resident advisors for periods ranging from a few weeks to a few years and in the form of technical and diagnostic studies, training courses, seminars, workshops, and "on-line" advice and support).

World Bank - WB

Since its inception in 1944, the WB has expanded from a single institution to a closely associated group of five development institutions. The WB's mission evolved from the International Bank for Reconstruction and Development (IBRD) as facilitator of post-war reconstruction and development to the present day mandate of worldwide poverty alleviation in conjunction with its affiliate, the International Development Association.

The WB is a vital source of financial and technical assistance to developing countries around the world and is made up of two unique development institutions owned by 185 member countries - the International Bank for Reconstruction and Development (IBRD) and the International Development Association (IDA) (There are also three more institutions closely associated with the WB, namely, International Finance Corporation (IFC), the Multilateral Investment Guarantee Agency (MIGA) and the International Centre for

Settlement of Investment Disputes (ICSID)). Each institution plays a different but supportive role in the WB's mission of global poverty reduction and the improvement of living standards. The IBRD focuses on middle income and creditworthy poor countries, while IDA focuses on the poorest countries in the world. Together the WB provides low-interest loans, interest-free credit, grants to developing countries for education, health, infrastructure, communications and many other purposes and also provides analysis, advice and information to the member countries. The WB does not operate for profit.

According to WB, globalization offers incredible opportunities. Yet exclusion, grinding poverty, and environmental damage create dangers. The ones that suffer most are those who have the least to start with – indigenous peoples, women in developing countries, the rural poor, Africans, and their children. Therefore, the World Bank Group assists countries to help themselves by catalyzing the capital and policies through a mix of ideas and experience, development of private market opportunities, and support for good governance and anti-corruption.

The WB's vision is to contribute to an inclusive and sustainable globalization - to overcome poverty, enhance growth with care for the environment, and create individual opportunity and hope and to advance ideas about international projects and agreements on trade, finance, health, poverty, education, and climate change so that they can benefit all, especially the poor seeking new opportunities. The process includes fund generation, loans, grants, analytic and advisory services and capacity building.

Organization for Economic Co-Operation and Development - OECD

The forerunner of the OECD was the Organization for European Economic Co-operation (OEEC). The OEEC was formed in 1947 to administer American and Canadian aid under the Marshall Plan for the reconstruction of Europe after World War II. Its headquarters were established in Paris in 1949.

The OECD took over from the OEEC in 1961. Since then, its missions have been to:

- Support sustainable economic growth,
- Boost employment,
- Raise living standards,
- Maintain financial stability,
- Assist other countries' economic development,
- Contribute to growth in world trade.

In order to contribute to the development of the world economy, the OECD's focus has progressively broadened to include a growing number of other countries, in addition to its 30 members who are committed to democracy and the market economy. It now shares its expertise and accumulated experience with more than 70 developing and emerging market economies. The OECD view on globalization may be best-defined with the speech of

Australian Treasurer Peter Costello at The Annual OECD Summit, 2000 which states "We don't have a choice as to whether or not to stop globalization. Our choice is how to manage it and how to manage it for the benefit of our citizens." In this framework, it could be said that the OECD views globalization as an inevitable process and just aims to regulate and manage the process.

World Trade Organization – WTO

The WTO has 151 members, accounting for over 97 per cent of world trade and is the only global international organization dealing with the rules of trade between nations that is the main catalyst of the process of globalization. At its heart are the WTO agreements, negotiated and signed by the bulk of the world's trading nations and ratified in their parliaments.

Currently there are WTO agreements on goods, services and intellectual property rights. The GATT is the principle rule-book for trade in goods. The WTO also provides dispute settlement and policy reviews. Main functions of the organization are as follows:

- Administering trade agreements,
- Acting as a forum for trade negotiations,
- Settling trade disputes,
- Reviewing national trade policies,
- Assisting developing countries in trade policy issues, through technical assistance and training programmes,
- Cooperating with other international organizations.

As the main purposes of the organization are to promote freer trade, fair competition and encourage development and economic reform, it is one of the main contributors of the process of economic globalization.

United Nations – UN

Another organization regulating globalization is the UN. Its roots go back to the International Telecommunication Union, 1865. The name "United Nations", coined by United States President Franklin D. Roosevelt, was first used in the "Declaration by United Nations" of 1 January 1942. Today the UN has 192 member states.

The organization is central to global efforts to solve problems that challenge humanity. Cooperating in this effort are more than 30 affiliated organizations, known together as the UN system. Day in and day out, the UN and its family of organizations work to promote respect for human rights, protect the environment, fight against disease and reduce poverty. With more than 70 per cent of the work of the UN system, one of the UN's central mandates is the promotion of higher standards of living, full employment, and conditions of economic and social progress and development. In order to achieve these goals, some tools are as follows:

- Grant free access to their markets for good produced in poor countries,
- Implement debt relief programme, including cancellation of all official debts of the heavily indebted poor countries, in return for those countries making demonstrable commitments to poverty reduction,
- Grant more generous development assistance,
- Work with pharmaceutical companies and other partners to develop an effective and affordable vaccine against HIV,
- Make special provision for the needs of Africa.

INTERNATIONAL INTEGRATIONS

International agreements that promote international trade are significant mediums of globalization. The most well-known integration is the European Union which constitutes integration besides a free-trade agreement or area. There are also other agreements which increase international trade. These kinds of integrations, whether free trade agreements or integrations, foster the globalization process by increasing trade, exchange of goods, services and labour and consequently cultures.

European Union - EU

Established in 1951 as the European Coal and Steel Community by the six founding members, the EU chronologically has established a common market, common policies, a single market and finally a monetary union. Today, the EU has 27 member states and acts in a wide range of policy areas - economic, social, regulatory and financial - where its actions are beneficial to the member states. These include:

- Solidarity policies (also known as cohesion policies) in regional, agricultural and social affairs and
- Innovation policies, which bring state-of-the-art technologies to fields such as environmental protection, research and development (R and D) and energy.

Europe's mission in the 21st century is to:

- Provide peace, prosperity and stability for its people,
- Overcome the divisions on the continent,
- Ensure that its people can live in safety,
- Promote balanced economic and social development,
- Meet the challenges of globalization and preserve the diversity of the peoples of Europe,
- Uphold the values that Europeans share, such as sustainable development and a sound environment, respect for human rights and the social market economy.

As a regional integration the EU is ahead of a free trade agreement or a free trade association. Therefore it is not a catalyst for globalization but the globalization itself in all areas and European integration will continue in the fields in which the member states consider it is in their best interests to work together within the traditional EU framework (on issues like trade, globalization, the single market, regional and social development, research and development, measures to promote growth and jobs and many others).

Asia-Pacific Economic Co-Operation - APEC

Since its inception in 1989, the APEC region has consistently been the most economically dynamic part of the world. Today APEC has 21 members. APEC works in three broad areas to meet the Bogor Goals of free and open trade and investment in the Asia-Pacific by 2010 for developed economies and 2020 for developing economies. Known as APEC's 'Three Pillars', APEC focuses on three key areas:

- Trade and Investment Liberalization (reduces and eventually eliminates tariff and non-tariff barriers to trade and investment)
- Business Facilitation (reduces the costs of business transactions, improves access to trade information and aligns policy and business strategies to facilitate growth, and free and open trade)
- Economic and Technical Cooperation (proves training and cooperation to build capacities in all APEC Member Economies)

The outcomes of these three areas enable APEC member economies to strengthen their economies by pooling resources within the region and achieving efficiencies. As a trade boosting integration, APEC is one of the reputable integrations that foster globalization.

North American Free Trade Agreement - NAFTA

The NAFTA is the trade bloc in North America created by the NAFTA and its two supplements, the North American Agreement on Environmental Cooperation (NAAEC) and the North American Agreement on Labour Cooperation (NAALC), whose members are Canada, Mexico, and the United States. It came into effect on January 1, 1994 (Mexico started full implementation in 2008) and it remains the largest trade bloc in the world in terms of combined GDP of its members.

NAFTA was an expansion of the earlier Canada-U.S. Free Trade Agreement of 1988. NAFTA eliminated the majority of tariffs on products traded among the USA, Canada and Mexico, and gradually phased out other tariffs over a 15-year period. Restrictions were to be removed from many categories, including motor vehicles, computers, textiles, and agriculture. The treaty also protects intellectual property rights (patents, copyrights, and trademarks), and outlines the removal of investment restrictions among the three countries. The treaty is trilateral in nature; the terms apply equally to all countries, in which stipulations, tariff reduction phase-out periods, and protection of selected industries, were negotiated on a bilateral basis. Provisions regarding worker and environmental protection were added later as a result of supplemental agreements signed in 1992.

European Free Trade Association - EFTA

EFTA is an intergovernmental organization set up for the promotion of free trade and economic integration to the benefit of its four member states: Iceland, Liechtenstein, Norway and Switzerland. The Association manages the EFTA Convention; EFTA's worldwide network of free trade and partnership agreements, and the European Economic Area Agreement (EEA).

EFTA Convention is set up in 1960 to provide a framework for the liberalization of trade in goods amongst its member states and updated in 2001 (called the Vaduz Convention).

EFTA's worldwide network of free trade and partnership agreements - consisting of EFTA, EEA, Free Trade Agreement and Joint Declaration of Cooperation plus on-going and potential FTAs - create one of the world's largest networks of free trade partners securing free access to markets of around 440 million consumers.

The EEA, which entered into force on 1 January 1994, brings together the 27 EU members and the three EFTA countries - Iceland, Liechtenstein and Norway - in a single internal market, referred to as the "Internal Market." The EEA Agreement provides for the inclusion of EU legislation that covers the four freedoms - the free movement of goods, services, persons and capital - throughout the 30 EEA States. In addition, the Agreement covers co-operation in other important areas such as research and development, education, social policy, the environment, consumer protection, tourism and culture, collectively known as "flanking and horizontal" policies. The Agreement guarantees equal rights and obligations within the Internal Market for citizens and economic operators in the EEA.

Others

ASEAN Free Trade Agreement (AFTA) was established in 1967 in Bangkok by the five original member countries, namely, Indonesia, Malaysia, Philippines, Singapore, and Thailand. Then Brunei Darussalam, Vietnam, Lao PDR, Myanmar and Cambodia have joint.

The ASEAN Declaration states that the aims and purposes of the association are:

- To accelerate economic growth, social progress and cultural development in the region and
- To promote regional peace and stability through abiding respect for justice and the rule of law in the relationship among countries in the region and adherence to the principles of the United Nations Charter.

Central European Free Trade Agreement (CEFTA) is another agreement which is between countries in Central and South-Eastern Europe. It was originally signed in 1992 by Poland, Hungary, Czech and Slovak Republics and entered into force in 1994. The parties of the CEFTA are: Albania, Bosnia and Herzegovina, Croatia, Republic of Macedonia, Moldova, Montenegro, Serbia and Kosovo. Former parties that left the agreement because of their EU membership are Bulgaria, the Czech Republic, Hungary, Poland, Romania, Slovakia and Slovenia. There are a lot of international integrations and free trade agreements in the world. Most of them are in favour of freer trade and therefore economic globalization.

FUTURE: QUA VADIS?

Despite the peace settlements signed after 2nd World War, the world entered a cold war process. At the essence of this contention that affected the whole world there were the contradicting economic structures, capitalism and communism. Even the countries who didn't want to place in any bloc were affected from this structure and for their interest had close relations with both zones.

Either capitalist or communist systems, they have developed in different directions with what their ideas and targets promise. Capitalism has developed by accepting material success and wealth as the measure of everything and material satisfaction of human as the basic motive. At the end it was successful but could not share this success with the public. Therefore the individuals that are desired to be rescued are depressed more and left alone. Individuals that feel this depression oriented to other things. On the other hand mercantilist state perception which takes the state as basis and accepts full responsibility of state for the society in order to retrieve equity to everybody disregarded individuals. The public depressed under the power of state and who could not achieve the promised heavens at the end surrendered from the ideals and operability of communism. Therefore in the period of about half a century both economic perception and the cohesive political systems recognized the need of change.

Although globalization constitutes an important leg of this change, there is no consensus on the definition and the effects of the concept "globalization". Public opinion on globalization is polarized due to the advantages and disadvantages of the process. Globalization is perceived as either a cure for all problems or the primary cause of these problems.

Globalization is neither a magic cure for the problems of national economies nor a plot for exploitation of workers or despoliation of environment by mega-corporations. Globalization is neither the return of colonialism, nor is it the arrival of world government. Globalization simply means an expansion of the range of possible commercial activities at the most fundamental level. The activities such as buying, selling, producing, borrowing and lending which were restricted by geographic technologic or legal barriers have become practical. Seeking and sorting through the possibilities opened up by globalization will require a great amount of effort, flexibility and change because globalization embodies such a vast and marvelous array of new economic opportunities.

Globalization will affect every country and individual both positively and negatively. While positive effects do not bear any threat and are desired by everyone, all the negative effects constitute the basis of anti-globalist movements. The basic item that anti-globalist movements are grounded on is the fact that the negative effects will affect fragile, weak and poor countries and persons first and then the whole mankind. Therefore the world should deliberate on the threats that globalization creates and try to manage the process. In this process the most important function belongs to international institutions.

If the future of globalization is analyzed in terms of statistics and world realizations the developing countries of BRICS (Brazil, Russia, India, China and South Africa) have the fastest growing information and communication technologies (ICT) markets in the world and the developments in these five countries have spill-over effects on OECD region. Between 2000 and 2005 with an annual increase over 19 per cent the ICT expenditures reached to $277 billion from $114 billion. Between 2000 and 2006 the annual ICT growth rate of expenditure was 5.6 per cent for the world and only 4.2 per cent for the OECD region and the share of OECD in the world market decreased form 89 per cent to 83 per cent.

The highest growth in ICT expenditure was experienced by the developing countries outside the OECD region. ICT expenditure of China that achieved an annual growth rate of 22 per cent in terms of nominal dollars is estimated to be $118 billion in 2005. Excluding China, the highest growth rates belong to 9 non-OECD countries like Russia (25 per cent annually) and India (23 per cent) between 2000 and 2005. the second group pf countries which have high growth rates include Indonesia, South Africa and East European OECD member countries.

In these circumstances, it is possible to say that the ICT demand of developing countries like China will continue and consequently the integration of the world economy will increase and globalization will intensify.

On the other hand as of 2000 an American consumes 2.1 fold more energy than a German, 12.1 fold than a Colombian, 28.9 fold than an Indian, 127 fold than a Haitian and 395 fold than an Ethiopian. These figures emphasize the inequality among people and this inequality has significant importance for the future of globalization and environment.

Divergence of incomes helps to explain the polarization in the world system between the region of peace and the region of chaos. The wealthy zone lives the wax of economic growth and the republican order of liberal tolerance and the technologic innovations that will substitute natural capital usage. Our age is the optimal era for those at the highest parts of income distribution in the prosperous countries. On the other hand in the low and medium income zone, mostly in Africa, Middle East, Central Asia, Russia and in some parts of East Asia, the governance capacity of many countries are stagnant or eroding. The people living in these countries can not find their access to even basic necessities while at the same time see people driving Mercedes – on TV if not outside their own windows.

New information technologies produce tools that threaten the stability of societies and crate a lot of unemployed and angry young people that threaten even the stability of the prosperous zone. Economic growth in poor countries often depletes natural resource and therefore future growth potential. More and more people see migration to prosperous zone as the only way of salvation. The importance of the "missing middle" is partly that the three quarter of world population in the third world must get to the first world in order appreciably to raise their incomes. There is not much of a middle world for them to migrate, and in any case average income in the middle world is only 4 times higher than average income in the third world; while average income in the first world is over 9 times higher.

As a result, the answer to the question whether the globalization process will create a wealthier world for all or a world that will have greater differences among countries and therefore unrests will be given by the process itself. Good management of the process will increase the chance of first scenario while ignorance or deferment of the problems will increase the risk of second scenario.

THE FUTURE OF GLOBALIZATION

Have you noticed that the nations of the world have become increasingly interconnected? Think about it. At the supermarket you can buy products from all over the earth—oranges from South Africa, olive oil from Greece, wine from Italy. You can purchase clothes made in Indonesia, Sri Lanka, or Malaysia. In the evening you turn on your Asian-made television set to watch your favorite programme. Every day you drive your American, Japanese, South Korean or German-made car to work. Call customer service to discuss your telephone bill and you may well be speaking to someone in India. If you live in a big city, you have likely encountered people who have immigrated to your country.

Surfing the Internet on your computer, you can keep up to date with news anywhere in the world, 24 hours a day, 7 days a week. Drought on the American and Canadian prairies affects the price of bread. Political unrest in the Ivory Coast influences the price of chocolate. Bad weather in Brazil affects the price of coffee. Acts of terrorism against the U.S. impact the New York stock markets. And political disputes between major oil-producing nations and their customers increase the price of gas.

Since the latter half of the 20th century, the international community has become more interconnected and interdependent in economic, cultural and environmental matters than ever. It seems the world is rapidly becoming a single community, a global village. Some see this as a good thing; others are not so sure. Then there are those who believe integration is the first step towards a "new world order," one in which sovereign nation states will be dissolved in favour of large trading blocs led by a super world government.

Where is this globalization trend leading? Will the world eventually become a single community?

HISTORY OF GLOBALIZATION

Globalization is the process by which nations become increasingly integrated. This is occurring primarily due to advances in technology that have enabled people, goods, money, data and ideas to travel the world much faster than before; and the reduction of trade and economic barriers, which has greatly increased trade between countries.

In recent years, globalization has become a hot topic, one that has been associated with trends such as the following:

- The rise and expansion of multinational corporations with business interests and employees in several countries, including McDonald's, Coca-Cola, Toyota, Sony, IBM, Unilever, Nike and Shell.
- The emergence of global financial markets in centers such as New York, London, Frankfurt and Hong Kong, providing businesses around the world with easier access to financing.
- Greater levels of immigration, changing the ethnic, cultural and religious composition of several countries and leading to the establishment of multicultural societies.
- The erosion of trade barriers between groups of nations, leading to the emergence of powerful trading blocs, with names such as NAFTA (the North American Free Trade Agreement), the European Union and the ASEAN (Association of Southeast Asian Nations).

Globalization is not new. Historically, people have left their surroundings and traveled to distant lands for four main reasons: *conquest* (the desire to control other countries); *prosperity* (the search for a better life); *exploration* (the desire to discover new lands); and *trade* (the desire to sell goods profitably). The primary agents of globalization in the past were soldiers, sailors, traders and explorers.

For thousands of years, traders carried their goods across oceans and continents and armies launched invasions on their rulers' orders. Powerful nations have brought new lands under their authority, integrating disparate nations, peoples and cultures into empires.

Earlier forms of globalization existed in the Egyptian, Medo-Persian, Babylonian, Greek and Roman empires. During the time of the Mongol empire in the Middle Ages, the famed "Silk Road" connected Central Asia and Europe, linking several civilizations.

The first steps towards globalizing as we know it today were taken in the 16th and 17th centuries when the Portuguese and Spanish empires spread into

Africa, the Americas and Asia seeking gold, silver and spices. The Dutch, French and British empires soon followed, with the Dutch East India Company becoming the world's first multinational privately-held company, in which ownership was divided into shares. This first wave of globalization was characterized by rapid growth in trade and investment between the European powers and their colonies, including the American colonies.

The first era of globalization began to break down with the advent of the First World War, and later collapsed between the two world wars, in part due to the raising of tariffs and increased immigration restrictions.

GLOBALIZATION TODAY

The end of the Second World War brought renewed life to globalization. Since 1950, the volume of world trade has increased by roughly 20 times from \$320 billion to \$6.8 trillion (USD). Between 1980 and 2000, flow of foreign investment had increased approximately twenty-fold, from \$57 billion to around \$1.3 trillion. This increase in trade and foreign investment allows consumers around the world to enjoy a broader selection of products.

In the years since WWII, a defining feature of globalization has been an international industrial and business structure built by multinational corporations. Many governments have adopted free market economic systems, negotiating reductions in barriers to commerce and establishing international agreements to promote trade in goods, services and investment.

As a result of the explosion of trade and technology, the current rate of globalization is unprecedented. Author and journalist Thomas Friedman stated that today's globalization is unique because what was once accomplished only by corporations is now being done by individuals, allowing them to reach around the world "farther, faster, cheaper, and deeper."

Examples are everywhere, which we experience every day. Internationally, millions eat Kentucky Fried Chicken, drink Pepsi, drive Hondas, listen to music on Sony mp3 players, and play sports wearing Reebok sneakers.

Nowadays, many companies outsource their manufacturing operations to developing nations. For example, American and European clothing companies employ workers in Indonesia to produce their products to be sold back home. Technology firms employ programmers in India to write programming code. Telecommunication companies place call centers in India to handle customer service.

At the Crossroads "Down Under"

Few countries have used globalization as effectively as Australia—a market that has been transformed by a commercial link with Asia, particularly China. As a result, for the past 15 years Australia's economy has grown at an average rate of 3.7 per cent per year and shows no sign of slowing down—despite having one of the world's highest minimum wages.

The *Christian Science Monitor* reports that in the early years of the 20th century, Australians were the richest people on earth, the result of the country's vast natural resources. However, their standard of living steadily declined, leaving in its wake high unemployment and inflation during the early 1980s. This convinced the government to remove its protectionist policies and force Australian companies to compete globally.

This decision set in motion a period of reform. In 1983, the Australian dollar was allowed to compete with other world currencies. In the banking industry, regulations were changed to make it easier and potentially more profitable for foreign banks to do business in Australia. Also, trade tariffs were slowly dismantled from the clothing, auto and wool industries. Major state-owned firms were privatized and sold, the most prominent of which were the phone company and national airline. Citizens were encouraged to buy shares in privatized companies, to the extent that today 55 per cent of adults own stocks—the highest rate in the world.

Interestingly, throughout all of the reforms, Australia continues to set minimum wages per industry. Benefits such as health care, pensions and prescription drugs are means tested, directing more to the poor than the wealthy.

Australia's economy has grown because of skyrocketing prices for its iron ore, coal and aluminum, which fuel China's factories. The cheaper prices of China's toys, appliances and other household products and office supplies have also helped raise living standards.

Of some concern is the fact, that even in the face of the overall rise in prosperity, the gap between rich and poor is growing. In 1995, the richest 1 per cent of the population earned 5 per cent of the national income, which increased to 9 per cent by 2006. These trends and impending changes by the government to slow minimum wage growth are stirring misgivings and protests.

A Controversial Topic

Those who support globalization point out that free trade enables companies from the rich industrialized countries to invest in poorer countries, providing jobs to local citizens and improvements to infrastructure. Many multinational corporations now reduce labour costs by outsourcing portions of their business operations to countries such as India and China. This has been particularly true of the manufacturing sector.

Foreign companies also provide wealth to local economies in the form of foreign currency when they buy local products and services. In many cases, they have built schools, colleges and hospitals for the local residents, enhancing the quality of life.

Advocates also contend that globalization allows for the mixing of people and cultures, further enabling the sharing of ideas, experiences and lifestyles. People can experience foods and other products not previously available in their own country. Overall, supporters of globalization argue that it has brought improved standards of living and quality of life to several countries. They point to examples such as China. As a result of opening its markets to the world, China's economy can claim an increase in per capita personal income from $1,420 in 1980 to $4,120 by 1999. In 1980, Americans earned 12.5 times as much as the Chinese per capita. By 1999, they were only earning 7.4 times as much.

Supporters cite globalization as having benefited countries in a number of ways, particularly poorer ones. For example, the percentage of people in developing countries living below $1 per day has halved in only 20 years; life expectancy in the developing world has almost doubled since WWII and is closing the gap with the developed world; between 1950 and 1999 global literacy increased from 52 per cent to 81 per cent.

But globalization has equally vocal opponents. In recent times, globalization has been blamed for a host of ills, including poverty in the Third World, job losses in industrialized countries and even the "Americanization" of other cultures. "Anti-globalists" contend that it operates only in the interests of the rich nations and multinational corporations. They argue that such corporations exploit workers in the developing world, subjecting them to poor working conditions in "sweat shops," and paying them salaries that they would not be allowed to get away with back home. They contend that the multinational profits are repatriated and little is invested in the communities whose labour and resources they consume.

These critics also say that the gap between the rich and poor nations is growing, and that globalization has not benefited poorer countries. Figures used frequently to back their position come from a variety of sources, including a report from the United Nations Development Programme. For example, the gap in incomes between the 20 per cent of the richest and poorest countries has grown from 30 to 1 in 1960 to 82 to 1 in 1995.

By the late 1990s, the fifth of the world's population living in the highest-income countries had:

- 86 per cent of the world's gross domestic product—the bottom fifth just 1 per cent.
- 82 per cent of world export markets—the bottom fifth just 1 per cent.
- 68 per cent of foreign direct investment—the bottom fifth just 1 per cent.
- 74 per cent of the world's telephone lines—the bottom fifth just 1.5 per cent.

These anti-globalists say this rising inequality is the result of market forces. They say that given free rein, market forces give the rich the power to add to their wealth. Therefore, they argue that large corporations invest in poor countries only because they can take advantage of low wage levels or so they can access their natural resources.

The Future

So what does the future hold? What will be the result of the increasingly interconnected state of the world's nations?

While there are many opinions, there is only one source that can give us the true answer—the Holy Bible. In it, God accurately foretold the rise and fall of the major nations throughout history, including the Babylonian, Medo-Persian, Greek and Roman empires (Daniel 2). He even prophesied the sudden rise of the American and British people to world prominence.

And God has foretold today's fast-paced interconnected world and its matchless advances in science and technology: "But you, O Daniel, shut up the words, and seal the book, even to the time of the end: *many shall run to and fro*, and *knowledge shall be increased*".

The Bible states that, in the future, a union of ten nations (or groups of nations) will arise, and replace America as the dominant world power. It will attack and defeat America and Britain, taking the survivors into captivity. This political, economic and military combine will be backed by a universal false church. It will become a world-leading trading bloc, possessing vast riches and trading all over the world in every product imaginable—even human beings! This politically influential religious entity, led by a charismatic figure, will usher in a temporary period of great wealth. Globalization will thrive during its reign to levels unseen in human history—prosperity will flourish, but not for all.

However, shortly after the rise of this ten-nation union, it will be replaced by a world-rulingSUPERGOVERNMENT that will usher in lasting peace, prosperity and security for all. Upon His triumphant Return, Jesus Christ will take over all the governments of men, and administer His government—the kingdom of God—throughout the earth. At that time, the world will become truly "one"—one with God.

True globalization will occur, but according to God's just standards. No more inequality. No more poverty. No more exploitation. Peace will abound. What a wonderful picture—soon to become a reality!

2

Critical Theory and World Politics

COLOMBIA'S CONFLICT AND THEORIES OF WORLD POLITICS

Among the multiple critiques of International Relations theory, its limited relevance for understanding the Third World's place in global affairs has gained increasing attention during the past decade. First, the end of the Cold War revealed a more complex world stage with a plurality of actors, problems and interests that had little to do with traditional interstate power relations. September 11 drove home like a sledgehammer the point that the world is about far more than the high politics of Western nations. Today, IR theory's poor ability to describe and explain, much less predict, the behaviour of states in the global South is recognized as one of its primary shortcomings. This in part accounts for the tepid reception that this body of theory has received within countries not counted among the great powers. Both academic and policy-making circles in the developing and less developed world are skeptical about a theoretical tradition whose claims to universalism not only ignore them, but also act to reify a global order within which they are destined to draw the short straw.

The Andean Region exemplifies this breach between contemporary IR theorizing and the multifarious problems besetting peripheral states and societies. Until very recently, the violence and social conflicts found in nearly every corner of the Andes were not even on IR's radar screen. The 40-year plus armed conflict in Colombia, the violent opposition to Hugo Chavez's populism, massive social protests in Bolivia and Peru, and Ecuador's persistent political and social instability have all been branded domestic issues, and thus not within the purview of systemic IR thinking. Worldwide transformations that have blurred the internal-external dichotomy, however, have prompted some to recognize what has long been common knowledge in the region: local conflicts and problems are completely enmeshed with complex global economic, social and political processes. Colombia's conflict is a case in point. Global markets for illicit drugs, links between Colombian armed actors and international criminal organizations, regional externalities of Colombian violence, the massive level of migration to the North, the explosion of the global third sector's presence in Colombia, increasing U.S. military involvement, and growing concerns of the international community about the deteriorating Colombian situation all illustrate the international face of this crisis.

What light might IR theory shed on a conflict that is estimated to result in 3,500 deaths a year, two thirds of which are civilian, that is responsible for 2.7 million displaced people and another 1 million plus international refugees, whose political economy is such that an average of seven kidnappings occur daily, and that has the country awash in numbing levels of violence and human rights abuses? IR theory is in the business of explaining and predicting violent conflict, as well as the behaviour of the world's member states in relation to conflict and stability.

Although critical and second-order theories of international relations have fundamentally different concerns, substantive theorizing must address what Michael Mann calls IR's "most important issue of all: the question of war and peace." Indeed, realist and liberal theories within the classical paradigm, which share a similar ontology, assumptions and premises, purport to do just that. Given that Kal Holsti's latest figures estimate that 97 per cent of the world's armed conflicts between 1945 and 1995 took place in either the traditional or the new Third World, a viable theoretical framework of world politics must be able to integrate the global periphery.

IR scholarship may or may not offer in its treatment of the Andean Region, and of the armed conflict in Colombia in particular. My commentary will be limited to three issues familiar to the developing world, as seen through the lens of Colombia's current crisis: the correlation of state weakness with violence and instability, the post-territorial nature of security threats, and the North-South power disparity. I will conclude with some observations on what this may tell us about the adequacy of the theories themselves.

STATE WEAKNESS

The sovereign state that lies at the heart of the Westphalian model is the building block of mainstream IR theory. Most theorizing about international politics characterizes the state in terms of power, understood as the capability of achieving national interests related to external security and welfare. Realist and liberal perspectives, and some versions of constructivism, are all concerned with explaining conflictual and cooperative relations among territorially distinct political units, even while their causal, or constitutive, arguments are quite different. Although Kenneth Waltz was taken to task for blithely claiming that states under anarchy were always "like units" with similar functions, preferences and behavioural patterns, much of international relations scholarship persists in a top-down, juridical view of statehood largely abstracted from internal features.

But international legal sovereignty may be the most that the advanced industrialized states have in common with states on the global periphery such as Colombia. First of all, Colombia's priority is internal security, not its power position relative to other states. Threats to the state originate within Colombian territory, not in neighboring countries. In spite of some longstanding border tensions and historical rivalries within the Andean Region, Colombia and its neighbors tend to be more concerned with the strength of domestic social movements and armed actors than they are with the international balance of power. Indeed, even in the absence of a regional balancer, strong democratic institutions, dense economic and political networks, or multilateral governance structures, inter-state wars in the region during the 20th century have been extremely rare. This no-war zone, or negative peace according to Arie Kacowicz, appears to be best explained by a shared normative commitment to maintaining a society of states and to peaceful conflict resolution, contradicting both material and systemic explanations of interstate behaviour.

State strength in much of the developing world is not measured in terms of military capability to defend or project itself externally, but rather according to the empirical attributes of statehood: the institutional provision of security, justice and basic services; territorial consolidation and control over population groups; sufficient coercive power to impose order and to repel challenges to state authority; and some level of agreement on national identity and social purpose. States in the Andean Region all receive low marks for the very features that mainstream IR theory accepts as unproblematic, and immaterial. Although Colombia is in no immediate danger of collapse, most indications point to a state that has become progressively weaker: the basic functions required of states are poorly and sporadically performed, central government control is non-existent in many jurisdictions, social cohesion is poor, and the fundamental rules of social order and authority are violently contested. Most importantly, the Colombian state fails the basic Weberian test of maintaining its monopoly over the legitimate use of force and providing security for its citizens.

Internal state weakness, ranging from impairment to outright collapse, is the common denominator of post-Cold War global violence and insecurity. It is also the permissive condition of Colombia's security emergency. Reduced state capacity underlies the more proximate causes of the violent competition with and among contending subnational groups, namely the FARC, ELN, paramilitaries, and narcotrafficking organizations. Recent efforts by the Alvaro Uribe administration to build up Colombia's military suggest movement towards state strengthening, although effective consolidation must go far beyond this one component of stateness. It remains to be seen whether in the long run Colombia's bloody conflict becomes a force for state creation in the Tillian tradition, or on the contrary a structure that has ritualized violent discord as a normal part of Colombian social life.

This erosion in capacity and competence has taken its toll on what is perhaps a state's most valuable asset—legitimacy. The Colombian state's mediocre performance and problem-solving record degrades central authority, reducing public compliance and policy options, and leading to a further deterioration in internal order as para-institutional forms of security and justice emerge. This dynamic has been exacerbated by new mechanisms of global governance and the proliferation of global actors within domestic jurisdictions increasingly perceived as legitimate alternatives to sovereign state authority. What Jessica Matthews describes as a "power shift" away from the state—up, down, and sideways—to suprastate, substate, and nonstate actors as part of the emergent world order may also involve a relocation of authority.

This is particularly apparent in the post-colonial and developing world where the state is less equipped to respond to internal challengers, and sovereignty's norm of exclusivity is more readily transgressed. In Colombia, alternative political communities such as transnational NGO's, church and humanitarian associations, and global organizations, as well as insurgent and paramilitary groups, are increasingly viewed as functional and normative substitutes for the state.

GLOBAL SECURITY DYNAMICS

At the same time that Colombia's security crisis is in great measure attributable to the empirical weakness of the state, it also highlights another dimension of the emerging global order: the complex interplay between domestic and international security domains. The globalization of security puts into sharp relief the growing discontinuity between fixed, territorial states and the borderless processes that now prevail in world politics. While Realists would point out that current events in North Korea and Iraq are eloquent reminders of the applicability of a traditional national security model in which state-on-state military threats predominate, concerns in Colombia reflect a somewhat different security paradigm.

First of all, insecurity in Colombia is experienced by multiple actors, including the state, the society at large, and particular subnational groups. Security values, in turn, vary according to the referent: national security interests, both military and non-military, exist alongside societal and individual security concerns. Colombian society not only seeks security against attacks, massacres, torture, kidnapping, displacement, and forced conscription, but also in the form of institutional guarantees related to democracy and the rule of law, and access to basic services such as education, employment and health care. Many of the internal risks that Colombia confronts are also enmeshed with regional, hemispheric and global security dynamics that are dominated by state and non-state actors.

While Colombia is typically viewed as being the in eye of the regional storm, the Colombian crisis is itself entangled with transregional and global security processes, including drug trafficking, the arms trade, criminal and terrorist networks, and U.S. security policies. The remarkable growth in the strength of Colombia's most destabilizing illegal groups during the 1990s, for instance, is directly attributed to their ability to generate revenue from activities related to the global market for illegal drugs.

Both the FARC and the paramilitaries capture rents from the cultivation, production and trade of cocaine and heroin, which finances their organizations, keeps them well stocked with arms also traded on regional and worldwide black markets, and sustains a pernicious conflict. These transactions occur within complex transnational criminal associations within and at the edges of the Andean region, which in turn are involved in global financial, crime, and even terrorist networks. Seen from this perspective, Colombia's war is not so internal after all: it actively involves dense transborder networks composed of an array of global actors. Such a post-sovereign security setting underscores the necessity for mainstream IR theorizing to go beyond its state-centered vision of world politics and to develop conceptual tools better equipped to deal with global realities.

POWER AND AUTHORITY ON THE PERIPHERY

IR theory's notion of formal anarchy coexists uneasily with relations of inequality and domination that pervade world order. While most states in the South would tell you that the exclusive authority with which the institution of sovereignty endows them is not quite equal to that of their more powerful northern associates, neo-realism and neoliberalism insist that the evident discrepancies among states are mere power differentials within a decentralized international system that lacks a central political authority. Thus hegemony and asymmetrical interdependence as such do not contradict the fundamental IR distinction between anarchy and hierarchy.

Some dominant-subordinate structures, such as the U.S.-Colombian relationship, may indeed be about more than material differences, however. The immense disparity in economic, political and military power has permitted Washington to impose its will in Colombia on a wide range of issues similar to a coercive hegemonic project.

Nevertheless, Colombian observance of American preferences in its foreign and internal security policy is not exclusively related to overt threats or quid pro quos. The rules of what Alexander Wendt and Daniel Friedheim call "informal empire" are such that inequality can also be characterized as a de facto authority structure. Authority implies that the U.S. exercises a form of social control over Colombia, and that in turn Colombian compliance cannot always be explained by fear of retribution or self-interest, but rather suggests some acceptance, no matter how rudimentary, of the legitimacy of U.S. power.

Ongoing practices that become embedded in institutional structures can create shared behavioral expectations and intersubjective understandings reflected in identities and preferences. Colombia's anti-drug posture, for example, that was in great measure shaped by Washington´s militarized war on drugs and aggressive extradition policy, has over time become internalized. Colombia has appropriated the prohibitionist discourse of the United States, and become an active agent in reproducing its own identity and interests vis-à-vis the illegality and danger of drugs.

It would be an exaggeration, however, to conclude that Colombia's behaviour on its shared agenda with the U.S. is completely consensual: the underlying power configuration is a constant reminder that Washington calls the shots. The U.S. reconstruction of Colombia's internal conflict into part of its war on global terror, with great uncertainty within the country about its implications for a negotiated settlement, is illustrative. U.S. preponderance can also lead to "increased incentives for unilateralism and bilateral diplomacy," at times directly against Colombian interests. Recent arm-twisting to grant immunity to American citizens and military in Colombia from prosecution for human rights violations under the International Criminal Court is a case in point. Still, material inequalities can obscure how third-dimensional power also operates in the informal authority relations between the United States and Colombia.

Conclusion

The Colombian situation suggests various themes which theories of world politics would be well advised to take into consideration. IR theory has been largely silent on the issues of state-making and state-breaking that reside at the heart of the Third World security problematic. In neglecting domestic contexts more broadly speaking, this body of theory is inadequate for explaining the relationship between violent "internal" conflicts and global volatility at the start of the 21st century.

These theories also have a blind spot when it comes to non-state actors in world politics. In overemphasizing states, realist theories in particular are hard pressed to adequately account for the countless sources of vulnerability of states and societies alike. Security threats, from terrorism to drug trafficking to AIDS, defy theoretical assumptions about great power politics and the state's pride of place in world order. Similarly, non-territorial global processes such as Colombia's security dynamics are not well conceptualized by conventional IR levels of analysis that spatially organize international phenomena according to a hierarchy of locations. Colombia's experience with sovereignty also calls into question the logic of anarchy in realist and liberal IR theorizing. Seen from a peripheral point of view, the notion of formal equality is little more than a rhetorical device that camouflages deep and persistent material and social inequalities in the international system. We thus arrive at the conundrum of a "stable" world order, in IR terms defined by the absence of war among the world's strongest states, wracked by violent conflict and immeasurable human suffering in peripheral regions. Perhaps most importantly, today's global security landscape should prompt us to rethink theories that by and large bracket the non-Western, developing domains and suppress their narratives.

The heterogeneity of the IR discipline cautions us against jettisoning the entire canon as flawed when it comes to the Third World, however. Constructivists' incorporation of a social dimension into an analysis of state identities and interests is a promising research agenda for analyzing non-material aspects of North-South relations. Institutionalism theory has also contributed to our understanding of the role of global institutions and norms in conflict resolution and cooperation in the Third World, and may offer insight into seemingly intractable conflicts such as Colombia's. Paradoxically, certain realist precepts also have utility for analyzing the international politics of developing states. The distribution of global economic, political and military power has an enormous impact on center and peripheral states alike. As we have seen, the inequality in U.S.-Colombian relations poses a serious challenge to multilateralism and mechanisms of global governance. In spite of the ongoing reconfiguration of the state in response to global transformations, the sovereign state has proved to be highly adaptive and resilient. Colombia's internal weakness, for example, is to be contrasted with the state's increasingly successful political and diplomatic agenda within the international community, even in the face of increasing global constraints. The complexities of Colombian security dynamics, which vividly illustrate a non-realist security landscape, nevertheless require that public policies prioritize, delineate and specify threats and responses largely in conventional, military terms. And finally, Colombia's efforts to recuperate state strength, or complete its unfinished state-making process, as the case may be, suggest that state power remains pivotal to internal, and thus global, order.

Rather than dismissing IR theory outright for its shortcomings in explaining the problems of countries such as Colombia, we may be better advised to look towards peripheral regions for what they can contribute to testing, revising, and advancing our theories of international politics. Perhaps the explosion of war-torn societies in the Third World and the implications this has for global order will inspire critical analysis of where the theories fail and what they have that is germane to analysis of international relations in the South. Just as there is no single theoretical orthodoxy in IR, neither is the Third World a like unit. With any luck, the diversity of these experiences will lead to new theorizing about world politics.

LIBERAL THEORIES OF WORLD POLITICS

This memo outlines the liberal approach to theorizing international relations. Like realism, institutionalism, or non-rational approaches, it is a name given to a family of related theories of international relations. Here it will not be used, as many use it in international relations, to designate theories that stress the importance of international institutions. Nor to designate theories that stress the importance of universal, altruistic or utopian values of a liberal sort, such as human rights or democracy. Nor to designate theories favored by left-wing ("liberal") political parties or policies in the US. Instead, it is a theory that stresses the role of the varied *social interests and values* of states, and their relevance for world politics.

Liberals argue that the universal condition of world politics is *globalization*. States are, and always have been, embedded in a domestic and transnational society, which creates incentives for economic, social and cultural interaction across borders. State policy may facilitate or block such interactions. Some domestic groups may benefit from or be harmed by such policies, and they pressure government accordingly for policies that facilitate realization of their goals. These social pressures, transmitted through domestic political institutions, define "state preferences" –that is, the set of substantive social purposes that motivate foreign policy. State preferences give governments an underlying stake in the international issues they face. Since the domestic and transnational social context in which states are embedded varies greatly across space and time, so do state preferences. Without such social concerns that transcend state borders, states would have no rational incentive to engage in world politics at all, but would simply devote their resources to an autarkic and isolated existence. To motivate conflict, cooperation, or any other costly foreign policy action, states must possess sufficiently intense state preferences. The resulting globalization-induced variation in social demands, and thus state preferences, is a fundamental cause of state behaviour in world politics. This is the central insight of liberal international relations theory. It can be expressed colloquially in various ways: *"What matters most is what states want, not how they get it."* –or- *"Ends are more important than means."*

Liberal theory is distinctive in the nature of the variables it privileges. The liberal focus on variation in socially-determined state preferences distinguishes liberal theory from other theoretical traditions: realism (focusing on variation in coercive power resources), institutionalism (focusing on information), and most non-rational approaches (focusing on patterns of beliefs about appropriate means-ends relationships). In explaining patterns of war, for example, liberals do not look to inter-state imbalances of power, bargaining failure due to private information or uncertainty, or particular non-rational beliefs or propensities of individual leaders, societies, or organizations. Liberals look instead to conflicting state preferences derived from hostile nationalist or political ideologies, disputes over appropriable economic resources, or exploitation of unrepresented political constituencies. For liberals, a necessary condition for war is that social pressures lead one or more "aggressor" states to possess "revisionist" preferences so extreme or risk-acceptant that other states are unwilling to submit.

Three specific variants of liberal theory are defined by particular types of preferences, their variation, and their impact on state behaviour. *Ideational liberal* theories link state behaviour to varied conceptions of desirable forms of cultural, political, socioeconomic order. *Commercial liberal* theories stress economic interdependence, including many variants of "endogenous policy theory." *Republican* liberal theories stress the role of domestic representative institutions, elites and leadership dynamics, and executive-legislative relations. Such theories were first conceived by prescient liberals such as Immanuel Kant, Adam Smith, John Stuart Mill, John Hobson, Woodrow Wilson, and John Maynard Keynes-writing well before the deep causes (independent variables) they stress (*e.g.* democratization, industrialization, nationalism, and welfare provision) were widespread.

This essay introduces the liberal approach in three steps. It presents two distinctive assumptions underlying and distinguishing liberal theories. Then it further explicates the three variants of liberal theory that follow from these assumptions. Finally, it reviews some distinctive strengths that liberal theories tend to share vis-à-vis other types of international relations theory.

TWO UNIQUE ASSUMPTIONS UNDERLYING LIBERAL THEORY

What basic assumptions underlie the liberal approach? Two assumptions liberal theory make are the assumptions of *anarchy* and *rationality*. Specifically, *states (or other political actors) exist in an anarchic environment* and *they generally act in a broadly rational way in making decisions*. The anarchy assumption means that political actors exist in the distinctive environment of international politics, without a world government or any other authority with a monopoly on the legitimate use of force. They must engage in self-help. The rationality assumption means that state leaders and their domestic supporters engage in foreign policy for the instrumental purpose of securing benefits provided by (or avoiding costs imposed by) actors outside of their borders, and in making such calculations, states seek to deploy the most cost-effective means to achieve whatever their ends (preferences) may be. Liberal theory shares the first (anarchy) assumption with almost all international relations theories, and it shares the second (rationality) assumption with realism and institutionalism, but not non-rationalist process theories.

Liberal theories are distinguished from other rationalist theories, such as realism and institutionalism, by two unique assumptions about world politics: (1) States represent social groups, whose views constitute state preferences; and (2) Interdependence among state preferences influences state policy. Let us consider each in turn.

Assumption One: States Represent Societal Preferences

The first assumption shared by liberal theories is that *states represent some subset of domestic society, whose views constitute state preferences*. For liberals, the state is a representative institution constantly subject to capture and recapture, construction and reconstruction, by domestic social coalitions. These social coalitions define state "preferences" in world politics at any point in time: the "tastes," "ends," "basic interests," or "fundamental social purposes" that underlie foreign policy. Political institutions constitute a critical "transmission belt" by which these interests of individuals and groups in civil society enter the political realm. All individuals and groups do not wield equal influence over state policy. To the contrary, their power varies widely, depending on the context. Variation in the precise nature of representative institutions and practices helps define which groups influence the "national interest." Some states may represent, ideal-typically, the preferences of a single tyrannical individual, a Pol Pot or Josef Stalin; others afford opportunities for broad democratic participation. Most lie in between. The precise preferences of social groups, weighted by their domestic power, shape the underlying goals ("state preferences") that states pursue in world politics. Sometimes, non-governmental organizations (NGOs) and other actors may form transnational alliances to assist social forces. "State-society relations"—the relationship between a state and its domestic (and transnational) society in which it is embedded—lies at the center of liberal theory.

Liberals believe that state preferences cannot be reduced to some simple metric or preference ordering, such as seeking "security" or "wealth". Most modern states are not Spartan: They compromise security or sovereignty in order to achieve other ends, or, indeed, just to save money. Nor do modern states uniformly seek "wealth." Instead they strike rather strike complex and varied trade-offs among economic, social and political goals. Nor, finally do they seek "power" in the sense of "domination": Many countries would clearly rather spend money on "butter" rather than "guns." To see how consequential the variation in goals can be, one need look no further than the implications for international relations of Germany's evolution from Adolf Hitler's preference for militant nationalism, fascist rule, autarky, and ruthless exploitation of German *Lebensraum* under *Das Dritte Reich* to the social compromise underlying the postwar *Bundesrepublik Deutschland*, which favored capitalist democracy, expanding German exports, and peaceful reunification. Similarly one can look at the striking change in policy between Maoist and post-Maoist China, Soviet and post-Soviet Russia, Imperial and post-Imperial Japan, and so on.

Assumption Two: Interdependence among State Preferences Influences State Behaviour

The second core assumption shared by liberal theories is that *the interdependence among of state preferences influences state behaviour.* Rather than treating preferences as a fixed constant, as do realists or institutionalists, liberals seek to explain variation in preferences and its significance for world politics. The precise distribution and nature of the "stakes" explains differences in state policy and behaviour. States, liberals argue, orient their behaviour to the precise nature of these underlying preferences: compatible or conflictual, intense or weak, and their precise scope. States require a "social purpose" — a perceived underlying stake in the matter at hand — in order to pay any attention to international affairs, let alone to provoke conflict, inaugurate cooperation, or take any other significant foreign policy action. If there is no such interdependence among state objectives, a rational state will conduct no international relations, satisfying itself with an isolated and autarkic existence. Conflictual goals increase the incentive for of political disputes. Convergence of underlying preferences creates the preconditions for peaceful coexistence or cooperation.

The critical theoretical link between state preferences, on the one hand, and state behaviour, on the other, is the concept of policy interdependence. Policy interdependence refers to the distribution and interaction of preferences—that is, the extent to which the pursuit of state preferences necessarily imposes costs and benefits (known as *policy externalities*) upon other states, independent of the "transaction costs" imposed by the specific strategic means chosen to obtain them. Depending on the underlying pattern of interdependence, each of the qualitative categories above, the form, substance, and depth of conflict and cooperation vary according to the precise nature and intensity of preferences.

The existence of some measure of divergent fundamental beliefs, scarcity of material goods, and inequalities in domestic political power among states and social actors renders inevitable some measure of pluralism and competition among and within states. Unlike realists such as Waltz and Morgenthau, liberals do not assume these divergent interests are uniformly zero-sum. At the same time, liberals reject the utopian notion (often attributed to them by realists) of an automatic harmony of interest among individuals and groups in international society. Nor do liberals argue, as realists like Morgenthau charge, believe that each state pursues an ideal goal, oblivious of what other states do. Liberals argue instead that each state seeks to realize distinct preferences or interests under constraints imposed by the different interests of other states. This distribution of preferences varies considerably. For liberals, this variation—not realism's distribution of capabilities or institutionalism's distribution of information—is of decisive causal importance in explaining state behaviour.

A few examples illustrate how liberal theories differ from realist, institutionalist or non-rational ones. We have already encountered the example of war in the introduction, in which liberals stress states with aggressive preferences, rather than imbalances of power, incomplete information, or non-rational beliefs and processes. Another illustration is trade policy. Economists widely agree that free trade is superior welfare-improving policy choice for states, yet trade protection is often practiced. To explain protectionism, liberals look to domestic social preferences. An important factor in almost all countries is the competitive position of affected economic sectors in global markets, which generates domestic and transnational distributional effects: Protectionism is generally backed by producers who are globally uncompetitive; free trade by producers who are globally competitive. Moreover, even if the state is a net beneficiary from free trade, domestic adjustment costs may be too high to tolerate politically, or may endanger other countervailing domestic social objectives, such as domestic social equality or environmental quality. Certain domestic political institutions, such as non-parliamentary legislative systems, which governed US trade policy before 1934, grant disproportionate power to protectionist interests.

This differs from realist explanations of trade protectionism, which tend to stress the role of "hegemonic power" in structuring trade liberalization, or the need to defend self-sufficient national security within the prevailing zero-sum geopolitical competition, perhaps by maintaining self-sufficiency or by aiding allies at the expense of purely economic objectives. Institutionalists might cite the absence of appropriate international institutions, or other means to manage the complex informational tasks and collective action problems—negotiation, dispute resolution, enforcement—required to manage free trade. Those who focus on non-rational theories (psychological, cultural, organizational, epistemic, perceptual or bureaucratic) might stress an ideological disposition to accept "mercantilist" theory, shared historical analogies, and the psychological predisposition to avoid losses.

To further illustrate the importance of patterns of policy interdependence, consider the following three circumstances: zero-sum, harmonious and mixed preferences. In the case of *zero-sum* preferences, attempts by dominant social groups in one state to realize their preferences through international action may necessarily impose costs on dominant social groups in other countries. This is a case of "zero-sum" preferences, similar to the "realist" world. Governments face a bargaining game with few mutual gains and a high potential for interstate tension and conflict. Many ancient cities and states, including those of Ancient Athens, often imposed imperial tribute on defeated neighbors or, in extremis, killed the male population, cast women and children into slavery, and repopulated the town with their own citizens—a situation approximating zero-sum conflict. Today, it might still be argued that there are certain cases—trade in agricultural goods by industrial democracies, for example—where entrenched national interests are so strong that no government seriously considers embracing free trade. In the case of *harmonious* preferences, where the externalities of unilateral policies are optimal (or insignificant) for others, there are strong incentives for quiet coexistence with low conflict and (at most) simple forms of interstate coordination. For example, advanced industrial democracies today no longer contemplate waging war on one another, and in some areas governments have agreed to mutual recognition of certain legal standards without controversy. One case of *mixed* preferences is bargaining, where states can achieve common gains (or avoid common losses, as with a war) if they agree to coordinate their behaviour, but may disagree strongly on the distribution of benefits or adjustment costs. Under such circumstances, one of the most important determinants of bargaining power is the intensity of the preferences of each party; the more intense their preference for a beneficial settlement, the more likely they are to make concessions (or employ coercive means) in order to achieve it. Another situation of mixed motives is a situation where interstate coordination can avoid significant risks and costs, as in agreement to avoid naval incidents at sea, or to share information on infectious diseases. In such situations, institutional pre-commitments and the provision of greater information can often improve the welfare of all parties.

Liberals derive several distinctive conceptions of power, very different from that of realism. One form of international influence, for liberals, stems from the interdependence among preferences that Keohane and Nye (*Power and Interdependence)* call "asymmetrical interdependence." All other things equal, the more interdependent a state is, the more intense its preference for a given outcome, the more power others potentially have over it; while the less a state wants something, the less a state cares about outcomes, the less intense its preferences, the less power others have over it. Situations of asymmetrical interdependence, where one state has more intense preference for an agreement than another, create bargaining power.

In trade negotiations, for example, smaller and poorer countries are often more dependent on trade and thus benefit more from free trade, and thus tend to have a weaker position and make more concessions in the course of negotiations. Enlargement of the European Union is a recent instance. Relative preference intensity can also influence the outcome of war, but in a different way. Nations are in fact rarely prepared to mortgage their entire economy or military in conflict, so their power depends not on their coercive power resources, but on their resolve or will. This is why smaller states often prevail over larger ones. Vietnam, for example, did not prevail over the US in the Vietnam War because it possessed more coercive power resources, but because it had a more intense preference at stake.

FROM ASSUMPTIONS TO THEORIES

Taken by themselves, these liberal assumptions—the international system is anarchic, states are rational, social pressures define state preferences, interdependence among preferences dictates state behaviour—are thin. They exclude most existing realist, institutionalist, and non-rational theories, but they do not, taken by themselves, define very precisely the positive content of liberal theory. Some might rightly complain that simply pointing to state preferences opens up an unmanageably wide range of hypothetical social influences on policy.

Yet, in practice, research has shown that, in practice, the range of viable liberal theories that test out empirically are relatively few, focused, and powerful. Three broad variants or categories of liberal theory exist: *ideational, commercial, and republican liberalism.* At the core of each lies a distinct conception of the social pressures and representative institutions that define state preferences, and the consequences for state behaviour. Some of these have proven, empirically, to be among the most powerful theories in international relations. Let us consider each in turn.

Ideational Liberalism: State Preferences Based on Domestic Social Values and Identities

Ideational liberalism views *domestic social identities and values* as basic determinants of state preferences. Drawing on a liberal tradition of political philosophy dating back to John Stuart Mill, Giuseppe Mazzini, Woodrow Wilson, and John Maynard Keyes, liberals defines social values as the set of preferences held by various individuals and groups in society concerning the proper scope and nature of legitimate state objectives. In particular, nations and groups within nations differ in their conceptions of what a legitimate domestic order is—that is, their conception of which social actors belong to the polity and what is owed them. Thus for liberals, ends that may appear universal—such as the defence of political sovereignty and national security—are not necessarily ends in themselves, but are justified only insofar as they are means to realize the specific underlying preferences of social actors concerning "legitimate social order." Some states, such as aggressive states like Hitler's Germany, willing place security and sovereignty at risk in order to achieve conquest. Other states may place security at risk to maintain peace or prosperity. None of these choices are necessarily "irrational"; they simply involve varying sets of social preferences.

Foreign policy, in the ideational liberal view, is an effort to realize these views domestically. Social actors provide support to the government in exchange for institutions that accord with their identity-based preferences and are therefore deemed "legitimate". Similarly, actors will sometimes advocate foreign policies that subvert the existing domestic social order. On the liberal view, the effect of conceptions of social legitimacy on state behaviour depends on patterns of interdependence among these ideals—in other words, on the transnational externalities created for others by attempts to realize those preferences in one place. Liberal theories predict that where national conceptions of legitimate borders, political institutions, and socioeconomic equality are compatible, generating positive or negligible externalities, peaceful coexistence is likely. Where social identities are incompatible and create significant negative externalities—as when one state views the promotion of its legitimate borders, political institutions, and socioeconomic standards as requiring aggression or demands *vis à vis* another state tension and zero-sum conflict is more likely. Where national claims can be made more compatible through reciprocal policy adjustment, efforts to cooperate explicitly through international institutions are more likely.

Some social preferences about a legitimate social order are particularly important, such as those pertaining to the proper location of national borders, the nature of political institutions, and the scope of socioeconomic regulation.

National Identity: One basic type of social identity concerns the scope of the "nation": specifically, the legitimate location of national borders and the allocation of citizenship rights. Where borders coincide with underlying patterns of identity, coexistence and even mutual recognition are more likely, but where there are inconsistencies between borders and underling patterns of identity—as there have been in the Balkans for over 100 years, in central Europe in the mid-19th century, and in many places in the world today—greater potential for interstate conflict exists. Over the last century and a half, from mid-nineteenth century nationalist uprisings to late twentieth-century national liberation struggles, the desire for national autonomy constitutes the most common issue over which wars have been fought and great power intervention has taken place. The Balkan conflicts preceding World War I and in the former Yugoslavia after the end of the Cold War are notorious examples. Not by chance is scenario planning for China/United States conflict focused almost exclusively on Taiwan—the one jurisdiction where borders and national identity (as well as political ideology) are subject to competing claims.

Political Ideology: The second basic type of social identity stems from individuals and group commitments to particular forms of political institutions. Where the realization of legitimate domestic political institutions in one jurisdiction threatens its realization in others (negative externalities), conflict is more likely. From Ancient Greece, where oligarchic and democratic factions in city-states used foreign policy to defend and advance their preferred form of government, to the French Revolution and nineteenth-century Concert of Europe, where monarchies used international cooperation to quash democratic and nationalist revolution, to the Second World War, where democracies and communists fought fascists, to the Cold War, when the United States and the Soviet Union were motivated by divergent political ideologies, disputes over political ideology have fueled international conflict.

Socioeconomic Regulation: The third basic type of social identity relevant for world politics stems from beliefs about legitimate socioeconomic regulation and redistribution. Modern liberal theories (in contrast to the *laissez faire* libertarianism sometimes labeled as quintessentially "liberal") have long recognized that societal preferences concerning the appropriate nature and level of regulation impose legitimate limits on transnational markets. Domestic and international markets are embedded in local social compromises concerning the provision of regulatory public goods. The extent to which countries can cooperate to liberalize markets, for example, depends on the level of conflict or convergence of views about immigration, social welfare, taxation, religious freedom, families, health and safety, environmental and consumer protection, cultural promotion, and many other domestic public goods. These issues have increasingly been the subjects of international economic negotiations. We often see odd domestic coalitions made up of idealists and materialists—so-called "Baptist-bootlegger" coalitions where those who favour regulation for public spirited reasons ("Baptists") ally with those who benefit in a material sense ("bootleggers")—around international economic issues. For example, we sometimes observe unions, uncompetitive business and environmentalists all supporting trade protection—for quite different reasons.

COMMERCIAL LIBERALISM: STATE PREFERENCES BASED ON ECONOMIC INTERESTS

Commercial liberal theories seek to explain the international behaviour of states based on the domestic and global market position of domestic firms, workers, and owners of assets. Commercial liberal theory posits that changes in the structure of the domestic and global economy alter the costs and benefits of transnational economic exchange, thus creating pressure on domestic governments to facilitate or block such exchanges through appropriate foreign economic and security policies.

Commercial liberal theory does not predict that economic incentives automatically generate universal free trade and peace, but focuses instead on the interplay between aggregate incentives and distributional consequences. The greater the economic benefits for powerful private actors, the greater their incentive, all other things equal, to press governments to facilitate such transactions; the more costly the adjustment imposed by the proposed economic exchanges, the more opposition is likely to arise. As Dani Rodrik has argued, contemporary trade liberalization generates domestic distributional shifts totaling many times aggregate welfare benefits. Losers generally tend to be better identified and organized than beneficiaries. A major source of protection, liberals predict, lies in uncompetitive, un diversified, and monopolistic sectors or factors of production. Their pressure induces a systematic divergence from laissez-faire policies-a tendency

Recognized by Adam Smith, who famously complained of mercantilism that "the contrivers of this whole mercantile system [are] the producers, whose interest has been so carefully attended to." This commercial liberal approach to analyzing conflict over foreign economic policy is distinct from those of realism (emphasizing security concerns and relative power), institutionalism (informational and institutional constraints on optimal interstate collective action), and constructivism (beliefs about "free trade"). Extensive research supports the view that free trade is most likely where strong competitiveness, extensive intra-industry trade or trade in intermediate goods, large foreign investments, and low asset specificity internalize the net benefits of free trade to powerful actors, reducing the influence of net losers from liberalization. Similar arguments can be used to analyze issues such as sovereign debt, exchange rate policy, agricultural trade policy, European integration, foreign direct investment, tax policy, and migration policy.

The effect of economic interdependence on security affairs varies with market incentives. A simple starting point is that the collateral damage of war disrupts economic activity: the more vulnerable and extensive such activity, the greater the cost. A more sophisticated cost-benefit calculation would take into account the potential economic costs and benefits of war. Where monopolies, sanctions, slavery, plunder of natural resources, and other forms of coercive extraction backed by state power are cost-effective means of elite wealth accumulation-as was true for most of human history-we should expect to see a positive relationship, between transnational economic activity and war. Where, conversely, private trade and investment within complex and well-established transnational markets provide a less costly means of accumulating wealth and one that cannot be cost-effectively appropriated-as is most strikingly the case within modern multinational investment and production networks-the expansion of economic opportunities will have a pacific effect. Along with the spread of democracy and relative absence of nationalist conflict, this distinguishes the current era from the period before the

First World War, when high levels of interdependence famously failed to deter war. We see in current Western relations with China a very deliberate strategy to encourage the slow evolution of social preferences in a pacific direction by encouraging trade. Eric Gartzke has recently argued that the "democratic peace" phenomenon can largely be explained in terms of a lack of economic and other motives for war. Even among developed economies, however, circumstances may arise where governments employ coercive means to protect international markets. This may take varied forms, as occurred under nineteenth-century empires or with pressure from business for the United States to enter the First World War to defend trade with the allies.

REPUBLICAN LIBERALISM: STATE PREFERENCES BASED ON SYSTEMS OF DOMESTIC REPRESENTATION

A final source of state preferences is the structure of domestic political representation. While ideational and commercial theories stress, respectively, particular patterns of underlying societal identities and interests related to globalization, republican liberal theory emphasizes the ways in which domestic institutions and practices aggregate and transmit such pressures, transforming them into state policy. The key variable in republican liberalism, which dates back to the theories of Kant, Wilson, and others, is the nature of domestic political representation, which helps determine *whose* social preferences dominate state policy—thereby defining the "national interest".

A simple consequence is that policy tends to be biased in favour of the governing coalitions or powerful domestic groups favored by representative institutions—whether those groups are administrators (rulers, armies, or bureaucracies) or societal groups that "capture" the state. Costs and risks are passed on to others. When particular groups with outlier preferences are able to formulate policy without providing gains for society as a whole, the result is likely to be inefficient and suboptimal policy for the policy as a whole. To the extent that most individuals and groups in society tend generally to be risk averse, the broader the range of represented groups, the less likely it is that they will support indiscriminate use of policy instruments, like war or autarky, that impose large net costs or risks on society as a whole. Democracies tend to be choosy about the wars they enter: Selecting lower cost war, not provoking great-power war, and fighting to win.

Republican liberal theory thereby helps to explain phenomena as diverse as the "democratic peace," modern imperialism, and international trade and monetary cooperation. Given the plausibility of the assumption that major war imposes net costs on society as a whole, it is hardly surprising that the most prominent republican liberal argument concerns the "democratic peace:' which one scholar has termed "as close as anything we have to an empirical law in international relations" –one that applies to tribal societies as well as modern states. From a liberal perspective, the theoretical interest in the "democratic peace" lies not in the greater transparency of democracies (a claim about information), the greater military power of democracies (a realist claim), or norms appropriate behaviour (a constructivist claim), but the distinctive preferences of democracies.

This is not, of course, to imply that broad domestic representation *necessarily* generates international cooperation. In specific cases, elite preferences in multiple states may be more convergent than popular ones. Moreover, the extent of bias in representation, not democracy per se, is the theoretically critical point. There exist conditions under which specific governing elites may have an incentive to represent long-term social preferences in a way that is less biased-for example, when they dampen nationalist sentiment, as may be the case in some democratizing regimes, or exclude powerful outlier special interests, as is commonly the case in trade policy.

The theoretical obverse of "democratic peace" theory is a republican liberal theory of war, which stresses risk -acceptant leaders and rent -seeking coalitions. There is substantial historical evidence that the aggressors who have provoked modern great-power wars tend either to be extremely risk-acceptant individuals, or individuals well able to insulate themselves from the costs of war, or both. Jack Snyder, for example, has refurbished Hobson's classic left-liberal analysis of imperialism-in which the military, uncompetitive foreign investors and traders, jingoistic political elites, and others who benefit from imperialism are particularly well placed to influence policy-by linking unrepresentative and extreme outcomes to log-rolling coalitions. Consistent with this analysis, the highly unrepresentative consequences of partial democratization, combined with the disruption of rapid industrialization and incomplete political socialization, suggest that democratizing states, if subject to these influences, may be particularly war-prone. This offers one answer to the paradox posed by James Fearon-namely, why rational states would ever enter into war rather than negotiate their way out.

Parallels to the "democratic peace" exist in political economy. We have seen that illiberal commercial policies-trade protection, monetary instability, and sectoral subsidization that may manifestly undermine the general welfare of the population-reflect pressure from powerful domestic groups. In part this power results from biases within representative institutions, such as the power of money in electoral systems, the absence or presence of insulated institutions. Consider the example of international trade.

As we saw in the preceding section, perhaps the most widespread explanation for the persistence of illiberal commercial policies, such as protection, monetary instability, and sectoral subsidization that may manifestly undermine the general welfare of the population, is pressure from powerful domestic groups. The power of such groups is often exacerbated by biases within representative institutions. Where the latter sort of biases exist—and it is seen in most contemporary representative institutions—special interest groups are likely to gain protection through tariffs, subsidies, favorable regulation, or competitive devaluation. Where policy makers are insulated from such pressures, which may involve less democratic—such as "fast track" provisions, executive agreements, and the United States Trade Representative—open policies are more viable. Ironically, in such cases, less "democratic" institutions, in the sense of less "populist" and "participatory" institutions, may in fact be more representative of society as a whole.

THE SCOPE OF THE LIBERAL PERSPECTIVE

We have seen that liberal theory is a coherent family of ideational, commercial and republican theories that share common assumptions about international relations. Such theories explain not only cooperation among liberal states, but pertain to liberal and non-liberal polities, conflictual and cooperative situations, security and political economy issues, and both individual foreign policy and aggregate behaviour. Such theories challenge the conventional presumption that realism is the simplest, most encompassing and most powerful of major IR theories. Although not all liberal theories are easy to specify, hypotheses about endogenous tariff setting, the democratic peace, and nationalist conflict suggest that liberalism generates many empirical arguments as powerful and parsimonious as those of realism. At first glance, some may object that the claim that state preferences or interests matter—that is, what states want shapes what they do—is trivial. Yet in fact the liberal approach is distinctively different than other widely advocated families of theories, which stress instead the distribution of coercive power, information, cultural beliefs and other characteristics of states.

Others may feel that stressing preferences may lead to an impossibly broad and vague approach, because thousands of factors might affect the social demands placed on a modern state. In practice, however, specific liberal theories turn out to be not just powerful but precise and focused as well. Fifty years ago Morgenthau launched the modern post-war field of international relations by proclaiming that international relations theory should avoid "two popular fallacies...the concern with motives...and the concern with ideological preferences." Liberalism seeks to theorize motives, ideologies and preferences—and the empirical data shows that it has done so successfully.

Theories based on the liberal approach can explain, moreover, a number of phenomena for which realist, institutionalist, and non-rational theories of international relations approaches lack a persuasive account.

First, the *liberal approach provides a plausible theoretical explanation for variation in the substantive content of foreign policy*. Neither realism nor institutionalism explains the changing substantive goals and purposes over which states conflict and cooperate. Both focus instead on formal causes, such as relative power, issue density, or the distribution of information—and on formal consequences, such as conflict and cooperation per se. By contrast, liberal theories provide a plausible explanation not just for conflict and cooperation, but for the substantive content of foreign policy.

Liberal IR theory offers plausible, parsimonious hypotheses to explain things like the difference between Anglo-American, Nazi, and Soviet plans for the post–World War II world; U.S. concern about a few North Korean, Iraqi, or Chinese nuclear weapons, rather than the greater arsenals held by Great Britain, Israel, and France; the substantial differences between within the Bretton Woods compromise of "embedded liberalism" and the period of "free trade imperialism" that preceded it, divergences between economic cooperation under the EC and NAFTA, and many other cases. Similarly, liberalism makes more sense of the sudden reversal of East–West relations, a shift made possible by the widespread view among Russian officials (so interview data reveal) that Germany was at once ethnically satisfied, politically democratic, and commercially inclined.

Second, *the liberal approach offers a plausible explanation for historical change in the international system.* The static quality of both realist and institutionalist theories, and their lack of persuasive explanations for fundamental long-term change in the nature of international politics, are recognized weaknesses. Global economic development over the past five hundred years has been closely related to greater per capita wealth, democratization, education systems that reinforce new collective identities, and greater incentives for trans-border economic transactions. Realist theory accords such shifts no theoretical importance, but analyzes enduring patterns of state behaviour reflecting cyclical shifts in power, as in the rise and decline of great powers. Liberal theories, by contrast, forge a direct causal link between economic, political, and social modernization and state behaviour in world politics. Hence, for example, it is significant to liberals that over the modern period the principles of international order have been decreasingly linked to dynastic legitimacy and increasingly to factors directly drawn from the three variants of liberalism: national self-determination and social citizenship, the increasing complexity of economic integration, and liberal democratic governance.

Third, following on from the second point, *the liberal approach offers a plausible explanation for the distinctiveness of modern international politics.* Among advanced industrial democracies, a stable form of interstate politics has emerged, grounded in reliable expectations of peaceful change, domestic rule of law, stable international institutions, and intensive societal interaction. Whereas realists offer no general explanation for the emergence of this distinctive mode of international politics, liberal theories argue that the emergence of a large and expanding bloc of pacific, interdependent, normatively satisfied states has been a precondition for such politics. Consider, for example, the current state of Europe. Unlike realist theories, for example, liberal theories explain the near total absence of competitive alliance formation among the leading democratic powers today.

From Unicausal to Multi-Causal Theory

We have seen that liberal assumptions about world politics offer a distinct foundation on which a number of powerful theories may be grounded. Yet any good historian, policy-maker or social scientist is instinctively—and rightly—suspicious of mono-causal explanations based on only a single theory. Surely world politics is more complex. What if we want to combine a liberal theory with other theories, liberal or non-liberal? Two final points are worth noting, both of which elaborate the various in which any given liberal theory can be combined with other theories.

First, *various liberal theories work well in tandem with one another.* Not only does liberal theory apply across a wide domain of circumstances, but its three variants—ideational, commercial, and republican liberalism—are mutually reinforcing. They are stronger taken together than separately. Not only do they share assumptions and causal mechanisms, but their empirical implications aggregate in interesting ways. It is widely accepted, for example, that economic development has a strong influence on the viability of democratic governance, with its pacific implications; liberal democratic governments tend in turn to support commerce, which promotes economic development. Such claims can be analytically reinforcing even where they do not make parallel predictions. Anomalies within one variant of liberal theory may be resolved by considering other variants. Positive movement along one liberal dimension—patterns of national identity, democratic participation, or transnational economic transactions—may condone or exacerbate the negative distortions along another liberal dimension.

Norman Angell, whose commercial liberal claims on the eve of World War I included a prediction -that war among major powers was obsolete, is often parodied by secondhand critics. Yet he does not deserve this. Angell staunchly maintained that his well-known "unprofitability of war" thesis in no way implies "the impossibility of war"—a doctrine he dismissed for republican liberal reasons (*i.e.* the fact that not all governments are representative) as a "ridiculous myth." Where representative bias permits special interests to control policy, aggregate incentives for welfare-improving trade are likely to have less effect. Recent studies reveal that the correlation between economic interdependence and peace holds far more strongly among liberal states. Conversely, where democratization heightens socioeconomic inequality, nationalist cleavages, uneven patterns of gains, and losses due to interdependence or extreme heterogeneity of interests—as may have occurred in the former Yugoslavia and other democratizing nations—it may exacerbate international economic and political conflict. Such interaction effects among liberal factors offer a promising area for more detailed analysis. Liberal theories are greater than the sum of their parts.

Second, *liberal theories are easily combined with other international relations theories, generating multi-causal explanations.* Surely there are cases in which a *combination* of liberal and other theories offers a better explanation of state behaviour than any single sort of theory alone, liberal or otherwise. In such cases, a *multicausal synthesis* is required. But an "anything goes" attitude will quickly lead to complexity. How can we discipline such a synthesis? What model should we use?

Most theorists believe we should synthesize theories by employing realism first (with preferences assumed to be invariant) and then introduce liberal theories to explain whatever is left over. The justification often given is that realist theories deal with the most "important" phenomena in international affairs, coercive threats to national security, and no state will pay attention to liberal factors until they resolve such classic *Realpolitik* issues. Yet such claims arbitrarily privilege realist explanations of any phenomena that might be explained by other theories—and liberal theories, as we have seen, do deal with essential matters of peace and war. Moreover, it is clear—as we have seen above—that conflict often comes about precisely because states have varied interests, and some aggressor states have privileged something above security, this violating the key assumptions of realism.

The truth is in fact the opposite: to the extent that both preferences and coercive other factors matter, *liberal theories enjoy analytical priority in any synthesis.* The assumption of rationality or purposive behaviour central to realism (like the "bounded rationality" claims of institutionalism) implies action on the basis of a prior, specific, and consistent set of preferences. Unless we know what these preferences are (that is, unless we know the extent to which states value the underlying stakes), we cannot assess realist or institutionalist claims linking variation in the particular means available to states (whether coercive capabilities or institutions) on interstate conflict or cooperation. Nor can we use non-rational decision-making theory to assess whether the means-ends calculations used to realize those interests are rational or not. Preferences determine the nature and intensity of the game that states are playing and thus are a primary determinant of which systemic theory is appropriate and how it should be specified.

Variation in state preferences often influences the way in which states make calculations about their strategic environment, whereas the converse—that the strategic situation leads to variation in state preferences—is inconsistent with the rationality assumption shared by all three theories. *In short, liberal theories explain when and why the assumptions about state preferences underlying realism or institutionalism hold.* The reverse is not the case, at least in the short term. In situations where these assumptions do not hold, realism and institutionalism (as well as some variants of constructivism) are not just of limited importance, they are theoretically irrelevant.

The priority of liberalism in multicausal models of state behaviour implies, furthermore, that collective state behaviour should be analyzed as a *two-stage process*. States first define preferences—a stage uniquely explained by liberal theories—and *only then* do they debate, bargain, or fight to particular agreements—a second stage explained by realist and/or institutionalist (as well as liberal) theories of strategic interaction. The two-stage model offers a general structure for research design and theoretical explanation. In those cases where liberal factors only influence strategic outcomes directly, through preferences and preference intensities, liberalism can be tested as a monocausal hypothesis against alternative realist or institutionalist factors. Liberal factors may also influence outcomes indirectly, because the nature of preferences helps determine the relative power and influence of states.. Recall that preferences do not simply shape outcomes, they tell us which realist or institutionalist factors are important and how they relate to state behaviour. In such cases, explaining (or at least controlling for) variation in state preferences is analytically prior to an analysis of strategic interaction. Without a prior analysis of preferences, only monocausal formulations of realist or institutionalist theory can be tested.

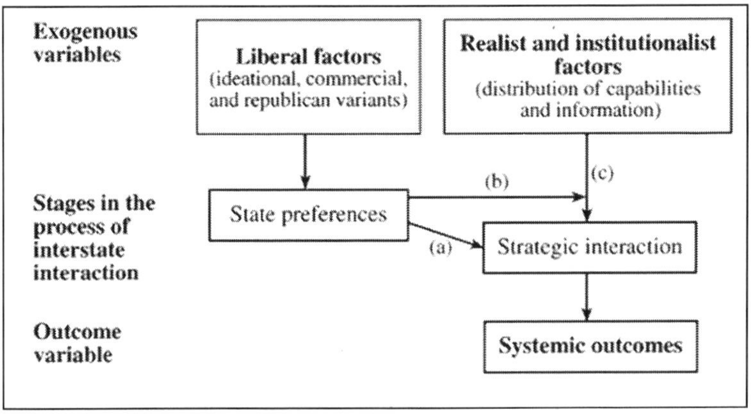

Fig. A two-stage model of state behaviour

The primacy of liberal theories in such multicausal explanations may appear to be an abstract admonition, yet it is of real practical importance in interpreting historical experience and current policy.

How are we to understand, for example, Woodrow Wilson's proposal for the League of Nations, often cited as the epitome of liberal "legalism" and "utopianism." At first glance, Wilson's proposal seems to reflect a naive confidence in international institutions.

Yet in fact it was a two-stage liberal proposal—and a realistic one at that. From the start, Wilson was skeptical about the *autonomous* influence of international institutions.

He cared little about their precise form, because he viewed them as no more than "a symbolic affirmation of the 'rightness' of democracies in their mutual relations." Thus, for example, his initial draft of the League Covenant included no provisions for international law or a supranational court; both were eventually added only at the insistence of more conservative (and more cynical) foreign and domestic politicians. He was skeptical that the League could ever actually override national decisions.

Instead what Wilson termed the "first point" to remember about the League was not institutionalist but liberal: Its membership was to be restricted to those countries enjoying republican government and national self-determination. Insofar as the League was to rely on public opinion, it was to be solely *democratic* public opinion. Based on a multicausal liberal analysis, Wilson explicitly identified a set of narrow preconditions under which collective security institutions could succeed.

The League, he argued, would function only if nationally self-determining democracy was a nearly universal form of government among great powers, which in turn controlled an overwhelming proportion of global military power. In 1917, Wilson believed this situation to be imminent: "There are not going to be many other kinds of nations for long.... The Hapsburgs and the Hohenzollerns are permanently out of business." Given Wilson's underlying theory, is it surprising that the League had become moribund by 1936, after twelve European countries had moved from democracy to dictatorship? Or that this shift isolated democratic France and Britain, exacerbating their oft-noted geopolitical dilemmas in Manchuria and Abyssinia? When a similar situation arose in the former Yugoslavia after 1989, in a world where almost all the great powers in the region were liberal democracies—as we have seen above—Western governments intervened to oppose aggression, while avoiding any hint of armed conflict among themselves. Indeed, the absence of serious conflict among Western powers over Yugoslavia—the "World War I scenario"—reflects in large part a shared perception that the geopolitical gains from conflict among democratic governments are low. In this sense, the interwar failure of the League, often cited as a realist refutation of utopian liberal *ideology,* in fact confirms liberal IR *theory.*

Multicausal liberalism helps to explain not only ambitious schemes for cooperation like collective security, but "realist" policy outcomes like power balancing and bipolar conflict. A form of multicausal liberalism underlay the post–World War II U.S. policy of containment—a policy traditionally treated as the embodiment of realism. Containment of the Soviet Union was never simply about power balancing. It was a liberal grand strategy, as made explicit after World War I by Wilson and John Dewey, then after World War II by George Kennan. Kennan, in this regard a liberal, linked the European threat to the nature of the Soviet regime; it is often forgotten that nine-tenths of the seminal "X" article was given over to an analysis of Soviet domestic beliefs. A Western military deterrent would be required, he argued, only until the Bolshevik revolution had run its course, whereupon the Soviet system would collapse of its own accord. The decisive Western actions in the Cold War, according to Kennan, were the reconstruction of Germany and Japan as capitalist democracies through policies like the Marshall Plan. The goal of the policy was the transformation of social purposes and state preferences in Western countries, neither of which would assume much importance in a purely realist analysis.

In the end, the conduct and conclusion of the Cold War proceeded precisely as Kennan's two-stage liberal model had predicted. Realist power balancing served throughout as a static, interim instrument to maintain the status quo, but shifting state preferences explain the outbreak and eventual passing of the conflict. By 1959, standing in a Moscow exhibit of kitchenware, Richard Nixon and Nikita Khrushchev declared that the Cold War would be won and lost not through relative military capabilities, but through the relative economic prowess and ideological attractiveness of the two superpowers.

Economic stagnation and a measure of ideological change in the East predated foreign policy change. If the West, as Khrushchev rashly promised, had been buried under the superior economic performance of the East, the outcome might well have been different. These examples demonstrate the ability of multicausal liberal theories to explain critical twentieth-century foreign policy decisions, such as those taken in 1918, 1947, and 1989, even when national security interests are fully engaged.

In interpreting such cases, the major difference between realist and liberal theories lies not, as is often claimed, in the observation that realist states are concerned about security threats, or even with balancing security threats. Both theories predict this under specific circumstances. Where the two families of theory genuinely differ is on the sources of security threats themselves, with realists attributing them to particular configurations of power (against which states balance), whereas liberals attribute them to extreme conflict among ideological, institutional, and material preferences. (For their part, Institutionalists attribute them to uncertainty and the failure of commitment strategies, and epistemic theorists to particular beliefs about the efficacy or appropriateness of specific policy responses.) If liberal theories contribute to explaining core realist cases such as bipolar conflict, there is good reason to believe that the most powerful influences in world politics today are not the deployment of military force or the construction of international institutions, but the quiet transformation of the domestic and transnational social values, interests, and institutions that underlie the widely varying preferences states bring to world politics.

THEORIES OF INTERNATIONAL RELATIONS

A theory of international relations is a set of ideas that explains how the international system works. Unlike an ideology, a theory of international relations is (at least in principle) backed up with concrete evidence. The two major theories of international relations are realism and liberalism.

NATIONAL INTEREST

Most theories of international relations are based on the idea that states always act in accordance with their national interest, or the interests of that particular state. State interests often include self-preservation, military security, economic prosperity, and influence over other states. Sometimes two or more states have the same national interest. For example, two states might both want to foster peace and economic trade. And states with diametrically opposing national interests might try to resolve their differences through negotiation or even war.

Realism

According to realism, states work only to increase their own power relative to that of other states. Realism also claims the following:

- The world is a harsh and dangerous place. The only certainty in the world is power. A powerful state will always be able to outdo—and outlast—weaker competitors. The most important and reliable form of power is military power.
- A state's primary interest is self-preservation. Therefore, the state must seek power and must always protect itself
- There is no overarching power that can enforce global rules or punish bad behaviour.
- Moral behaviour is very risky because it can undermine a state's ability to protect itself.
- The international system itself drives states to use military force and to war. Leaders may be moral, but they must not let moral concerns guide foreign policy.
- International organizations and law have no power or force; they exist only as long as states accept them.

Politicians have practiced realism as long as states have existed. Most scholars and politicians during the Cold War viewed international relations through a realist lens. Neither the United States nor the Soviet Union trusted the other, and each sought allies to protect itself and increase its political and military influence abroad. Realism has also featured prominently in the administration of George W. Bush.

Machiavelli

One of the best-known realist thinkers is the notorious Niccolo Machiavelli. In his book *The Prince* (1513), he advised rulers to use deceit and violence as tools against other states. Moral goals are so dangerous, he wrote, that to act morally will bring about disaster. He also gave advice about how to deal with conflicts among neighboring states and how to defend one's homeland. Machiavelli's name has become synonymous with nasty and brutal politics.

Liberalism

Liberalism emphasizes that the broad ties among states have both made it difficult to define national interest and decreased the usefulness of military power. Liberalism developed in the 1970s as some scholars began arguing that realism was outdated. Increasing globalization, the rapid rise in communications technology, and the increase in international trade meant that states could no longer rely on simple power politics to decide matters. Liberal approaches to international relations are also called *theories of complex interdependence.* Liberalism claims the following:

- The world is a harsh and dangerous place, but the consequences of using military power often outweigh the benefits. International cooperation is therefore in the interest of every state.

- Military power is not the only form of power. Economic and social power matter a great deal too. Exercising economic power has proven more effective than exercising military power.
- Different states often have different primary interests.
- International rules and organizations can help foster cooperation, trust, and prosperity.

Example: Relations among the major Western powers fit a model of complex interdependence very well. The United States has significant disagreements with its European and Asian allies over trade and policy, but it is hard to imagine a circumstance in which the United States would use military power against any of these allies. Instead, the United States relies on economic pressure and incentives to achieve its policy aims.

Idealism

Idealism is a specific school of liberalism that stresses the need for states to pursue moral goals and to act ethically in the international arena. Idealists believe that behaviour considered immoral on an interpersonal level is also immoral in foreign policy. Therefore, idealists argue that dishonesty, trickery, and violence should be shunned. In the United States, idealism has usually been associated with the Democratic Party since World War I.

Example: As he negotiated the treaty to end World War I in 1918, Woodrow Wilson worked to promote democracy and national self-determination. Wilson's idealism led him to push hard for the creation of the League of Nations, an international organization that would fight aggression and protect the weak from the strong, in 1919. Scholars use the term Wilsonianto describe a person or group who advocates promoting democracy overseas in the name of idealism.

3

War on Terror — Global Issues

It was with disbelief and shock that people around the world saw footage of the terrorist attacks in the US on on September 11, 2001 when the planes-turned-missiles slammed into the World Trade Center towers and damaged the Pentagon.

This ultimately resulted in the US declaring and waging a war on "terror". Osama Bin Laden was eventually tracked down and killed some 10 years later. But the way the war on terror has been conducted has led to many voicing concerns about the impact on civil liberties, the cost of the additional security focused changes, the implications of the invasions and wars in Iraq and Afghanistan, and more.

10 YEARS SINCE THE 9-11 TERRORIST ATTACKS

It is now over a decade since the terrorist attacks in the US, simply dubbed "9-11" shocked the world, and ushered in a global "war on terror".

And looking back, what has the US to show for its decade of effort? Has it been winning the war on terror? It depends how it is measured. The killing of Osama Bin Laden was of course a major success. But the cost of vengeance (instead of justice) has also been high:

- A further turn towards hatred and a rise in those who think most Muslims are terrorists, that Islam is a threat to the world, etc.
- Wars that have seen far more than the 3,500 deaths that the US saw, and a self-fulfilling prophecy; creating more anger and resentment against the US, more potential terrorists, and the complete opposite of what the neo-cons wanted; global downturn and US decline instead consolidating their power and position in the world.
- Over 6,000 US soldiers killed in wars in Afghanistan and Iraq. Possibly 100 times that number of civilians in those countries (in Iraq, at an early point, there was an estimated range of 400,000 to 900,000 civilian deaths, which of course Bush had to reject, claiming it used flawed techniques, even though it used estimation techniques his own government agencies taught others to use).

And also worryingly, as *Inter Press Service* (IPS) correspondent Jim Lobe notes, Al Qaeda's project for ending the "American Century" appears to have largely succeeded:

Al Qaeda appears to have largely succeeded in its hopes of accelerating the decline of U.S. global power, if not bringing it to the brink of collapse.

That appears to be the strong consensus of the foreign-policy elite which, with only a few exceptions, believes that the administration of President George W. Bush badly "over-reacted" to the attacks and that that over-reaction continues to this day.

Jim Lobe, Al Qaeda's Project for Ending the American Century Largely Succeeded, Inter Press Service, September 8, 2011

The rest of Jim Lobe's article provides a useful summary of why Bush's focus on Iraq (under the clearly false and fear-mongering excuses of weapons of mass destruction and links to terrorism), instead of tackling terrorism, was "perhaps the single-most disastrous foreign policy decision by a U.S. president in the past decade, if not the past century." This is because it allowed the Taliban to regroup in Afghanistan leading to more expensive military operations and strengthening Al Qaeda's resolve further. Meanwhile, various US actions in Iraq and elsewhere damaged its reputation around the world.

The above summary also matches concerns (in the section on Bush Losing the War on Terror) which was written quite some time ago, so it did not have to take a decade to look back and see a change in course should have been possible. But maybe the impact of the enormous cost this would have (US tax payers have had to fork out trillions of dollars) was somewhat unimaginable?

The costs have been staggering in almost every respect. The estimated three to 4.4 trillion dollars Washington has incurred either directly or indirectly in conducting the "global war on terror" account for a substantial portion of the fiscal crisis that transformed the country's politics and brought it to the edge of bankruptcy last month.

And while the U.S. military remains by far the strongest in the world, its veil of invincibility has been irreparably pierced by the success with which rag-tag groups of guerrillas have defied and frustrated it.

Jim Lobe, Al Qaeda's Project for Ending the American Century Largely Succeeded, Inter Press Service, September 8, 2011

For many years even before 9-11, neo-conservatives had called for the US to consolidate its position in the world as the sole superpower and dominate further. 9-11 appeared to give them an excuse to push these ideas further and their ideology permeated throughout top-level thinking of the Bush Administration. It is therefore quite ironic, as Jim Lobe also notes, that "leading the charge [for such an aggressive foreign policy approach] were precisely those hawks whose fondest wish was to extend, rather than cut short, Washington's global hegemony."

By framing this as a war on "terror" (which, as a concept can almost never end), an excuse is now afforded to all governments to put in place tough security measured on any potentially flimsy basis. And the predicted "war" on civil liberties and human rights has unfortunately proven true as human rights organizations around the world feared from the start of the war on terror.

If the US public mood at the time was understandably full of anger and vengeance as well as shock and disbelief, it also reflects badly on US society that voices for more measured and appropriately calculated responses could be drowned out; an individual acting in a regrettable way due to a moment of anger is very different than an entire state apparatus (that should have time to think things through more thoroughly) doing that.

Maybe it could be argued that with hindsight it is easy to make these criticisms. Unfortunately, however, these concerns were there from the start, and re-iterated many times by many people and organizations during the past decade. But not all have wanted vengeance. Many families of the victims of the 9-11 atrocity have campaigned for a more peaceful approach to combating terrorism, for example.

Accompanying this has been media propaganda, media manipulation, sensationalism, sound-bite journalism and all the various other problems that have minimized coverage of deeper issues and understanding while allowing various claims to go almost unchallenged.

The rest of the article below started shortly after the 9-11 attacks in 2001 and was updated a few times up to 2007. It barely covered any details but still showed these numerous concerns from so many people and organizations were already there and are still relevant.

REACTION TO THE SEPTEMBER 11, 2001 EVENTS

With disbelief and shock around the world people saw the news footage of the events on September 11, 2001 when the planes-turned-missiles slammed into the World Trade Center towers and into the Pentagon. What is probably the worst terrorist attack on the United States, was totally inexcusable and roundly condemned.

Some 3000 were killed. *Initial fears were that it was over 6000»*

The subsequent bombing of Afghanistan to attack Osama Bin Laden's Al Qaeda terrorist network and the Taliban for harboring them has also led to some 3,500 civilian deaths, according to an independent study released at the beginning of December 2001. The ghastly terrorist attacks led to a mixture of political, social and economic reaction around the world.

Hatred and anti-Islam sentiment, (without distinguishing the despotic militants from ordinary Muslims) increased, even though most of the Muslim communities around the world condemned this act.

While visible efforts were seen by politicians to try to separate terrorists from Muslims in general, it has not been easy. On the one hand, after years of economic and geopolitical history, there are some aspects of distrust, while on the other hand, extremists in the Muslim and Christian communities are adding to the antagonisms. For example, during the height of the shock and anger to the September 11 attacks, extremist tendencies in the West resulted in beatings and even killings of Muslims. Even non-Muslims that just happened to have long beards or in some way resembled Taliban/Al Qaeda members were targeted. Others saw this as "proof" that Islam is inherently violent or that it is the primary threat to the rest of the world, etc. On the Muslim side, there have also been equally extreme reactions, from support of these terrorist acts to even being convinced that this was some sort of Zionist conspiracy to blame Muslims! In both cases these seem to be a minority of people with such extreme views but of course the concern is always that it will increase over time.

There was no question that there was going to be some sort of retaliation and response from the United States. One could not have expected them seriously to refrain from wanting to take revenge. Yet the fear was in what form this revenge would be and how it would be carried out as well as what the impact on ordinary Afghans would be, who have already suffered at the hands of the Taliban and outside forces for years.

In addition, some eight months after the attacks it was revealed in the mainstream press around the world that the CIA had warned George Bush of the threats weeks before September 11. This caused an uproar in many places, including the United States Congress, where members demanded more information to understand if all those deaths could have been prevented.

RESULTING "WAR ON TERROR"

The terrible events of September 11 saw the considerable quieting of what was until then growing domestic and international criticism of the Bush Administration. The September 11 events resulted in a "war on terror" which saw support for Bush and his popularity soar at the time.

Up to September 11, 2001, the Bush administration was being criticized around the world for its stances on various issues domestically and internationally. Even European and other allies were very critical of positions on numerous global issues.

But even before the Bush Administration, throughout the world, many nations and groups of people had expressed their frustrations at how U.S. foreign policies had affected them on all sorts of issues, ranging from economic/ globalization issues that have deepened poverty and/or inequality for most people around the world; geopolitics/arms/missile defence; environmental issues and so on. Protests either directly, or indirectly at U.S. policies have occurred all around the world—especially on globalization issues—as mentioned on this web site.

Yet that cannot be an excuse for the atrocity of September 11 as it killed many innocent people. At the same time, people have correctly pointed out that when other regions around the world have faced similar terrorist attacks, the outpouring of concern and condemnation has not been as much. The *Washington Post* (September 12, 2001) even dared to admit this at such a sensitive time shortly after the attacks.

However, behind the unity of the American people in the shock of September 11, a heightened sense of security resulted with concerns reverberating throughout the world. Many were concerned about the resulting crackdown of freedoms and civil liberties in various nations. Many worried that various countries around the world would also use this "war on terror" as an excuse to pursue more aggressive options on their own citizens.

For example, consider the concerns Amnesty International raised in October 2001, shortly after the September 11, 2001 attacks: "In the name of fighting 'international terrorism', governments have rushed to introduce draconian new measures that threaten the human rights of their own citizens, immigrants and refugees.... Governments have a responsibility to ensure the safety of their citizens, but measures taken must not undermine fundamental human rights standards.

It appears that some of the initiatives currently being discussed or implemented may be used to curb basic human rights and to suppress internal opposition. Some of the definitions of 'terrorism' under discussion are so broad that they could be used to criminalize anyone out of favour with those in power and criminalize legitimate peaceful exercise of the right to freedom of expression and association. They could also put at risk the right to privacy and threaten the rights of minorities and asylum-seekers."

In May 2003, Amnesty International charged, "The 'war on terror', far from making the world a safer place, has made it more dangerous by curtailing human rights, undermining the rule of international law and shielding governments from scrutiny. It has deepened divisions among people of different faiths and origins, sowing the seeds for more conflict. The overwhelming impact of all this is genuine fear—among the affluent as well as the poor."

In January 2004, one of the essays comprising the World Report 2004 from *Human Rights Watch* raised concerns about human rights in the U.S.:

Justice cannot exist without respect for human rights. As stated in the preamble of the Universal Declaration of Human Rights, "recognition of the inherent dignity and of the equal and inalienable rights of all members of the human family is the foundation of freedom, justice and peace in the world." The Bush administration's rhetoric acknowledges human rights and insists that the fight against terrorism is a fight to preserve "the non-negotiable demands of human dignity, the rule of law, limits on the power of the state—and equal justice," as President Bush told the graduating class of the West Point military academy in June 2002. But the Bush administration's actions contradict such fine words. Taken together, the Bush administration's anti-terrorism practices represent a stunning assault on basic principles of justice, government accountability, and the role of the courts.

... Confronted with a difficult and complex battle against international terrorism, the United States must not relinquish its traditions of justice and public accountability. The United States has long held itself up as the embodiment of good government. But it is precisely good governance—and its protection of human rights—that the Bush administration is currently jeopardizing with its post-September 11 anti-terrorist policies.

Alison Parker and Jamie Fellner, Above the Law: Executive Power after September 11 in the United States, World Report 2004, Human Rights Watch, January 2004 [Emphasis Added]

Even in the U.S. some of the resulting policies on how suspects will be treated, on how access to personal information will be made available for security concerns and so on, led to debates at all levels on what is considered an attack on civil liberties, and what is reasonable for security. On the foreign policy arena, there was increasing concern that the U.S. would be able to use the "war on terror" to pursue aggressive policies that were previously criticized by many other people. This can range from economic, to political and even military policies. The Iraq war was one such example, where among other things, the concern of terrorism was used to justify a war against Iraq, even though the terrorism links were not real.

Also of importance, with its loose definition of terror, there is concern that the "war on terror", will also affect all those working honestly for peace and social justice for all, as even they will come under scrutiny for perhaps appropriately criticizing policies of any number of nations and organizations around the world, including those from the West.

Interestingly, the prevention of a renowned constitutional lawyer and former US Marine revealed that *peace* marchers and those who criticized George Bush could find themselves on the US government's no-fly list. In early 2007, Walter Murphy, a constitutional law scholar and professor emeritus of politics at Princeton University (described as "the most distinguished constitutional scholars of the 20th century") had criticized the Bush administration for abusing the US Constitution. Shortly after that as he tried to fly somewhere he was stopped by authorities because he was on the "terrorist watch list" as they had put it. He recounted a conversation with some authorities during this incident:

"Have you been in any peace marches?" And then, before I could answer, he says, "We ban a lot of people from flying for that." And then I said, "No, but I did give a speech attacking George Bush." And he said, "Oh, that will do it."

Walter Murphy, Is Princeton Professor and Retired Marine on Government No-Fly List for Criticizing the White House?, Democracy Now!, April 12, 2007

That *peace* marchers would be on terrorist watch lists seems shocking. However, in some regards, this revelation is not as surprising as it may first seem. For years it has been suspected that this happens—around the world, not just in the US. In addition, towards the end of 2006, it was revealed that the Pentagon is keeping secret surveillance on peaceful protest activities. Furthermore, thousands have been mistakenly put on the no-fly list, and it is very hard to know why and get off it.

Amnesty International continued their criticism in their Report 2004, noting that both "governments and armed groups have launched a war on global values, destroying the human rights of ordinary people:"

Violence by armed groups and increasing violations by governments have combined to produce the most sustained attack on human rights and international humanitarian law in 50 years. This was leading to a world of growing mistrust, fear and division.

... Amnesty International strongly condemned armed groups responsible for atrocities such as the March 11 bombing in Madrid and the bomb attack on the United Nations building in Iraq on 19 August 2003.... Violent attacks on civilians and on institutions established to provide solutions to conflict and insecurity ... represented a significant new threat to international justice.

Report 2004: War on global values, Amnesty International, May 26, 2004

But Amnesty also harshly criticized governments of powerful and influential nations, including the United States:

"But it is also frightening that the principles of international law and the tools of multilateral action which could protect us from these attacks are being undermined, marginalized or destroyed by powerful governments," said Irene Khan [Secretary General of Amnesty International].

"Governments are losing their moral compass, sacrificing the global values of human rights in a blind pursuit of security. This failure of leadership is a dangerous concession to armed groups."

"The global security agenda promoted by the US Administration is bankrupt of vision and bereft of principle. Violating rights at home, turning a blind eye to abuses abroad and using pre-emptive military force where and when it chooses has damaged justice and freedom, and made the world a more dangerous place."

The "war on terror" and the war in Iraq has encouraged a new wave of human rights abuse and diverted attention from old ones ... while many governments are openly pursuing repressive agendas.

"While governments have been obsessed with the threat of weapons of mass destruction in Iraq, they have allowed the real weapons of mass destruction—injustice and impunity, poverty, discrimination and racism, the uncontrolled trade in small arms, violence against women and abuse of children—to go unaddressed," said Irene Khan.

Report 2004: War on global values, Amnesty International, May 26, 2004

Many might feel they are willing to give up some of their rights for more security, but as Irene Khan notes "Human rights matter because they offer a powerful and compelling vision of a better and fairer world, and a concrete plan of how to get there. These global values of justice are the most effective route to security and peace." The "war on terror" has in some respects, led to what has been described as a "war on freedom".

WAR ON TERROR

The War on Terror (WOT), also known as the Global War on Terrorism (GWOT), is a term applied to the international military campaign that started after the 11 September 2001 terrorist attacks on the United States. The campaign led to an international campaign to eliminate al-Qaeda and other militant organizations. The United States and many other NATO and non-NATO nations participated in the campaign.

The phrase "War on Terror" was first used by U.S. President George W. Bush on 20 September 2001. The Bush administration and the western media have since used the term to argue a global military, political, lawful, and conceptual struggle against both organizations designated terrorist and regimes accused of supporting them. It was originally used with a particular focus on Muslim countries associated with Islamic terrorism organizations including al-Qaeda and like-minded organizations.

Although the term War on Terror is no longer officially used by the administration of U.S. President Barack Obama (which prefers the term Overseas Contingency Operation), it is still commonly used by politicians, the media and in some official governmental aspects, including the US military's Global War on Terrorism Service Medal.

ETYMOLOGY

The phrase "War on Terror" has been used to specifically refer to the ongoing military campaign led by the US, UK and their allies against organizations and regimes identified by them as terrorist, and excludes other independent counter-terrorist operations and campaigns such as those by Russia and India. The conflict has also been referred to by names other than the War on Terror. It has also been known as:

- World War III
- World War IV (assuming the Cold War was World War III)
- Bush's War on Terror
- The Long War
- The Global War of Terror
- The War Against al-Qaeda

History of the name

In 1984, the Reagan Administration used the term "war against terrorism" as part of an effort to pass legislation that was designed to freeze assets of terrorist groups and marshal the forces of government against them. Author Shane Harris asserts this was a reaction to the 1983 Beirut barracks bombing.

The concept of America at war with terrorism may have begun on 11 September 2001 when Tom Brokaw, having just witnessed the collapse of one of the towers of the World Trade Center, declared "Terrorists have declared war on [America]."

On 16 September 2001, at Camp David, President George W. Bush used the phrase *war on terrorism* in an unscripted and controversial comment when he said, "This crusade – this war on terrorism – is going to take a while,... " Bush later apologized for this remark due to the negative connotations the term *crusade* has to people, *e.g.* of Muslim faith. The word*crusade* was not used again. On 20 September 2001, during a televised address to a joint session of congress, Bush stated that, "(o)ur 'war on terror' begins with al-Qaeda, but it does not end there.

It will not end until every terrorist group of global reach has been found, stopped and defeated." Bush did not say when he expected this would be achieved. In April 2007 the British government announced publicly that it was abandoning the use of the phrase "War on Terror" as they found it to be less than helpful. This was explained more recently by Lady Eliza Manningham-Buller. In her 2011Reith lecture, the former head of MI5 said that the 9/11 attacks were "a crime, not an act of war." "So I never felt it helpful to refer to a war on terror."

US President Barack Obama has rarely used the term, but in his inaugural address on 20 January 2009, he stated "Our nation is at war, against a far-reaching network of violence and hatred." In March 2009 the Defence Department officially changed the name of operations from "Global War on Terror" to "Overseas Contingency Operation" (OCO). In March 2009, the Obama administration requested that Pentagon staff members avoid use of the term, instead using "Overseas Contingency Operation". Basic objectives of the Bush administration "war on terror", such as targeting al Qaeda and building international counterterrorism alliances, remain in place. In December 2012, Jeh Johnson, the General Counsel of the Department of Defence, stated that the military fight will be replaced by a law enforcement operation when speaking at Oxford University, predicting that al Qaeda will be so weakened to be ineffective, and has been "effectively destroyed", and thus the conflict will not be an armed conflict under international law. In May 2013, Obama stated that the goal is "to dismantle specific networks of violent extremists that threaten America"; which coincided with the US Office of Management and Budget having changed the wording from "Overseas Contingency Operations" to "Countering Violent Extremism" in 2010.

The rhetorical war on terror

Because the actions involved in the "war on terrorism" are diffuse, and the criteria for inclusion are unclear, political theorist Richard Jackson has argued that "the 'war on terrorism' therefore, is simultaneously a set of actual practices—wars, covert operations, agencies, and institutions—and an accompanying series of assumptions, beliefs, justifications, and narratives—it is an entire language or discourse."

Jackson cites among many examples a statement by John Ashcroft that "the attacks of September 11 drew a bright line of demarcation between the civil and the savage".

Administration officials also described "terrorists" as hateful, treacherous, barbarous, mad, twisted, perverted, without faith, parasitical, inhuman, and, most commonly, evil. Americans, in contrast, were described as brave, loving, generous, strong, resourceful, heroic, and respectful of human rights.

Both the term and the policies it denotes have been a source of ongoing controversy, as critics argue it has been used to justify unilateral preventive war, human rights abuses and other violations of international law.

PRECURSOR TO THE 9/11 ATTACKS

The origins of al-Qaeda can be traced to the Soviet war in Afghanistan (December 1979 – February 1989). The United States, United Kingdom, Saudi Arabia, Pakistan, and the People's Republic of China supported the Islamist Afghanmujahadeen guerillas against the military forces of the Soviet Union and the Democratic Republic of Afghanistan.

A small number of "Afghan Arab" volunteers joined the fight against the Soviets, including Osama bin Laden, but there is no evidence they received any external assistance. In May 1996 the group World Islamic Front for Jihad Against Jews and Crusaders (WIFJAJC), sponsored by bin Laden (and later re-formed as al-Qaeda), started forming a large base of operations inAfghanistan, where the Islamist extremist regime of the Taliban had seized power earlier in the year.

In February 1998, Osama bin Laden signed a fatwâ, as head of al-Qaeda, declaring war on the West and Israel, later in May of that same year al-Qaeda released a video declaring war on the US and the West.

Following the bombings of US embassies in Kenya and Tanzania, US President Bill Clinton launched Operation Infinite Reach, a bombing campaign in Sudan and Afghanistan against targets the US asserted were associated with WIFJAJC, although others have questioned whether a pharmaceutical plant in Sudan was used as a chemical warfare plant.

The plant produced much of the region's antimalarial drugs and around 50 per cent of Sudan's pharmaceutical needs.The strikes failed to kill any leaders of WIFJAJC or the Taliban.

Next came the 2000 millennium attack plots, which included an attempted bombing of Los Angeles International Airport. In October 2000 the USS Cole bombing occurred, followed in 2001 by the 11 September 2001 attacks.

U.S. OBJECTIVES

The Authorization for Use of Military Force Against Terrorists or "AUMF" was made law on September 14, 2001, to authorize the use of United States Armed Forces against those responsible for the attacks on September 11, 2001. It authorized the President to use all necessary and appropriate force against those nations, organizations, or persons he determines planned, authorized, committed, or aided the terrorist attacks that occurred on September 11, 2001, or harbored such organizations or persons, in order to prevent any future acts of international terrorism against the United States by such nations, organizations or persons. Congress declares this is intended to constitute specific statutory authorization within the meaning of section 5(b) of the War Powers Resolution of 1973.

The George W. Bush administration defined the following objectives in the War on Terror:

1. Defeat terrorists such as Osama bin Laden, Abu Musab al-Zarqawi and demolish their organizations
2. Identify, locate and demolish terrorists along with their organizations
3. Deny sponsorship, support and sanctuary to terrorists
    1. End the state sponsorship of terrorism
    2. Establish and maintain an international standard of accountability with regard to combating terrorism
    3. Strengthen and sustain the international effort to combat terrorism
4. Work with willing and able states
5. Enable weak states
6. Persuade reluctant states
7. Compel unwilling states
8. Interdict and disorder material support for terrorists
9. Abolish terrorist sanctuaries and havens
    4. Diminish the underlying conditions that terrorists seek to exploit
        1. Partner with the international community to strengthen weak states and prevent (re)emergence of terrorism
        2. Win the war of ideals
    5. Defend US citizens and interests at home and abroad
        1. Integrate the National Strategy for Homeland Security
        2. Attain domain awareness
        3. Enhance measures to ensure the integrity, reliability, and availability of critical, physical, and information-based infrastructures at home and abroad
        4. Implement measures to protect US citizens abroad
        5. Ensure an integrated incident management capability

U.S. AND NATO-LED MILITARY OPERATIONS

OPERATION ACTIVE ENDEAVOUR

Operation Active Endeavour is a naval operation of NATO started in October 2001 in response to the September 11 attacks. It operates in the Mediterranean and is designed to prevent the movement of militants or weapons of mass destruction and to enhance the security of shipping in general. The operation has also assisted Greece with its prevention of illegal immigration.

Operation Enduring Freedom

Operation Enduring Freedom is the official name used by the Bush administration for the War in Afghanistan, together with three smaller military actions, under the umbrella of the Global War on Terror. These global operations are intended to seek out and destroy any al-Qaeda fighters or affiliates.

Operation Enduring Freedom – Afghanistan

On 20 September 2001, in the wake of the 11 September attacks, George W. Bush delivered an ultimatum to the Taliban government of Afghanistan to turn over Osama bin Laden and al-Qaeda leaders operating in the country or face attack. The Taliban demanded evidence of bin Laden's link to the 11 September attacks and, if such evidence warranted a trial, they offered to handle such a trial in an Islamic Court. The US refused to provide any evidence.

Subsequently, in October 2001, US forces (with UK and coalition allies) invaded Afghanistan to oust the Taliban regime. On 7 October 2001, the official invasion began with British and US forces conducting airstrike campaigns over enemy targets. Kabul, the capital city of Afghanistan, fell by mid-November. The remaining al-Qaeda and Taliban remnants fell back to the rugged mountains of eastern Afghanistan, mainly Tora Bora. In December, Coalition forces (the US and its allies) fought within that region. It is believed that Osama bin Laden escaped into Pakistan during the battle.

In March 2002, the US and other NATO and non-NATO forces launched Operation Anaconda with the goal of destroying any remaining al-Qaeda and Taliban forces in the Shah-i-Kot Valley and Arma Mountains of Afghanistan. The Taliban suffered heavy casualties and evacuated the region.

The Taliban regrouped in western Pakistan and began to unleash an insurgent-style offensive against Coalition forces in late 2002.Throughout southern and eastern Afghanistan, firefights broke out between the surging Taliban and Coalition forces. Coalition forces responded with a series of military offensives and an increase in the amount of troops in Afghanistan. In February 2010, Coalition forces launched Operation Moshtarak in southern Afghanistan along with other military offensives in the hopes that they would destroy the Taliban insurgency once and for all. Peace talks are also underway between

Taliban affiliated fighters and Coalition forces. TheUnited States and other NATO and non-NATO forces are planning to withdraw from Afghanistan by the end of 2014.

Operation Enduring Freedom – Philippines

In January 2002, the United States Special Operations Command, Pacific deployed to the Philippines to advise and assist the Armed Forces of the Philippines in combating Filipino Islamist groups. The operations were mainly focused on removing the Abu Sayyafgroup and Jemaah Islamiyah (JI) from their stronghold on the island of Basilan. The second portion of the operation was conducted as a humanitarian programme called "Operation Smiles." The goal of the programme was to provide medical care and services to the region of Basilan as part of a "Hearts and Minds" programme.

Operation Enduring Freedom – Horn of Africa

This extension of Operation Enduring Freedom was titled OEF-HOA. Unlike other operations contained in Operation Enduring Freedom, OEF-HOA does not have a specific organization as a target. OEF-HOA instead focuses its efforts to disrupt and detect militant activities in the region and to work with willing governments to prevent the Re-emergence of militant cells and activities.

In October 2002, the Combined Joint Task Force - Horn of Africa (CJTF-HOA) was established in Djibouti at Camp Lemonnier. It contains approximately 2,000 personnel including US military and special operations forces (SOF) and coalition force members,Combined Task Force 150 (CTF-150).

Task Force 150 consists of ships from a shifting group of nations, including Australia, Canada, France, Germany, Italy, Netherlands, Pakistan, New Zealand and the United Kingdom. The primary goal of the coalition forces is to monitor, inspect, board and stop suspected shipments from entering the Horn of Africa region and affecting the US' Operation Iraqi Freedom.

Included in the operation is the training of selected armed forces units of the countries of Djibouti, Kenya and Ethiopia in counter-terrorism and counter-insurgency tactics. Humanitarian efforts conducted by CJTF-HOA include rebuilding of schools and medical clinics and providing medical services to those countries whose forces are being trained.

The programme expands as part of the Trans-Saharan Counterterrorism Initiative as CJTF personnel also assist in training the armed forces of Chad, Niger, Mauritaniaand Mali. However, the War on Terror does not include Sudan, where over 400,000 have died in an ongoing civil war.

On 1 July 2006, a Web-posted message purportedly written by Osama bin Laden urged Somalis to build an Islamic state in the country and warned western governments that the al-Qaeda network would fight against them if they intervened there.

Somalia has been considered a "failed state" because its official central government was weak, dominated by warlords and unable to exert effective control over the country. Beginning in mid-2006, the Islamic Courts Union (ICU), an Islamist faction campaigning on a restoration of "law and order" through Sharia law, had rapidly taken control of much of southern Somalia.

On 14 December 2006, the US Assistant Secretary of State Jendayi Frazer claimed al-Qaeda cell operatives were controlling the Islamic Courts Union, a claim denied by the ICU.

By late 2006, the UN-backed Transitional Federal Government (TFG) of Somalia had seen its power effectively limited to Baidoa, while the Islamic Courts Union controlled the majority of southern Somalia, including the capital of Mogadishu. On 20 December 2006, the Islamic Courts Union launched an offensive on the government stronghold of Baidoa, and saw early gains before Ethiopia intervened in favour of the government.

By 26 December, the Islamic Courts Union retreated towards Mogadishu, before again retreating as TFG/Ethiopian troops neared, leaving them to take Mogadishu with no resistance. The ICU then fled to Kismayo, where they fought Ethiopian/TFG forces in the Battle of Jilib.

The Prime Minister of Somalia claimed that three "terror suspects" from the 1998 United States embassy bombings are being sheltered in Kismayo. On 30 December 2006, al-Qaeda deputy leader Ayman al-Zawahiri called upon Muslims worldwide to fight against Ethiopia and the TFG in Somalia.

On 8 January 2007, the US launched the Battle of Ras Kamboni by bombing Ras Kamboni using AC-130 gunships.

On 14 September 2009, US Special Forces killed two men and wounded and captured two others near the Somali village of Baarawe. Witnesses claim that helicopters used for the operation launched from French-flagged warships, but that could not be confirmed. A Somali based al-Qaida affiliated group, the Al-Shabaab, has confirmed the death of "sheik commander" Saleh Ali Saleh Nabhan along with an unspecified number of militants. Nabhan, a Kenyan, was wanted in connection with the 2002 Mombasa attacks.

Operation Enduring Freedom – Trans Sahara

Operation Enduring Freedom – Trans Sahara (OEF-TS) is the name of the military operation conducted by the US and partner nations in the Sahara/Sahel region of Africa, consisting of counter-terrorism efforts and policing of arms and drug trafficking across central Africa.

The conflict in northern Mali began in January 2012 with radical Islamists (affiliated to al-Qaeda) advancing into northern Mali. The Malian government had a hard time maintaining full control over their country. The fledgling government requested support from the international community on combating the Islamic militants. In January 2013, France intervened on behalf of the Malian government's request and deployed troops into the region. They launched

Operation Serval on 11 January 2013, with the hopes of dislodging the al-Qaeda affiliated groups from northern Mali.

Iraq

Iraq had been listed as a State sponsor of terrorism by the US since 1990, when Saddam Hussein invaded Kuwait. Iraq had also been on the list from 1979 to 1982; it was removed so that the US could provide material support to Iraq in its war with Iran. Hussein's regime had proven to be a problem for the UN and Iraq's neighbors due to its use of chemical weaponsagainst Iranians and Kurds in the 1980s.

Iraqi no-fly zones

Following the ceasefire agreement that suspended hostilities (but not officially ended) in the 1991 Gulf War, the United States and its allies instituted and began patrolling Iraqi no-fly zones, to protect Iraq's Kurdish and Shi'a Arab population—both of which suffered attacks from the Hussein regime before and after the Gulf War—in Iraq's northern and southern regions, respectively. US forces continued in combat zone deployments through November 1995 and launched Operation Desert Fox against Iraq in 1998 after it failed to meet US demands of "unconditional cooperation" in weapons inspections.

In the aftermath of Operation Desert Fox, during December 1998, Iraq announced that it would no longer respect the no-fly zones and resumed its attempts to shoot down US aircraft.

Operation Iraqi Freedom

The Iraq War began in March 2003 with an air campaign, which was immediately followed by a U.S.-led ground invasion. The Bush administration stated the invasion was the "serious consequences" spoken of in the UNSC Resolution 1441, partially on the basis of Iraq possessing weapons of mass destruction. The Bush administration also stated the Iraq war was part of the War on Terror, something later questioned or contested.

Baghdad, Iraq's capital city, fell in April 2003 and Saddam Hussein's government quickly dissolved. On 1 May 2003, Bush announced that major combat operations in Iraq had ended. However, an insurgency arose against the U.S.-led coalition and the newly developing Iraqi military and post-Saddam government. The insurgency, which included al-Qaeda affiliated groups, led to far more coalition casualties than the invasion. Other elements of the insurgency were led by fugitive members of President Hussein's Ba'ath regime, which included Iraqi nationalists and pan-Arabists. Many insurgency leaders are Islamists and claim to be fighting a religious war to Re-establish the Islamic Caliphate of centuries past. Iraq's former president, Saddam Hussein was captured by U.S. forces in December 2003. He was executed in 2006.

In 2004, the insurgent forces grew stronger. The US conducted attacks on insurgent strongholds in cities like Najaf and Fallujah.

In January 2007, President Bush presented a new strategy for Operation Iraqi Freedom based upon counter-insurgency theories and tactics developed by General David Petraeus. The Iraq War troop surge of 2007 was part of this "new way forward" and, along with US backing of Sunni groups it had previously sought to defeat, has been credited with a widely recognized dramatic decrease in violence by up to 80 per cent.

Operation New Dawn

The war entered a new phase on 1 September 2010, with the official end of US combat operations. The last U.S. troopsexited Iraq on 18 December 2011.

OPERATION INHERENT RESOLVE

In a major split in the ranks of Al Qaeda's organization, the Iraqi franchise, known as Al Qaeda in Iraq covertly invaded Syria and the Levant and began participating in the ongoing Syrian Civil War, gaining enough support and strength to re-invade Iraq's western provinces under the name of the Islamic State of Iraq and the Levant, taking over much of the country in ablitzkrieg-like action and combining the Iraq insurgency and Syrian Civil War into a single conflict. Due to their extreme brutality and a complete change in their overall ideology, Al Qaeda's core organization in Central Asia eventually denounced ISIS and directed their affiliates to cut off all ties with this organization. Many analysts believe that because of this schism, Al Qaeda and ISIL is now in a competition to retain the title of the world's most powerful terrorist organization.

The Obama administration began to Re-engage in Iraq with a series of airstrikes aimed at ISIS beginning on 10 August 2014. On 9 September 2014 President Obama said that he had the authority he needed to take action to destroy the militant group known as the Islamic State of Iraq and the Levant and thus did not require additional approval from Congress. The following day on September 10, 2014 President Barack Obama made a televised speech about ISIL, which he stated "Our objective is clear: We will degrade, and ultimately destroy, ISIL through a comprehensive and sustained counterterrorism strategy,".

Obama has authorized the deployment of additional U.S. Forces into Iraq, as well as authorizing direct military operations against ISIL within Syria. On the night of September 21/22 the United States, Saudi Arabia, Bahrain, the UAE, Jordan and Qatar started air attacks against ISIS in Syria.

In October 2014, it was reported that the U.S. Department of Defence considers military operations against ISIL as being under Operation Enduring Freedom in regards to campaign medal awarding. On 15 October, the military intervention became known as "Operation Inherent Resolve".

OTHER MILITARY OPERATIONS

FIGHTING IN PAKISTAN

Following the 11 September 2001 attacks, former President of Pakistan Pervez Musharraf sided with the US against the Taliban government in Afghanistan after an ultimatum by then US President George W. Bush. Musharraf agreed to give the US the use of three airbases for Operation Enduring Freedom. United States Secretary of State Colin Powell and other US administration officials met with Musharraf. On 19 September 2001, Musharraf addressed the people of Pakistan and stated that, while he opposed military tactics against the Taliban, Pakistan risked being endangered by an alliance of India and the US if it did not cooperate. In 2006, Musharraf testified that this stance was pressured by threats from the US, and revealed in his memoirs that he had "war-gamed" the United States as an adversary and decided that it would end in a loss for Pakistan.

On 12 January 2002, Musharraf gave a speech against Islamic extremism. He unequivocally condemned all acts of terrorism and pledged to combat Islamic extremism and lawlessness within Pakistan itself. He stated that his government was committed to rooting out extremism and made it clear that the banned militant organizations would not be allowed to resurface under any new name. He said, "the recent decision to ban extremist groups promoting militancy was taken in the national interest after thorough consultations. It was not taken under any foreign influence".

In 2002, the Musharraf-led government took a firm stand against the jihadi organizations and groups promoting extremism, and arrested Maulana Masood Azhar, head of the Jaish-e-Mohammed, and Hafiz Muhammad Saeed, chief of the Lashkar-e-Taiba, and took dozens of activists into custody. An official ban was imposed on the groups on 12 January. Later that year, the Saudi born Zayn al-Abidn Muhammed Hasayn Abu Zubaydah was arrested by Pakistani officials during a series of joint US-Pakistan raids. Zubaydah is said to have been a high-ranking al-Qaeda official with the title of operations chief and in charge of running al-Qaeda training camps.Other prominent al-Qaeda members were arrested in the following two years, namely Ramzi bin al-Shibh, who is known to have been a financial backer of al-Qaeda operations, and Khalid Sheikh Mohammed, who at the time of his capture was the third highest-ranking official in al-Qaeda and had been directly in charge of the planning for the 11 September attacks.

In 2004, the Pakistan Army launched a campaign in the Federally Administered Tribal Areas of Pakistan's Waziristan region, sending in 80,000 troops. The goal of the conflict was to remove the al-Qaeda and Taliban forces in the region.

After the fall of the Taliban regime many members of the Taliban resistance fled to the Northern border region of Afghanistan and Pakistan where the

Pakistani army had previously little control. With the logistics and air support of the United States, the Pakistani Army captured or killed numerous al-Qaeda operatives such as Khalid Sheikh Mohammed, wanted for his involvement in the USS Cole bombing, the Bojinka plot, and the killing of *Wall Street Journal* reporter Daniel Pearl.

The United States has carried out a campaign of Drone attacks on targets all over the Federally Administered Tribal Areas. However, thePakistani Taliban still operates there. To this day it's estimated that 15 US soldiers were killed while fighting al-Qaeda and Taliban remnants in Pakistan since the War on Terror began. Osama bin Laden, the founder of al-Qaeda, was killed on 2 May 2011, during a raid conducted by the United States special operations forces in Abbottabad, Pakistan.

FIGHTING IN YEMEN

The United States has also conducted a series of military strikes on al-Qaeda militants in Yemen since the War on Terror began. Yemen has a weak central government and a powerful tribal system that leaves large lawless areas open for militant training and operations. Al-Qaida has a strong presence in the country. The US, in an effort to support Yemeni counter-terrorism efforts, has increased their military aid package to Yemen from less than $11 million in 2006 to more than $70 million in 2009, as well as providing up to $121 million for development over the next three years.

FIGHTING IN KASHMIR

In a 'Letter to American People' written by Osama bin Laden in 2002, he stated that one of the reasons he was fighting America is because of its support of India on the Kashmir issue. While on a trip to Delhi in 2002, U.S. Secretary of Defence Donald Rumsfeld suggested that Al-Qaeda was active in Kashmir, though he did not have any hard evidence. An investigation in 2002 unearthed evidence that Al-Qaeda and its affiliates were prospering in Pakistan-administered Kashmir with tacit approval of Pakistan's National Intelligence agencyInter-Services Intelligence. A team of Special Air Service and Delta Force was sent into Indian-administered Kashmir in 2002 to hunt for Osama bin Laden after reports that he was being sheltered by the Kashmiri militant group Harkat-ul-Mujahideen. U.S. officials believed that Al-Qaeda was helping organize a campaign of terror in Kashmir in order to provoke conflict between India and Pakistan. Fazlur Rehman Khalil, the leader of the Harkat-ul-Mujahideen, signed al-Qaeda's 1998 declaration of holy war, which called on Muslims to attack all Americans and their allies. In 2006, Al-Qaeda claimed they had established a wing in Kashmir; this worried the Indian government.Al-Qaeda has strong ties with the Kashmir militant groups Lashkar-e-Taiba and Jaish-e-Mohammed in Pakistan. While on a visit to Pakistan in January 2010, U.S. Defence secretary Robert Gates stated that Al-Qaeda was seeking to destabilize the region and planning to provoke a nuclear war between India and Pakistan. In September 2009, a U.S. Drone strike reportedly killed Ilyas Kashmiri, who was the chief of Harkat-ul-Jihad al-Islami, a Kashmiri militant group associated with Al-Qaeda. Kashmiri was described by Bruce Riedel as a 'prominent' Al-Qaeda member, while others described him as the head of military operations for Al-Qaeda. Waziristan had now become the new battlefield for Kashmiri militants, who were now fighting NATO in support of Al-Qaeda.

On 8 July 2012, Al-Badar Mujahideen, a breakaway faction of Kashmir centric terror group Hizbul Mujahideen, on conclusion of their two-day Shuhada Conference called for mobilisation of resources for continuation of jihad in Kashmir.

INTERNATIONAL MILITARY SUPPORT

The invasion of Afghanistan is seen to have been the first action of this war, and initially involved forces from the United States, the United Kingdom, and the Afghan Northern Alliance.

Since the initial invasion period, these forces were augmented by troops and aircraft from Australia, Canada, Denmark, France, Italy, Netherlands, New Zealand and Norway amongst others. In 2006, there were about 33,000 troops in Afghanistan.

On 12 September 2001, less than 24 hours after the 11 September attacks in New York City and Washington, D.C., NATO invoked Article 5 of the North Atlantic Treaty and declared the attacks to be an attack against all 19 NATO member countries. Australian Prime MinisterJohn Howard also declared that Australia would invoke the ANZUS Treaty along similar lines.

In the following months, NATO took a wide range of measures to respond to the threat of terrorism. On 22 November 2002, the member states of the Euro-Atlantic Partnership Council (EAPC) decided on a Partnership Action Plan against Terrorism, which explicitly states, "EAPC States are committed to the protection and promotion of fundamental freedoms and human rights, as well as the rule of law, in combating terrorism." NATO started naval operations in the Mediterranean Sea designed to prevent the movement of terrorists or weapons of mass destruction as well as to enhance the security of shipping in general called Operation Active Endeavour.

Support for the US cooled when America made clear its determination to invade Iraq in late 2002. Even so, many of the "coalition of the willing" countries that unconditionally supported the US-led military action have sent troops to Afghanistan, particular neighboring Pakistan, which has disowned its earlier support for the Taliban and contributed tens of thousands of soldiers to the conflict. Pakistan was also engaged in the War in North-West Pakistan (Waziristan War). Supported by US intelligence, Pakistan was attempting to remove the Taliban insurgency and al-Qaeda element from the northern tribal areas.

INTERNATIONAL SECURITY ASSISTANCE FORCE

December 2001 saw the creation of the NATO-led International Security Assistance Force (ISAF) to assist the Afghan Transitional Administration and the first post-Taliban elected government. With a renewed Taliban insurgency, it was announced in 2006 that ISAF would replace the US troops in the province as part of Operation Enduring Freedom.

The British 16th Air Assault Brigade (later reinforced by Royal Marines) formed the core of the force in southern Afghanistan, along with troops and helicopters from Australia, Canada and the Netherlands. The initial force consisted of roughly 3,300 British, 2,000 Canadian, 1,400 from the Netherlands and 240 from Australia, along with special forces from Denmark andEstonia and small contingents from other nations. The monthly supply of cargo containers through Pakistani route to ISAF in Afghanistan is over 4,000 costing around 12 billion in Pakistani Rupees.

AL-QAEDA ATTACKS AND FAILED PLOTS SINCE 9/11

Since 9/11, Al-Qaeda and other affiliated radical Islamist groups have executed attacks in several parts of the world where the conflict is not taking place. Whereas countries like Pakistan have suffered hundreds of attacks killing tens of thousands and displacing many more.

- The 2002 Bali bombings in Indonesia were committed by various members of Jemaah Islamiyah, an organization linked to Al-Qaeda.
- The 2003 Casablanca bombings were carried out by Salafia Jihadia, an Al-Qaeda affiliate.
- After the 2003 Istanbul bombings, Turkey charged 74 people with involvement, including Syrian Al-Qaeda member Loai al-Saqa.
- The 2004 Madrid train bombings in Spain were "inspired by" Al-Qaeda, though no direct involvement has been established.
- The 7 July 2005 London bombings in the United Kingdom were perpetrated by 4 homegrown terrorists, one of whom appeared in an edited video with a known Al-Qaeda operative, though the British government denies Al-Qaeda involvement.
- Al Qaeda claimed responsibility for the 11 April 2007 Algiers bombings in Algeria.
- The 2007 Glasgow International Airport attack in the United Kingdom was carried out by a pair of bombers whose laptops and suicide notes included videos and speeches referencing Al-Qaeda, though no direct involvement was established.
- The 2009 Fort Hood shooting in the United States was committed by Nidal Malik Hasan, who had been in communication with Anwar al-Awlaki, though the Department of Defence classifies the shooting as an incidence of workplace violence.

- Morocco blames Al-Qaeda for the 2011 Marrakech bombing, though Al-Qaeda denies involvement.
- 2012 Toulouse and Montauban shootings in France were committed by Mohammed Merah, who reportedly had familial ties to Al-Qaeda, along with a history of petty crime and psychological issues. Merah claimed ties to Al-Qaeda, though French authorities deny any connection.
- To date, no one has been convicted for the 2012 U.S. Consulate attack in Benghazi in Libya and no one has claimed responsibility. Branches of Al-Qaeda, Al-Qaeda affiliates, and individuals "sympathetic to Al-Qaeda" are blamed.

There may also have been several additional planned attacks that were not successful.

- 2004 financial buildings plot (United States and the United Kingdom)
- 21 July 2005 London bombings (United Kingdom)
- 2006 Toronto terrorism plot (Canada)
- 2006 transatlantic aircraft plot involving liquid explosives carried onto commercial airplanes
- 2006 Hudson River bomb plot (United States)
- 2007 Fort Dix attack plot (United States)
- 2007 London car bombs (United Kingdom)
- 2007 John F. Kennedy International Airport attack plot (United States)
- 2009 Bronx terrorism plot (United States)
- 2009 New York Subway and United Kingdom Plot (United States and the United Kingdom)
- 2009 Christmas Bomb Plot (United States)
- 2010 Times Square car bombing attempt (United States)
- 2010 cargo plane bomb plot (United States)
- 2010 Portland car bomb plot (United States)
- 2011 Manhattan terrorism plot (United States)
- 2013 VIA Rail Canada terrorism plot (Canada)

U.S. MILITARY AID TO OTHER COUNTRIES

Pakistan

In the three years before the attacks of 11 September, Pakistan received approximately US$9 million in American military aid. In the three years after, the number increased to US$4.2 billion, making it the country with the maximum funding post 9/11. Such a huge inflow of funds has raised concerns in the Indian press that these funds were given without any accountability, as the end uses not being documented, and that large portions were used to suppress civilians' human rights and to purchase weapons to contain domestic problems like the Balochistan unrest.

POST 9/11 EVENTS INSIDE THE UNITED STATES

In addition to military efforts abroad, in the aftermath of 9/11 the Bush Administration increased domestic efforts to prevent future attacks. Various government bureaucracies that handled security and military functions were reorganized. A new cabinet-level agency called the United States Department of Homeland Security was created in November 2002 to lead and coordinate the largest reorganization of the US federal government since the consolidation of the armed forces into the Department of Defence.

The Justice Department launched the National Security Entry-Exit Registration System for certain male non-citizens in the US, requiring them to register in person at offices of the Immigration and Naturalization Service.

The USA PATRIOT Act of October 2001 dramatically reduces restrictions on law enforcement agencies' ability to search telephone, e-mail communications, medical, financial, and other records; eases restrictions on foreign intelligence gathering within the United States; expands theSecretary of the Treasury's authority to regulate financial transactions, particularly those involving foreign individuals and entities; and broadens the discretion of law enforcement and immigration authorities in detaining and deporting immigrants suspected of terrorism-related acts.

The act also expanded the definition of terrorism to include domestic terrorism, thus enlarging the number of activities to which the USA PATRIOT Act's expanded law enforcement powers could be applied. A new Terrorist Finance Tracking Programme monitored the movements of terrorists' financial resources (discontinued after being revealed by *The New York Times*). Global telecommunication usage, including those with no links to terrorism, is being collected and monitored through the NSA electronic surveillance programme. The Patriot Act is still in effect.

Political interest groups have stated that these laws remove important restrictions on governmental authority, and are a dangerous encroachment on civil liberties, possibleunconstitutional violations of the Fourth Amendment. On 30 July 2003, the American Civil Liberties Union (ACLU) filed the first legal challenge against Section 215 of the Patriot Act, claiming that it allows the FBI to violate a citizen's First Amendment rights, Fourth Amendment rights, and right to due process, by granting the government the right to search a person's business, bookstore, and library records in a terrorist investigation, without disclosing to the individual that records were being searched. Also, governing bodies in a number of communities have passed symbolic resolutions against the act.

In a speech on 9 June 2005, Bush said that the USA PATRIOT Act had been used to bring charges against more than 400 suspects, more than half of whom had been convicted. Meanwhile the ACLU quoted Justice Department figures showing that 7,000 people have complained of abuse of the Act. The Defence

Advanced Research Projects Agency (DARPA) began an initiative in early 2002 with the creation of the Total Information Awareness programme, designed to promote information technologies that could be used in counter-terrorism. This programme, facing criticism, has since been defunded by Congress.

By 2003, 12 major conventions and protocols were designed to combat terrorism. These were adopted and ratified by a number of states. These conventions require states to co-operate on principal issues regarding unlawful seizure of aircraft, the physical protection of nuclear materials, and the freezing of assets of militant networks.

In 2005, the UN Security Council adopted Resolution 1624 concerning incitement to commit acts of terrorism and the obligations of countries to comply with international human rights laws. Although both resolutions require mandatory annual reports on counter-terrorism activities by adopting nations, the United States and Israel have both declined to submit reports. In the same year, the United States Department of Defenceand the Chairman of the Joint Chiefs of Staff issued a planning document, by the name "National Military Strategic Plan for the War on Terrorism", which stated that it constituted the "comprehensive military plan to prosecute the Global War on Terror for the Armed Forces of the United States...including the findings and recommendations of the 9/11 Commission and a rigorous examination with the Department of Defence".

On 9 January 2007, the House of Representatives passed a bill, by a vote of 299–128, enacting many of the recommendations of the 9/11 Commission The bill passed in the US Senate, by a vote of 60–38, on 13 March 2007 and it was signed into law on 3 August 2007 by President Bush. It became Public Law 110-53. In July 2012, US Senate passed a resolution urging that the Haqqani Network be designated a foreign terrorist organisation.

The Office of Strategic Influence was secretly created after 9/11 for the purpose of coordinating propaganda efforts, but was closed soon after being discovered. The Bush administration implemented the Continuity of Operations Plan (or Continuity of Government) to ensure that US government would be able to continue in catastrophic circumstances.

Since 9/11, extremists made various attempts to attack the United States, with varying levels of organization and skill. For example, vigilant passengers aboard a transatlantic flight prevented Richard Reid, in 2001, and Umar Farouk Abdulmutallab, in 2009, from detonating an explosive device.

Other terrorist plots have been stopped by federal agencies using new legal powers and investigative tools, sometimes in cooperation with foreign governments.

Such thwarted attacks include:

- The 2001 shoe bomb plot
- A plan to crash airplanes into the US Bank Tower (aka Library Tower) in Los Angeles

- The 2003 plot by Iyman Faris to blow up the Brooklyn Bridge in New York City
- The 2004 Financial buildings plot, which targeted the International Monetary Fund and World Bank buildings in Washington, D.C., the New York Stock Exchange and other financial institutions
- The 2004 Columbus Shopping Mall Bombing Plot
- The 2006 Sears Tower plot
- The 2007 Fort Dix attack plot
- The 2007 John F. Kennedy International Airport attack plot
- The New York Subway Bombing Plot and 2010 Times Square car bombing attempt

The Obama administration has promised the closing of the Guantanamo Bay detention camp, increased the number of troops in Afghanistan, and promised the withdrawal of its troops from Iraq.

CASUALTIES

According to Joshua Goldstein, an international relations professor from the American University, The Global War on Terror has seen fewer war deaths than any other decade in the past century.

There is no widely agreed on figure for the number of people that have been killed so far in the War on Terror as it has been defined by the Bush Administration to include the war in Afghanistan, the war in Iraq, and operations elsewhere. Some estimates include the following:

- Iraq Body Count project documented 110,937–121,227 civilian deaths from violence from March 2003 to December 2012.
- 110,600 deaths in total according to the Associated Press from March 2003 to April 2009.
- 151,000 deaths in total according to the Iraq Family Health Survey.
- Opinion Research Business (ORB) poll conducted 12–19 August 2007 estimated 1,033,000 violent deaths due to the Iraq War. The range given was 946,000 to 1,120,000 deaths. A nationally representative sample of approximately 2,000 Iraqi adults answered whether any members of their household (living under their roof) were killed due to the Iraq War. 22 per cent of the respondents had lost one or more household members. ORB reported that "48 per cent died from a gunshot wound, 20 per cent from the impact of a car bomb, 9 per cent from aerial bombardment, 6 per cent as a result of an accident and 6 per cent from another blast/ordnance."
- Between 392,979 and 942,636 estimated Iraqi (655,000 with a confidence interval of 95 per cent), civilian and combatant, according to the second Lancet survey of mortality.
- A minimum of 62,570 civilian deaths reported in the mass media up to 28 April 2007 according to Iraq Body Count project.

- 4,409 US military dead (929 non-hostile deaths), and 31,926 wounded in action during Operation Iraqi Freedom. 66 US Military dead (28 non-hostile deaths), and 295 wounded in action during Operation New Dawn.
- Afghanistan: between 10,960 and 49,600
- 16,725–19,013 civilians killed according to Cost of War project from 2001 to 2013
- According to Marc W. Herold's extensive database, between 3,100 and 3,600 civilians were directly killed by US Operation Enduring Freedom bombing and Special Forces attacks between 7 October 2001 and 3 June 2003. This estimate counts only "impact deaths"—deaths that occurred in the immediate aftermath of an explosion or shooting—and does not count deaths that occurred later as a result of injuries sustained, or deaths that occurred as an indirect consequence of the US airstrikes and invasion.
- In an opinion article published in August 2002 in the magazine The Weekly Standard, Joshua Muravchik of the American Enterprise Institute, questioned Professor Herold's study entirely on the basis of one single incident that involved 25–93 deaths. He did not provide any estimate his own.
- In a pair of January 2002 studies, Carl Conetta of the Project on Defence Alternatives estimates that "at least" 4,200–4,500 civilians were killed by mid-January 2002 as a result of the war and Coalition airstrikes, both directly as casualties of the aerial bombing campaign, and indirectly in the resulting humanitarian crisis.
- His first study, "Operation Enduring Freedom: Why a Higher Rate of Civilian Bombing Casualties?", released 18 January 2002, estimates that, at the low end, "at least" 1,000–1,300 civilians were directly killed in the aerial bombing campaign in just the 3 months between 7 October 2001 to 1 January 2002. The author found it impossible to provide an upper-end estimate to direct civilian casualties from the Operation Enduring Freedom bombing campaign that he noted as having an increased use of cluster bombs. In this lower-end estimate, only Western press sources were used for hard numbers, while heavy "reduction factors" were applied to Afghan government reports so that their estimates were reduced by as much as 75 per cent.
- In his companion study, "Strange Victory: A critical appraisal of Operation Enduring Freedom and the Afghanistan war", released 30 January 2002, Conetta estimates that "at least" 3,200 more Afghans died by mid-January 2002, of "starvation, exposure, associated illnesses, or injury sustained while in flight from war zones", as a result of the war and Coalition airstrikes.

- In similar numbers, a Los Angeles Times review of US, British, and Pakistani newspapers and international wire services found that between 1,067 and 1,201 direct civilian deaths were reported by those news organizations during the five months from 7 October 2001 to 28 February 2002. This review excluded all civilian deaths in Afghanistan that did not get reported by US, British, or Pakistani news, excluded 497 deaths that did get reported in US, British, and Pakistani news but that were not specifically identified as civilian or military, and excluded 754 civilian deaths that were reported by the Taliban but not independently confirmed.
- According to Jonathan Steele of *The Guardian* between 20,000 and 49,600 people may have died of the consequences of the invasion by the spring of 2002.
- 2,046 US military dead (339 non-hostile deaths), and 18,201 wounded in action.
- Pakistan: Between 1467 and 2334 people were killed in U.S. drone attacks as of 6 May 2011. tens of thousands have been killed by terrorist attacks, millions displaced.
- Somalia: 7,000+
- In December 2007, The Elman Peace and Human Rights Organization said it had verified 6,500 civilian deaths, 8,516 people wounded, and 1.5 million displaced from homes in Mogadishu alone during the year 2007.
- USA
- 1 June 2009, Pvt. William Andrew Long was shot and killed by Abdulhakim Muhammad, while outside a recruiting facility in Little Rock AR.
- On 5 November 2009, Nidal Malik Hasan shot and killed 13 people and wounded more than 30 others in Fort Hood, Texas.

Total American casualties from the War on Terror (this includes fighting throughout the world):

US Military killed	6,639
US Military wounded	50,422
US DoD Civilians killed	16
US Civilians killed (includes 9/11 and after)	3,000 +
US Civilians wounded/injured	6,000 +
Total Americans killed (military and civilian)	**9,655 +**
Total Americans wounded/injured	**56,422 +**
Total American casualties	**66,077 +**

The United States Department of Veterans Affairs has diagnosed more than 200,000 American veterans with PTSD since 2001.

Costs

A March 2011 Congressional report estimated spending related to the war through fiscal year 2011 at $1.2 trillion, and that spending through 2021 assuming a reduction to 45,000 troops would be $1.8 trillion. A June 2011 academic report covering additional areas of spending related to the war estimated it through 2011 at $2.7 trillion, and long term spending at $5.4 trillion including interest.

Expense	CRS/CBO (Billions US$):	Watson (Billions constant US$):
FY2001-FY2011		
War appropriations to DoD	1208.1	1311.5
War appropriations to DoS/USAid	66.7	74.2
VA medical	8.4	13.7
VA disability		18.9
Interest paid on DoD war appropriations		185.4
Additions to DoD base spending		362.2-652.4
Additions to Homeland Security base spending		401.2
Social costs to veterans and military families to date		295-400
Subtotal:	**1283.2**	**2662.1-3057.3**
FY2012-future		
FY2012 DoD request		118.4
FY2012 DoS/USAid request		12.1
Projected 2013–2015 war spending		168.6
Projected 2016–2020 war spending		155
Projected obligations for veterans' care to 2051		589-934
Additional interest payments to 2020		1000
Subtotal:	**454.1**	**2043.1-2388.1**
Total:	**1737.3**	**4705.2-5445.4**

Criticism

Criticism of the War on Terror addresses the issues, morality, efficiency, economics, and other questions surrounding the War on Terror and made against the phrase itself, calling it a misnomer. The notion of a "war" against "terrorism" has proven highly contentious, with critics charging that it has been exploited by participating governments to pursue long-standing policy / military objectives, reduce civil liberties, and infringe upon human rights. It is argued that the term war is not appropriate in this context (as in War on Drugs), since there is no identifiable enemy, and that it is unlikely international terrorism can be brought to an end by military means.

Other critics, such as Francis Fukuyama, note that "terrorism" is not an enemy, but a tactic; calling it a "war on terror", obscures differences between conflicts such as anti-occupation insurgents and international mujahideen. With a military presence in Iraq andAfghanistan and its associated collateral damage Shirley Williams maintains this increases resentment and terrorist threats against the West. There is also perceived U.S. hypocrisy, media induced hysteria, and that differences in foreign and security policy have damaged America's image in most of the world.

WAR ON TERROR TRANSFORMING CONTEMPORARY POLITICS

The War on Terror has changed the world of international politics greatly. Old traditions and customs such as the respect for state sovereignty and the formal equality of states have been shaken. Humanitarian intervention and concerns for human security have been forced into the background, and the human rights and liberty of citizens of all nations are being threatened by the War on Terror.

This essay will evaluate the extent to which the War on Terror, started by the US in the aftermath of the terrorist attacks of September 11th 2001, is changing contemporary politics, and how. It will briefly look at the situation before the War on Terror began, and will then examine the ways in which the War on Terror has influenced the freedoms of citizens and how liberty has been affected by the desire for security and protection. The changes to the international community that have occurred and the damage that has been done to the stability of the system will be examined. The changes in priorities and objectives on an international level will be analysed with the change from intervention for humanitarianism to intervention for security. The essay will then move on to the probable future consequences of the war and will then take a look at how the War on Terror may continue to shape politics.

At the end of the Cold War, the United States of America was left as the single most powerful nation in the world. The victory of capitalism over communism had resulted in a dramatic shift from realism as the dominant theory in international relations, to liberalism. Realism had failed to anticipate the end of the Cold War, and had instead predicted a continual balance of power between the USSR and the USA.

Liberal academics such as Francis Fukuyama heralded an 'end of history', a new world in which liberal democracy, having been proved to be the most effective system of government, will spread across the globe and will result in a peaceful, united world. Liberals believe that democracy has a unique trait in that it is an inherently peaceful system, as there is yet to be a war between liberal democratic nations. They argue that this is because liberal democracies form links between each other, initially through trade alliances and economic interdependence. They predicted that states themselves will become more interdependent and unified because democracies are ruled by the individual citizens within them, who are much more likely to want to benefit from trading with another nation rather than declaring war against them. And in the post-Cold War world, this seemed to be occurring.

Liberals in the post-Cold War period pointed to international organisations such as the European Union, the North Atlantic Treaty Organisation, the World Trade Organisation, Interpol, and of course the United Nations, as well as many other organisations, as symbols of the ability of states to cooperate and work together for mutual gain. They envisaged an international system of collaboration and union.

Ever since the 1600s the international community has adhered to the principles of Westphalian Sovereignty. In this view sovereignty is the right of all governments to rule their nations as they see fit, free of external challenge (although they were never granted the right to abuse their citizens). The Westphalian tradition saw that international order and stability were of great importance, but to achieve this states had to respect one another's right to govern. In the 20th century however, Westphalian sovereignty began to be challenged by the growing concern that states are not always able or willing to protect their citizens' human rights. Indeed, in the 20th century alone 262 million people were killed by their own governments: six times more than the number of people killed in battle with foreign governments.

After the Cold War, Humanitarianism became a very powerful force, which resulted in numerous interventions. The humanitarian failures in Rwanda and the NATO bombing of Yugoslavia prompted international organisations and politicians to re-evaluate the meaning of sovereignty and the responsibility for states to intervene in the governing of other nations when human rights and human security is threatened. The humanitarian movement of the 1990s started to crack the norms of non-intervention and traditional views of sovereignty, which the terrorist attacks of 9/11 and the subsequent War on Terror have shattered.

The events on September 11th 2001 had a great impact on nations all over the globe. It shook the core assumptions that had shaped international politics, and demonstrated that in the modern world threats to security are present on all levels, not only from states, but from individuals from anywhere in the world. 9/11 made it obvious how interconnected the world had become, and how no nation can cut itself off from the rest of the world. It showed how space and territory were no longer boundaries which protected states, as dangers can come from anywhere. It can also be seen that 9/11 showed that the military strength, size of a nation's high tech arsenal, and geostrategic power provides little protection from the new globalised terrorists, who were able to cause such chaos using only parcel knives to seize control of an aeroplane.

In America the terrorist attacks sparked a great amount of shock, fear, sadness, and also hatred. In the eyes of the West, the world had become divided into good and evil, and a vast series of new threats and dangers came into focus. Although terrorism was nothing new at the time, there had never been a terrorist attack which had received such media attention. The US reacted to the attacks with the declaration of a 'war on terror' to eliminate the terrorist networks which had grown around the world. It was widely recognised that terrorist networks tended to thrive in failed, rogue or unstable states, and so these states became the focus of intervention.

The interventions in Afghanistan in 2001 and Iraq in 2003 were not humanitarian however. Certainly, the US did intend to remove two ruthless regimes that had butchered and oppressed their people. The invasion of Afghanistan was also argued by Donald Rumsfeld as being in line with previous interventions in Kosovo, Bosnia, Somalia, Northern Iraq and Kuwait 'for the purpose of denying hostile regimes the opportunity to oppress their own people and other people.'

The key difference between the invasions in the War on Terror and previous humanitarian interventions are, as Paul Heinbecker the Canadian Ambassador to the UN described, the interventions in Kosovo and East Timor were based on concern for the vulnerable 'other, whereas Afghanistan and Iraq were fought for the protection of the 'self'. Indeed, before the invasion of Iraq the crisis was described with little focus on the suffering of civilians within Iraq, but on the threat that the nation posed to other nations. It was only after support for the war diminished and the weakness of the links between Al Qaida and Saddam Hussein was exposed that humanitarian arguments were used for justification. However, it can be argued that the threat of terrorism is actually rather minor when compared to other threats to human security around the world. Poverty and underdevelopment and the problems they cause, as well as natural disasters, wars, crime, and even car accidents are arguably greater threats to survival. Indeed, the terrorist attacks of 9/11 killed nearly three thousand people in one day, whereas at least as many children die every day of avoidable intestinal diseases such as dysentery and diarrhoea caused mainly by impure water, and in late 2006 there were a similar number of people dying every month in the insurgency and sectarian violence in Iraq. Interventions are now no longer about saving the lives of citizens of other nations, and are now all about security.

The War on Terror has caused severe damage to the concept of state sovereignty and has set a very dangerous precedent for arguments of legitimate intervention. This damage to sovereignty could well lead to the lowering of legal, psychological, and political barriers to the use of force against other nations for all manner of purposes. This might have initiated a 'frame shattering, norm changing process' which will reduce them further. An example of this is in Russia's decision to invade Georgia, to which Vladimir Putin compared the US invasion of Iraq:

"They [the Americans] of course had to hang Saddam Hussein for destroying several Shia villages. But the current Georgian rulers who in one hour simply wiped 10 Ossetian villages from the face of the earth, the Georgian rulers which used tanks to run over children and the elderly, which threw civilians into cellars and burnt them – they [Georgian leaders] are players that have to be protected."

The perceived threat of terrorism has provided impetus for pre-emptive intervention against states that show the symptoms of one which may become a breeding ground for terrorists; this has meant that the target of the War on Terror is not limited to terrorist networks, but states which are perceived as having the conditions which may spread terrorism, and it has enabled the US to invade before the target state has, or imminently will, attack. This presents a very serious challenge to the principles of sovereignty, as it gives states the justification to change, interfere and intervene in how a state is governed. This has the potential of eroding the normative framework of the use of force enshrined in the UN Charter and shakes international law and the core principles of the UN, both in its defiance of the traditional views towards sovereignty and the challenging of the boundaries of the legitimate use of force. Speaking in 1956 US Secretary of State John Foster argued that 'The violent armed attack by three members of the United nations upon a fourth cannot be treated as anything but a grave error inconsistent with the principles and purposes of the Charter' however this is a growing occurrence in the War on Terror.

The War on Terror has also treated states unequally, which is undermining the formal equality of states protected in the UN Charter. The Bush doctrine has granted some states (such as France, Israel and India the right to provide for their defence as they see fit, but not others (such as Iran etc). The war has also strained relationships between the US and the other members of the coalition that invaded Iraq, and many other members of the UN including allies such as France and Germany. This strain, combined with the damages to the principles of the United Nations could cause a fracturing of the international community.

The effects of the War on Terror are not limited to the realm of states however. The internal politics of the states fighting the war have also changed. Before 9/11 the surveillance and biometric industry was steadily growing, but growth was restricted by concerns for liberty and privacy. However, since the start of the War on Terror, security and surveillance technology has seen a massive surge in usage. Zureik showed that within weeks of the attack on the World Trade Centre, the US Congress introduced seventeen new bills with measures to increase border security and impose stricter regulations on migration and travel. Many countries have seen similar increases in surveillance of their own citizens, particularly the UK, which may now have more CCTV cameras per capita than anywhere else, and over 4.8 million cameras in operation.

The War on Terror has encouraged states to police their borders far more cautiously with a myriad of security checks needed in travelling between nations and far stricter regulations on who is allowed to travel. The movements of people anywhere is now very closely watched, and the government now has the power to locate and track the behaviour of virtually anyone through the use of technologies such as CCTV, border control, GPS, bank transactions, and even mobile phones can be used by the state to locate and trace members of the public. On top of this, the content of phone calls and e-mails can be monitored and used by intelligence agencies. The War on Terror has sparked numerous policies to be undertaken and legislations enforced which would have never previously been even considered due to the threat that they pose to human rights. One example is the US PATRIOT Act, which enables security services to search a suspect's home or place of work, record conversations, and monitor phone lines, e-mails and financial records without the knowledge or permission of the individual concerned or a court order. Another is the torture and rendition of people in Guantanamo Prison and other such places as well as the imprisonment of well over 100,000 people without trial. There have been similar actions taken in the UK also, such as new legislation giving security forces much greater powers to detain and interrogate terrorism suspects. There have even been allegations made recently that the UK has had knowledge of, and assisted the torture of British citizens and terrorism suspects in overseas prisons.

This authoritarian approach to security is a worrying trend which has compromised liberty and human rights around the world, especially those of foreign nationals and refugees, who are now not only discriminated against and blamed for scrounging welfare and stealing jobs, but are also accused of playing a role in the globalised terrorist network. The War on Terror has lead to migrants being subjected to racism and distrust, as well as deprivation of their human rights. They can now be detained on charges which they cannot defend against as they are not always told what they are accused of having done. These changes show a broad shift of Western societies to becoming 'control states', nations in which individuals are tightly regulated and controlled by the state and other institutions in all areas of life. The movement and behaviour of citizens has become restricted and people are constantly surveilled.

It can be argued that the War on Terror may not actually have a weakening effect on the state as an entity despite the damage that it has done to sovereignty in many cases. Indeed, the War on Terror may have actually made the state stronger. The concept of pharmacotic war is the idea that war can have a 'healing' effect on a nation that can remove internal disorder, restore authority and legitimacy of government, and create union and consensus among a nation's people. Larry George argues that this is the case in the War on Terror. But pharmacotic war is far from a good thing, it requires the identification of an enemy, usually a scapegoat on whom the troubles of the state can be pinned. This practice was used in Nazi Germany, the Soviet Union, apartheid Africa, the 1970s military dictatorships of Chile and Argentina, and now in the nations fighting the War on Terror.

The War on Terror mirrors the model of previous pharmacotic wars, with a political crisis facing the community in which a violent, 'symbolically resonant violation' occurs. Examples of this are the Boston massacre, Fort Sumter, Lusitania, Pearl Harbour, and Tonkin Gulf scenarios in which innocent lives are lost and others are endangered. This leads to the identification and demonization of an external enemy leading to a punitive military response against the perceived threat. The effect of this on contemporary politics is the depoliticisation of issues and actions which are viewed as being necessary for the safety and survival of the state. The War on Terror has granted the Bush Administration the support of the US citizens and much of the international community to police the oil fields and pipelines in Central Asia, provide security for a pipeline from the Caspian Sea to the Arabian Sea, to become militarily involved in the civil war in Georgia and Uzbekistan, to support Moscow's repression of the Chechen rebellion and Israel's actions in the West Bank, to support the Philippine government's conflict with Islamist rebels, to support the undemocratic Saudi royal family, it has transformed the counternarcotics programme in Colombia into an element of the War on Terror, to adopt an aggressive foreign policy towards North Korea and Iran, and, of course, the invasions of Afghanistan and Iraq.

The War on Terror has clearly had a considerable effect on international and domestic politics. Whether or not the changes thus far experienced will gather momentum and lead to the complete breakdown of international community and law and order, however, remains to be seen. Although the US has succeeded in going against the will of the UN (and breaching international law) it is questionable whether it will be able to continue to do so for much longer. With the US' status as the global hegemon in the international system being gradually lost due to its failures in dealing with terrorism, it may have to become more careful with its power and try to appease the rest of the United Nations. Indeed, the Obama administration is much less eager to follow the precedence set by the Bush doctrine, and even the use of the term 'war on terror' is falling into disuse.

However, the precedence that the War on Terror has set for the rest of the world may continue to change international politics. The excuse of counter-terrorism in establishing authoritarian policies and in intervening other nations is a popular, and evidently effective one, and the damage to state sovereignty, international law and may see breakdown of the United Nations and the international community. So the War on Terror may have begun to wind to a close, but the effects of it may continue to change the world dramatically.

ISLAMIC STATE OF IRAQ AND THE LEVANT

The Islamic State of Iraq and the Levant, also translated as the Islamic State of Iraq and Syria, also known by the Arabic acronym Da^ish and self-proclaimed as the Islamic State(IS), is a Sunni, extremist, jihadist rebel group controlling territory in Iraq and Syria. It has been designated as a terrorist organization by the United Nations, the European Union, the United Kingdom, the United States, Australia, Canada, Turkey, Saudi Arabia, Indonesia, the UAE and Israel.

The group originated as *Jama'at al-Tawhid wal-Jihad* in 1999, becoming *Tanzim Qaidat al-Jihad fi Bilad al-Rafidayn*, commonly known as Al-Qaeda in Iraq (AQI) in 2004. Following the 2003 invasion of Iraq, AQI took part in the Iraqi insurgency against coalition forces and Iraqi security forces. In 2006, AQI joined other Sunni insurgent groups to form the Mujahideen Shura Council, which consolidated further into the Islamic State of Iraq (ISI) shortly afterwards. ISI gained a significant presence in Al Anbar, Nineveh,Kirkuk and other areas, but around 2008, its violent methods, including suicide attacks on civilian targets and the widespread killing of prisoners, led to a backlash from Sunni Iraqis and other insurgent groups and to temporary decline.

In April 2013, the group changed its name to the Islamic State of Iraq and the Levant. It grew significantly under the leadership ofAbu Bakr al-Baghdadi, who was subsequently criticized by al-Zawahri, but by November 2014, ISIL controlled a third of Iraq and Syria. After entering the Syrian Civil War, it established a large presence in the Syrian governorates of Ar-Raqqah, Idlib, Deir ez-Zor and Aleppo. ISIL had close links to al-Qaeda until February 2014 when, after an eight-month power struggle, al-Qaeda cut all ties with the group, citing its failure to consult and "notorious intransigence".

The group's original aim was to establish an Islamic state in Sunni-majority regions of Iraq. Following its involvement in the Syrian Civil War, this expanded to include controlling Sunni-majority areas of Syria. It then proclaimed a worldwide caliphate on 29 June 2014, Abu Bakr al-Baghdadi—known by his supporters as Amir al-Mu'minin, Caliph Ibrahim—was named its caliph, and the group was renamed the Islamic State. As caliphate it claims religious authority over all Muslims worldwide, and aims to bring most traditionally Muslim-inhabited regions of the world under its legislative control, beginning with the Levant region, which approximately covers Syria, Jordan, Israel, Palestine, Lebanon, Cyprus, and part of southern Turkey. Groups in Sinai and eastern Libya have declared allegiance to ISIL.

The United Nations and Amnesty International have accused the group of grave human rights abuses, and Amnesty International has found it guilty of ethnic cleansing on a "historic scale". The group's actions, authority and theological interpretations have beenwidely criticized around the world and notably within the Muslim community.

ISIS is widely known for uploading videos of beheadings onto the internet.

HISTORY

Names

The group has had various names since it was established.

1. The group was founded in 1999 by Abu Musab al-Zarqawi under the name "The Organization of Monotheism and Jihad" (JTJ).

2. In October 2004, al-Zarqawi swore loyalty to Osama bin Laden and changed the group's name to "The Organization of Jihad's Base in Mesopotamia", commonly known as Al-Qaeda in Iraq. (AQI). Although the group has never called itself Al-Qaeda in Iraq, this has been its informal name over the years.
3. In January 2006, AQI merged with several other Iraqi insurgent groups to form the Mujahideen Shura Council. Al-Zarqawi was killed in June 2006.
4. On 12 October 2006, the Mujahideen Shura Council merged with several more insurgent factions, and on 13 October the establishment of the Islamic State of Iraq (ISI) was announced. Abu Abdullah al-Rashid al-Baghdadi and the Egyptian Abu Ayyub al-Masri became the leaders of the group. When they were killed in a US–Iraqi operation in April 2010, they were succeeded by Abu Bakr al-Baghdadi, the current leader of ISIL.
5. On 8 April 2013, having expanded into Syria, the group adopted the name Islamic State of Iraq and the Levant, also known as Islamic State of Iraq and al-Sham. These names are translations of the Arabic name being a description of the Levant or Greater Syria— sometimes shortened to ("the Islamic State"). The translated names are commonly abbreviated as ISIL or ISIS.
6. The name Danish is often used by ISIL's Arabic speaking detractors. It is based on the Arabic letters dâl, alif, ˆayn, and shîn, which form the acronym. There are many different spellings of this acronym which is similar to the word "crush". ISIL considers the name Daˆish derogatory and reportedly uses flogging as a punishment for those who use it in ISIL-controlled areas.
7. On 14 May 2014, the United States Department of State announced its decision to use "Islamic State of Iraq and the Levant" (ISIL) as the group's primary name.Which of these acronyms should be used to designate the group, ISIL or ISIS, has been debated, but concluded: "In the larger battlefield ofcopy style controversies, the distinction between ISIS or ISIL is not so great."
8. On 29 June 2014, the group renamed itself the Islamic State (IS) and declared its government a caliphate.

Foundation of the Group (1999–2006)

Following the 2003 US-led invasion of Iraq, the Jordanian Salafi Jihadist Abu Musab al-Zarqawi and his militant group Jama'at al-Tawhid wal-Jihad, founded in 1999, achieved notoriety in the early stages of the Iraq insurgency, by not only carrying out attacks on coalition forces but conducting suicide attacks on civilian targets and beheading hostages.

Al-Zarqawi's group grew in strength and attracted more fighters, and in October 2004 it officially pledged allegiance to Osama bin Laden's al-Qaeda network, changing its name to Tanzim Qaidat al-Jihad fi Bilad al-Rafidayn, also known as Al-Qaeda in Iraq (AQI). Attacks by the group on civilians, the Iraqi Government and security forces continued to increase over the next two years—see list of major resistance attacks in Iraq. In a letter to al-Zarqawi in July 2005, al-Qaeda's deputy leader Ayman al-Zawahiri outlined a four-stage plan to expand the Iraq War, which included expelling US forces from Iraq, establishing an Islamic authority, as caliphate, spreading the conflict to Iraq's secular neighbors, and engaging in theArab–Israeli conflict.

In January 2006, AQI merged with several smaller Iraqi insurgent groups under an umbrella organization called the Mujahideen Shura Council (MSC). This was claimed by Brian Fishman in the Annals of the American Academy of Political and Social Science to be little more than a media exercise and an attempt to give the group a more Iraqi flavour and perhaps to distance al-Qaeda from some of al-Zarqawi's tactical errors, notably the 2005 bombings by AQI of three hotels in Amman. On 7 June, al-Zarqawi was killed in a US airstrike and was succeeded as leader of the group by the Egyptian militant Abu Ayyub al-Masri.

On 12 October 2006, the Mujahideen Shura Council joined four more insurgent factions and the representatives of a number of Iraqi Arab tribes, and together they swore the traditional Arab oath of allegiance known as *$-ilf al-Mum-ayyabîn* ("Oath of the Scented Ones"). During the ceremony, the participants swore to free Iraq's Sunnis from what they described as Shia and foreign oppression, and to further the name of Allah and restore Islam to glory.

On 13 October 2006, the Mujahideen Shura Council declared the establishment of the Islamic State of Iraq (ISI), comprising Iraq's six mostly Sunni Arab governorates, with Abu Omar al-Baghdadi being announced as its Emir. Al-Masri was given the title of Minister of War within the ISI's ten-member cabinet. The declaration of statehood was met with hostile criticism, not only from ISI's jihadist rivals in Iraq, but from leading jihadist ideologues outside the country.

As Islamic State of Iraq (2006–2013)

According to a study compiled by US intelligence agencies in early 2007, the ISI—also known as AQI—planned to seize power in the central and western areas of the country and turn it into a Sunni Islamic state. The group built in strength and at its height enjoyed a significant presence in the Iraqi governorates of Al Anbar, Nineveh, Kirkuk, most of Salah ad Din, parts of Babil, Diyala and Baghdad, and claimed Baqubah as a capital city.

However, by late 2007, violent and indiscriminate attacks directed by rogue AQI elements against Iraqi civilians had severely damaged the group's image and caused a loss of support among the population, thus isolating it. In a major blow to AQI, many former Sunni militants who had previously fought alongside the group started to work with the US armed forces. The US troops surge supplied the military with more manpower for operations targeting the group, resulting in dozens of high-level AQI members being captured or killed.

Al-Qaeda seemed to have lost its foothold in Iraq and appeared to be severely crippled. During 2008, a series of US and Iraqi offensives managed to drive out the AQI-aligned insurgents from their former safe havens, such as the Diyala and Al Anbar governorates and the embattled capital of Baghdad, to the area of the northern city of Mosul, the latest of the Iraq War's major battlegrounds. By 2008, the ISI was describing itself as being in a state of "extraordinary crisis". Its violent attempts to govern its territory led to a backlash from Sunni Iraqis and other insurgent groups and a temporary decline in the group, which was attributable to a number of factors, notably the Anbar Awakening.

In late 2009, the commander of the US forces in Iraq, General Ray Odierno, stated that the ISI "has transformed significantly in the last two years. What once was dominated by foreign individuals has now become more and more dominated by Iraqi citizens". On 18 April 2010, the ISI's two top leaders, Abu Ayyub al-Masri and Abu Omar al-Baghdadi, were killed in a joint US-Iraqi raid near Tikrit. In a press conference in June 2010, General Odierno reported that 80 per cent of the ISI's top 42 leaders, including recruiters and financiers, had been killed or captured, with only eight remaining at large. He said that they had been cut off from al-Qaeda's leadership in Pakistan, and that improved intelligence had enabled the successful mission in April that led to the killing of al-Masri and al-Baghdadi; in addition, the number of attacks and casualty figures in Iraq for the first five months of 2010 were the lowest since 2003.

On 16 May 2010, Abu Bakr al-Baghdadi was appointed the new leader of the Islamic State of Iraq. Al-Baghdadi replenished the group's leadership, many of whom had been killed or captured, by appointing former Ba'athist military and intelligence officers who had served during the Saddam Hussein regime. These men, nearly all of whom had spent time imprisoned by the US military, came to make up about one-third of Baghdadi's top 25 commanders. One of them was a former Colonel, Samir al-Khlifawi, also known as Haji Bakr, who became the overall military commander in charge of overseeing the group's operations.

In July 2012, al-Baghdadi released an audio statement online announcing that the group was returning to the former strongholds from which US troops and their Sunni allies had driven them prior to the withdrawal of US troops. He also declared the start of a new offensive in Iraq called *Breaking the Walls*, which was aimed at freeing members of the group held in Iraqi prisons. Violence in Iraq began to escalate that month, and by July 2013 monthly fatalities had exceeded 1,000 for the first time since April 2008. The*Breaking the Walls* campaign culminated in July 2013, with the group carrying out simultaneous raids on Taji and Abu Ghraib prison, freeing more than 500 prisoners, many of them veterans of the Iraqi insurgency.

AS ISLAMIC STATE OF IRAQ AND THE LEVANT (2013–2014)

Declaration and Dispute with al-Nusra Front

In March 2011, protests began in Syria against the government of Bashar al-Assad. In the following months, violence between demonstrators and security forces led to a gradual militarisation of the conflict. In August 2011, Abu Bakr al-Baghdadi began sending Syrian and Iraqi ISI members experienced in guerilla warfare across the border into Syria in order to establish an organization inside the country. Led by a Syrian known as Abu Muhammad al-Jawlani, this group began to recruit fighters and establish cells throughout the country. On 23 January 2012, the group announced its formation as *Jabhat al-Nusra li Ahl as-Sham*—Jabhat al-Nusra—more commonly known as the al-Nusra Front. al-Nusra grew rapidly into a capable fighting force, with popular support among Syrians opposed to the Assad regime.

On 8 April 2013, al-Baghdadi released an audio statement in which he announced that al-Nusra Front had been established, financed and supported by the Islamic State of Iraq and that the two groups were merging under the name "Islamic State of Iraq and Al-Sham". Al-Jawlani issued a statement denying the merger and complaining that neither he nor anyone else in al-Nusra's leadership had been consulted about it. In June 2013, Al Jazeera reported that it had obtained a letter written by al-Qaeda's leader Ayman al-Zawahiri, addressed to both leaders, in which he ruled against the merger, and appointed an emissary to oversee relations between them to put an end to tensions. In the same month, al-Baghdadi released an audio message rejecting al-Zawahiri's ruling and declaring that the merger was going ahead. In October 2013, al-Zawahiri ordered the disbanding of ISIL, putting al-Nusra Front in charge of jihadist efforts in Syria, but al-Baghdadi contested al-Zawahiri's ruling on the basis of Islamic jurisprudence, and his group continued to operate in Syria. In February 2014, after an eight-month power struggle, al-Qaeda disavowed any relations with ISIL.

According to journalist Sarah Birke, there are "significant differences" between al-Nusra Front and ISIL. While al-Nusra actively calls for the overthrow of the Assad government, ISIL "tends to be more focused on establishing its own rule on conquered territory". ISIL is "far more ruthless" in building an Islamic state, "carrying out sectarian attacks and imposing sharia law immediately". While al-Nusra has a "large contingent of foreign fighters", it is seen as a home-grown group by many Syrians; by contrast, ISIL fighters have been described as "foreign 'occupiers'" by many Syrian refugees. It has a strong presence in central and northern Syria, where it has instituted sharia in a number of towns. The group reportedly controlled the four border towns of Atmeh, al-

Bab, Azaz and Jarablus, allowing it to control the entrance and exit from Syria into Turkey.Foreign fighters in Syria include Russian-speaking jihadists who were part of Jaish al-Muhajireen wal-Ansar (JMA). In November 2013, the JMA's Chechen leader Abu Omar al-Shishani swore an oath of allegiance to al-Baghdadi; the group then split between those who followed al-Shishani in joining ISIL and those who continued to operate independently in the JMA under new leadership.

In May 2014, Ayman al-Zawahiri ordered al-Nusra Front to stop attacks on its rival ISIL. In June 2014, after continued fighting between the two groups, al-Nusra's branch in the Syrian town of Al-Bukamal pledged allegiance to ISIL.

In mid-June 2014, ISIL captured the Trabil crossing on the Jordan–Iraq border, the only border crossing between the two countries. ISIL has received some public support in Jordan, albeit limited, partly owing to state repression there, but has undertaken a recruitment drive in Saudi Arabia, where tribes in the north are linked to those in western Iraq and eastern Syria.

Conflicts With Other Groups

In January 2014, rebels affiliated with the Islamic Front and the US-trained Free Syrian Army launched an offensive against ISIL militants in and around the city of Aleppo in Syria.

AS ISLAMIC STATE (2014–PRESENT)

On 29 June 2014, ISIL removed "Iraq and the Levant" from its name and began to refer to itself as the "Islamic State", proclaiming itself caliphate and naming Abu Bakr al-Baghdadi as caliph. The declaration as caliphate has been criticized and ridiculed by Muslim scholars and rival Islamists inside and outside the occupied territory.

Analysts described dropping the reference to region in its new name as widening the group's scope, and terrorism analyst Laith Alkhouri believed that after capturing many areas in Syria and Iraq the Islamic State had felt this was a suitable opportunity to take control of the global jihadist movement.

In June and July 2014, Jordan and Saudi Arabia moved troops to their borders with Iraq, after Iraq lost control of, or withdrew from, strategic crossing points that had then come under the control of the Islamic State. There was speculation that Iraqi Prime Minister Nouri al-Maliki had ordered a withdrawal of troops from the Iraq–Saudi crossings in order "to increase pressure on Saudi Arabia and bring the threat of Isis over-running its borders as well".

In July 2014, Boko Haram leader Abubakar Shekau declared support for the new caliphate and Caliph Ibrahim. In August, Shekau announced that Boko Haram had captured the Nigerian town of Gwoza. Shekau announced: "Thanks be to God who gave victory to our brethren in Gwoza and made it a state among the Islamic states". Boko Haram launched an offensive in Adamawa and Borno States in northeastern Nigeria in September, following the example of the Islamic State.

In July 2014, the Islamic State recruited more than 6,300 fighters, according to the Syrian Observatory for Human Rights, some of whom were thought to have previously fought for the Free Syrian Army.

On 3 August 2014, the Islamic State captured the towns of Zumar, Sinjar and Wana in northern Iraq.

The need for food and water of thousands of Yazidis, having fled up a mountain out of fear for approaching hostile ISIL militants, and the threat of genocide to Yazidis and others as announced by ISIL, together with protecting Americans in Iraq and supporting Iraq in its fight against the Islamic State, were reasons for the US to launch a humanitarian mission on 7 August 2014 to aid those Yazidis on that mountain and to start an aerial bombing campaign in Iraq on 8 August against the Islamic State—one step in a new escalation of mutually hostile rhetoric and actions between these two war opponents of 2003. Nevertheless, the United Nations concluded in September and October that ISIL had killed thousands of Yazidis in that region in August.

On 11 October 2014, ISIL dispatched 10,000 militants from Syria and Mosul to capture the Iraqi capital city of Baghdad, and Iraqi Army forces and Anbar tribesmen threatened to abandon their weapons if the US did not send in ground troops to halt ISIL's advance. On 13 October, ISIL fighters advanced to within 25 kilometers (15.5 miles) of the Baghdad Airport.

At the end of October 2014, radical militants in control of the Libyan city of Derna pledged their allegiance to Abu Bakr al-Baghdadi, thus making Derna the first city outside Syria and Iraq a part of the so-called Islamic State caliphate.

On 2 November 2014, in response to the US-led airstrikes, representatives from Ahrar ash-Sham attended a significant meeting with the al-Nusra Front, the Khorasan Group, the Islamic State of Iraq and the Levant, and Jund al-Aqsa, which sought to unite several hard line groups against the US-led Coalition and other moderate Syrian Rebel groups. On 10 November 2014, the Egyptian terrorist group Ansar Bait al-Maqdis also pledged its allegiance to ISIL.

TIMELINE LATEST EVENTS

An excerpt of recent events in the timeline is shown below:

- 26 October: during the Siege of Kobani, ISIL failed for the fourth time to capture the border gate with Turkey in the northern al-Jomrok neighborhood. The Iraqi army retook four villages in the Himreen mountains. Two bombs killed five people and wounded 15 in Baghdad.
- 27 October: ISIL car bombings killed 27 Iraqi soldiers and Shia militamen and wounded 60 in Jurf al-Sakhar, and killed 15 civilians and wounded 23 in Baghdad. The U.S. Air Force launched 11 more air strikes in Iraq and Syria. The Lebanese Army took the last positions held by ISIL militants in Tripoli, after 11 Lebanese soldiers, eight civilians and 22 militants were killed in three days of battle; 162 militants were captured. ISIL released another video with British

hostageJohn Cantlie, in which he claimed that the city of Kobani was mostly under ISIL control, with only a few pockets of Kurdish resistance remaining. He also claimed that the Battle of Kobani was "largely over", and that ISIL forces were mostly mopping up in the city. The captions in the video, displaying the Turkish flags at the border, claimed that it was filmed by one of the four ISIL drones. However, the video has been deemed to be ISIL propaganda, especially since analysts claim that it was filmed about a week earlier. Additionally, 200 Iraqi Kurdish forces will soon arrive in Kobani as reinforcements, via the Syrian-Turkish border.

- 29 October: Australian ISIL leader and recruiter Mohammad Ali Baryalei was confirmed to have been killed. Fifty Free Syrian Army and 150 Kurdish Peshmerga reinforcements reached Kobani. The US launched 14 air strikes in Iraq and Syria between 28 and 29 October. Two-hundred and twenty members of the Albu Nimr tribe were executed by ISIL, 70 in Hit and 150 in Ramadi. ISIL forces captured three gas wells east of Palmyra in Homs province, and killed 30 Syrian Army soldiers in an attack on the Shaer gas field. A suicide bomber killed five policemen and wounded 18 civilians in Youssifiyah near Baghdad. ISIL released the last 25 of a group of 150 Kurdish children previously kidnapped from Kobani. The Iraqi Army retook six villages near Baiji.
- 30 October: ISIL captured the Shaer gas field near Homs, Syria. Norway announced that it would send 120 soldiers to Iraq to help train the Iraqi Army to fight ISIL.
- 31 October: The UN stated that overall 15,000 foreign fighters had joined ISIL in Iraq and Syria. While battle raged in Baiji between ISIL and the Iraqi Army and Shia militia, bombings killed 15 people and wounded 34 in and near Baghdad. Abu Bakr al-Baghdadi was proclaimed caliph of the "Islamic Caliphate of Derna" established by jihadists in Derna, Libya.
- The UN reported that at least 1,273 Iraqis—856 civilians and 417 members of the security forces—were killed "by violence" during October (379 civilians in Baghdad alone) and that 2,010 were wounded, not counting the casualties in Anbar province and other ISIL-held areas.

November 2014

- 1 November: ISIL executed 50–67 more displaced members of the Albu Nimr tribe, in the village of Ras al-Maa. Thirty-five bodies of members of the same tribe were found in another mass grave. News spread that ISIL had started rounding up and killing former police and army officer in areas under its control—especially Mosul—in order to prevent possible uprisings. Among those killed were Colonels Mohammed Hassan and Issa Osman. Suicide bombers and car bombings killed at least 24 people and wounded dozens in the Baghdad area. Ten US airstrikes were launched in Syria and Iraq.

- 2 November: ISIL killed 50–75 more members of the Albu Nimr tribe in Ras al-Maa and Haditha and 17 were kidnapped. Overall, 322 members of the Albu Nimr tribe had been killed by 2 November. Car bombings killed 44 Shia pilgrims and wounded 75 in Baghdad. Also, in response to the US-led airstrikes, representatives from Ahrar ash-Sham attended a significant meeting with the al-Nusra Front, the Khorasan Group, the Islamic State of Iraq and the Levant, and Jund al-Aqsa, which sought to unite several hard-line groups against the US-led Coalition and other moderate Syrian Rebel groups.
- 3 November: ISIL claimed to have captured the Jahar gas field in Homs province, Syria. After ransoms had been paid, 234 Yazidis kidnapped in August were released. Canadian planes launched their first airstrikes against ISIL near Fallujah. US planes launched 14 airstrikes between November 2 and 3. ISIL executed 36 more members of the Albu Nimr tribe in Ras al-Maa.
- 4 November: ISIL released 93 Syrian Kurds kidnapped by the group in February.
- 5 November: A leader of the Albu Nimr tribe stated that 540 members of the tribe had been killed by ISIL. US allies conducted 23 airstrikes in Syria, Iraq – military between 3 and 5 November in Iraq and Syria. The Syrian Army and militia recaptured the Jhar and Mahr gas fields near Homs from ISIL.
- 7 November: Car bombings in Baiji, which had been partly reconquered by the Iraqi Army, killed eight servicemen and policemen—among them Faisal Malek—and wounded 15. The US decided to send 1,500 more troops to Iraq.
- 8 November: A US airstrike killed 50 ISIL militants near Mosul; rumors spread that Abu Bakr al-Baghdadi may have been killed or seriously wounded in the attack.Twenty-seven ISIL fighters were poisoned by Syrian rebels who had infiltrated as cooks into the Fath El-Shahel camp; twelve were killed. Six car bombings killed 40 people and wounded 90 in Baghdad and Ramadi.
- 9 November: The Syrian Air Force bombed the ISIL-held town of Al-Bab in Aleppo province, killing 21 and wounding over 100.
- 10 November: Seventy more members of the Albu Nimr tribe were killed by ISIL near Hit. The main Egyptian terrorist group operating in Sinai Ansar Beit al-Maqdispledged allegiance to ISIL. RAF drones were launched in their first airstrikes against ISIL in Iraq.

- 11 November: A car bombing killed eight people and wounded 13 in Baiji, which had been largely recaptured by the Iraqi Army; more car bombings killed nine people and wounded 24 in and near Baghdad.
- 14 November: The Iraqi Army reconquered the city of Baiji from ISIL. Car bombings killed 17 people and wounded 57 in Baghdad.
- 16 November: ISIL released a video showing a beheaded American hostage Peter Kassig, and the beheading of 15 Syrian Army prisoners.
- 19 November: Kurdish fighters captured six buildings from Islamic State militants besieging the Syrian town of Kobanî on Tuesday, and seized a large haul of their weapons and ammunition, a group monitoring the war said. Also, ISIL control of the town was reduced to 20 per cent.

List of ISIL members

- Abu Bakr al-Baghdadi (Leader since 2010, various titles)
- Abu Muslim al-Turkmani (Deputy Leader in Iraq)
- Abu Ali al-Anbari (Deputy Leader in Syria)
- Abu Mohammad al-Adnani (official spokesperson)

more:

IDEOLOGY AND BELIEFS

ISIL is a Sunni extremist group. It follows an extreme interpretation of Islam, promotes religious violence, and regards those who do not agree with its interpretations as infidels or apostates.

ISIL's ideology originates in the branch of modern Islam that aims to return to the early days of Islam, rejecting later "innovations" in the religion which it believes corrupt its original spirit. It condemns later caliphates and the Ottoman Empire for deviating from what it calls pure Islam and hence has been attempting to establish its own caliphate.

ISIL's philosophy is well represented by the symbolism in the Black Standard variant, the legendary battle flag of Muhammad, it as adopted. The flag shows the seal of theMuhammad within a white circle, with the phrase above it, "There is no God but Allah." Such symbolism has been said to point to ISIL's belief that it represents no less than the restoration of the caliphate of early Islam, with all of the political, religious and eschatological ramifications that this would imply.

According to some observers, ISIL emerged from the ideology of the Muslim Brotherhood, the first post-Ottoman Islamist group dating back to the late 1920s in Egypt. It adheres to global jihadist principles and follows the hard-line ideology of al-Qaeda and many other modern-day jihadist groups. However, other sources trace the group's roots not to the Islamism of the Muslim Brotherhood and the more mainstream jihadism of al-Qaeda, but to Wahhabism. *The New York Times* wrote:

For their guiding principles, the leaders of the Islamic State, also known as ISIS or ISIL, are open and clear about their almost exclusive commitment to the Wahhabi movement of Sunni Islam. The group circulates images of Wahhabi religious textbooks from Saudi Arabia in the schools it controls. Videos from the group's territory have shown Wahhabi texts plastered on the sides of an official missionary van.

ISIL seeks to revive the original Wahhabi project of the restoration of the caliphate governed by strict Salafist doctrine, and following Wahhabi tradition, it condemns the followers of secular law as disbelievers, putting the current Saudi regime in that category.

ISIL's use of violence to purify the community of unbelievers comes from the Wahhabi tradition. Bernard Haykel has described Abu Bakr al-Baghdadi's creed as "a kind of untamed Wahhabism", saying, "For Al Qaeda, violence is a means to an ends; for ISIS, it is an end in itself".

The destruction by ISIL in July 2014 of the tomb and shrine of the prophet Yunus—Jonah in Christianity—the 13th century mosque of Imam Yahya Abu al-Qassimin, the 14th century shrine of prophet Jerjis—St George to Christians—and the attempted destruction of the Hadba minaret at the 12th century Great Mosque of Al-Nuri have been described as "an unchecked outburst of extreme Wahhabism".

According to *The New York Times*, "All of the most influential jihadist theorists are criticizing the Islamic State as deviant, calling its self-proclaimed caliphate null and void" and have denounced it for its beheading of journalists and aid workers. ISIL is widely denounced by a broad range of Islamic clerics including Al-Qaeda-oriented and Saudi clerics

Salafists such as ISIL believe that only a legitimate authority can undertake the leadership of jihad, and that the first priority over other areas of combat, such as fighting non-Muslim countries, is the purification of Islamic society. For example, when it comes to the Israeli–Palestinian conflict, since ISIL regards the Palestinian Sunni group Hamas as apostates who have no legitimate authority to lead jihad, it regards fighting Hamas as the first step towards confrontation with Israel.

Sunni critics, including Salafi and jihadist muftis such as Adnan al-Aroor and Abu Basir al-Tartusi, say that ISIL and related terrorist groups are not Sunnis, but modern-dayKhawarij—Muslims who have stepped outside the mainstream of Islam—serving an imperial anti-Islamic agenda. Other critics of ISIL's brand of Sunni Islam include Salafists who previously publicly supported jihadist groups such as al-Qaeda, for example the Saudi government official Saleh Al-Fawzan, known for his extremist views, who claims that ISIL is a creation of "Zionists, Crusaders and Safavids", and the Jordanian-Palestinian writer Abu Muhammad al-Maqdisi, the former spiritual mentor to Abu Musab al-Zarqawi, who was released from prison in Jordan in June 2014 and accuses ISIL of driving a wedge between Muslims.

Goals

Since 2004, the group's goal has been the foundation of an Islamic state in the Levant. Specifically, ISIL has sought to establish itself as a caliphate, an Islamic state led by a group of religious authorities under a supreme leader—caliph—who is believed to be the successor to Muhammad.

In June 2014, ISIL published a document in which it claimed to have traced the lineage of its leader Abu Bakr al-Baghdadi back to Muhammad. That same month, ISIL removed "Iraq and the Levant" from its name and began to refer to itself as the "Islamic State", declaring a worldwide caliphate and naming al-Baghdadi as its caliph. By declaring itself as caliphate, al-Baghdadi was demanding the allegiance of all devout Muslims according to Islamic jurisprudence—fiqh. Shaykh Abu Muhammad al-Adnani al-Shami, spokesperson for ISIL, described the establishment of the caliphate as "a dream that lives in the depths of every Muslim believer" and "the abandoned obligation of the era", while ISIL stated: "The legality of all emirates, groups, states and organizations becomes null by the expansion of the khilafah's [caliphate's] authority and arrival of its troops to their areas." ISIL thus rejects the political divisions (colonies) established by Western powers at the end of World War I in the Sykes–Picot Agreement as it absorbs territory in Syria and Iraq. ISIL's current goal is to consolidate the territorial gains it has made, to establish an Islamic state, and to expand its caliphate throughout the Levant region and beyond.

TERRITORIAL CLAIMS

ISIL divides the territory which it controls or aspires to control into provinces—*wilayah*.

Iraq

When the group announced the establishment of the Islamic State of Iraq in 2006, it claimed authority over seven Iraqi provinces:Baghdad, Al Anbar, Diyala, Kirkuk, Salah al-Din, Nineveh, and parts of Babil. It later created the province of Fallujah from territory which it already controlled.

Syria

In April 2014, the group claimed nine Syrian provinces, covering most of the country and lying largely along existing provincial boundaries: Al Barakah, Al Kheir, Ar-Raqqah, Al Badiya, Halab, Idlib, Hama, Damascus, and the Coast. A new province was created in August 2014 called al-Furat—"Euphrates"—which incorporates territory on both sides of the Syria–Iraq border.

Expansion in November 2014

On 13 November 2014, al-Baghdadi released an audio-recording in which he stated: "We announce to you the expansion of the Islamic State to new countries, to the countries of the Haramayn [Saudi Arabia], Yemen, Egypt, Libya [and] Algeria". In these countries he announced the creation of five new *wilayah* or provinces, each with a governor, while nullifying all local jihadist groups. These areas were singled out because the group had a strong base in them from which it could carry out attacks. However, according to analyst Aaron Zelin from the Washington Institute for Near East Policy, only the groups in Sinai and Libya exercise any territorial control and the pledges from Saudi Arabia, Libya and Yemen are anonymous and not from known terrorist groups.This nullification is a direct challenge to al-Qaeda-backed groups, as al-Baghdadi's declaration suggests that the official branches of al-Qaeda—such as AQAP in Saudi Arabia and Yemen and AQIM in Algeria and Libya—-are now illegitimate if they do not submit to his claimed authority.

Libya

The city of Derna has been a major source of fighters in the Syrian Civil War and Iraq Insurgency. During early 2014, a number of leading ISIL fighters arrived in Derna. In the next few months, they united many local militant factions under their leadership and declared war on anyone who opposed them, killing judges, civic leaders and other opponents, including local militants who rejected their authority. On 5 October 2014, the ISIL-linked militants, who then fully controlled the city, gathered to pledge allegiance to Abu Bakr al-Baghdadi. These events are seen by ISIL and its opponents as a model for ISIL expansion outside Iraq and Syria. ISIL calls this territory Barqa province, using a term denoting eastern Libya.

Egypt (Sinai)

The Egyptian militant group Ansar Bayt al-Maqdis swore allegiance to ISIL in November 2014. After al-Baghdadi's speech on 13 November, the group changed its name to *Sinai Province*, on the Twitter feed claiming to represent the group.

Saudi Arabia

Al-Bagdadi called for the overthrow of the Saudi Royal Family and criticized the Kingdom's participation in the US-led coalition against ISIL. ISIL calls the KSA provinceHaramayn or "The Two Sanctuaries".

GOVERNANCE

The group is headed and run by Abu Bakr al-Baghdadi, called caliph, with a cabinet of advisers. There are two deputy leaders, Abu Muslim al-Turkmani for Iraq and Abu Ali al-Anbari for Syria, and 12 local governors in Iraq and Syria. Beneath the leaders are councils on finance, leadership, military matters, legal matters—including decisions on executions—foreign fighters' assistance, security, intelligence and media. In addition, a Shura council has the task of ensuring that all decisions made by the governors and councils comply with the group's interpretation of sharia.

The Wall Street Journal estimated in September 2014 that 8 million Iraqis and Syrians live in areas controlled by ISIL. Ar-Raqqah in Syria is the *de facto* headquarters and is said to be a test case of ISIL governance. As of September 2014, governance in Ar-Raqqah has been under the total control of ISIL where it has rebuilt the structure of modern government in less than a year. Former government workers from the Assad regime maintain their jobs after pledging allegiance to ISIL. Institutions, restored and restructured, are providing services. The Ar-Raqqah dam continues to provide electricity and water. Foreign expertise supplements Syrian officials in running civilian institutions. Only the police and soldiers are ISIL fighters, who receive confiscated lodging previously owned by non-Sunnis and others who fled. Welfare services are provided, price controls established, and taxes imposed on the wealthy. ISIL runs a soft power programme in the areas under its control in Iraq and Syria, which includes social services, religious lectures and *da'wah*—proselytizing—to local populations. It also performs public services such as repairing roads and maintaining the electricity supply.

Exporting oil from oilfields captured by ISIL brings in tens of millions of dollars. One US Treasury official has estimated that ISIL earns US$1 million a day from the export of oil. Much of the oil is sold illegally in Turkey. Dubai-based energy analysts have put the combined oil revenue from ISIL's Iraqi-Syrian production as high as US$3 million per day. ISIL also extracts wealth through taxation and extortion.

British security expert Frank Gardner has concluded that ISIL's prospects of maintaining control and rule are greater in 2014 than they were in 2006. Despite being as brutal as before, ISIL has become "well entrenched" among the population and is not likely to be dislodged by ineffective Syrian or Iraqi forces. It has replaced corrupt governance with functioning locally controlled authorities, services have been restored and there are adequate supplies of water and oil. With Western-backed intervention being unlikely, the group will "continue to hold their ground" and rule an area "the size of Pennsylvania for the foreseeable future", he said. Further solidifying ISIL rule is the control of wheat production, which is roughly 40 per cent of Iraq's production. ISIL has maintained food production, crucial to governance and popular support.

Diktats, Influences and Pressures

In Mosul, ISIL has implemented a sharia school curriculum which bans the teaching of art, music, national history, literature and Christianity. Although Charles Darwin's theory of evolution has never been taught in Iraqi schools, the subject has been banned from the school curriculum. Patriotic songs have been declared blasphemous, and orders have been given to remove certain pictures from school textbooks. Iraqi parents have largely boycotted schools in which the new curriculum has been introduced. After capturing cities in Iraq, ISIL issued guidelines on how to wear clothes and veils. ISIL warned women in the city of Mosul to wear full-face veils or face severe punishment. A cleric told Reuters in Mosul that ISIL gunmen had ordered him to read out the warning in his mosque when worshippers gathered. ISIL ordered the faces of both male and female mannequins to be covered, in an order which also banned the use of naked mannequins. In Ar-Raqqah the group uses its two battalions of female fighters in the city to enforce compliance by women with its strict laws on individual conduct.

ISIL released 16 notes labeled "Contract of the City", a set of rules aimed at civilians in Nineveh. One rule stipulated that women should stay at home and not go outside unless necessary. Another rule said that stealing would be punished by amputation. In addition to banning the sale and use of alcohol—which is customary in Muslim culture—ISIL has banned the sale and use of cigarettes and hookah pipes. It has also banned "music and songs in cars, at parties, in shops and in public, as well as photographs of people in shop windows".

According to *The Economist*, dissidents in the ISIL capital of Ar-Raqqah report that "all 12 of the judges who now run its court system... are Saudis". Saudi practices also followed by the group include the establishment of religious police to root out "vice" and enforce attendance at salat prayers, the widespread use of capital punishment, and the destruction of or conversion to other uses of Christian churches and non-Sunni mosques. Christians living in areas under ISIL control who want to remain in the "caliphate" face three options: converting to Islam, paying a religious levy, jizya, or death. "We offer them three choices: Islam; the dhimma contract – involving payment of jizya; if they refuse this they will have nothing but the sword", ISIL said. ISIL had already set similar rules for Christians in Ar-Raqqah, once one of Syria's more liberal cities.

HUMAN RIGHTS ABUSES

In early September 2014, the United Nations Human Rights Council agreed to send a team to Iraq and Syria to investigate the abuses and killings being carried out by the ISIL on "an unimaginable scale". Prince Zeid bin Ra'ad, the newly appointed UN High Commissioner for Human Rights, urged world leaders to step in to protect women and children suffering at the hands of ISIL militants, who he said were trying to create a "house of blood". He appealed to the international community to concentrate its efforts on ending the conflict in Iraq and Syria.

There have been many reports of the group's use of death threats, torture and mutilation to compel conversion to Islam, the killing of clerics who refuse to pledge allegiance to the Islamic State, mass killing of prisoners of war and civilians, and sexual enslavement of Iraqi women and girls, predominantly from the minority Christian and Yazidi communities.

War Crimes Accusations and Findings

In July 2014, the BBC reported the United Nations' chief investigator as stating: "Fighters from the Islamic State in Iraq and the Levant (Isis) may be added to a list of war crimes suspects in Syria." By June 2014, according to United Nations reports, ISIL had killed hundreds of prisoners of war and killed over 1,000 civilians.

In August 2014, the UN accused ISIL of committing "mass atrocities" and war crimes, including the mass killing of up to 250 Syrian Army soldiers near Tabqa Air base. Other known killing of military prisoners took place in Camp Speicher (1,095–1,700 Iraqi soldiers shot and "thousands" more "missing") and the Shaer gas field(200 Syrian soldiers shot). In November 2014 the U.N. Commission of Enquiry on Syria said that ISIS was committing crimes against humanity.

Religious and Minority Group Persecution

ISIL compels people in the areas it controls, under the penalty of death, torture or mutilation, to declare Islamic creed, and live according to its interpretation of Sunni Islam andsharia law. It directs violence against Shia Muslims, indigenous Assyrian, Chaldean, Syriac and Armenian Christians, Yazidis, Druze, Shabaks and Mandeans in particular.

Amnesty International has found ISIL guilty of the ethnic cleansing of ethnic and religious minority groups in northern Iraq on a "historic scale". In a special report released on 2 September 2014, it describes how ISIL has "systematically targeted non-Arab and non-Sunni Muslim communities, killing or abducting hundreds, possibly thousands, and forcing more than 830,000 others to flee the areas it has captured since 10 June 2014". Among these people are Assyrian Christians, Turkmen Shia, Shabak Shia, Yazidis, Kaka'i andSabean Mandeans, who have lived together for centuries in Nineveh province, large parts of which are now under ISIL's control.

Among the known killings of religious and minority group civilians carried out by ISIL are those in the villages and towns of Quiniyeh (70–90 Yazidis killed), Hardan (60 Yazidis killed), Sinjar (200–500 Yazidis killed), Ramadi Jabal (60–70 Yazidis killed), Dhola (50 Yazidis killed), Khana Sor (100 Yazidis killed), Hardan (250–300 Yazidis killed), al-Shimal(dozens of Yazidis killed), Khocho (400 Yazidis killed and 1,000 abducted), Jadala (14 Yadizis killed) and Beshir (700 Shia Turkmen killed), and others committed nearMosul (670 Shia inmates of the Badush prison killed), and in Tal Afar prison, Iraq (200 Yazidis killed for refusing conversion). The UN estimated that 5,000 Yazidis were killed by ISIL during the takeover of parts of northern Iraq in August 2014.

In late May 2014, 150 Kurdish boys from Kobani aged 14–16 were abducted and subjected to torture and abuse, according to Human Rights Watch. In the Syrian towns of Ghraneij, Abu Haman and Kashkiyeh 700 members of the Sunni

Al Sheitaat tribe were killed for attempting an uprising against ISIL control. The UN reported that in June 2014 ISIL had killed a number of Sunni Islamic clerics who refused to pledge allegiance to it.

Treatment of civilians

During the Iraqi conflict in 2014, ISIL released dozens of videos showing its ill treatment of civilians, many of whom had apparently been targeted on the basis of their religion or ethnicity. Navi Pillay, UN High Commissioner for Human Rights, warned of war crimes being committed in the Iraqi war zone, and disclosed one UN report of ISIL militants murdering Iraqi Army soldiers and 17 civilians in a single street in Mosul. The United Nations reported that in the 17 days from 5 to 22 June, ISIL killed more than 1,000 Iraqi civilians and injured more than 1,000. After ISIL released photographs of its fighters shooting scores of young men, the United Nations declared that cold-blooded "executions" by militants in northern Iraq almost certainly amounted to war crimes.

ISIL's advance in Iraq in mid-2014 was accompanied by continuing violence in Syria. On 29 May, ISIL raided a village in Syria and at least 15 civilians were killed, including, according to Human Rights Watch, at least six children. A hospital in the area confirmed that it had received 15 bodies on the same day. The Syrian Observatory for Human Rights reported that on 1 June, a 102-year-old man was killed along with his whole family in a village in Hama province.

ISIL has recruited Iraqi children to its ranks, who can be seen with masks on their faces and guns in their hands patrolling the streets of Mosul.

Sexual violence and slavery allegations

According to one report, ISIL's capture of Iraqi cities in June 2014 was accompanied by an upsurge in crimes against women, including kidnap and rape. *The Guardian* reported that ISIL's extremist agenda extended to women's bodies and that women living under their control were being captured and raped. Fighters are told that they are free to have sex and rape non-Muslim captive women. Hannaa Edwar, a leading women's rights advocate in Baghdad who runs an NGO called Iraqi Al-Amal Association (IAA), said that none of her contacts in Mosul were able to confirm any cases of rape. However, another Baghdad-based women's rights activist, Basma al-Khateeb, said that a culture of violence existed in Iraq against women generally and felt sure that sexual violence against women was happening in Mosul involving not only ISIL but all armed groups.

During a meeting with Nouri al-Maliki, British Foreign Minister William Hague said with regard to ISIL: "Anyone glorifying, supporting or joining it should understand that they would be assisting a group responsible for kidnapping, torture, executions, rape and many other hideous crimes". According to Martin Williams in *The Citizen*, some hard-lineSalafists apparently regard extramarital sex with multiple partners as a legitimate form of holy war and it is "difficult to reconcile this with a religion where some adherents insist that women must be covered from head to toe, with only a narrow slit for the eyes".

Haleh Esfandiari from the Woodrow Wilson International Center for Scholars has highlighted the abuse of local women by ISIL militants after they have captured an area. "They usually take the older women to a makeshift slave market and try to sell them. The younger girls... are raped or married off to fighters", she said, adding, "It's based on temporary marriages, and once these fighters have had sex with these young girls, they just pass them on to other fighters." Speaking of Yazidi women captured by ISIS,Nazand Begikhani said "[t]hese women have been treated like cattle... They have been subjected to physical and sexual violence, including systematic rape and sex slavery. They've been exposed in markets in Mosul and in Raqqa, Syria, carrying price tags." Yazidi girls in Iraq allegedly raped by ISIL fighters have committed suicide by jumping to their death from Mount Sinjar, as described in a witness statement.

A United Nations report issued on 2 October 2014, based on 500 interviews with witnesses, said that ISIL took 450–500 women and girls to Iraq's Nineveh region in August where "150 unmarried girls and women, predominantly from the Yazidi and Christian communities, were reportedly transported to Syria, either to be given to ISIL fighters as a reward or to be sold as sex slaves". In mid-October, the UN confirmed that 5,000–7,000 Yazidi women and children had been abducted by ISIL and sold into slavery.In November 2014 *The New York Times* reported on the accounts given by five who escaped ISIL of their captivity and abuse. In its digital magazine *Dabiq*, ISIL explicitly claimed religious justification for enslaving Yazidi women.

Attacks on members of the press

The Committee to Protect Journalists says "Without a free press, few other human rights are attainable." ISIL has attacked local journalists creating what Reporters Without Borders calls "news blackholes" in areas controlled by ISIL. In December 2013 two suicide bombers stormed TV station Salaheddin headquarters killing five journalists, after accusing the station of "distorting the image of Iraq's Sunni community." Reporters Without Borders (RSF) and his family said that on September 7, 2014 ISIL seized and on October 11 publicly beheaded Raad al-Azzawi (or Azzaoui), 37, a TV Salaheddin cameraman from the village of Samra, east of Tikrit. Fighters have reportedly been given written direction to kill or capture journalists. According to the Journalistic Freedoms Observatory (JFO), as of October 2014 ISIL was holding nine journalists and has nine others under close observation in Mosul and Salahuddin province.

During 2013 and into 2014 an ISIL unit nicknamed the Beatles acquired and held 12 western journalists hostage along with aid workers and other foreign hostages for a total of 23 or 24 known hostages. A Polish journalist Marcin

Suder was captured in July 2013 but escaped four months later.They executed American journalists James Foley and Steven Sotloff and released beheading videos. Eight of the other journalists were released for ransoms: Danish journalist Daniel Rye Ottosen, French journalists Didier François, Edouard Elias, Nicolas Hénin, and Pierre Torres, and Spanish journalists Marc Marginedas, Javier Espinosa, and Ricardo García Vilanova. They continue to hold British journalist John Cantlie and a female aid worker hostage.

CRITICISM

The group has attracted widespread criticism internationally for its extremism, from governments and international bodies such as the United Nations and Amnesty International.

ISIL has been at the receiving end of severe criticism from other Muslims, especially religious scholars and theologians.

In late August 2014, the Grand Mufti of Saudi Arabia, Abdul-Aziz ibn Abdullah Al ash-Sheikh, condemned the Islamic State and al-Qaeda saying, "Extremist and militant ideas and terrorism which spread decay on Earth, destroying human civilization, are not in any way part of Islam, but are enemy number one of Islam, and Muslims are their first victims".

In late September 2014, 126 Sunni imams and Islamic scholars, primarily Sufi, from around the Muslim world signed an open letter to the Islamic State's leader Abu Bakr al-Baghdadi, explicitly rejecting and refuting his group's interpretations of Islamic scriptures, the Qur'an and hadith, used by it to justify its actions. "[You] have misinterpreted Islam into a religion of harshness, brutality, torture and murder... this is a great wrong and an offence to Islam, to Muslims and to the entire world", the letter states. It rebukes the Islamic State for its killing of prisoners, describing the killings as "heinous war crimes" and its persecution of the Yazidis of Iraq as "abominable". Referring to the "self-described 'Islamic State'", the letter censures the group for carrying out killings and acts of brutality under the guise of jihad—holy struggle—saying that its "sacrifice" without legitimate cause, goals and intention "is not jihad at all, but rather, warmongering and criminality". It also accuses the group of instigating fitna—sedition—by instituting slavery under its rule in contravention of the anti-slavery consensus of the Islamic scholarly community. Other scholars have described the group as not Sunnis, but Khawarij.

On 24 September 2014, United Nations Secretary-General Ban Ki-Moon stated: "As Muslim leaders around the world have said, groups like ISIL – or Da'ish — have nothing to do with Islam, and they certainly do not represent a state. They should more fittingly be called the "Un-Islamic Non-State"."

The group's declaration of a caliphate has been criticized and its legitimacy disputed by Middle Eastern governments, other jihadist groups, and Sunni Muslim theologians and historians. Qatar-based TV broadcaster and theologian Yusuf al Qaradawi stated: "[The] declaration issued by the Islamic State is void under sharia and has dangerous consequences for the Sunnis in Iraq and for the revolt in Syria", adding that the title of caliph can "only be given by the entire Muslim nation", not by a single group.

The group was described as a cult in a Huffington Post column by Steven Hassan, a notable authority on the subject of cults.

Two days after the beheading of Hervé Gourdel, hundreds of Muslims gathered in the Grand Mosque of Paris to show solidarity against the beheading. The protest was lead by the leader of the French Council of the Muslim Faith, Dalil Boubakeur, and was joined by thousands of other Muslims around the country under the slogan "Not in my name". French president François Hollande said Gourdel's beheading was "cowardly" and "cruel", and confirmed that airstrikes would continue against ISIL in Iraq. Hollande also called for three days of national mourning, with flags flown at half-mast throughout the country and said that security would be increased throughout Paris.

The Islamic State is mocked on social media web sites such as Twitter and YouTube, with the use of hashtags, mock recruiting ads, fake news articles and YouTube videos.One parody, by a Palestinian TV satire show, portrays the Islamic State as "buffoon-like hypocrites", and has had more than half a million views on YouTube.

"Islamic State", criticism of use of this name

No nation recognises the group as a sovereign state. Many object to using the name "Islamic State" owing to the far-reaching political and religious authority which that name implies. The United Nations Security Council, the United States, Canada, Turkey, Australia, Russia, the United Kingdom and other countries generally call the group "ISIL", while much of the Arab world and France use the Arabic acronym "Dâˆish".

In late August 2014, a leading Islamic educational institution, Dar al-Ifta al-Misriyyah in Egypt, advised Muslims to stop calling the group "Islamic State" and instead refer to it as "Al-Qaeda Separatists in Iraq and Syria" or "QSIS", because of the militant group's "un-Islamic character". However, despite widespread news coverage of al-Misriyyah's proclamation, the name "QSIS" failed to become commonly used.

When addressing the United Nations Security Council in September 2014, Australian Prime Minister Tony Abbott summarized the widespread objections to the name "Islamic State" thus: "To use this term [Islamic State] is to dignify a death cult; a death cult that, in declaring itself a caliphate, has declared war on the world". The group is very sensitive about its name. "They will cut your tongue out even if you call them Isis—you have to say 'Islamic State'", said a woman in ISIL-controlled Mosul. In mid-October 2014, representatives of the Islamic Society of Britain, the Association of British Muslims and the UK's Association of Muslim Lawyers proposed that "'Un-Islamic State' (UIS) could be an accurate and fair alternative name to describe this group and its agenda", further stating, "We need to work together and make sure that these fanatics don't get the propaganda that they feed off."

PROPAGANDA AND SOCIAL MEDIA

ISIL is known for its extensive and effective use of propaganda. It uses a version of the Muslim Black Standard flag and developed an emblem which has clear symbolic meaning in the Muslim world.

In November 2006, shortly after the group's rebranding as the "Islamic State of Iraq", the group established the al-Furqan Institute for Media Production, which produces CDs, DVDs, posters, pamphlets, and web-related propaganda products. ISIL's main media outlet is the I'tisaam Media Foundation, which was formed in March 2013 and distributes through the Global Islamic Media Front(GIMF). In 2014, ISIL established the al-Hayat Media Center, which targets a Western audience and produces material in English, German, Russian and French. From July 2014, al-Hayat began publishing a digital magazine called *Dabiq*, in a number of different languages including English. According to the magazine, its name is taken from the town of Dabiq in northern Syria, which is mentioned in a hadith about Armageddon. In 2014 ISIL also launched the Ajnad Media Foundation, which releases jihadist audio chants.

ISIL's use of social media has been described by one expert as "probably more sophisticated than [that of] most US companies".It regularly takes advantage of social media, particularly Twitter, to distribute its message by organizing hashtag campaigns, encouraging Tweets on popular hashtags, and utilizing software applications that enable ISIL propaganda to be distributed to its supporters' accounts. Another comment is that "ISIS puts more emphasis on social media than other jihadi groups.... They have a very coordinated social media presence." In August 2014, Twitter administrators shut down a number of accounts associated with ISIL. ISIL recreated and publicized new accounts the next day, which were also shut down by Twitter administrators. The group has attempted to branch out into alternative social media sites, such as Quitter, Friendica and Diaspora; Quitter and Friendica, however, almost immediately worked to remove ISIL's presence from their sites.

On 19 August 2014, a propaganda video showing the beheading of US photojournalist James Foley was posted on the Internet. ISIL claimed that the killing had been carried out in revenge for the US bombing of ISIL targets. The video promised that a second captured US journalist Steven Sotloff would be killed next if the airstrikes continued. On 2 September 2014, ISIL released a video purportedly showing their beheading of Sotloff. In the video the executioner says, "I'm back, Obama, and I'm back because of your arrogant foreign policy towards the Islamic State, because of your insistence on continuing your bombings and on Mosul Dam, despite our serious warnings. So just as your missiles continue to strike our people, our knife will continue to strike the necks of your people." The next scene shows the same executioner holding the orange jumpsuit of another prisoner and saying, "We take this opportunity to warn those governments that enter this evil alliance of America against the Islamic State to back off and leave our people alone." On 13 September 2014, ISIL released a similar video purportedly showing the beheading of David Cawthorne Haines, a British aid worker whom they had been holding hostage.

In a switch from its former practices, ISIL's media arm imposed a social media blackout on 27 September 2014, fearing that tweets and posts would give away military positions. ISIL has also attempted to present a more "rational argument" in its series of "press release/discussions" performed by hostage/captive John Cantlie and posted on YouTube. In its most recent "Cantlie presentation", various current and former US officials were quoted, such as US President Barack Obama and former CIA station chiefMichael Scheuer.

FINANCES

In 2014, the RAND Corporation carried out a study of 200 documents—personal letters, expense reports and membership rosters—that had been captured from Al-Qaeda in Iraq and the Islamic State of Iraq. It found that from 2005 until 2010, outside donations amounted to only 5 per cent of the group's operating budgets, with the rest being raised within Iraq. In the time-period studied, cells were required to send up to 20 per cent of the income generated from kidnapping, extortion rackets and other activities to the next level of the group's leadership. Higher-ranking commanders would then redistribute the funds to provincial or local cells that were in difficulties or needed money to conduct attacks. The records show that the Islamic State of Iraq was dependent on members from Mosul for cash, which the leadership used to provide additional funds to struggling militants in Diyala, Salahuddin and Baghdad.

In mid-2014, Iraqi intelligence extracted information from an ISIL operative which revealed that the organization had assets worth US$2 billion, making it the richest jihadist group in the world. About three quarters of this sum is said to be represented by assets seized after the group captured Mosul in June 2014; this includes possibly up to US$429 million looted from Mosul's central bank, along with additional millions and a large quantity of gold bullion stolen from a number of other banks in Mosul.However, doubt was later cast on whether ISIL was able to retrieve anywhere near that sum from the central bank, and even on whether the bank robberies had actually occurred.

Today the majority of the group's funding comes from the production and sale of energy. It controls around 300 oil wells in Iraq alone. At its peak it operated 350 oil wells in Iraq, but lost 45 to foreign airstrikes. It has captured 60 per cent of Syria's total production capacity. About one fifth of its total capacity is in operation. It earns US$2.5 million a day by selling 50,000 to 60,000 barrels of oil. Foreign sales rely on a long-standing black market through Turkey. Many of the smugglers and corrupt Turkish border guards who helped

Saddam Hussain to evade sanctions are helping ISIL to export oil and import cash. Energy sales include selling electric power from captured power plants in northern Syria. Some of this electricity is reportedly sold back to the Syrian government.

Sales of artifacts may be the second largest source of funding, according to an article in Newsweek. More than a third of Iraq's important sites are under ISIL's control. It looted the irreplaceable 9th century B.C. grand palace of the Assyrian king Ashurnasirpal II at Kalhu. Tablets, manuscripts and cuneiforms were sold, worth hundreds of millions of dollars. Stolen artifacts are smuggled into Turkey and Jordan. Abdulamir al-Hamdani, an archaeologist from SUNY Stony Brook, says ISIL is "looting of the very roots of humanity, artifacts from the oldest civilizations in the world."

The group routinely practises extortion, by demanding money from truck drivers and threatening to blow up businesses, for example. Robbing banks and gold shops has been another source of income.

ISIL is widely reported as receiving funding from private donors in the Gulf states, and the governments oflraq and Iran have repeatedly accused Saudi Arabia and Qatar of financing and supporting the group. Ahead of the conference of the US-led anti-ISIL coalition held in Paris in September 2014, France's foreign minister acknowledged that a number of countries at the table had "very probably" financed ISIL's advances.

Although Iran and Iraqi Prime Minister Nouri al-Maliki have accused Saudi Arabia and Qatar of funding the group, there is reportedly no evidence that this is the case. However, US SenatorJohn McCain has praised Saudi Arabia's Bandar bin Sultan for supporting forces fighting Bashar al-Assad's regime in Syria—"Thank God for the Saudis and Prince Bandar", he said to CNN—and according to *The Atlantic*, ISIL may have been a major part of Bandar's covert-ops strategy in Syria. Unregistered charity organizations are used as fronts for ISIL's funding. Using aliases on Facebook's WhatsApp andKik, the individuals and organizations arc untraccablc. Disguised as "humanitarian charity," funds are transferred to ISIL's operations. Saudi Arabia has imposed a blanket ban on unauthorized donations destined to Syria as the only means of stopping such funding.

Since 2012, ISIL has produced annual reports giving numerical information on its operations, somewhat in the style of corporate reports, seemingly in a bid to encourage potential donors.

In November 2014, ISIL announced that they intend to mint their own gold, silver and copper coins based on the coins minted by the Caliphate of Uthman. However, it is unclear where they plan on getting the materials. They have stated that the coins wwould be worth their weight in gold, silver or copper respectively.However, these currencies are not yet legal tender, or in production. The prototypes have included various different imagery. Prototype gold coins containing images of seven wheat stalks, mentioned in the Quran, while another showed a map of the world, referencing ISIL's belief that Islam will one day rule the world. Prototype silver coins have been shown with pictures of a minaret, symbolizing the city of Damascus, Syria, referenced by The Prophet Muhammad. Another displays a sword and shield, referencing a holy war. A different silver coin carries the symbol of the Al-Aqsa Mosque inJerusalem, revered as Islam's third-holiest place. The copper coins display a crescent moon and three palm trees. They are planned to be inscribed with an Arabic phrase that translates to, "The ISIL / A Caliphate Based on the Doctrine of the Prophet".

ANALYSIS

After significant setbacks for the group during the latter stages of the coalition forces' presence in Iraq, by late 2012 it was thought to have renewed its strength and to have more than doubled the number of its members to about 2,500, and since its formation in April 2013, ISIL grew rapidly in strength and influence in Iraq and Syria. Analysts have underlined the deliberate inflammation of sectarian conflict between Iraqi Shias and Sunnis during the Iraq War by various Sunni and Shia players as the root cause of ISIL's rise. The post-invasion policies of the international coalition forces have also been cited as a factor, with Fanar Haddad, a research fellow at the National University of Singapore's Middle East Institute, blaming the coalition forces during the Iraq War for "enshrining identity politics as the key marker of Iraqi politics".

By 2014, ISIL was increasingly being viewed as a militia rather than as a terrorist group. As major Iraqi cities fell to ISIL in June 2014, Jessica Lewis, a former US army intelligence officer at the Institute for the Study of War, described ISIL as "not a terrorism problem anymore", but rather "an army on the move in Iraq and Syria, and they are taking terrain. They have shadow governments in and around Baghdad, and they have an aspirational goal to govern. I don't know whether they want to control Baghdad, or if they want to destroy the functions of the Iraqi state, but either way the outcome will be disastrous for Iraq." Lewis has called ISIL "an advanced military leadership". She said, "They have incredible command and control and they have a sophisticated reporting mechanism from the field that can relay tactics and directives up and down the line. They are well-financed, and they have big sources of manpower, not just the foreign fighters, but also prisoner escapees."

According to the Institute for the Study of War, ISIL's 2013 annual report reveals a metrics-driven military command, which is "a strong indication of a unified, coherent leadership structure that commands from the top down". Middle East Forum's Aymenn Jawad Al-Tamimi said, "They are highly skilled in urban guerrilla warfare while the new Iraqi Army simply lacks tactical competence." Seasoned observers point to systemic corruption within the Iraq Army, seeing it as little more than a system of patronage, and have attributed to this its spectacular collapse as ISIL and its allies took over large swaths of Iraq in June 2014. While officials fear that ISIL may either inspire attacks in the United States by sympathizers or by those returning after joining ISIL, US intelligence agencies find there is no immediate threat or specific plots. US Defence Secretary Chuck Hagel sees an "imminent threat to every interest we have", but former top counterterrorism adviser Daniel Benjamin has derided such alarmist talk as a "farce" that panics the public. Some news commentators—the international newspaper columnist Gwynne Dyer, for example—and samples of public opinion, such as surveys by NPR, have advocated a strong but measured response to ISIL's recent provocative acts.

Conspiracy Theories in the Arab World

Conspiracy theorists in the Arab world have advanced rumors that the US is secretly behind the existence and emboldening of ISIL, as part of an attempt to further destabilize the Middle East. After such rumors became widespread, the US embassy in Lebanon issued an official statement denying the allegations, calling them a complete fabrication. Others are convinced that ISIL leader Abu Bakr al-Baghdadi is an Israeli Mossad agent and actor called Simon Elliot. The rumors claim that NSA documents leaked by Edward Snowden reveal this connection. Snowden's lawyer has called the story "a hoax".

MILITARY AND ARMS

Estimates of the size of ISIL's military vary widely from tens of thousands up to 200,000 fighters, with the latter estimate being the most recent one, as of November 2014.

Conventional weapons

ISIL relies mostly on captured weapons, with major sources being Saddam Hussein's Iraqi stockpiles (during the 2003-11 Iraq insurgency) and from government and opposition forces in the Syrian Civil War and Post-US withdrawal Iraqi insurgency. The captured weapons, including armor, guns, surface to air missiles, and even some aircraft, enabled rapid territorial growth and facilitated the capture of additional equipment.

Non-conventional weapons

ISIL captured nuclear materials from Mosul University in July 2014 but is unlikely to be able to weaponize it. They have used chemical weapons in Iraq and Syria. ISIL has a long history of using truck and car bombs, suicide bombers, and IEDs.

SUPPORT

Turkey

Turkey has been accused of supporting or colluding with ISIL, especially by Syrian Kurds. According to journalist Patrick Cockburn, there is "strong evidence for a degree of collaboration" between the Turkish intelligence services and ISIL, although the "exact nature of the relationship... remains cloudy". David L. Phillips of Columbia University's Institute for the Study of Human Rights, who compiled a list of allegations and claims accusing Turkey of assisting ISIL, writes that these allegations "range from military cooperation and weapons transfers to logistical support, financial assistance, and the provision of medical services". Several ISIL fighters and commanders have claimed Turkey supports ISIL.

Turkey has been further criticized for allowing individuals from outside the region to enter its territory and join ISIL in Syria. With many Islamist fighters passing through Turkey to fight in Syria, Turkey has been accused of becoming a transit country for such fighters and has been labeled the "Gateway to Jihad". Turkish border patrol officers are reported to have deliberately overlooked those entering Syria upon the payment of a small bribe. A report by Sky News exposed documents showing that passports of foreign Islamists wanting to join ISIL by crossing into Syria had been stamped by the Turkish government. An ISIL commander stated that "most of the fighters who joined us in the beginning of the war came via Turkey, and so did our equipment and supplies", adding that ISIL fighters received treatment in Turkish hospitals.

Foreign fighters

There are many foreign fighters in ISIL's ranks. In June 2014, *The Economist* reported that "ISIS may have up to 6,000 fighters in Iraq and 3,000–5,000 in Syria, including perhaps 3,000 foreigners; nearly a thousand are reported to hail from Chechnya and perhaps 500 or so more from France, Britain and elsewhere in Europe". Chechen leader Abu Omar al-Shishani, for example, was made commander of the northern sector of ISIL in Syria in 2013. According to *The New York Times*, in September 2014 there were more than 2,000 Europeans and 100 Americans among ISIL's foreign fighters. As of mid-September 2014, around 1,000 Turks had joined ISIL, and as of October 2014, 2,400–3,000 Tunisians had joined the group. An ISIL deserter alleged that foreign recruits were treated with less respect than Arabic-speaking Muslims by ISIL commanders and were placed in suicide units if they lacked otherwise useful skills.

4

Global Issues of National Defence And Security

Defence technologists are most successful when they hone in on specific problems. The Pentagon's research agencies and their contractors were asked in 2003 to come up with ways to foil roadside bombs in Iraq and Afghanistan, and although they did not defeat the threat entirely, they did produce a number of useful detectors, jammers and other counter-explosive systems. More recently, military researchers received marching orders to help tackle the so-called "anti-access area-denial" threats, which is Pentagon-speak for enemy weapons that could be used to shoot down U.S. fighters and attack Navy ships. The next wave of national security threats, however, might be more than the technology community can handle. They are complex, multidimensional problems against which no degree of U.S. technical superiority in stealth, fifth-generation air warfare or night-vision is likely to suffice.

The latest intelligence forecasts by the Obama administration and other sources point to five big challenges to U.S. and global security in the coming decades. Biological Weapons: The White House published in 2009 a National Strategy for Countering Biological Threats with an underlying theme that biological weapons eventually will be used in a terrorist attack. To prevent deadly viruses from being turned into mass-casualty weapons, officials say, one of the most difficult challenges is obtaining timely and accurate insight on potential attacks. The Defence Threat Reduction Agency has a team of researchers working these problems. But they worry that the pace of research is too slow to keep up with would-be terrorists. Nukes: Large stockpiles of nuclear weapons are tempting targets for nation-states or groups set on attacking the United States and its allies, officials assert. Black-market trade in sensitive nuclear materials is a particular concern for U.S. security agencies. "The prospect that al-Qaida or another terrorist organization might acquire a nuclear device represents an immediate and extreme threat to global security," says an administration report. No high-tech sensors exist to help break up black markets, detect and intercept nuclear materials in transit and there are no financial tools to disrupt this dangerous trade. A much-hyped Department of Homeland Security effort to detect radioactive materials at U.S. ports has been plagued by technical hiccups. Analysts believe that although a full-up nuclear weapon would be nearly impossible for an al-Qaida like group to build, a more likely scenario would be a low-yield "dirty bomb" that could be made with just a few grams of radioactive material. Cyber-Attacks: The drumbeats of cyberwarfare have been sounding for years. Network intrusions are widely viewed as one of the most serious potential national security, public safety and economic challenges. Technology, in this case, becomes a double-edge sword. "The very technologies that empower us to lead and create also empower individual criminal hackers, organized criminal groups, terrorist networks and other advanced nations to disrupt the critical infrastructure that is vital to our economy, commerce, public safety, and military," the White House says. The cybersecurity marketplace is flooded with products that promise quick fixes but it is becoming clear that the increasing persistence and sophistication of attacks will require solutions beyond the traditional. Climate Change: The national security ramifications of climate change are severe, according to Defence Secretary Leon Panetta.

While the topic of climate change has been hugely politicized, Panetta casts the issue as a serious security crisis. "In the 21st century, we recognize that climate change can impact national security — ranging from rising sea levels, to severe droughts, to the melting of the polar caps, to more frequent and devastating natural disasters that raise demand for humanitarian assistance and disaster relief," Panetta said. The administration projects that the change wrought by a warming planet will lead to new conflicts over refugees and resources and catastrophic natural disasters, all of which would require increased U.S. military support and resources. The scientific community, in this area, cannot agree on what it will take to reverse this trend. There is agreement, though, that there is no silver bullet. Transnational Crime: U.S. defence and law-enforcement agencies see transnational criminal networks as national security challenges. These groups cause instability and subvert government institutions through corruption, the administration says.

"Transnational criminal organizations have accumulated unprecedented wealth and power through the drug trade, arms smuggling, human trafficking, and other illicit activities. ... They extend their reach by forming alliances with terrorist organizations, government officials, and some state security services." Even the United States' sophisticated surveillance technology is not nearly enough to counter this threat, officials say. In this special report, National Defence examines the top five threats in greater detail. Bio-Threats The public health community's dream is to make the arrival and spread of communicable diseases as easy to predict and track as the weather. Just as a meteorologist spots the seeds of a hurricane off the African coast, and begins to plot its possible path as it makes its way towards the Caribbean, a global bio-surveillance network would allow officials to detect a bio-weapon or the emergence of a deadly flu virus in China and track it as it spreads throughout the world. Measures could then be taken to quickly develop and distribute vaccines. Despite the onset of the information age, where a doctor in Asia could theoretically inform a centralized information clearinghouse on the other side of the world of a new virus within seconds, realizing this dream is years away, experts at a recent National Defence Industrial Association Biosurveillance conference said. Making diseases as predictable as the weather is a lofty goal, but the weather analogy is an imperfect one, said Steve Bennett, director of the Department of Homeland Security's National Biosurveillance Integration Center. To start, the medical community doesn't have all the prediction models that weather watchers can use to plug data into. They just don't exist. "Prediction is a pretty difficult thing to achieve," he said. "Real-time situational awareness, I think we can get close."

Congress established the center in 2007 to pull together the efforts of 12 federal agencies and departments that are charged with tracking diseases. Its goal is to "rapidly identify, characterize, localize and track a biological event of national concern; integrate and analyze data relating to human health, animal, plant, food, water, and environmental domains; and to disseminate alerts and pertinent information."

The Defence Department's Defence Threat Reduction Agency, the Centers for Disease Control and Prevention, the Departments of Health and Human Services and Agriculture are all among the entities that track diseases. "I think there was this idea in 2007 when that law was stood up ... there was this thought that there were these databases all around the federal government and the states and all we had to do was put $100 million into an IT system and hook it all together, and out comes wisdom," Bennett said. The databases don't exist, or they exist in spreadsheets on different systems, and they are not structured at all, he said. Five years after the law was passed, Bennett still spends the bulk of his time visiting other agencies to keep tabs on what is happening.

"It is people and relationships. I wish there was a more technical solution, but that is kind of the way it is," he said. As far as developing a real-time global picture of what diseases are spreading and where, there seem to be more questions than answers. "Right now the sum of biosusurveillance is based on ambiguous data. And to go from ambiguous data to a decision is a very difficult thing to do," said C. Nicole Rosenzweig, a research biologist at the Army's Edgewood Chemical Biological Center in Maryland. How do analysts take something that is at some level, research, and assess it as though we have complete confidence in it? she asked. "A lot of research will have to go into this," she added. Information technology systems that could collect and coordinate the data and give public health officials a picture of where diseases are emerging is only one part of the problem. The main issue is that the policies and procedures on how to do this have yet to be worked out. Harshini Mukundan, a scientist in the chemical division at Los Alamos National Laboratory, said diseases emerge in food, humans and animals. "They are all interconnected and having separate agencies monitoring each [one] defeats the cause," she added. Who owns the biosurveillance data? she asked. Is it going to be governments or the World Health Organization? "It is hard to envision what the system will look like and how exactly it will function. ... We need some direction on that from the government to start imagining how it will be implemented," Mukundan added. Bennett said: "There are lot of systemic issues that we need to fix, process issues, authority issues, things that can make decisions faster." Laurie Garrett, a policy analyst and senior fellow for global health at the Council on Foreign Relations, said all the technical problems could be solved in five to 10 years, "but I don't believe we have the capacity or the will to implement" them. The political crisis in the United States today means it is difficult to get any kind of decision from the federal government. Many state legislatures are suffering from similar gridlock, she said. "Are the problems bureaucratic, financial or policy? The answer is 'yes,' [to] all three," she said. Transparency has been an issue on the federal government's end. For example, it issued a gag order on federal scientists during the 2001 anthrax attacks. "As a result, on the local level, they were operating almost blind and did not have vital information," she said. Meanwhile, the government may be turning to the public for help. Health and Human Services recently sponsored a grand challenge asking competitors to use Twitter to create a web-based application that would compile the top five trending illnesses in a geographic area and distribute the findings to state and local public health officials. Bennett said there is valuable data contained in insurance claims. Such forms have geo-location tags and could help public health officials to see where diseases are cropping up. But then there are privacy issues. "I don't need to know specific patient information....I need to know general trends."

The national security community may not need to know the kinds of data that would intrude on personal privacy, he added. Jason Pargas, special assistant to the director at the Defence Threat Reduction Agency's chemical and biological technologies directorate, said he believes that these issues will all be worked out in five to 10 years. He is in the research-and-development community, so he has to be an optimist, he said.

Prediction models, applied math and computing may converge to where disease forecasts could become possible, he said. But governments need to see the public as a partner. "If you engage the public, you will have a much more redundant, highly, highlyeffective system," he said. Nuclear Weapons

Still at the top of the list of the most terrifying threats to the United States are nuclear weapons. The nation has spent an almost incalculable amount of money over the past six decades to find them, monitor them, and destroy the means by which they are delivered. Open source information suggests there is still a lot of work to be done.

Research into hitting an intercontinental ballistic missile bearing a nuclear warhead with another missile began in the Eisenhower administration 50 years ago. Yet today, this can still only be accomplished under the most controlled circumstances with questions remaining on whether decoys could easily defeat the "hitting a bullet with a bullet" scenario.

President Reagan's dead-end effort to shoot down missiles from space, better known as Star Wars, came to naught. The Airborne Laser programme, which envisioned destroying missiles on the launch pad by using directed energy shot from an aircraft, also came to a halt. The mutually assured destruction doctrine offset these defensive shortcomings. But as many analysts have noted, non-state actors such as terrorist groups, if they were to get their hands on a nuke, don't play by those rules. More recently, the Department of Homeland Security abandoned a programme to develop Advanced Spectroscopic Portals that could detect a smuggled warhead inside a shipping container.

The congressional mandate to scan every container entering the United States means that this effort will continue, although on a smaller scale. Less overt is the detection problem. Who has nukes? And where are they? The answer is: underground. North Korea's nuclear weapons programme is hidden deep in its mountains, as are Iran's alleged efforts. Army Lt. Gen. Ronald L. Burgess Jr., director of the Defence Intelligence Agency in his annual threat assessment released in February before his retirement, said underground facilities that may hide missiles and weapons of mass destruction are "spreading." Finding, assessing, mapping and ultimately destroying a hard and deep buried target — HDBT in military lingo — has become an increasingly difficult challenge for the military and spy communities, Air Force Lt. Col. Craig Baker, wrote in an Army War College paper, "The Strategic Importance of Defeating Underground Facilities." The two communities have placed a great deal of emphasis on tackling this problem during the last decade, he wrote. Most of it has been carried out with little attention. Despite the low profile, the military has been taking the problem seriously.

"America's potential adversaries have realized that current non-nuclear penetrating weapons are relatively ineffective in destroying underground facilities," Baker wrote. Weapons of mass destruction programmes are now underground in an effort to remain out of reach. New commercial tunneling technologies have also made underground bunkers less expensive to build, he noted. The National Reconnaissance Office, National Geo-Spatial Intelligence Agency and the Air Force all need sensors to detect nuclear weapons, as well as the underground bunkers where they are hiding. The Air Force's Technical Applications Center, based at Patrick Air Force Base, Fla., has been tasked with searching for nuclear weapons and verifying treaties. Much of its work is classified. If the U.S. is to pre-emptively destroy a nuclear weapons programme, it will require intelligence on where these weapons are located and how deep underground they are stored. An effort to destroy an underground complex may require repeated bombings by massive ordnance penetrator.

These can only be carried by B-2 bombers, and only one at a time. Jeffrey Richelson, senior fellow at the National Security Archives, a research institute that pries secret documents out of the government through Freedom of Information Act requests, said, "We obviously need weapons that can penetrate through certain depths, through certain hardness. But whether they can even build them to attain certain levels of destruction, I just don't know ... I'm not even sure the people in the Defence Department know. They are guessing, trying to figure it out using various models."

Then comes the difficult question of battlefield damage assessment. Some things could be determined from outside, such as whether a bombing campaign collapsed an entrance. But since there may be an incomplete picture of what was inside a deeply buried bunker in the first place, it would be hard to know if a strike was successful, he said. Documents show that the Defence Department and intelligence community over the past decade have been taking this problem seriously.

"It has become more prominent and more important in recent years," Richelson said. Baker's paper identified more than $1 billion being spent tackling underground facility defeat issues during fiscal years 2009 and 2010. There is some good news. The Comprehensive Nuclear Test Ban Treaty, signed by most countries, has yet to be ratified. But it has helped create a robust global network that can monitor clandestine underground nuclear weapon detonations. A National Academies report released in 2000 spelled out the shortcomings signees would have in attempting to detect tests. On a typical day, the Earth experiences hundreds of earthquakes and large mine blasts.

The seismic clutter made it difficult to detect underground nuclear explosions, said Paul Richards, a Colombia University emeritus professor of geophysics and seismology at a Center for Science, Technology and Security Policy briefing on Capitol Hill. A follow-up report released this year showed remarkable progress over the last decade. Hundreds of seismic and air-sniffing sensors have been placed all over the world, and countries have done a better job of sharing their legacy seismic sensor data with those who monitor the treaty, he said.

The radioactive particles released by the Fukushima Daiichi Nuclear Plant accident last year were detected all over the globe and as far as South America, said Robert Werzi, who maintains the Comprehensive Test Ban Treaty Organization's 80 radionuclide air monitors. If a sensor detects a manmade radioactive particle, analysts can then determine how many days old it is, backtrack the weather patterns, and pinpoint its origins, he said. Officials believe the network of seismic sensors is good enough to detect 90 percent of any clandestine attempt to test a nuclear weapon that is over 1 kiloton. The lower the yield is on a test, the less effective it is. Richards said it is necessary "to consider how well nuclear tests can be carried out evasively."

There is a need for a continuing research-and-development programme to improve the network of sensors, he added. "The goal of the monitoring effort is to drive ever downwards the yield of anything that might go undetected or identified," he said. The Future of Cyber-Wars Army Gen. Keith Alexander, commander of U.S. Cyber Command, sees a day in the not too distant future when attacks on computer networks cross the line from theft and disruption to "destruction." And this chaos will not all take place in the digital world of ones and zeroes. He is referring to remote adversaries taking down infrastructure such as power grids, dams, transportation systems and other sectors that use computer-based industrial controls.

The last decade has seen mostly exploitation by adversaries, or the theft of money and intellectual property. Next came distributed denial of service attacks when hackers overwhelm networks and disrupt operations of businesses or other organizations, Alexander said at a recent Woodrow Wilson Center panel discussion on cybersecurity. Other than intercontinental ballistic missiles and acts of terrorism, an adversary seeking to reach out and harm the United States has only one other option: destructive cyber-attacks, Alexander said. This could result in loss of life and damage to the economy on par with what occurred after 9/11.

"All of that is within the realm of the possible," he said. "I believe that is coming our way. We have to be out in front of this," Alexander said. How to thwart such attacks is the problem the nation is facing. Most of the Internet's infrastructure through which malware is delivered is in the private sector's hands. So too are the banking, energy, transportation and other institutions that are vulnerable to the attacks. During the past year, there have been 200 attacks on core critical infrastructures in the transportation, energy, and communication industries reported to the Department of Homeland Security, said Sen. Susan Collins, R-Maine, and ranking member of the Senate Homeland Security and Governmental Affairs Committee. "And that is only the tip of the iceberg. Undoubtedly there are more that have not been reported," she said during the panel. "In this case, the dots have already been connected. The alarm has already been sounded, and we know it is only a matter of when, not whether we have a catastrophic attack," she said. Alexander, Collins and others are advocating for a more coordinated national effort to share information on cyberthreats. Cyber Command and the National Security Agency have loads of expertise, but can't always share classified information, or cross lines when it comes to the privacy of U.S. citizens. The rest of the federal government has bits and pieces of information, and different responsibilities. Private sector companies are sometimes reluctant to disclose attacks for fear of upsetting shareholders or opening themselves up to lawsuits. Legislation co-sponsored by Collins to help pave the way for better information sharing died in Congress last summer. Despite having poured countless amounts of money into cybersecurity on both the federal and private levels, there is still a lot to be learned about the threat, said one analyst. "Why do we have a cyberwar community? Because we haven't mastered cyber," said Martin Libicki, senior management scientist at Rand Corp.

The main problem is that computers were originally seen as something to be "tinkered" with, Libicki said. "We've built the most important infrastructure on things that were made to be toys," said Libicki. Being toys, computer systems from the start have gaps and vulnerabilities needing to be patched. "Every cyber-attack is a reflection of some vulnerability in the system," said Libicki. Greg Giaqunito, an analyst at Forecast International, said it's not enough to defend the nation from attacks, offensive capabilities are required. Increasingly, the United States is taking more proactive measures against adversaries and initiating activity, Giaqunito said. "We are actually taking proactive action against other adversaries, so it's not only protecting ourselves, but the U.S. taking more proactive stances and actually initiating some activity against U.S. adversaries," he said. Over the next few years, the hackers will become more sophisticated, said Charles Croom, vice president of cyber security solutions at Lockheed Martin Information Systems and Global Solutions.

This doesn't necessarily mean that the technologies are becoming more advanced — even the most sophisticated threats often use known vulnerabilities and malware, Croom said — but the adversaries have become more effective. Lockheed Martin's Security Intelligence Center has over the last 10 years compiled a database of patterns and hacking groups. This information can help analysts as they work to stop threats. While innovation in technology is important, Croom said the backbone of its security system is its analysts. A shortage of network security experts continues to be a problem in both government and the private sector.

Alexander said because of the poor economy, he isn't having a problem attracting and retaining service personnel and civilian employees to Cyber Command now, but that won't always be the case. Incentives and bonuses may be needed to retain experts, he said. Duke Ayers, programme manager of SAIC's CyberNEXS initiative, a live-training programme that focuses on cyber education, said,

"We know that we're not developing people fast enough in cyber or the technical skills." SAIC, along with other partners such as the University of Texas at San Antonio, developed the CyberNEXS programme that gives immediate feedback to participants as they pursue cyber-education. Industry, the Defence Department and the Air Force Association have also teamed up to work on the CyberPatriot programme, a nationwide high school-level competition intended to motivate high school students to get involved in the cybersecurity sector early and to cultivate talent. Industry has also formed partnerships with academia to help stop attacks. In 2009, Northrop Grumman started its Cybersecurity Research Consortium, which includes Carnegie Mellon, MIT and Purdue University. There they investigate the various security threats that face the economy and national security and work on solutions that can help stop them, said Mike Papay, vice president of Cyber Initiatives at Northrop Grumman Information Systems.

With cybersecurity, Papay said, government and industry need to work together from the beginning during the procurement process. This, he said, is one way to reduce costs and achieve better cybersecurity. "It's not just about acquiring pure cybersystems anymore; it's about acquiring UAV's, radars, ships, etc, where cyber needs to be embedded to ensure mission success. Government and industry need to consider cyber in almost everything they do," said Papay.

Despite all these initiatives, Collins struck a pessimistic tone, especially when it comes to the federal government's response. "In all the years that I have been working on homeland security issues, I can't think of another area where the threat is greater, and we have done less," she said.

Climate Change For the U.S. military, climate change is a "ring-road" issue that surrounds its future strategic planning. No matter which way the Defence Department turns, U.S. global interests will eventually intersect with the effects of a warming planet, analysts said. While politicians debate the legitimacy of climate science, the Defence Department has recognized it has a practical, hard-security interest in tackling issues like its energy footprint, said David Michel, director of environmental security at the Stimson Center. "There's no tree-hugging, sandal-wearing, granola eating aspects to the military's approach," Michel told National Defence. "The water-food-energy nexus of issues caused by climate change is going to be a rising challenge for the military and the national security strategy reflects that." The military will have an ever-increasing need for sensors and observation platforms to keep constant watch on how climate change manifests itself through weather and ecological phenomena, said Michel.

"These technologies are increasingly particularized and specialized," he said. "We need to make sure that all of our eyes in the sky are not only looking at North Korea, for instance, but gathering a wealth of data from many areas. We need an inclusive data network to which many different observation technologies contribute." At the ends of the Earth, where climate change is already noticeable in receding ice caps, the same technologies are needed to monitor the melt, said Heather Conley, director of the Europe Programme at the Center for Strategic and International Studies. The Coast Guard will also need new ships that can patrol the cold waters of the Arctic, to provide a constant presence in what could become the world's newest contested open ocean, she said. The 2010 Quadrennial Defence Review lists resource scarcity, climate change, disease, and demographics as "enduring trends" that threaten national security.

The challenge for the U.S. military, as it shifts its primary focus to the Pacific Ocean, will be balancing its response to acute events with a chronic, sustained preparedness for the long-term effects of climate change, Michel said. The Pacific already averages 70,000 annual deaths to natural disasters ranging from floods to typhoons and earthquakes. "We're likely to see more of those sorts of acute events," Michel said. "But even at the same frequency and strength as we see them today ... as populations continue to grow, as urbanization along coastlines continues, more people will be exposed." The U.S. military has a unique ability to provide infrastructure at nearly a moment's notice when disaster strikes. A single carrier strike group can provide medical supplies, lift capabilities and communications to a country devastated by a catastrophic event, as it did after a massive earthquake ravaged Haiti in 2010. The Marine Corps, along with the Navy, has pledged that disaster relief and humanitarian aid will be two of their main duties within a Pacific-centered security strategy. The chronic results of climate change are more challenging. Funneling resources to combat a problem that might not manifest for decades is a hard sell, especially with constrained budgets, Conley said. But phenomena associated with climate change like persistent drought, violent flooding and agricultural disruption are real and immediate concerns for many of the nations the United States partners with around the world, Michel said. The effects are also causing the most disruption in some of the world's most politically unstable regions — Southern Asia, Sub-Saharan Africa, South America. "To the extent that climate change is an issue for our partners ... it is going to become an issue for us," Michel said. "The military is also aware that ... climate impacts could be accelerants of instability in the countries where we have political interests or strategic concerns." There are opportunities also associated with a warming planet. Some effects like the melting polar ice caps are regrettable ecologically but potentially a windfall for global commerce, said Conley.

A receding Arctic icecap could mean the Northwest and Northeast passages and Russia's Northern Sea Route could remain open longer in summer. Eventually they could remain navigable to commercial shipping year-round. The National Snow and Ice Data Center in September announced that the polar ice cap shrank over the summer months to the smallest area in the 33 years that records have been kept — just 1.5 million square miles at its nadir.

"We're really seeing a dramatic acceleration of Arctic ice melt," Conley said. "As the ice recedes, there are increases in commercial and other human activity. It also opens new sources of oil and gas and tourist opportunities in new waters." The implications of the sudden availability of natural resources and shipping lanes through the Arctic have drawn much attention from nations spanning the globe. The obvious players — the eight-member Arctic Council, which includes the United States, Canada, Denmark, Finland, Norway, Russia, Sweden and Iceland — are concerned about border security where a sea of ice once did the work for them. Other nations as far away as India and China are trying to gain admission to the council to advocate for their interests in shipping through an open Arctic, which could lessen by a third the time and cost of trans-oceanic shipping, said Conley.

For those and other reasons, the U.S. military "is just as interested in the decline of polar ice as the polar bear people," Michel said. It is another instance where the military, by addressing a practical challenge to national security, can have a positive ecological impact, like the Navy being a champion of biofuels. Navy officials view renewable energy as a means of bringing down the cost of operations. The Marines care less about curbing global warming than they do about keeping fuel and water convoys off vulnerable roads. But the net result of sustainable resource programmes is a significant reduction in the military's carbon footprint, Michel said.

In the Arctic, however, the United States is woefully unprepared for the challenge. The Coast Guard has a single operational icebreaker and the military hasn't built one for more than 30 years. "This summer, when Shell Oil attempted to drill offshore in the Arctic, they were able to bring more assets to bear than the U.S. Coast Guard could ever hope to muster," Conley said. "When we need resources, we borrow them from other countries. By the time there is a crisis there, we won't have the ability to address it." There are other strikes against U.S.

polar preparedness. Because the disappearance of the ice cap is a long-term issue that may not have consequences for decades, it is difficult to interest policymakers and even more difficult to pin down funding for infrastructure and ships, Conley said. The Arctic is also an area where 20 federal agencies have some role, creating headaches for strategists and diplomatic efforts to manage competition there. "Coordination of Arctic policy is a nightmare on a good day," she said.

In the Arctic, as in Asia and the Pacific, the United States will be forced to acknowledge and address climate change, if it is to uphold its professed role as a global power to secure and maintain the free-flow of public goods, Michel said. "If we say climate change is one of our major concerns that is going to shape the 21st century and then we ignore it, the international community will notice," he said.

Transnational Crime/Terror Well before the May killing of Osama bin Laden at the hands of U.S. Navy SEALs, the terrorist organization he headed had become a dispersed, loosely linked network of international terror and criminal groups. Add to that the existing transnational trafficking in narcotics, weapons and people, and the recipe yields a complicated problem for U.S. military and law enforcement agencies at home and abroad. "We're going to continue to have this transnational, non-standard set of threats and everything that goes with that," said Garry Reid, principal deputy assistant secretary of defence for special operations, during a discussion of future SOF operations at the annual Air and Space conference in September.

"Those threats are going to persist in multiple environments over the next 10-plusyears." Countering those threats is made all the more difficult given that the U.S. military can't take its eye off state-level actors to fight non-state, non-standard actors. "Our national defence focus and clearly the focus of our Special Operations Command has got to equally be on ... high-end threats and state competitors of the future," Reid said. Events like the Arab Spring have created power vacuums and ungoverned lands where criminals and terrorist groups are able to operate with impunity. While much of the U.S. military's attention has been on the Middle East, anti-U.S. terror groups and al-Qaida sympathizers have spread elsewhere. Today, the arc of instability, from West to East Africa to Pakistan to Bangladesh has any number of al-Qaida copycat sympathizers, Arnaud de Borchgrave, senior adviser and director of the

Transnational Threats Project at the Center for Strategic and International Studies, wrote in January. Illegal trade is "increasingly converging with ideologically-motivated networks, fostering a new generation of hybrid threats," according to information from the project's web site. Mali and Libya were two examples given by Reid of places where those two forces are converging. A coup last year in Mali left the country's inhospitable north largely ungoverned. "Bandits and kidnappers" have since set up shop.

Al-Qaida in the Islamic Maghreb has reared its head in Mali, operating without constraint in the arid north, some of the most inhospitable terrain on earth. "Al-Qaida branched into there a few years ago and showed mixed results with proselytizing their ideology," Reid said. "They have not posed a transnational threat per se to attack the United States homeland, but they are of growing concern to our interests in the region." The group draws its origins from desert bandits and smugglers taking advantage of a power vacuum to advance their and al-Qaida's interests.

The instability in Libya has afforded them an opportunity to spread their beliefs there also, Reid said. They gain a significant amount of resources from kidnapping for ransom — tens of millions of dollars go into their treasure chests. For al-Qaida, kidnapping to fund terrorist activities is a relatively new brand of criminality, he said. These are small-scale crimes with regional implications for which military intervention is not well suited. They call instead for foreign military engagement by special operations forces, which have been overstretched this last decade, and for which no respite is in sight, Reid said. "We see ourselves being pretty busy in the future," he said. The situation calls, as many others do, for technologies that are force multipliers, like intelligence, surveillance and reconnaissance platforms that are easily deployed and operated by militaries short on resources. There are "issues of partner-nation absorption," of what portion of the enforcement burden native societies and militaries can take on, Reid said. Technologies like unmanned aerial vehicles and persistent border surveillance can enhance that absorption, he said.

But it is "not as simple as providing a piece of kit and waving goodbye," he said. "How do we allow a small nation to have the advantage of these capabilities? These technologies will have to be scalable." Simply handing over or lending the U.S. military's large and complicated unmanned aerial vehicles and surveillance systems won't do. Once criminal activity is detected, the host nation must be have the will and training to curtail it. That will require a steady presence of SOF personnel in remote parts of the world. Distributed operations of that nature and scope call for a secure communications network the United States doesn't currently have, Reid said. The transnational threat also hits close to home. The United States is the world's primary market for illicit drugs. They flow over the nation's land and maritime borders by the ton and government agencies catch only about a third of what's smuggled, Gen. Douglas Fraser, then the commander of U.S.

Southern Command, told defence reporters in March. An estimated 1,200 to 1,500 metric tons of illegal drugs are produced in South and Central America each year, Fraser said. Of that, about 60 percent eventually makes it to the United States, he said. Here again, intelligence, surveillance and reconnaissance technologies can help. But eyes in the sky can only spy, and in South America are often hampered by rain forests.

In countries like Colombia and Honduras, criminals hide beneath a triple-canopy rain forest through which current sensors cannot penetrate, Fraser said. "That's really a [research-and-development] effort right now.... We have not gotten to a penetrative capability yet." UAVs, however, cannot interdict drugs or smugglers once they are found. The Coast Guard and Navy need more ships for that task, or other weapon systems that both spot and stop illegal drug and gun trafficking, he said.

But technology is not always the silver bullet, Fraser said. Just as in North Africa, countering transnational threats in South America is accomplished by using some technologies like maritime radar but is best done through direct cooperation with regional allies and old-fashioned word-of-mouth intelligence gathering, he said. While UAVs have developed rapidly because of successes in Iraq and Afghanistan — Reid credits many of SOF's "most public successes" on their spying abilities — they aren't necessarily the best platform for every job, Fraser said.

NATIONAL DEFENCE STRATEGY OF THE UNITED STATES OF AMERICA

AMERICA'S SECURITY IN THE 21ST CENTURY

A Changing Security Environment

Uncertainty is the defining characteristic of today's strategic environment. We can identify trends but cannot predict specific events with precision. While we work to avoid being surprised, we must posture ourselves to handle unanticipated problems-we must plan with surprise in mind.

We contend with uncertainty by adapting to circumstances and influencing events. It is not enough to react to change. This strategy focuses on safeguarding U.S. freedoms and interests while working actively to forestall the emergence of new challenges.

Mature and Emerging Challenges

"America is now threatened less by conquering states than we are by failing ones. We are menaced less by fleets and armies than by catastrophic technologies in the hands of the embittered few." - *National Security Strategy, September 2002*

The U.S. military predominates in the world in *traditional* forms of warfare. Potential adversaries accordingly shift away from challenging the United States through *traditional*military action and adopt asymmetric capabilities and methods. An array of *traditional, irregular, catastrophic, and disruptive* capabilities and methods threaten U.S. interests:

- *Traditional* challenges are posed by states employing recognized military capabilities and forces in well understood forms of military competition and conflict.
- *Irregular* challenges come from those employing "unconventional" methods to counter the traditional advantages of stronger opponents.
- *Catastrophic* challenges involve the acquisition, possession, and use of WMD or methods producing WMD like effects.
- *Disruptive* challenges may come from adversaries who develop and use breakthrough technologies to negate current U.S. advantages in key operational domains.

These categories overlap. Actors proficient in one can be expected to try to reinforce their position with methods and capabilities drawn from others.

Indeed, recent experience indicates that the most dangerous circumstances arise when we face a complex of challenges. For example, our adversaries in Iraq and Afghanistan presented both *traditional* and *irregular* challenges. Terrorist groups like al Qaeda are *irregular* threats but also actively seek catastrophic capabilities. North Korea at once poses*traditional, irregular*, and *catastrophic* challenges. Finally, in the future, the most capable opponents may seek to combine truly disruptive capacity with *traditional, irregular*, or*catastrophic* forms of warfare.

Traditional challenges. These challenges are most often associated with states employing armies, navies, and air forces in long-established forms of military competition.*Traditional* military challenges remain important, as many states maintain capabilities to influence security conditions in their region. However, allied superiority in traditional domains, coupled with the costs of traditional military competition, drastically reduce adversaries' incentives to compete with us in this arena. As formidable as U.S. capabilities are against *traditional* opponents, we cannot ignore the challenges that such adversaries might present. Traditional challenges require us to maintain sufficient combat capability in key areas of military competition.

Irregular challenges. Increasingly sophisticated *irregular* methods *e.g.*, terrorism and insurgency challenge U.S. security interests. Adversaries employing irregular methods aim to erode U.S. influence, patience, and political will. Irregular opponents often take a long term approach, attempting to impose prohibitive human, material, financial, and political costs on the United States to compel strategic retreat from a key region or course of action.

Two factors have intensified the danger of *irregular* challenges: the rise of extremist ideologies and the absence of effective governance.

Political, religious, and ethnic extremism continues to fuel conflicts worldwide.

The absence of effective governance in many parts of the world creates sanctuaries for terrorists, criminals, and insurgents. Many states are unable, and in some cases unwilling, to exercise effective control over their territory or frontiers, thus leaving areas open to hostile exploitation.

Our experience in the war on terrorism points to the need to reorient our military capabilities to contend with such irregular challenges more effectively.

Catastrophic challenges. In the face of American dominance in *traditional* forms of warfare, some hostile forces are seeking to acquire *catastrophic* capabilities, particularly weapons of mass destruction (WMD). Porous international borders, weak international controls, and easy access to information related technologies facilitate these efforts. Particularly troublesome is the nexus of transnational terrorists, proliferation, and problem states that possess or seek WMD, increasing the risk of WMD attack against the United States.

Proliferation of WMD technology and expertise makes contending with *catastrophic* challenges an urgent priority. Even a single *catastrophic*attack against the United States or an ally would be unacceptable. We will place greater emphasis on those capabilities that enable us to dissuade others from acquiring catastrophic capabilities, to deter their use and, when necessary, to defeat them before they can be employed.

Disruptive challenges. In rare instances, revolutionary technology and associated military innovation can fundamentally alter long-established concepts of warfare. Some potential adversaries are seeking *disruptive* capabilities to exploit U.S. vulnerabilities and offset the current advantages of the United States and its partners.

Some *disruptive* breakthroughs, including advances in biotechnology, cyber operations, space, or directed energy weapons, could seriously endanger our security. As such breakthroughs can be unpredictable, we should recognize their potential consequences and hedge against them.

Changing Relationships

Alongside the four security challenges are far reaching changes in the international system:

- We continually adapt our defence partnerships.
- Key states face important decisions that will affect their strategic position.
- Some problem states will continue to pose challenges, while others could realize that their current policies undermine their own security.
- Hostile, non state actors have substantial numbers, capability, and, influence.

International partnerships. International partnerships continue to be a principal source of our strength. Shared principles, a common view of threats, and commitment to cooperation provide far greater security than we could achieve on our own. Unprecedented cooperation in the war on terrorism is an example of the benefit of strong international partnerships.

Today, the United States and its partners are threatened not just by enemies who seek to oppose us through traditional means, but also by an active spectrum of non traditional challenges. Key U.S. relationships around the globe are adapting and broadening in response to these changes. Also, we have significantly expanded our circle of security partners around the world.

Key states. Several key states face basic decisions about their roles in global and regional politics, economics, and security, and the pace and direction of their own internal evolution.

These decisions may change their strategic position in the world and their relationship with the United States. This uncertainty presents both opportunities and potential challenges for the United States. Some states may move towards greater cooperation with the United States, while others could evolve into capable regional rivals or enemies.

Over time, some rising powers may be able to threaten the United States and our partners directly, rival us in key areas of military and technological competition, or threaten U.S. interests by pursuing dominance over key regions. In other cases, if adverse economic, political, and demographic trends continue, large capable states could become dangerously unstable and increasingly ungovernable, creating significant future challenges.

While remaining alert to the possibility of renewed great power competition, recent developments in our relations with states like Russia and China should encourage a degree of hope. As the President's National Security Strategy states, "Today, the international community has the best chance since the rise of the nation state in the seventeenth century to build a world where great powers compete in peace instead of continually prepare for war."

Problem states. Problem states will continue to undermine regional stability and threaten U.S. interests. These states are hostile to U.S. principles. They commonly squander their resources to benefit ruling elites, their armed forces, or extremist clients. They often disregard international law and violate international agreements. Problem states may seek WMD or other destabilizing military capabilities. Some support terrorist activities, including by giving terrorists safe haven.

As recently demonstrated by Libya, however, some problem states may recognize that the pursuit of WMD leaves them less, not more, secure.

Significant non state actors. Countering the military capabilities of state competitors alone cannot guarantee U.S. security. Challenges today emanate from a variety of state and non state sources. The latter are a diverse collection of terrorists, insurgents, paramilitaries, and criminals who seek to undermine the legitimate governance of some states and who challenge the United States and its interests.

ASSUMPTIONS FRAMING THE STRATEGY

This strategy is built on key assumptions about the world, the nature of U.S. strengths and vulnerabilities, and the opportunities and challenges we may see in the coming decade.

Our Strengths:

The United States will continue to enjoy a number of advantages:

- We will retain a resilient network of alliances and partnerships.
- We will have no global peer competitor and will remain unmatched in traditional military capability.
- We will maintain important advantages in other elements of national power-*e.g.*, political, economic, technological, and cultural.
- We will continue to play leading roles on issues of common international concern and will retain influence worldwide.

Our Vulnerabilities

Nevertheless, we have vulnerabilities:

- Our capacity to address global security challenges alone will be insufficient.
- Some allies and partners will decide not to act with us or will lack the capacity to act with us.
- Our leading position in world affairs will continue to breed unease, a degree of resentment, and resistance.
- Our strength as a nation state will continue to be challenged by those who employ a strategy of the weak using international fora, judicial processes, and terrorism.
- We and our allies will be the principal targets of extremism and terrorism.

Natural forces of inertia and resistance to change will constrain military transformation

Our Opportunities

The future also offers opportunities:

- The end of the Cold War and our capacity to influence global events open the prospect for a new and peaceful state system in the world.
- Positive developments in Iraq and Afghanistan strengthen U.S. influence and credibility.
- Problem states themselves will increasingly be vulnerable to the forces of positive political and economic change.
- Many of our key partners want to deepen our security relationships with them.

- New international partners are seeking integration into our system of alliances and partnerships.

Our Challenges

In the framework of the four mature and emerging challenges outlined earlier, we will contend with the following particular challenges:

- Though we have no global peer, we will have competitors and enemies-state and non state.
- Key international actors may choose strategic paths contrary to the interests of the United States.
- Crises related to political stability and governance will pose significant security challenges. Some of these may threaten fundamental interests of the United States, requiring a military response.
- Internationally-even among our closest partners-threats will be perceived differently, and consensus may be difficult to achieve.

An Active Defence

All this necessitates an active defence of the nation and its interests, as explained below and in the *National Military Strategy*.

NATIONAL SECURITY

National security is the requirement to maintain the survival of the state through the use of economic power, diplomacy, power projectionand political power. The concept developed mostly in the United States after World War II. Initially focusing on military might, it now encompasses a broad range of facets, all of which impinge on the non-military or economic security of the nation and the values espoused by the national society. Accordingly, in order to possess national security, a nation needs to possess economic security, energy security,environmental security, etc. Security threats involve not only conventional foes such as other nation-states but also non-state actors such asviolent non-state actors, narcotic cartels, multinational corporations and non-governmental organisations; some authorities include natural disasters and events causing severe environmental damage in this category.

Measures taken to ensure national security include:

- using diplomacy to rally allies and isolate threats
- marshalling economic power to facilitate or compel cooperation
- maintaining effective armed forces
- implementing civil defence and emergency preparedness measures (including anti-terrorism legislation)
- ensuring the resilience and redundancy of critical infrastructure
- using intelligence services to detect and defeat or avoid threats and espionage, and to protect classified information
- using counterintelligence services or secret police to protect the nation from internal threats

DEFINITIONS

There is no single universally accepted definition of *national security*. The variety of definitions provide an overview of the many usages of this concept. The concept still remains ambiguous, having originated from simpler definitions which initially emphasised the freedom from military threat and political coercion to later increase in sophistication and include other forms of non-military security as suited the circumstances of the time.

A typical dictionary definition, in this case from the Macmillan Dictionary (online version), defines the term as "the protection or the safety of a country's secrets and its citizens" emphasising the overall security of a nation and a nation state. Walter Lippmann, in 1943, defined it in terms of war saying that "a nation has security when it does not have to sacrifice its legitimate ínterests to avoid war, and is able, if challenged, to maintain them by war". A later definition by Harold Lasswell, a political scientist, in 1950, looks at national security from almost the same aspect, that of external coercion:

"The distinctive meaning of national security means freedom from foreign dictation." Arnold Wolfers (1960), while recognising the need to segregate the subjectivity of the conceptual idea from the objectivity, talks of threats to *acquired values*:

"An ambiguous symbol meaning different things to different people. National security objectively means the absence of threats to acquired values and subjectively, the absence of fear that such values will be attacked."

The 1996 definition propagated by the National Defence College of India accretes the elements of national power:

"National security is an appropriate and aggressive blend of political resilience and maturity, human resources, economic structure and capacity, technological competence, industrial base and availability of natural resources and finally the military might."

Harold Brown, U.S. Secretary of Defence from 1977 to 1981 in the Carter administration, enlarged the definition of national security by including elements such as economic and environmental security:

"National security then is the ability to preserve the nation's physical integrity and territory; to maintain its economic relations with the rest of the world on reasonable terms; to preserve its nature, institution, and governance from disruption from outside; and to control its borders."

In Harvard University history professor Charles Maier's definition of 1990, national security is defined through the lens of national power:

"National security... is best described as a capacity to control those domestic and foreign conditions that the public opinion of a given community believes necessary to enjoy its own self-determination or autonomy, prosperity and wellbeing." According to Prabhakaran Paleri, author of National Security, Imperatives and Challenges, national security may be defined as:

The measurable state of the capability of a nation to overcome the multi-dimensional threats to the apparent well-being of its people and its survival as a nation-state at any given time, by balancing all instruments of state policy through governance,that can be indexed by computation, empirically or otherwise,and is extendable to global security by variables external to it."

ORIGIN

The origin of the modern concept of "national security" as a philosophy of maintaining a stable nation state can be traced to the Peace of Westphalia, wherein the concept of asovereign state, ruled by a sovereign, became the basis of a new international order of nation states. It was Thomas Hobbes in his 1651 work *Leviathan* who stated that citizens yield to a powerful sovereign who in turn promises an end to civil and religious war, and to bring forth a lasting peace, and give him the right to conduct policy, including wage war or negotiate for peace for the good of the "commonwealth", *i.e.*, a mandate for national security. The Clausewitzian view of diplomacy and war being the instruments of furthering national cause, added to the view of national security being sought by nations by exercising self-interest at all times. This view came to be known as "classical realism" in international relations.

Immanuel Kant, in his 1795 essay "Perpetual Peace: A Philosophical Sketch" (Zum ewigen Frieden. Ein philosophischer Entwurf. (German)), proposed a system where nation-states and dominating national interests were replaced by an enlightened world order, a community of mankind where nation-states subsumed the national interests under the rule of the international law because of rational insight, common good and moral commitment. National security was achieved by this voluntary accession by the leadership to a higher order than the nation-state, *viz.* "international security". Thus was born the "idealism" school of international relations.

As an academic concept, national security can be seen as a recent phenomenon which was first introduced in the United States after World War II, and has to some degree replaced other concepts that describe the struggle of states to overcome various external and internal threats. The term was used during discourse on war, for example, Walter Lippmann in 1943 criticized an unwillingness of political pundits to discuss "the foundations of national security" in a time of peace. However, the earliest mention of the term *national security*, can be traced to 1790 in Yale University in reference to its relation with domestic industries.

ELEMENTS OF NATIONAL SECURITY

As in the case of national power, the military aspect of security is an important, but not the sole, component of national security. To be truly secure, a nation needs other forms of security. Authorities differ in their choice of nation security elements. Besides the military aspect of security, the aspects of diplomacy or politics; society; environment; energy and natural resources; and economics are commonly listed. The elements of national security corelate closely to the concept of the elements of national power. Romm (1993) lists security from narcotic cartels, economic security, environmental security and energy security as the non-military elements of national security.

MILITARY SECURITY

This is traditionally, the earliest recognised form of national security. Military security implies the capability of a nation to defend itself, and/or deter military aggression. Alternatively, military security implies the capability of a nation to enforce its policy choices by use of military force. The term "military security" is considered synonymous with "security" in much of its usage. One of the definitions of security given in the *Dictionary of Military and Associated Terms*, may be considered a definition of "military security":

A condition that results from the establishment and maintenance of protective measures that ensure a state of inviolability from hostile acts or influences.

—Dictionary of Military and Associated Terms

Political Security

The political aspect of security has been offered by Barry Buzan, Ole Wæver, Jaap de Wilde as an important component of national security, Political security is about the stability of the social order. Closely allied to military security and societal security, other components proposed in a framework for national security in their book "Security: a new framework for analysis", it specifically addresses threats to sovereignty. System referent objects are defined, such as nation-states, nations, transnational groups of political importance including tribes, minorities, some religious organisations, systems of states such as the European Union and the United Nations, besides others. Diplomacy, negotiation and other interactions form the means of interaction between the objects,

Economic Security

Historically, conquest of nations has made conquerors rich through plunder, access to new resources and enlarged trade by controlling a conquered nations' economy. In today's complex system of international trade, characterised by multi-national agreements, mutual inter-dependence and availability of natural resources etc., the freedom to exercise choice of policies to develop a nation's economy in the manner desired, invites economic security. Economic security today forms, arguably, as important a part of national security as military security. The creation and protection of jobs that supply defence and non-defence needs are vital to national security. Third world countries are less secure due to lack of employment for their citizens.

Environmental Security

Environmental security deals with environmental issues which threaten the national security of a nation in any manner. The scope and nature of environmental threats to national security and strategies to engage them are a subject of debate.

While all environmental events are not considered significant of being categorised as threats, many transnational issues, both global and regional would affect national security. Romm (1993) classifies these as:

- *Transnational environmental problems that threaten a nation's security, in its broad defined sense.* These include global environmental problems such as climate change due to global warming, deforestation and loss of biodiversity, etc.
- *Environmental or resource problems that threaten a nation's security, traditionally defined.* These would be problems whose outcomes would result in conventional threats to national security as first or higher order outcomes. Such disputes could range from heightened tension or outright conflict due to disputes over water scarcity in the Middle East, to illegal immigration into the United States caused by the failure of agriculture in Mexico. The genocide in Rwanda, indirectly or partly caused by rise in population and dwindling availability of farmland, is an example of the extremity of outcome arising from problems of environmental security.
- *Environmentally threatening outcomes of warfare, e.g.* Romans destroyed the fields of Carthage by pouring salt over them; Saddam Hussein's burning of oil wells in the Gulf War; the use of Agent Orange by the UK in the Malayan Emergency and the USA in the Vietnam War for defoilating forests for military purposes.

Security of Energy and Natural Resources

A resource has been defined as:

"...a support inventory... biotic or abiotic, renewable or expendable,... for sustaining life at a heightened level of well-being."

—Prabhakaran Paleri (2008)

Resources include water, sources of energy, land and minerals. Availability of adequate natural resources is important for a nation to develop its industry and economic power. Lack of resources is a serious challenge for Japan to overcome to increase its national power. In the Persian Gulf War of 1991, fought over economic issues, Iraq capturedKuwait in order to capture its oil wells, among other reasons. Water resources are subject to disputes between many nations, including the two nuclear powers, India andPakistan. Nations attempt to attain energy and natural resource security by acquiring the needed resources by force, negotiation and commerce.

Cybersecurity

Recently, cybersecurity began to be viewed as a pressing national security issue. Electronic information systems are vital for maintaining a national security of any state. Possible unauthorized access to the critical governmental infrastructures by state and non-state entities can create a serious threat and have a negative impact on political, economic and military security of a given nation. In the United States, the Bush Administration in January 2008, initiated the Comprehensive National Cybersecurity Initiative (CNCI). It introduced a differentiated approach, such as: identifying existing and emerging cybersecurity threats, finding and plugging existing cyber vulnerabilities, and apprehending actors that trying to gain access to secure federal information systems. President Obama issued a declaration that the "cyber threat is one of the most serious economic and national security challenges we face as a nation" and that "America's economic prosperity in the 21st century will depend on cybersecurity."

Empowerment of Women

Hillary Clinton has stated that "The countries that threaten regional and global peace are the very places where women and girls are deprived of dignity and opportunity". She has noted that countries where women are oppressed are places where the "rule of law and democracy are struggling to take root" and that when women's rights as equals in society are upheld, the society as a whole changes and improves, which in turn enhances stability in that society, which in turn contributes to global society

COUNTRY-BY-COUNTRY PERSPECTIVES

UNITED KINGDOM

The primary body responsible for coordinating national security policy in the UK is the National Security Council (United Kingdom). It was created in May 2010 by the newcoalition government of the Conservative Party (UK) and Liberal Democrats. The National Security Council is a committee of the Cabinet of the United Kingdom and was created as part of a wider reform of the national security apparatus. The included the creation of a National Security Adviser (United Kingdom) and a National Security Secretariat to support the National Security Council.

UNITED STATES

National Security Act of 1947

The concept of national security became an official guiding principle of foreign policy in the United States when the National Security Act of 1947 was signed on July 26, 1947 byU.S. President Harry S. Truman. As amended in 1949, this Act:

- created important components of American national security, such as the precursor to the Department of Defence);
- subordinated the military branches to the new cabinet level position of Secretary of Defence;
- established the National Security Council and the Central Intelligence Agency;

Notably, the Act did *not* define national security, which was conceivably advantageous, as its ambiguity made it a powerful phrase to invoke whenever issues threatened by other interests of the state, such as domestic concerns, came up for discussion and decision. The notion that national security encompasses more than just military security was present, though understated, from the beginning. The Act established the National Security Council so as to "advise the President on the integration of domestic, military and foreign policies relating to national security".

While not defining the "interests" of national security, the Act does establish, within the National Security Council, the "Committee on Foreign Intelligence", whose duty is to conduct an annual review "identifying the intelligence required to address the national security interests of the United States *as specified by the President*" (emphasis added).

Gen. Maxwell Taylor's essay of 1974 titled "The Legitimate Claims of National Security" has this to say:

The national valuables in this broad sense include current assets and national interests, as well as the sources of strength upon which our future as a nation depends. Some valuables are tangible and earthy; others are spiritual or intellectual. They range widely from political assets such as the Bill of Rights, our political institutions and international friendships, to many economic assets which radiate worldwide from a highly productive domestic economy supported by rich natural resources. It is the urgent need to protect valuables such as these which legitimizes and makes essential the role of national security.

Obama Administration

The U.S. Armed Forces defines national security of the United States in the following manner:

A collective term encompassing both national defence and foreign relations of the United States. Specifically, the condition provided by: a. a military or defence advantage over any foreign nation or group of nations; b. a favorable foreign relations position; or c. a defence posture capable of successfully resisting hostile or destructive action from within or without, overt or covert.

In 2010, the White House included an all-encompassing world-view in a national security strategy which identified "security" as one of the country's "four enduring national interests" that were "inexorably intertwined":

"To achieve the world we seek, the United States must apply our strategic approach in pursuit of four enduring national interests:

- *Security:* The security of the United States, its citizens, and U.S. allies and partners.
- *Prosperity:* A strong, innovative, and growing U.S. economy in an open international economic system that promotes opportunity and prosperity.
- *Values:* Respect for universal values at home and around the world.
- *International Order:* An international order advanced by U.S. leadership that promotes peace, security, and opportunity through stronger cooperation to meet global challenges.

Each of these interests is inextricably linked to the others: no single interest can be pursued in isolation, but at the same time, positive action in one area will help advance all four."

— *National Security Strategy*, Executive Office of the President of the United States (May 2010)

NATIONAL SECURITY STATE

To reflect on institutionalization of new bureaucratic infrastructures and governmental practices in the post-World War II period in the U.S., when a culture of semi-permanent military mobilization brought around the National Security Council, the CIA, the Department of Defence, and the Joint Chiefs of Staff, national-security researchers apply a notion of a *national security state*:

During and after WorldWar II, US leaders expanded the concept of national security and used its terminology for the first time to explain America's relationship to the world. For most of US history, the physical security of the continental United States had not been in jeopardy. But by 1945, this invulnerability was rapidly diminishing with the advent of long-range bombers, atom bombs, and ballistic missiles. A general perception grew that the future would not allow time to mobilize, that preparation would have to become constant. For the first time, American leaders would have to deal with the essential paradox of national security faced by the Roman Empire and subsequent great powers: Si vis pacem, para bellum — If you want peace, prepare for war.

—David Jablonsky

NATIONAL SECURITY AND RIGHTS AND FREEDOMS

The measures nearly universally adopted around the world to maintain national security in the face of the possible threats has led to ongoing dialectic struggle, particularly inliberal democracies, between government authority and civil and human rights. These are natural tensions of the process of maintaining self-determination and sovereignty and keeping the rights and freedoms of individuals.

Although national security measures are imposed to protect society as a whole, many such measures may restrict the rights and freedoms of individuals in society. Where the exercise of national security laws and powers is not subject to good governance, the rule of law, and strict checks and balances, there is a risk that *national security* may simply serve as a pretext for suppressing unfavorable political and social views. Measures which may ostensibly serve a national security purpose, such as mass surveillance, andcensorship of mass media, could ultimately lead to an Orwellian dystopia.

In the United States, the controversial USA Patriot Act and other governmental actions has brought the issues of rights and freedoms to citizen's attention. Among questions raised: to what extent for the sake of national security individual rights and freedoms can be restricted, and how the restriction of civil rights for the sake of national security be justified in an absence of war.

Functional Aspects

Because of the highly competitive nature of nation states and the fluid state of world order, national security preparedness depends as much on routine technical measures and operational procedures as on central decision making. This ranges from information protection to state secrets to weaponry to international negotiation strategies.

Any given national security apparatus runs on combination of management practices and technical capabilities. Emerging issues such as proliferation, failing states, climate change and global terrorism increasingly dominate the reality of competition between nation states. All of these lead to the need to have a clear understanding of the technical issues underlying national security in order to create and sustain the national security institutions that may ultimately affect the future of a nation state.

NUCLEAR WEAPON

A nuclear weapon is an explosive device that derives its destructive force from nuclear reactions, either fission or a combination of fission and fusion. Both reactions release vast quantities of energy from relatively small amounts of matter. The first fission ("atomic") bomb test released the same amount of energy as approximately 20,000 tons of TNT. The firstthermonuclear ("hydrogen") bomb test released the same amount of energy as approximately 10,000,000 tons of TNT.

A thermonuclear weapon weighing little more than 2,400 pounds (1,100 kg) can produce an explosive force comparable to the detonation of more than 1.2 million tons (1.1 million tonnes) of TNT. Thus, even a small nuclear device no larger than traditional bombs can devastate an entire city by blast, fire, and radiation. Nuclear weapons are considered weapons of mass destruction, andtheir use and control have been a major focus of international relations policy since their debut.

As of 2014, only two nuclear weapons have been used in the course of warfare, both times by the United States near the end of World War II. On 6 August 1945, a uranium gun-type fission bomb code-named "Little Boy" was detonated over the Japanese city of Hiroshima. Three days later, on 9 August, a plutonium implosion-type fission bomb code-named "Fat Man" was exploded over the Japanese city ofNagasaki. These two bombings resulted in the deaths of approximately 200,000 civilians and military personnel from acute injuries sustained from the explosions. The role of the bombings in Japan's surrender, and their ethical status, remain the subject of scholarly and popular debate.

Since the bombings of Hiroshima and Nagasaki, nuclear weapons have been detonated on over two thousand occasions for testing purposes and demonstrations. Only a few nations possess such weapons or are suspected of seeking them. The only countries known to have detonated nuclear weapons—and that acknowledge possessing such weapons—are (chronologically by date of first test) the United States, the Soviet Union (succeeded as a nuclear power by Russia), the United Kingdom, France, the People's Republic of China, India, Pakistan, and North Korea. Israel is also widely believed to possess nuclear weapons, though it does not acknowledge having them. One state, South Africa, fabricated nuclear weapons in the past, but as its apartheid regime was coming to an end, it disassembled its arsenal, acceded to the Nuclear Non-Proliferation Treaty, and accepted full-scope international safeguards. The Federation of American Scientists estimates there are more than 17,000 nuclear warheads in the world as of 2012, with around 4,300 of them considered "operational", ready for use.

TYPES

There are two basic types of nuclear weapons: those that derive the majority of their energy from nuclear fission reactions alone, and those that use fission reactions to begin nuclear fusion reactions that produce a large amount of the total energy output.

Fission Weapons

All existing nuclear weapons derive some of their explosive energy from nuclear fission reactions. Weapons whose explosive output is exclusively from fission reactions are commonly referred to as atomic bombs or atom bombs(abbreviated as A-bombs). This has long been noted as something of a misnomer, as their energy comes from the nucleus of the atom, just as it does with fusion weapons.

In fission weapons, a mass of fissile material (enriched uranium or plutonium) is assembled into a supercritical mass—the amount of material needed to start an exponentially growing nuclear chain reaction—either by shooting one piece of sub-critical material into another (the "gun" method) or by compressing using explosive lenses a sub-critical sphere of material using chemical explosives to many times its original density (the "implosion" method). The latter approach is considered more sophisticated than the former and only the latter approach can be used if the fissile material is plutonium.

A major challenge in all nuclear weapon designs is to ensure that a significant fraction of the fuel is consumed before the weapon destroys itself. The amount of energy released by fission bombs can range from the equivalent of just under a ton of TNT, to upwards of 500,000 tons (500 kilotons) of TNT.

All fission reactions necessarily generate fission products, the radioactive remains of the atomic nuclei split by the fission reactions. Many fission products are either highly radioactive (but short-lived) or moderately radioactive (but long-lived), and as such are a serious form of radioactive contamination if not fully contained. Fission products are the principal radioactive component of nuclear fallout.

The most commonly used fissile materials for nuclear weapons applications have been uranium-235 and plutonium-239. Less commonly used has been uranium-233.Neptunium-237 and some isotopes of americium may be usable for nuclear explosives as well, but it is not clear that this has ever been implemented, and even their plausible use in nuclear weapons is a matter of scientific dispute.

Fusion Weapons

The other basic type of nuclear weapon produces a large proportion of its energy in nuclear fusion reactions. Such fusion weapons are generally referred to as thermonuclear weapons or more colloquially as hydrogen bombs (abbreviated as H-bombs), as they rely on fusion reactions between isotopes of hydrogen (deuterium and tritium). All such weapons derive a significant portion, and sometimes a majority, of their energy from fission. This is because a fission weapon is required as a "trigger" for the fusion reactions, and the fusion reactions can themselves trigger additional fission reactions.

Only six countries—United States, Russia, United Kingdom, People's Republic of China, France and India—have conducted thermonuclear weapon tests. (Whether India has detonated a "true", multi-staged thermonuclear weapon is controversial.)Thermonuclear weapons are considered much more difficult to successfully design and execute than primitive fission weapons. Almost all of the nuclear weapons deployed today use the thermonuclear design because it is more efficient.

Thermonuclear bombs work by using the energy of a fission bomb to compress and heat fusion fuel. In the Teller-Ulam design, which accounts for all multi-megaton yield hydrogen bombs, this is accomplished by placing a fission bomb and fusion fuel (tritium, deuterium, or lithium deuteride) in proximity within a special, radiation-reflecting container. When the fission bomb is detonated, gamma rays and X-rays emitted first compress the fusion fuel, then heat it to thermonuclear temperatures. The ensuing fusion reaction creates enormous numbers of high-speed neutrons, which can then induce fission in materials not normally prone to it, such as depleted uranium. Each of these components is known as a "stage", with the fission bomb as the "primary" and the fusion capsule as the "secondary". In large, megaton-range hydrogen bombs, about half of the yield comes from the final fissioning of depleted uranium.

Virtually all thermonuclear weapons deployed today use the "two-stage" design described above, but it is possible to add additional fusion stages—each stage igniting a larger amount of fusion fuel in the next stage. This technique can be used to construct thermonuclear weapons of arbitrarily large yield, in contrast to fission bombs, which are limited in their explosive force. The largest nuclear weapon ever detonated—the Tsar Bomba of the USSR, which released an energy equivalent of over 50 million tons (50 megatons) of TNT—was a three-stage weapon. Most thermonuclear weapons are considerably smaller than this, due to practical constraints from missile warhead space and weight requirements.

Fusion reactions do not create fission products, and thus contribute far less to the creation of nuclear fallout than fission reactions, but because all thermonuclear weapons contain at least one fission stage, and many high-yield thermonuclear devices have a final fission stage, thermonuclear weapons can generate at least as much nuclear fallout as fission-only weapons.

Other Types

There are other types of nuclear weapons as well. For example, a boosted fission weapon is a fission bomb that increases its explosive yield through a small amount of fusion reactions, but it is not a fusion bomb. In the boosted bomb, the neutrons produced by the fusion reactions serve primarily to increase the efficiency of the fission bomb.

Some weapons are designed for special purposes; a neutron bomb is a thermonuclear weapon that yields a relatively small explosion but a relatively large amount of neutron radiation; such a device could theoretically be used to cause massive casualties while leaving infrastructure mostly intact and creating a minimal amount of fallout. The detonation of any nuclear weapon is accompanied by a blast of neutron radiation. Surrounding a nuclear weapon with suitable materials (such as cobalt or gold) creates a weapon known as a salted bomb. This device can produce exceptionally large quantities of radioactive contamination.

Research has been done into the possibility of pure fusion bombs: nuclear weapons that consist of fusion reactions without requiring a fission bomb to initiate them. Such a device might provide a simpler path to thermonuclear weapons than one that required development of fission weapons first, and pure fusion weapons would create significantly less nuclear fallout than other thermonuclear weapons, because they would not disperse fission products. In 1998, the United States Department of Energy divulged that the United States had, "...made a substantial investment" in the past to develop pure fusion weapons, but that, "The U.S. does not have and is not developing a pure fusion weapon", and that, "No credible design for a pure fusion weapon resulted from the DOE investment". Most variation in nuclear weapon design is for the purpose of achieving different yields for different situations, and in manipulating design elements to attempt to minimize weapon size.

Antimatter, which consists of particles resembling ordinary matter particles in most of their properties but having opposite electric charge, has been considered as a trigger mechanism for nuclear weapons. A major obstacle is the difficulty of producing antimatter in large enough quantities, and there is no evidence that it is feasible beyond the military domain. However, the U.S. Air Force funded studies of the physics of antimatter in the Cold War, and began considering its possible use in weapons, not just as a trigger, but as the explosive itself. A fourth generation nuclear weapon design is related to, and relies upon, the same principle as Antimatter-catalyzed nuclear pulse propulsion.

WEAPONS DELIVERY

Nuclear weapons delivery—the technology and systems used to bring a nuclear weapon to its target—is an important aspect of nuclear weapons relating both to nuclear weapon design and nuclear strategy. Additionally, development and maintenance of delivery options is among the most resource-intensive aspects of a nuclear weapons programme: according to one estimate, deployment costs accounted for 57 per cent of the total financial resources spent by the United States in relation to nuclear weapons since 1940.

Historically the first method of delivery, and the method used in the two nuclear weapons used in warfare, was as a gravity bomb, dropped from bomber aircraft. This is usually the first method that countries developed, as it does not place many restrictions on the size of the weapon and *weapon miniaturization*requires considerable weapons design knowledge. It does, however, limit attack range, response time to an impending attack, and the number of weapons that a country can field at the same time.

With the advent of miniaturization, nuclear bombs can be delivered by both strategic bombers and tacticalfighter-bombers, allowing an air force to use its current fleet with little or no modification. This method may still be considered the primary means of nuclear weapons delivery; the majority of U.S. nuclear warheads, for example, are free-fall gravity bombs, namely the B61.

More preferable from a strategic point of view is a nuclear weapon mounted onto a missile, which can use a ballistic trajectory to deliver the warhead over the horizon. Although even short-range missiles allow for a faster and less vulnerable attack, the development of long-range intercontinental ballistic missiles(ICBMs) and submarine-launched ballistic missiles (SLBMs) has given some nations the ability to plausibly deliver missiles anywhere on the globe with a high likelihood of success.

More advanced systems, such as multiple independently targetable Re-entry vehicles (MIRVs), can launch multiple warheads at different targets from one missile, reducing the chance of a successful missile defence. Today, missiles are most common among systems designed for delivery of nuclear weapons. Making a warhead small enough to fit onto a missile, though, can be difficult.

Tactical weapons have involved the most variety of delivery types, including not only gravity bombs and missiles but also artillery shells,land mines, and nuclear depth charges and torpedoes for anti-submarine warfare. An atomic mortar was also tested at one time by the United States. Small, two-man portable tactical weapons (somewhat misleadingly referred to as suitcase bombs), such as the Special Atomic Demolition Munition, have been developed, although the difficulty of combining sufficient yield with portability limits their military utility.

NUCLEAR STRATEGY

Nuclear warfare strategy is a set of policies that deal with preventing or fighting a nuclear war. The policy of trying to prevent an attack by a nuclear weapon from another country by threatening nuclear retaliation is known as the strategy of nuclear deterrence. The goal in deterrence is to always maintain a second strike capability (the ability of a country to respond to a nuclear attack with one of its own) and potentially to strive for first strike status (the ability to completely destroy an enemy's nuclear forces before they could retaliate). During the Cold War, policy and military theorists in nuclear-enabled countries worked out models of what sorts of policies could prevent one from ever being attacked by a nuclear weapon, and developed weapon game theory models that create the greatest and most stable deterrence conditions.

Fig. The now decommissioned United States' Peacekeeper missile was anICBM developed to entirely replace theminuteman missile in the late 1980s. Each missile, like the heavier liftRussian SS-18 Satan, could contain up to ten nuclear warheads (shown in red), each of which could be aimed at a different target. A factor in the development of MIRVs was to make complete missile defence very difficult for an enemy country.

Different forms of nuclear weapons delivery allow for different types of nuclear strategies. The goals of any strategy are generally to make it difficult for an enemy to launch a pre-emptive strike against the weapon system and difficult to defend against the delivery of the weapon during a potential conflict. Sometimes this has meant keeping the weapon locations hidden, such as deploying them on submarines or land mobile transporter erector launchers whose locations are very hard for an enemy to track, and other times, this means protecting them by burying them in hardened missile silo bunkers.

Other components of nuclear strategies have included using missile defence (to destroy the missiles before they land) or implementation of civil defence measures (using early-warning systems to evacuate citizens to safe areas before an attack). Note that weapons designed to threaten large populations, or to generally deter attacks are known as *strategic weapons.* Weapons designed for use on a battlefield in military situations are called *tactical weapons.*

There are critics of the very idea of nuclear strategy for waging nuclear war who have suggested that a nuclear war between two nuclear powers would result in mutual annihilation. From this point of view, the significance of nuclear weapons is purely to deter war because any nuclear war would immediately escalate out of mutual distrust and fear, resulting in mutually assured destruction. This threat of national, if not global, destruction has been a strong motivation for anti-nuclear weapons activism.

Critics from the peace movement and within the military establishment have questioned the usefulness of such weapons in the current military climate. According to an advisory opinion issued by the International Court of Justice in 1996, the use of (or threat of use of) such weapons would generally be contrary to the rules of international law applicable in armed conflict, but the court did not reach an opinion as to whether or not the threat or use would be lawful in specific extreme circumstances such as if the survival of the state were at stake.

Another deterrence position in nuclear strategy is that nuclear proliferation can be desirable. This view argues that, unlike conventional weapons, nuclear weapons successfully deter all-out war between states, and they succeeded in doing this during the Cold War between the U.S. and the Soviet Union. In the late 1950s and early 1960s, Gen. Pierre Marie Gallois of France, an adviser to Charles DeGaulle, argued in books like *The Balance of Terror: Strategy for the Nuclear Age* (1961) that mere possession of a nuclear arsenal, what the French called the *force de frappe*, was enough to ensure deterrence, and thus concluded that the spread of nuclear weapons could increase international stability. Some very prominent neo-realist scholars, such as the late Kenneth Waltz, formerly a Political Science at UC Berkeley and Adjunct Senior Research Scholar atColumbia University, and John Mearsheimer of University of Chicago, have also argued along the lines of Gallois. Specifically, these scholars have advocated some forms of nuclear proliferation, arguing that it would decrease the likelihood of total war, especially in troubled regions of the world where there exists a unipolar nuclear weapon state. Aside from the public opinion that opposes proliferation in any form, there are two schools of thought on the matter: those, like Mearsheimer, who favour selective proliferation,and those of Kenneth Waltz, who was somewhat more non-interventionist.

The threat of potentially suicidal terrorists possessing nuclear weapons (a form of nuclear terrorism) complicates the decision process. The prospect of mutually assured destruction may not deter an enemy who expects to die in the confrontation. Further, if the initial act is from a stateless terrorist instead of a sovereign nation, there is no fixed nation or fixed military targets to retaliate against. It has been argued by the New York Times, especially after the September 11, 2001 attacks, that this complication is the sign of the next age of nuclear strategy, distinct from the relative stability of the Cold War. In 1996, the United States adopted a policy of allowing the targeting of its nuclear weapons at terrorists armed with weapons of mass destruction.

Robert Gallucci, president of the John D. and Catherine T. MacArthur Foundation, argues that although traditional deterrence is not an effective approach towards terrorist groups bent on causing a nuclear catastrophe, Gallucci believes that "the United States should instead consider a policy of expanded deterrence, which focuses not solely on the would-be nuclear terrorists but on those states that may deliberately transfer or inadvertently lead nuclear weapons and materials to them. By threatening retaliation against those states, the United States may be able to deter that which it cannot physically prevent.".

Graham Allison makes a similar case, arguing that the key to expanded deterrence is coming up with ways of tracing nuclear material to the country that forged the fissile material. "After a nuclear bomb detonates, nuclear forensics cops would collect debris samples and send them to a laboratory for radiological analysis. By identifying unique attributes of the fissile material, including its impurities and contaminants, one could trace the path back to its origin." The process is analogous to identifying a criminal by fingerprints. "The goal would be twofold: first, to deter leaders of nuclear states from selling weapons to terrorists by holding them accountable for any use of their own weapons; second, to give leader every incentive to tightly secure their nuclear weapons and materials."

GOVERNANCE, CONTROL, AND LAW

Because of the immense military power they can confer, the political control of nuclear weapons has been a key issue for as long as they have existed; in most countries the use of nuclear force can only be authorized by the head of government or head of state.

In the late 1940s, lack of mutual trust was preventing the United States and the Soviet Union from making ground towards international arms control agreements. The Russell–Einstein Manifesto was issued in London on July 9,

1955 by Bertrand Russell in the midst of the Cold War. It highlighted the dangers posed by nuclear weapons and called for world leaders to seek peaceful resolutions to international conflict. The signatories included eleven pre-eminent intellectuals and scientists, including Albert Einstein, who signed it just days before his death on April 18, 1955. A few days after the release, philanthropist Cyrus S. Eaton offered to sponsor a conference—called for in the manifesto—in Pugwash, Nova Scotia, Eaton's birthplace. This conference was to be the first of the Pugwash Conferences on Science and World Affairs, held in July 1957.

By the 1960s steps were being taken to limit both the proliferation of nuclear weapons to other countries and the environmental effects ofnuclear testing. The Partial Test Ban Treaty (1963) restricted all nuclear testing to underground nuclear testing, to prevent contamination from nuclear fallout, whereas the Nuclear Non-Proliferation Treaty (1968) attempted to place restrictions on the types of activities signatories could participate in, with the goal of allowing the transference of non-military nuclear technology to member countries without fear of proliferation.

In 1957, the International Atomic Energy Agency (IAEA) was established under the mandate of the United Nations to encourage development of peaceful applications for nuclear technology, provide international safeguards against its misuse, and facilitate the application of safety measures in its use. In 1996, many nations signed the Comprehensive Test Ban Treaty, which prohibits all testing of nuclear weapons. A testing ban imposes a significant hindrance to nuclear arms development by any complying country. The Treaty requires the ratification by 44 specific states before it can go into force; as of 2012, the ratification of eight of these states is still required.

Additional treaties and agreements have governed nuclear weapons stockpiles between the countries with the two largest stockpiles, the United States and the Soviet Union, and later between the United States and Russia. These include treaties such as SALT II (never ratified), START I (expired), INF, START II (never ratified), SORT, and New START, as well as non-binding agreements such as SALT I and the Presidential Nuclear Initiatives of 1991. Even when they did not enter into force, these agreements helped limit and later reduce the numbers and types of nuclear weapons between the United States and the Soviet Union/Russia.

Nuclear weapons have also been opposed by agreements between countries. Many nations have been declared Nuclear-Weapon-Free Zones, areas where nuclear weapons production and deployment are prohibited, through the use of treaties. The Treaty of Tlatelolco (1967) prohibited any production or deployment of nuclear weapons in Latin America and the Caribbean, and the Treaty of Pelindaba (1964) prohibits nuclear weapons in many African countries. As recently as 2006 a Central Asian Nuclear Weapon Free Zone was established amongst the former Soviet republics of Central Asia prohibiting nuclear weapons. In the middle of 1996, the International Court of Justice, the highest court of the United Nations, issued an Advisory Opinion concerned with the "Legality of the Threat or Use of Nuclear Weapons". The court ruled that the use or threat of use of nuclear weapons would violate various articles of international law, including the Geneva Conventions, theHague Conventions, the UN Charter, and the Universal Declaration of Human Rights. In view of the unique, destructive characteristics of nuclear weapons, the International Committee of the Red Cross calls on States to ensure that these weapons are never used, irrespective of whether they consider them lawful or not.

Additionally, there have been other, specific actions meant to discourage countries from developing nuclear arms. In the wake of the tests by India and Pakistan in 1998, economic sanctions were (temporarily) levied against both countries, though neither were signatories with the Nuclear Non-Proliferation Treaty. One of the stated *casus belli* for the initiation of the 2003 Iraq War was an accusation by the United States that Iraq was actively pursuing nuclear arms (though this was soon discovered not to be the case as the programme had been discontinued). In 1981, Israel had bombed a nuclear reactor being constructed in Osirak, Iraq, in what it called an attempt to halt Iraq's previous nuclear arms ambitions; in 2007, Israel bombed another reactor being constructed in Syria.

In 2013, Mark Diesendorf says that governments of France, India, North Korea, Pakistan, UK, and South Africa have used nuclear power and/or research reactors to assist nuclear weapons development or to contribute to their supplies of nuclear explosives from military reactors.

Disarmament

Nuclear disarmament refers to both the act of reducing or eliminating nuclear weapons and to the end state of a nuclear-free world, in which nuclear weapons are completely eliminated.

Beginning with the 1963 Partial Test Ban Treaty and continuing through the 1996 Comprehensive Test Ban Treaty, there have been many treaties to limit or reduce nuclear weapons testing and stockpiles. The 1968 Nuclear Non Proliferation Treaty has as one of its explicit conditions that all signatories must "pursue negotiations in good faith" towards the long-term goal of "complete disarmament". The nuclear weapon states have largely treated that aspect of the agreement as "decorative" and without force.

Only one country—South Africa—has ever fully renounced nuclear weapons they had independently developed. The former Soviet republics of Belarus, Kazakhstan, and Ukraine returned Soviet nuclear arms stationed in their countries to Russia after the collapse of the USSR.

Proponents of nuclear disarmament say that it would lessen the probability of nuclear war occurring, especially accidentally. Critics of nuclear disarmament say that it would undermine the present nuclear peace and deterrence and would lead to increased global instability. Various American elder statesmen, who were in office during the Cold War period, have been advocating the elimination of nuclear weapons. These officials include Henry Kissinger, George Shultz, Sam Nunn, and William Perry. In January 2010, Lawrence M. Krauss stated that "no issue carries more importance to the long-term health and security of humanity than the effort to reduce, and perhaps one day, rid the world of nuclear weapons". In the years after the end of the Cold War, there have been numerous campaigns to urge the abolition of nuclear weapons, such as that organized by the Global Zero movement, and the goal of a "world without nuclear weapons" was advocated by United States PresidentBarack Obama in an April 2009 speech in Prague. A CNN poll from April 2010 indicated that the American public was nearly evenly split on the issue.

Some analysts have argued that nuclear weapons have made the world relatively safer, with peace through deterrence and through thestability–instability paradox, including in south Asia. Kenneth Waltz has argued that nuclear weapons have helped keep an uneasy peace, and further nuclear weapon proliferation might even help avoid the large scale conventional wars that were so common prior to their invention at the end of World War II. But former Secretary Henry Kissinger says there is a new danger, which cannot be addressed by deterrence: "The classical notion of deterrence was that there was some consequences before which aggressors and evildoers would recoil. In a world of suicide bombers, that calculation doesn't operate in any comparable way". George Shultz has said, "If you think of the people who are doing suicide attacks, and people like that get a nuclear weapon, they are almost by definition not deterrable".

United Nations

The UN Office for Disarmament Affairs (UNODA) is a department of the United Nations Secretariat established in January 1998 as part of the United Nations Secretary-GeneralKofi Annan's plan to reform the UN as presented in his report to the General Assembly in July 1997.

Its goal is to promote nuclear disarmament and non-proliferation and the strengthening of the disarmament regimes in respect to other weapons of mass destruction, chemicaland biological weapons. It also promotes disarmament efforts in the area of conventional weapons, especially land mines and small arms, which are often the weapons of choice in contemporary conflicts.

CONTROVERSY

Ethics

Even before the first nuclear weapons had been developed, scientists involved with the Manhattan Project were divided over the use of the weapon. The role of the two atomic bombings of the country in Japan's surrender and the U.S.'s ethical justification for them has been the subject of scholarly and popular debate for decades. The question of whether nations should have nuclear weapons, or test them, has been continually and nearly universally controversial.

Notable nuclear weapons accidents

- February 13, 1950: a Convair B-36B crashed in northern British Columbia after jettisoning a Mark IV atomic bomb. This was the first such nuclear weapon loss in history.
- 7 June 1960: the 1960 Fort Dix IM-99 accident destroyed a Boeing CIM-10 Bomarc nuclear missile and shelter and contaminated the BOMARC Missile Accident Site in New Jersey.
- 24 January 1961: the 1961 Goldsboro B-52 crash occurred near Goldsboro, North Carolina. A B-52 Stratofortress carrying two Mark 39 nuclear bombs broke up in mid-air, dropping its nuclear payload in the process.
- 1965 Philippine Sea A-4 crash, where a Skyhawk attack aircraft with a nuclear weapon fell into the sea. The pilot, the aircraft, and the B43 nuclear bomb were never recovered. It was not until the 1980s that the Pentagon revealed the loss of the one-megaton bomb.
- January 17, 1966: the 1966 Palomares B-52 crash occurred when a B-52G bomber of the USAF collided with a KC-135 tanker during mid-air refuelling off the coast of Spain. The KC-135 was completely destroyed when its fuel load ignited, killing all four crew members. The B-52G broke apart, killing three of the seven crew members aboard.Of the four Mk28 type hydrogen bombs the B-52G carried, three were found on land near Almería, Spain. The non-nuclear explosives in two of the weapons detonated upon impact with the ground, resulting in the contamination of a 2-square-kilometer (490-acre) (0.78 square mile) area by radioactive plutonium. The fourth, which fell into the Mediterranean Sea, was recovered intact after a 2½-month-long search.
- January 21, 1968: the 1968 Thule Air Base B-52 crash involved a United States Air Force (USAF) B-52 bomber. The aircraft was carrying four hydrogen bombs when a cabin fire forced the crew to abandon the aircraft. Six crew members ejected safely, but one who did not have an ejection seat was killed while trying to bail out. The bomber crashed onto sea ice in Greenland, causing the nuclear payload to rupture and disperse, which resulted in widespread radioactive contamination.

Nuclear fallout

Over 500 atmospheric nuclear weapons tests were conducted at various sites around the world from 1945 to 1980. Radioactive fallout from nuclear weapons testing was first drawn to public attention in 1954 when the Castle

Bravo hydrogen bomb test at the Pacific Proving Grounds contaminated the crew and catch of the Japanese fishing boat *Lucky Dragon*. One of the fishermen died in Japan seven months later, and the fear of contaminated tuna led to a temporary boycotting of the popular staple in Japan. The incident caused widespread concern around the world, especially regarding the effects of nuclear fallout and atmospheric nuclear testing, and "provided a decisive impetus for the emergence of the anti-nuclear weapons movement in many countries".

As public awareness and concern mounted over the possible health hazards associated with exposure to the nuclear fallout, various studies were done to assess the extent of the hazard. A Centers for Disease Control and Prevention/ National Cancer Institute study claims that fallout from atmospheric nuclear tests would lead to perhaps 11,000 excess deaths amongst people alive during atmospheric testing in the United States from all forms of cancer, including leukemia, from 1951 to well into the 21st century.As of March 2009, the U.S. is the only nation that compensates nuclear test victims. Since the Radiation Exposure Compensation Act of 1990, more than $1.38 billion in compensation has been approved. The money is going to people who took part in the tests, notably at the Nevada Test Site, and to others exposed to the radiation.

Public opposition

Peace movements emerged in Japan and in 1954 they converged to form a unified "Japanese Council Against Atomic and Hydrogen Bombs". Japanese opposition to nuclear weapons tests in the Pacific Ocean was widespread, and "an estimated 35 million signatures were collected on petitions calling for bans on nuclear weapons".

In the United Kingdom, the first Aldermaston March organised by the Campaign for Nuclear Disarmament(CND) took place at Easter 1958, when, according to the CND, several thousand people marched for four days from Trafalgar Square, London, to the Atomic Weapons Research Establishment close to Aldermaston in Berkshire, England, to demonstrate their opposition to nuclear weapons. The Aldermaston marches continued into the late 1960s when tens of thousands of people took part in the four-day marches.

In 1959, a letter in the *Bulletin of Atomic Scientists* was the start of a successful campaign to stop the Atomic Energy Commission dumpingradioactive waste in the sea 19 kilometres from Boston. In 1962, Linus Pauling won the Nobel Peace Prize for his work to stop the atmospheric testing of nuclear weapons, and the "Ban the Bomb" movement spread.

In 1963, many countries ratified the Partial Test Ban Treaty prohibiting atmospheric nuclear testing. Radioactive fallout became less of an issue and the anti-nuclear weapons movement went into decline for some years. A resurgence of interest occurred amid European and Americanfears of nuclear war in the 1980s.

COSTS AND TECHNOLOGY SPIN-OFFS

According to an audit by the Brookings Institution, between 1940 and 1996, the U.S. spent $8.75 trillion in present day terms on nuclear weapons programmes. 57 percent of which was spent on building nuclear weapons delivery systems. 6.3 percent of the total, $549 billion in present day terms, was spent on environmental remediation and nuclear waste management, for example cleaning up theHanford site, and 7 percent of the total, $615 billion was spent on making nuclear weapons themselves.

NON-WEAPONS USES

Civil Engineering and Energy Production

Fig. The 1962 Sedan nuclear testformed a crater 100 m (330 ft) deep with a diameter of about 390 m (1,300 ft), as a means of investigating the possibilities of using peaceful nuclear explosions for large-scale earth moving. The 140 kiloton Soviet Chagan (nuclear test), comparable in yield to the Sedan test of 104 kt, formed Lake Chagan, reportedly used as a watering hole for cattle and human swimming.

Apart from their use as weapons, nuclear explosives have been tested and used for various non-military uses. These have included large-scale earth moving and the creation of artificial bays. Due to the inability of the physicists to reduce the fission fraction of small, approximately 1 kiloton, yield nuclear devices that would have been required for many civil engineering projects, when long term health and clean-up costs from fission products were included in the cost, there was virtually no economic advantage over conventional explosives, except for potentially the very largest of projects.

At the peak of the Atomic Age, the United States Federal government initiated Operation Plowshare, involving "peaceful nuclear explosions". The United States Atomic Energy Commission chairman announced that the

Plowshares project was intended to "highlight the peaceful applications of nuclear explosive devices and thereby create a climate of world opinion that is more favorable to weapons development and tests". The Operation Plowshare programme included 27 nuclear tests designed towards investigating these non-weapons uses from 1961 through 1973.

The Qattara Depression Project, as developed by Professor Friedrich Bassler who during his appointment to the West German ministry of economics in 1968 put forth a plan to create a Saharan lake and hydroelectric power station by blasting a tunnel between the Mediterranean sea and the Qattara Depression in Egypt, an area that lies below sea level.

The core problem of the entire project was the water supply to the depression. Calculations by Bassler showed that digging a canal or tunnel would be too expensive, therefore Bassler determined that the use of nuclear explosive devices, to excavate the canal or tunnel, would be the most economical. The Egyptian government declined to pursue the idea.

The Soviet Union's Nuclear Explosions for the National Economy was a programme in the Soviet Union that investigated non-weapons uses of nuclear explosions. These included one 30 kiloton explosion being used to close the Uzbekistani *Urtabulak* gas well in 1966 that had been blowing since 1963, and a few months later a 47 kiloton explosive was used to seal a higher pressure blowout at the nearby *Pamuk*gas field.

The public records for devices that produced the highest proportion of their yield via fusion-only reactions are possibly the Soviet peaceful nuclear explosions of the 1970s, with 98 per cent of their 15 kiloton explosive yield being derived from fusion reactions, a total fission fraction of 0.3 kilotons in a 15 kt device.

The repeated detonation of nuclear devices underground in salt domes, in a somewhat analogous manner to the explosions that power a car internal combustion engine(in that it would be a heat engine) has also been proposed as a means of fusion power, in what is termed PACER. Other investigated uses for peaceful nuclear explosions were underground detonations to stimulate, by a process analogous to fracking, the flow of petroleum and natural gas in tight formations, this was most developed in the Soviet Union, with an increase in the production of many well heads being reported.

Physics

The discovery and synthesis of new chemical elements by nuclear transmutation, and their production in the necessary quantities to allow the studying of their properties, was carried out in nuclear explosive device testing. For example, the discovery of the short lived einsteinium andfermium, both created under the intense neutron flux environment within thermonuclear explosions, followed the first Teller-Ulam thermonuclear device test - Ivy Mike. The rapid capture of so many neutrons required in the synthesis of einsteinium would provide the needed direct experimental confirmation of the so-called r-process, the multiple neutron absorptions needed to explain the cosmic nucleosynthesis (production) of all heavy chemical elements heavier than nickel on the periodic table, in supernova explosions, before beta decay, with the r-process explaining the existence of many stable elements in the universe.

The worldwide presence of new isotopes from atmospheric testing beginning in the 1950s led to the 2008 development of a reliable way to detect art forgeries. Paintings created after that period may contain traces of caesium-137 and strontium-90, isotopes that did not exist in nature before 1945. (Fission products were produced in the natural nuclear fission reactor at Oklo about 1.7 billion years ago, but these decayed away before the earliest known human painting.)

Both climatology and particularly aerosol science, a subfield of atmospheric science, were largely created to answer the question of how far and wide fallout would travel.

Similar to radioactive tracers used in hydrology and materials testing, fallout and the neutron activation of nitrogen gas served as a radioactive tracer that was used to measure and then help model global circulations in the atmosphere by following the movements of fallout aerosols.

After the Van Allen Belts surrounding Earth were published about in 1958, James Van Allen suggested that a nuclear detonation would be one way of probing the magnetic phenomenon, data obtained from the August 1958 Project Argus test shots, a high altitude nuclear explosioninvestigation, were vital to the early understanding of Earth's magnetosphere.

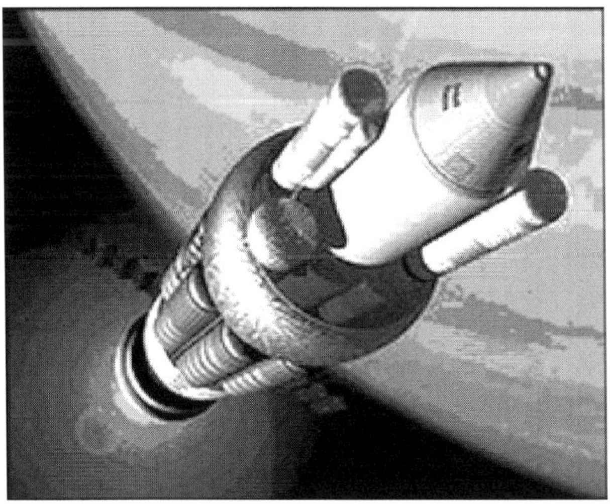

Fig. An artist's conception of the NASAreference design for the Project Orionspacecraft powered by nuclear pulse propulsion.

Soviet nuclear physicist and Nobel peace prize recipient Andrei Sakharov also proposed the idea that earthquakes could be mitigated and particle accelerators could be made by utilizing nuclear explosions, with the latter created by connecting a nuclear explosive device with another of his inventions, the explosively pumped flux compression generator, to accelerate protons to collide with each other to probe their inner workings, an endeavor that is now done at much lower energy levels with non-explosive superconducting magnets in CERN.

Sakharov suggested to replace the copper coil in his MK generators by a big superconductor solenoid to magnetically compress and focus underground nuclear explosions into a shaped charge effect. He theorized this could focus 10 positively chargedprotons per second on a 1 mm surface, then envisaged making two such beams collide in the form of a supercollider.

Underground nuclear explosive data from peaceful nuclear explosion test shots have been used to investigate the composition of Earth'smantle, analogous to the exploration geophysics practice of mineral prospecting with chemical explosives in "deep seismic sounding"reflection seismology.

Project A119, proposed in the 1960s, which as Apollo scientist Gary Latham explained, would have been the detonating of a "smallish" nuclear device on the Moon in order to facilitate research into its geologic make-up. Analogous in concept to the comparatively low yield explosion created by the water prospecting (LCROSS)Lunar Crater Observation and Sensing Satellite mission, which launched in 2009 and released the "Centaur" kinetic energy impactor, an impactor with a mass of 2,305 kg (5,081 lb), and an impact velocity of about 9,000 km/h (5,600 mph), releasing the kinetic energy equivalent of detonating approximately 2 tons of TNT (8.86 GJ).

Propulsion use

Although likely never achieving orbit due to aerodynamic drag, the first macroscopic object to obtain Earth orbital velocity was a "manhole cover" propelled by the detonation of test shot Pascal-B, before sputnik obtained orbital velocity, and also successfully became the first satellite, in October 1957. The use of a subterranean shaft and nuclear device to propel an object to escape velocity has since been termed a "thunder well".

The direct use of nuclear explosives, by using the impact of propellant plasma from a nuclear shaped charge acting on a pusher plate, has also been seriously studied as a potential propulsion mechanism for space travel.

Edward Teller, in the United States, proposed the use of a nuclear detonation to power an explosively pumped *soft* X-ray laser as a component of a ballistic missile defence shield, this would destroy missile components by transferring momentum to the vehicles surface by laser ablation. This ablation process is one of the damage mechanisms of a laser weapon, but it is also the basis of pulsed laser propulsion for spacecraft.

Ground flight testing by Professor Leik Myrabo, using a non-nuclear, conventionally powered pulsed laser test-bed, successfully lifted a lightcraft72 meters in altitude by a method similar to ablative laser propulsion in 2000. A powerful solar system based *soft* X-ray, to ultraviolet, laser system has been calculated to be capable of propelling an interstellar spacecraft, by the light sail principle, to 11 per cent of the speed of light. In 1972 it was also calculated that a 1 Terawatt, 1-km diameter x-ray laser with 1 angstrom wavelength impinging on a 1-km diameter sail, could propel a spacecraft to Alpha Centauri in 10 years.

Asteroid impact avoidance

A proposed means of averting an asteroid impacting with Earth, assuming low lead times between detection and Earth impact, is to detonate one, or a series, of nuclear explosive devices, on, in, or in a stand-off proximity orientation with the asteroid, with the latter method occurring far enough away from the incoming threat to prevent the potential fracturing of the near-Earth object, but still close enough to generate a high thrust laser ablation effect.

A 2007 NASA analysis of impact avoidance strategies using various technologies stated:

Nuclear stand-off explosions are assessed to be 10-100 times more effective than the non-nuclear alternatives analyzed in this study. Other techniques involving the surface or subsurface use of nuclear explosives may be more efficient, but they run an increased risk of fracturing the target near-Earth object. They also carry higher development and operations risks.

Analysis of the uncertainty involved in nuclear device asteroid deflection shows that the ability to protect the planet does not imply the ability to also target the planet, which is the case with all non-nuclear alternatives, such as the controversial gravity tractor technology.

A nuclear explosion that changed an asteroid's velocity by 10 m/s (±20 per cent) would be adequate to push it out of an Earth-impacting orbit. However, if the uncertainty of the velocity change is more than a few plus or minus percent, there would be no chance of directing the asteroid to a particular target.

However, if the need arises to use nuclear explosive devices to prevent an asteroid impact event, it may face the legal issue that theUnited Nations Committee on the Peaceful Uses of Outer Space and the 1996 Comprehensive Nuclear-Test-Ban Treaty ban nuclear weapons in space.

INDIAN BALLISTIC MISSILE DEFENCE PROGRAMME

The Indian Ballistic Missile Defence Programme is an initiative to develop and deploy a multi-layered ballistic missile defencesystem to protect India from ballistic missile attacks.

Introduced in light of the ballistic missile threat from Pakistan and China, it is a double-tiered system consisting of two interceptor missiles, namely the Prithvi Air Defence (PAD) missile for high altitude interception, and the Advanced Air Defence (AAD) Missile for lower altitude interception. The two-tiered shield should be able to intercept any incoming missile launched 5,000 kilometres away.

Fig. Launching of Advanced Air Defence (AAD) missile

PAD was tested in November 2006, followed by AAD in December 2007. With the test of the PAD missile, India became the fourth country to have successfully developed an Anti-ballistic missile system, after United States, Russia, Israel. On 6 March 2009, India again successfully tested its missile defence shield, during which an incoming "enemy" missile was intercepted at an altitude of 75 km.

BACKGROUND

Since the early 90s, India has faced the threat of ballistic missile attacks from Pakistan against which it has fought multiple wars in the past and also from China. With the heightening of tensions in the region, and in response to Pakistan's deployment of M-11 missiles bought from China, in August 1995, the Indian Government procured six batteries of Russian S-300 Surface-to-air missiles to protect New Delhi and other cities.

In May 1998, India for the second time (since its first test in 1974) tested nuclear weapons, followed by Pakistan with its first ever nuclear test. With Pakistan's testing of nuclear weapons and missile delivery systems, this threat intensified. India has also developed and tested missile delivery systems.

In 1999, the Kargil War between India and Pakistan became the first direct conflict between two declared nuclear powers. As the war progressed, the first hint of the possible use of a nuclear weapon was on 31 May, when Pakistani foreign secretary Shamshad Ahmad made a statement warning that an escalation of the limited conflict could lead Pakistan to use "any weapon" in its arsenal.

This was immediately interpreted as an obvious threat of a nuclear retaliation by Pakistan in the event of an extended war. The leader ofPakistan's senate noted that "the purpose of developing weapons becomes meaningless if they are not used when they are needed." Some experts believe that following nuclear tests in 1998, Pakistani military was emboldened by its nuclear deterrent cover to markedly increase coercion against India.

Development of an anti-ballistic missile system began in late 1999, suggesting that India initiated the programme in light of Pakistan's eschewing of a nuclear No first usepolicy and heightened tensions during the Kargil war including a possibility of full scale nuclear war.

DEVELOPMENT

Phase 1

Development of the anti-ballistic missile system began in 1999. Around 40 public and private companies were involved in the development of the systems. They include Bharat Electronics Ltd and Bharat Dynamics Ltd, Astra Microwave, ASL, Larsen and Toubro, Vem Technologies Private Limited and KelTech. Development of the LRTR and MFCR (Multi-function Fire Control Radar) was led by Electronics and Radar Development Establishment (LRDE).

Defence Research and Development Laboratory (DRDL) developed the mission control software for the AAD missile. Research Centre, Imarat (RCI) developed navigation, electromechanical actuation systems and the active radar seeker. Advanced System Laboratory (ASL) provided the motors, jet vanes and structures for the AAD and PAD. High Energy Materials Research Laboratory (HEMRL) supplied the propellants for the missile.

Description

The two-tiered BMD System consists of the PAD, which will intercept missiles at exo-atmospheric altitudes of 50-80 km and the AAD missile for interception at endoatmospheric altitudes of up to 30 km. The deployed system would consist of many launch vehicles, radars, Launch Control Centres (LCC) and the Mission Control Centre (MCC). All these are geographically distributed and connected by a secure communication network.

The MCC is the software intensive system of the ballistic missile defence system. It receives information from various sources such as radars and satellites which is then processed by ten computers which run simultaneously. The MCC is connected to all other elements of the defence through a WAN. MCC performs target classification, target assignment and kill assessment. It also acts as a decision support system for the commander. It can also decide the number of interceptors required for the target for an assured kill probability.

After performing all these functions, the MCC assigns the target to the LCC of a launch battery. The LCC starts computing the time to launch the interceptor based upon information received from a radar based on the speed, altitude and flight path of the target. LCC prepares the missile for launch in real time and carries out ground guidance computation.

After the interceptor is launched, it is provided target information from the radar through a datalink. When the interceptors close onto the target missile, it activates the radar seeker to search for the target missile and guides itself to intercept the target. Multiple PAD and AAD interceptors can be launched against a target for high kill probability.

Prithvi Air Defence (PAD) / Pradyumna Ballistic Missile Interceptor

The Prithvi Air Defence (PAD) is an anti-ballistic missile developed to intercept incoming ballistic missiles outside the atmosphere (exo-atmospheric). Based on the Prithvi missile, PAD is a two-stage missile with a maximum interception altitude of 80 km (50 mi). The first stage is a Solid fuelled motor while the second stage is Liquid fuelled. It has manoeuvre thrusters which can generate a lateral acceleration of more than 5 *g*s at 50 km (31 mi) altitude. Guidance is provided by an intertial navigation system with mid-course updates from LRTR and active radar homing in the terminal phase. PAD has capability to engage the 300 to 2,000 km (190 to 1,240 mi) class of ballistic missiles at a speed of Mach 5.

LRTR is the target acquisition and fire control radar for the PAD missile. It is an active phased array radar having capability to track 200 targets at a range of 600 km (370 mi). The PAD missile has also been called *Pradyumna*.

Further development led to the improvement of the interception range to the 80 to 50 km (50 to 31 mi) range. The improved missile will utilise a gimbaled directional warhead, a technology that until now has only been used by the US and Russia. This technology allows for a smaller warhead to destroy the target missile.

Prithvi Air Defence Exercise

The PADE (Prithvi Air Defence Exercise) was conducted on November 2006 in which a PAD missile successfully intercepted a modified Prithvi-II Missile at an altitude of 50 km (31 mi). The Prithvi-II ballistic missile was modified successfully to mimic the trajectory of M-11 missiles.

DRDO plans to test the anti-ballistic shield against missiles with a range of 1,500 km (930 mi). The test will be conducted with a modified Prithvi missile launched from a naval ship and the anti-ballistic missile launched from Wheeler Island. The interception of the target missile will take place at approximately 80 km (50 mi) altitude.

On 6 March 2009 DRDO carried out a second successful test of the PAD interceptor missile. The target used was ship launched Dhanush missile which followed the trajectory of a missile with range of a 1,500 km (930 mi). The target was tracked by Swordfish (LRTR) radar and destroyed by the PAD at 75 km (47 mi) altitude.

On 6 March 2011 DRDO successfully test-fired interceptor missile from Advanced Air Defence (AAD) which destroyed a 'hostile' target ballistic missile, a modified Prithvi, at an altitude of 16 km over the Bay of Bengal. Advanced Air Defence (AAD) missile positioned at Wheeler Island, about 70 km across sea from Chandipur, received signals from tracking radars installed along the coastline and travelled through the sky at a speed of 4.5 Mach to destroy it.

Advanced Air Defence (AAD)/Ashwin Ballistic Missile Interceptor

Advanced Air Defence (AAD) is an anti-ballistic missile designed to intercept incoming ballistic missiles in the endo-atmosphere at an altitude of 30 km (19 mi).

AAD is a single-stage, solid-fuelled missile. Guidance is similar to that of PAD: it has an inertial navigation system, midcourse updates from ground based radar and active radar homing in the terminal phase. It is 7.5 m (25 ft) tall, weighs around 1.2 t (1.2 long tons; 1.3 short tons) and a diameter of less than 0.5 m (1 ft 8 in).

On 6 December 2007, AAD successfully intercepted a modified Prithvi-II missile acting as an incoming ballistic missile enemy target.

The endo-atmospheric interception was carried out at an altitude of 15 km (9.3 mi). The interceptor and all the elements performed in a copy book fashion validating the endo-atmospheric layer of the defence system. The launch was also shown through a video link at a control room of DRDO at Bhawan, Delhi.

The sequence of events of the test was as follows. At 11 am the Prithvi missile lifted off from Launch Complex III at the Integrated Test Range (ITR) at Chandipur Odisha. Radars at Konark, Paradip detected the missile and were continuously tracking it.

The target information was sent to MCC for further processing. MCC classified the target, calculated the trajectory of the missile and assigned the target to a AAD battery located on Wheeler Island, 70 km (43 mi) across the sea from Chandipur. The AAD was launched when the Prithvi reached an apogee of 110 km (68 mi). The AAD with the help of midcourse updates and its terminal seeker manoeuvres itself towards the target. AAD makes a direct hit at an altitude of 15 km (9.3 mi) and at a speed of Mach 4. Radars detected formation of a large number of tracks, signifying that the target had broken into multiple pieces. The thermal cameras located on Wheeler Island also picked up the direct hit through thermal images.

Due to two successful interceptor missile tests carried out by India, the scientists have said that the AAD missile could be modified into a new extended range (up to 150 km (93 mi)) surface-to-air missile that could be possibly named as 'Ashvin'.

On 15 March 2010, AAD interceptor missile test from the Odisha coast on Monday was aborted, as the target missile deviated from its path and plunged into the sea.

The AAD missile was to intercept the target at an altitude of 15 to 20 km over the sea. The target, a Prithvi missile, fired at 10:02 am from a mobile launcher from the Integrated Test Range Complex-3 at Chandipur-on-Sea, 15 km from here, deviated from its trajectory after travelling about 11 km and fell into the sea.

On 26 July 2010, AAD was successfully test-fired from the Integrated Test Range (ITR) at Wheeler Island off the Odisha's east coast.

On 6 March 2011, India launched its indigenously developed interceptor missile from the Odisha coast. India successfully test-fired its interceptor missile which destroyed a 'hostile' target ballistic missile, a modified Prithvi, at an altitude of 16 km over the Bay of Bengal. the interceptor, Advanced Air Defence (AAD) missile positioned at Wheeler Island, about 70 km across sea from Chandipur, received signals from tracking radars installed along the coastline and travelled through the sky at a speed of 4.5 Mach to destroy it. As the trial was aimed at achieving the desired result with precision, the interceptor missile had its own mobile launcher, secure data link for interception, independent tracking and homing capabilities and sophisticated radars. "It was a fantastic launch.

The trial, conducted from two launch sites of ITR off Orissa coast for developing a full fledged multi-layer Ballistic Missile Defence (BMD) system, was fully successful," he said.

On 10 February 2012, AAD was again successfully test-fired from Wheeler Island off the state coast near Dhamra in Bhadrak district, about 170 km from Bhubaneswar.

On 23 November 2012, India again successfully testfired its home-made supersonic Advanced Air Defence (AAD) interceptor missile from a defence base off the coast of the eastern state of Odisha. "The test-firing was part of India's efforts to create a missile defence shield against incoming enemy missiles. The AAD interceptor missile, which was fired from the Wheeler Island off the Odishan coast, successfully destroyed mid-air an incoming ballistic missile launched from the Integrated Test Range in Chandipur, about 70 km from the Wheeler Island."

Swordfish RADAR

Swordfish is the target acquisition and fire control radar for the BMD system. The LRTR currently has a range of 600 km (370 mi) to 800 km (500 mi) and can spot objects as small as a cricket ball. The DRDO plans to upgrade the capacity of Swordfish to 1,500 km by 2011.

Phase 2

Two new anti ballistic missiles that can intercept IRBMs are being developed. These high speed missiles (AD-1 and AD-2) are being developed to intercept ballistic missiles with a range of around 5,000 km (3,100 mi). The test trials of these two systems are expected to take place in 2011. The new missile will be similar to the THAAD missile deployed by the USA.

These missiles will travel at hypersonic speeds and will require radars with scan capability of over 1,500 km (930 mi) to successfully intercept the target.On 6 May 2012, Dr V K Saraswat while confirming the completion of Phase-I added that Phase-II would be completed by 2016 to protect against missiles having range up to 5000 km. India is also planning to develop a laser based weapon system as part of its defence to intercept and destroy missiles soon after they are launched towards the country. DRDO's Air Defence Programme Director V K Saraswat says its ideal to destroy a ballistic missile carrying nuclear or conventional warheads in its boost phase. Saraswat further added that it will take another 10–15 years for the premier defence research institute to make it usable on the ground.

PDV

In 2009, reports emerged of a new missile named the PDV. The DRDO is developing a new Prithvi interceptor missile codenamed PDV. It will be a two-stage missile and both the stages will be powered by solid propellants. It will have an innovative system for controlling the vehicle at an altitude of more than 150 km The PDV is intended to replace the existing PAD in the PAD/AAD combination. It will have an IIR seeker for its kill vehicle as well. The PDV will replace the PAD with a far more capable missile and will complete the Phase 1 of the BMD system, allowing it to be operational by 2013. Whereupon Phase 2 development will take over for protection against missiles of the 5,000 km (3,100 mi) range class. The first test flight of the missile was expected in 2010. The PDV is designed to take out the target missile at altitudes above 150 km (93 mi). The first PDV was successfully test fired on 27 April 2014.

Cooperation Offered by United States

According to US Deputy Defence Secretary Ashton Carter, there is a potential for co-operation with India to develop a Ballistic Missile Defence (BMD) shield. "That is an important potential area for our future cooperation," Carter said while on his visit to India in July 2012.

DEPLOYMENT

According to scientist V K Saraswat of DRDO the missiles will work in tandem to ensure a hit probability of 99.8 percent. On 6 May 2012, Dr V K

Saraswat confirmed that Phase-I is complete and can be deployed to protect two Indian cities at a short notice. He also added that Phase-I is comparable to PAC-3 system.

New Delhi, the national capital, and Mumbai, have been selected for the ballistic missile defence shield. After successful implementation in Delhi and Mumbai, the system will be used to cover other major cities in the country. This shield can destroy incoming ballistic missiles launched from as far as 2,500 km away. When the Phase II is completed and PDV is developed, the two anti-ballistic missiles can intercept targets up to 5,000 km both at exo and endo-atmospheric (inside the atmosphere) regions. The missiles will work in tandem to ensure a hit probability of 99.8 per cent.

5

Issues in International Political Economy

INTERNATIONAL POLITICAL ECONOMY

International political economy (IPE), also known as global political economy (GPE), is an academic discipline within political science that analyzes economics andinternational relations. As an interdisciplinary field, it draws on many distinct academic schools, most notably political science and economics, also sociology, history, and cultural studies.

The academic boundaries of IPE are flexible, and along with acceptable epistemologies are the subject of robust debate. This debate is essentially framed by the discipline's status as a new and interdisciplinary field of study. Despite such disagreements, most scholars can concur that IPE ultimately is concerned with the ways in which political forces (states, institutions, individual actors, etc.) shape the systems through which economic interactions are expressed, and conversely the effect that economic interactions (including the power of collective markets and individuals acting both within and outside them) have upon political structures and outcomes.

IPE scholars are at the center of the debate and research surrounding globalization, both in the popular and academic spheres. Other topics that command substantial attention among IPE scholars are international trade (with particular attention to the politics surrounding trade deals, but also significant work examining the results of trade deals),international development (poverty and the role of institutions in development), international finance, global markets, political risk, multi-state cooperation in solving trans-border economic problems, and the structural balance of power between and among states and institutions. Unlike the broader field international relations, power is understood to be both economic and political, which are interrelated in a complex manner.

ORIGIN

It has been predominantly considered by authors such as Benjamin Cohen (2008) that IPE emerged as a heterodox approach to international studies during the 1970s as the1973 world oil crisis and the breakdown of the Bretton Woods system alerted academics, particularly in the U.S., of the importance, contingency, and weakness of the economic foundations of the world order. IPE scholars such as Susan Strange asserted that earlier studies of international relations had placed excessive emphasis on law, politics, anddiplomatic history. Similarly, neo-classical economics was accused of abstraction and being ahistorical. Drawing heavily on historical sociology and economic history, IPE proposed a fusion of economic and political analysis. In this sense, both Marxist and liberal IPE scholars protested against the reliance of Western social science on the territorialstate as a unit of analysis, and stressed the international system..

TRADITIONAL APPROACHES

Academic courses, journals, and text books generally cover the various view points from which policy recommendations originate and will endeavour to provide an ideologically neutral presentation of the field of study. Following a precedent set by one of the founding text books of the discipline, individuals and organisations engaged in promoting particular policies, as well as many scholars active in this field, are commonly grouped into one of three worlds views, all of which have existed long before IPE emerged as a distinct academic discipline.

These categories are liberal, realist, and Marxist. Constructivism may be classed as a fourth high level view, although scholars such as Ravenhill have grouped it as a sub-class of the Marxist approach.

The liberal category is relatively unified, while the realist and Marxist views capture a vast range of outlooks. Widely shared views are found only at the highest level of abstraction:

The 'liberal' view believes in freedom for private powers at the expense of public power (government). It asserts that markets, free from the distortions caused by government controls and regulation, naturally will harmonise demand and supply of scarce resources resulting in the best possible world for populations at large.

The 'realist' view (formerly commonly labelled "nationalist") accepts the power of free markets to deliver favourable outcomes, but holds that optimum conditions generally are obtained with moderately strong public power exerting some regulatory control.

The 'Marxist' view believes that only robust application of strong public power can check innate tendencies for private power to benefit elites at the expense of populations at large.

The 'constructivist' view assumes that the domain of international economic interactions is not value-free, and that economic and political identities, in addition to material interests, are significant determinants of economic action.

The Liberal Approach

In economic terms, Liberalism is an approach associated with classical economics, neo-classical economics, Austrian School economics, and Chicago school economics.

History

The Liberal approach often is wrongly traced to the work of Adam Smith. Economics, as some may claim, has been viewed as dawning with the *Smithian* revolution against Mercantilism.

The liberal view point generally has been strong in Western academia since it was first articulated by Smith in the eighteenth century. Only during the 1940s to early 1970s did an alternative system, Keynesianism, command wide support in universities.

Keynes was concerned chiefly with domestic macroeconomic policy, however in IPE terms his mature views fall largely into the Realist camp, in that Keynes called for a middle way between public and private power and favoured a managed system of global finance for which he was one of the two chief architects at Bretton Woods. The Keynesian consensus was challenged successfully with attacks launched byFriedrich Hayek's Austrian School and Milton Friedman's Chicago School as early as the 1950s, which by the 1970s had succeeded in displacing Keynes as the dominant influence.

Keynes's approach to international relations, including his thinking on the economic causes of war and economic means of promoting peace, has received further attention with the onset of the global financial crisis and recession since 2008, especially through the work of Donald Markwell.

In policy making terms Western governments have generally pursued mixed agendas drawing on both the liberal and realist view point. This has been the case from the dawning of modern commerce to the present day, although there have been periods where one or the other school had gained temporary ascendency. Sometimes the period leading up to 1914 is described as a golden age of classical economics, but in practice governments continued to be partially influenced by mercantilist ideology, and following WW1 economic freedom was constricted.

After World War II the Bretton Woods system was established, reflecting the political orientation described as Embedded liberalism. This has been described as a compromise between the realist and liberal viewpoints, in that it allowed governments to manage international finance, while still allowing considerable freedom of action for private commerce. In 1971 President Richard Nixon began the rolling back of the Bretton Woods system and until 2008 the trend has been for increasing liberalization of international trade and finance. Domestically, the Atlantic nations since the 1970s and large Asian states such as China and India since the 1990s also have largely pursued a mixture of realist and liberal policies. The only close to wholesale implementations of the liberal viewpoint being carried out is by smaller developing nations, often with some degree of coercion by actors such as the U.S. treasury or IMF, who have been able to apply financial pressure when the developing nations faced various crises.

During 2008, liberal influences began to wane in the wake of the 2008–2009 Keynesian resurgence which the *Financial Times* described as a "stunning reversal of the orthodoxy of the past several decades". From later 2008 world leaders have also been increasingly calling for a New Bretton Woods System.

The realist view

Within IPE the Realist approach was commonly labeled nationalism until the first decade of the twenty-first century. Historically the earliest distinct school of thought in this category was mercantilism. Contemporary examples of the realist approaches are statism and developmentalism.

History

The mercantilist view largely characterised policies pursued by state actors from the emergence of the modern economy in the fifteenth century up to the mid-twentieth century. Sovereign states would compete with each other to accumulate bullion either by achieving trade surpluses or by conquest. This wealth could then be used to finance investment in infrastructure and to enhance military capability. The contemporary realist view generally agrees with liberals in viewing international trade as a win-win phenomenon where firms should be allowed to collaborate or compete depending on market forces. The chief point of contention with liberals is that realists assert national interests can be served best by protecting new industries from foreign competition with high tariffs until they've built up the capability to compete on the world market. One of the earliest formal expressions of this view was found in Alexander Hamilton's 'Report on Manufacturers' which he wrote for the U.S. government in 1791.

After WWII a notable success story for the developmentalist approach was found in South America where high levels of growth and equity were achieved partly as a result of policies originating from Raul Prebisch and economists he trained, who were assigned to governments around the continent. After the liberal view re-established its ascendancy in the 1970s, it has been asserted that high levels of growth resulted from generally favourable international conditions rather than the Realist policies.

A contemporary statement of the Realist view is strategic trade theory, and there has been much debate as to whether the policies it suggests could be effective in solving some of the issues with globalisation, such as persistent north/south inequality divide.

The Marxist view

This category has been used to group together an array of different approaches which sometimes have very little in common with Marx's focus on class, but which all believe in a strong role for public power. Labels for approaches within this category include: feminist, radical, structuralist, critical, underdevelopment and 'world systems'. Broadly the Marxist approach is associated with Heterodox economics.

History

Marx's Das Kapital was published in 1867 and an economic system based on his ideas was implemented after the Russian Revolution of 1917. Since the collapse of the Soviet union and the COMECON trading bloc in 1991 no major group of trading partners or even single large economy has been run along Marxist lines. Problems with a Marxist command economy are seen as including the very high informational demands required for the efficient allocation of resources and corruptive tendencies of the very high degree of public power need to govern the process.

Few academics currently promote classical Marxist views, especially in America, but there are a few exceptions in Europe. More popular perspectives include feminist, environmental and radical – developmentalist. The social – constructivist view is an unusual school of thought sometimes grouped into this category. Rather than focus on the tradition factors affecting trade such as distribution of resources, technology, and infrastructure, it emphasises the role of dialogue and debate in determining future developments in international trade and globalisation.

Criticisms of the Traditional Divide into the Liberal, Nationalist, and Marxist Views

Critics have asserted there is now too much variation in the different viewpoints grouped into each category, especially those under the Nationalist and Marxist headings. Also, the names can be considered misleading for the general public. The labels nationalist and Marxist have negative connotations, with many of the perspectives grouped under the Marxist label having very little to do with the classical Marxist position. Many advocates within the nationalist tradition, being themselves strongly opposed to nationalism in the commonly understood fascist or racist sense, and some professors, have replaced the label "nationalist" with "realist" in their most recent books and courses.

The Constructivist View

Constructivism is an emerging field in international political economy. In general, the constructivist view propounds that material interests, which are central to liberal, realist, and Marxist views, are not sufficient to explain patterns of economic interactions or policies, and that economic and political identities are significant determinants of economic action.

American vs. British IPE

Benjamin Cohen provides a detailed intellectual history of IPE identifying American and British camps. The Americans are positivist and attempt to develop intermediate level theories that are supported by some form of quantitative evidence. British IPE is more "interpretivist" and looks for "grand theories". They use very different standards of empirical work. Cohen sees benefits in both approaches. A special edition of *New Political Economy* has been issued on The 'British School' of IPE and a special edition of the *Review of International Political Economy* (RIPE) on American IPE.

One forum for this was the "2008 Warwick RIPE Debate: 'American' versus 'British' IPE" where Cohen, Mark Blyth, Richard Higgott, and Matthew Watson followed up the recent exchange in RIPE. Higgott and Watson in particular, queried the appropriateness of Cohen's categories.

INTERNATIONAL TRADE AND STATE SECURITY

International economic structures range from complete autarky to complete market openness. This structure has undergone numerous changes since the beginning of the nineteenth century. The state-power theory as put into perspective by Stephen Krasner (1976), explains that the structure of international trade is determined by the interests and power of states acting to maximize their aggregate national income, social stability, political power and economic growth. Such state interests can be achieved under free trade.

The relationship between these interests and the level of openness depends upon the economic power of states. Power is dependent upon a states size and level of economic development.

Krasner contends that distributions of potential power may vary from multipolar to hegemonic; and different international trading structures are made of either of these. The key to this argument is that a hegemonic distribution of potential economic power is likely to result in an open trading system. Since states act to maximize their aggregate economic utility, maximum global welfare is achieved under free trade. Neoclassical trade theory posits that the greater the degree of openness in the international trading system, the greater the level of aggregate economic income.

THEORETICAL PERSPECTIVES

Realism

Robert Gilpin and Stephen Krasner are advocates of the realist tradition, which emphasises the hegemonic system. The hegemonic system contends that there are states that are much larger and more developed than their trading partners and therefore, the costs and benefits of openness are not symmetrical for all members of the system. Krasner (1976) contends that the hegemonic state will have a preference for an open structure because it will increase its aggregate national income and power.

Realism emphasizes states' demands for power and security. Military force is therefore, the most important power resource. States must rely ultimately on their own resources and must strive to maintain their power positions in the system, even at high economic costs. For realism, the most important variables are the economic and military strength of hegemonic states; and international hostilities are mainly because of variations in the distribution of political-military capabilities between states.

Hegemonic Stability

The theory of hegemonic stability by the realist school argues that dominance of one country is necessary for the existence of an open and stable international economy. The relationship between hegemony and an open, stable economy has been challenged by some scholars "As US behaviour during the interwar period illustrates, the possession of superior resources by a nation does not translate automatically into great influence or beneficial outcomes for the world."

Development Policy

Realist trade encourages Import substitution industrialization (ISI) replacing imports with domestic production. Realism recognises that trade regulations can be used to correct domestic distortions and to promote new industries. Under realism, states possess a high degree of discretionary power to influence many variables and prices in the economy. The government influences the distribution of investment, thus protecting national industries.

International Institutions

Realists with their focus on power and the struggle for survival in an anarchical world, criticize the role of international institutions that govern the world economy, such as theWorld Bank, World Trade Organization (WTO), EU, and the International Monetary Fund (IMF). Scholars argue that the influence exerted by international institutions is dependent upon the states that form part of them, and therefore international institutions have little independent impact. Accordingly, the realist school emphasises the impact of state power over the strength of the institution per se.

Liberalism

The liberal tradition consists of two schools of thought on the causes of peace, one emphasises representative government and international institutions and the other advocates global markets and economic development. Liberalism traces back to Immanuel Kant. Kantian Liberalism posits that democracy, economic interdependence and international organisations are optimal solutions for reducing the incidence of conflict. It is not individual factors, which lead to a more peaceful world, but rather all three elements working in conjunction, which eliminates conflict.

Oneal and Russett's (2001) research design has become a standard choice of replications in studies assessing the Kantian peace triangle where democracies tend to be interdependent and members of the same International Government Organisations (IGOs). Their research is consistent with the argument that democratic peace advocates economic interdependence and a joint need to attain membership in IGOs in order to prevent the incidence of conflict. However, the empirical findings on the Kantian peace triangle as a joint force to eliminate conflict presents some limitations, as one study found that the three Kantian peace variables are less robust in explaining leaders' conflict behaviour. Keohane and Nye (2000) go further to include the lack of additional components in this theory including environmental and military measurements.

Trade

Liberals emphasise two main aspects of the benefits of trade. First, trade promotes states to work together and cooperatively, reinforcing peaceful relations among trading partners. The second benefit is based on the expected utility model of trade and conflict which emphasises the potential economic consequences of a disruption in trade. Countries are therefore deterred from initiating conflict against a trading partner for fear of losing the welfare gains associated with trade.

Interdependence

Liberals argue that economic interdependence between states reduces conflict because conflict discourages commerce.

Recent cost-benefit calculations of trade take into account information as an important component in the explanation of the pacifying aspect of economic interdependence. Through open trade, states reveal their intentions and capabilities and thus "relations become more transparent and reduce uncertainty."

Furthermore, economic interdependence makes costly signals possible. If military action did not entail loss, national leaders would not be able to communicate their capabilities and resolve. This acts as a deterrent and promotes peace between states. "Mechanisms that facilitate the transmission of credible information across international boundaries limit bargaining failure, enhancing interstate peace."

There is some disagreement about the interdependence liberal thesis among some scholars. Kenneth Waltz, for example, argues that since "close interdependence means closeness of contact and raises the prospect of at least occasional conflict... the [liberal] myth of interdependence... asserts a false belief about the conditions that may promote peace."

Despite the scrutiny, there is a long-held position that economic interdependence has a pacifying effect on interstate relations, evidenced by research conducted by Oneal and Russett 1999 and Xiang et al. 2007.

According to the liberal view, the costly nature of conflict is central to contemporary bargaining theory.

Keohane and Nye (1987) put forth four conditions that make the use of force by large states costly:

1. Risks of nuclear escalation
2. Resistance by people in poor or weak countries
3. Uncertain and possibly negative effects on the achievement of economic goals
4. Domestic opinion opposed to the human costs of the use of force

Development Policy

Liberal trade encourages export led growth (ELG), leaving traders and consumers dependent on foreign markets. Liberals argue that these actors have an incentive to avoid hostilities with their trading partners, since any disruption in commercial relations would be costly.

International Institutions

International institutions are a key feature of the liberal peace, because they represent credible signals of resolve to defend member states in times of crisis, regulate state behaviour, facilitate communication and create common security interests between member states.

THE ARGUMENT ABOUT TRADE AND CONFLICT

The relationship between international trade and conflict has been a source of controversy among international relations scholars. Some scholars argue that trade does not reduce conflict even though conflict reduces trade; while others report that international trade fosters a peaceful disposition among states, which are less likely to resort to armed conflict in times of crisis.

The argument that open trade inhibits conflict dates back to the classical liberal movement of free trade and world peace. This view argues that increasing interaction among traders and consumers (interdependence) promotes peace; free trade fosters a sense of international community that reduce interstate conflict and tensions. Liberals posit that free markets and economic development contribute to a reduction in interstate conflict. The contrasting contemporary view is that open trade dampens political conflict by promoting economic dependence. Economic dependence has negative consequences for interstate conflict. Albert O. Hirschman (1945) for example, has pointed out that the "gains from trade do not accrue to states proportionately and the distribution of these gains can affect interstate power relations. Moreover, shifts in power relations are widely regarded as a potent source of military conflict."

ECONOMIC INTERDEPENDENCE

Economic interdependence and greater openness exposes domestic economies to the exigencies of the world market. Social instability is therefore increased by exposure to international competition. This negative force undermines the Kantian peace and remains a cause for concern in international conflict. Although this concern seems legitimate given the economic disparities between developed and developing countries, studies fail to provide comprehensive empirical evidence.

Another view at odds with liberalism is that technological innovation and industrialization increase the ability of some countries to exercise power. As trade flows and the level of interdependence increases, so do the incentives for states to take military actions to reduce their economic vulnerability.

The adverse effect of trade on state security is difficult to determine, however the more competition, the more aggressive the environment. Openness and competition increases social instability because domestic prices need to adjust to changes in international prices. Consistent with the realists view that states are essentially always in conflict, social instability and resource competition are motives for conflict and states will rely on the use of force to attain their own political goals and interests.

The Role of Military Power

A number of international relations scholars, notably Xiang, Xu and Keteku 2007; Mearsheimer 2001, recognise the role of military power in initiating conflict, as well as the role militarily powerful countries play in international trade. One argument suggests that militarily capable countries are more likely to have the motivation to initiate armed conflict due to their awareness of their capabilities and to their confidence in achieving favourable outcomes.

A second argument suggests that power facilitates trade. Third, there are positive benefits from economic interdependence on military power. Finally, the economic stature of a country determines both the military power and level of trade of that country, hinting that economic powerful states trade more. Because powerful countries are better positioned to take advantage of the benefits resulting from international trade and to transform welfare gains into military power, they also are more likely to use force when their positions are threatened. Similarly, Gartzke and Hewitt (2010) argue that the "extension of economic and other interests beyond national borders increases incentives to police relevant regions and exercise influence, sometimes through force."

Unequal Peace

The motives for conflict, which historically were concentrated among the powerful and their ambitious challengers, are today clustered among the poor, and between the poor and the rich (Gartzke and Hewitt (2010). Theory has prompted to inequality as a potential source of internal conflict. "Inequalities within the same countries has increased, not through impoverishment of the masses, but because while wealth is created many people remain left behind in poverty. Thus, we have an unequal peace." Around 60 countries suffer not only from low GDP per capita but also low or negative growth. These countries tend to be caught in armed conflict among other development traps. Some argue that the evidence surrounding inequality and conflict remains inconclusive, calling for further empirical studies.

Studies show that states with the most dissimilar interests possess a motive for conflict but whether they experience conflict (or not) depends on external determinants of bargaining success or failure. These determinants include uncertainty about the balance of power, opponent's resolve as well as policy dissimilarities between competing states. Interests are important determinants of whether conflict occurs. According to Gartzke and Hewitt (2010), promoting democratic interests, or even imposing them for peace, is not likely to reduce conflict "it may even lead to a weakening of the actual determinants of liberal peace", thereby increasing interstate tensions. Contemporary research demonstrates that promoting free markets and economic development helps mitigate conflict and promote peace

CAPITALIST PEACE

The capitalist peace thesis suggests that free markets and economic development contribute to a reduction in interstate conflict.

Research on the capitalist peace has chosen to pursue the liberal political economy school, with a particular focus on Kant's Perpetual Peace. The same set of theoretical frameworks that evolved in democratic peace research now asserts itself in the capitalist peace.

The capitalist peace sees capitalism as creating conditions to make war more costly and therefore undesirable by trading states. Traditional interpretations of the capital peace contend that development and global markets will eventually eliminate resource competition as a motive for war. This view was eventually deemed outdated, as "it became clear that needed raw materials would continue to make their way to industrial centers through free markets, rather than through mercantilist autarkies.

The capitalist theory contends that as economies become stronger, prosperous capitalist states no longer need to threaten one another over access to inputs to production. Consequently, the security dilemma loses its relevance. Scholars like Michael Mousseau argue that democracies are only peaceful in pairs. Other research has demonstrated that the democratic peace is even more exclusive than previously imagined, limiting the finding to developed democracies. Gartzke and Hewitt (2010) challenged this by demonstrating that it is economic development and market freedoms, rather than political liberty that result in interstate peace.

Deterrent effect of institutional ties

International Government Organisations (IGOs) are designed to promote cooperation and inhibit political disputes. Institutional ties promote the exchange of information about the economic gains and losses of participating member states, thereby reducing uncertainty about the distribution of benefits.

Regional institutions also present great influence in addressing issues beyond trade. Regional economic institutions help develop trade expectations for the future. "High economic stakes that states have in the continuation and growth of economic activity in the context of economic regionalism lead to a security community in which states develop a genuine interest in not only keeping peace with each other, but also defending their relationship against outside aggressors." In addition to their role in dispute settlement, regional arrangements can deter aggressors from targeting institutionally connected states.

Aydin (2010) makes an important contribution to the extended deterrence literature and economic peace research through his empirical study on the deterrent effect of economic integration. This study shows that trade has a general deterrent effect on attackers when the target is economically integrated with potential defenders through regional trade institutions. When trade is conducted in an institutionalised setting it can have political implications beyond bilateral interdependence.

Research shows that economic integration decreases the opportunities to fight and enhances the opportunities to intervene in crisis. Mansfield and Pevehouse present strong evidence that "the combination of PTA membership (preferential trading arrangements) and a high level of trade is quite likely to discourage belligerence."

Many PTAs have become venues for addressing political disputes between participants and fostering cooperation. Observers have widely acknowledged, for example, thatASEAN has helped to manage tensions in Southeast Asia. Mercado Comun del Sur (MERCOSUR) has done likewise, improving political-military relations throughout the southern cone. The reciprocal nature of this system helps guarantee that economic concessions made by one state will be repaid, rather than exploited by its counterpart.

INTERNATIONAL INVESTMENT FLOWS

Another area to add to the existing literature on economic integration is the impact of militarized conflict on foreign investment.

Bussman's (2010) contribution to the liberal notion that conflict inhibits foreign investment, complements the liberal peace arguments in conflict studies. Bussman's research shows that international conflict reduces international investment flows considerably.

Bussman contends that "as with trade, foreign investment could be an important factor in promoting peace. States might avoid violent conflict in order not to deter foreign investors." By ensuring political stability, states can thus create an environment that is desirable to foreign investors. It is therefore, in the best interest of states to keep away from belligerent behaviour as they could potentially miss out on the welfare gains associated with foreign investment.

As a result, states that benefit from foreign direct investment flows are less likely to experience the onset of militarized conflict.

MONEY LAUNDERING

Money laundering is the process in which the proceeds of crime are transformed into ostensibly legitimate money or other assets.However, in a number of legal and regulatory systems the term money laundering has become conflated with other forms of financial crime, and sometimes used more generally to include misuse of the financial system (involving things such as securities, digital currencies, credit cards, and traditional currency), including terrorism financing, tax evasion and evading of international sanctions. Most anti-money laundering laws openly conflate money laundering (which is concerned with *source* of funds) with terrorism financing (which is concerned with *destination* of funds) when regulating the financial system.

Money obtained from certain crimes, such as extortion, insider trading, drug trafficking, illegal gambling and tax evasion is "dirty". It needs to be cleaned to appear to have derived from non-criminal activities so that banks and other financial institutions will deal with it without suspicion. Money can be laundered by many methods, which vary in complexity and sophistication.

Different countries may or may not treat tax evasion or payments in breach of international sanctions as money laundering. Some jurisdictions differentiate these for definition purposes, and others do not. Some jurisdictions define money laundering as obfuscating sources of money, either intentionally or by merely using financial systems or services that do not identify or track sources or destinations.

Other jurisdictions define money laundering to include money from activity that *would have been* a crime in that jurisdiction, even if it were legal where the actual conduct occurred. This broad brush of applying the term "money laundering" to merely incidental, extraterritorial, or simply privacy-seeking behaviours has led some to label it "financial thoughtcrime". Many regulatory and governmental authorities issue estimates each year for the amount of money laundered, either worldwide or within their national economy. In 1996, theInternational Monetary Fund estimated that two to five percent of the worldwide global economy involved laundered money. The Financial Action Task Force on Money Laundering (FATF), an intergovernmental body set up to combat money laundering, stated, "Overall, it is absolutely impossible to produce a reliable estimate of the amount of money laundered and therefore the FATF does not publish any figures in this regard." Academic commentators have likewise been unable to estimate the volume of money with any degree of assurance. Various estimates of the scale of global money laundering are sometimes repeated often enough to make some people regard them as factual—but no researcher has overcome the inherent difficulty of measuring an actively concealed practice.

Regardless of the difficulty in measurement, the amount of money laundered each year is in the billions (US dollars) and poses a significant policy concern for governments.As a result, governments and international bodies have undertaken efforts to deter, prevent, and apprehend money launderers. Financial institutions have likewise undertaken efforts to prevent and detect transactions involving dirty money, both as a result of government requirements and to avoid the reputational risk involved. Issues relating to money laundering have existed as long as there have been large scale criminal enterprises. Modern anti-money laundering laws have developed along with the modern War on Drugs. In more recent times anti-money laundering legislation is seen as adjunct to the financial crime of terrorist financing in that both crimes usually involve the transmission of funds through the financial system (although money laundering relates to where the money has come *from*, and terrorist financing relating to where the money is going *to*).

METHODS

Money laundering is commonly defined as occurring in three steps: the first step involves introducing cash into the financial system by some means ("placement"); the second involves carrying out complex financial transactions to camouflage the illegal source ("layering"); and the final step entails acquiring wealth generated from the transactions of the illicit funds ("integration"). Some of these steps may be omitted, depending on the circumstances; for example, non-cash proceeds that are already in the financial system would have no need for placement.

Money laundering takes several different forms, although most methods can be categorized into one of a few types. These include "bank methods, smurfing [also known as structuring], currency exchanges, and double-invoicing".

- Structuring: Often known as *smurfing*, this is a method of placement whereby cash is broken into smaller deposits of money, used to defeat suspicion of money laundering and to avoid anti-money laundering reporting requirements. A sub-component of this is to use smaller amounts of cash to purchase bearer instruments, such as money orders, and then ultimately deposit those, again in small amounts.

- Bulk cash smuggling: This involves physically smuggling cash to another jurisdiction and depositing it in a financial institution, such as an offshore bank, with greater bank secrecy or less rigorous money laundering enforcement.
- Cash-intensive businesses: In this method, a business typically involved in receiving cash uses its accounts to deposit both legitimate and criminally derived cash, claiming all of it as legitimate earnings. Service businesses are best suited to this method, as such businesses have no variable costs, and it is hard to detect discrepancies between revenues and costs. Examples are parking buildings, strip clubs, tanning beds, car washes and casinos.
- Trade-based laundering: This involves under- or overvaluing invoices to disguise the movement of money.
- Shell companies and trusts: Trusts and shell companies disguise the true owner of money. Trusts and corporate vehicles, depending on the jurisdiction, need not disclose their true, beneficial, owner. Sometimes referred to by the slang term *rathole* though that term usually refers to a person acting as the fictitious owner rather a business entity.
- Round-tripping: Here, money is deposited in a controlled foreign corporation offshore, preferably in a tax haven where minimal records are kept, and then shipped back as aforeign direct investment, exempt from taxation. A variant on this is to transfer money to a law firm or similar organization as funds on account of fees, then to cancel the retainer and, when the money is remitted, represent the sums received from the lawyers as a legacy under a will or proceeds of litigation.
- Bank capture: In this case, money launderers or criminals buy a controlling interest in a bank, preferably in a jurisdiction with weak money laundering controls, and then move money through the bank without scrutiny.
- Casinos: In this method, an individual walks into a casino with cash and buys chips, plays for a while, and then cashes in the chips, taking payment in a check, or just getting a receipt, claiming it as gambling winnings.
- Other gambling: Money is spent on gambling, preferably on higher odds. The wins are shown if the source for money is asked for, while the losses are hidden.
- Real estate: Someone purchases real estate with illegal proceeds and then sells the property. To outsiders, the proceeds from the sale look like legitimate income. Alternatively, the price of the property

is manipulated: the seller agrees to a contract that underrepresents the value of the property, and receives criminal proceeds to make up the difference.

- Black salaries: A company may have unregistered employees without a written contract and pay them cash salaries. Dirty money might be used to pay them.
- Tax amnesties: For example, those that legalize unreported assets in tax havens and cash
- Fictitious loans
- A goal of money laundering is to be able to use the dirty money for private consumption. If unable to use it openly, the traditional way to keep the dirty money near is hiding it as cash at home or other places. A more modern method is a credit card connected to a tax haven bank.

ENFORCEMENT

Anti-money laundering (AML) is a term mainly used in the financial and legal industries to describe the legal controls that require financial institutions and other regulated entities to prevent, detect, and report money laundering activities. Anti-money laundering guidelines came into prominence globally as a result of the formation of the Financial Action Task Force (FATF) and the promulgation of an international framework of anti-money laundering standards. These standards began to have more relevance in 2000 and 2001, after FATF began a process to publicly identify countries that were deficient in their anti-money laundering laws and international cooperation, a process colloquially known as "name and shame".

An effective AML programme requires a jurisdiction to have criminalized money laundering, given the relevant regulators and police the powers and tools to investigate; be able to share information with other countries as appropriate; and require financial institutions to identify their customers, establish risk-based controls, keep records, and report suspicious activities.

Criminalizing Money Laundering

The elements of the crime of money laundering are set forth in the United Nations Convention Against Illicit Traffic in Narcotic Drugs and Psychotropic Substances andConvention against Transnational Organized Crime. It is defined as knowingly engaging in a financial transaction with the proceeds of a crime for the purpose of concealing or disguising the illicit origin of the property from governments.

The Role of Financial Institutions

While banks operating in the same country generally have to follow the same AML laws and regulations, financial institutions all structure their AML efforts slightly different.Today, most financial institutions globally, and many non-financial institutions, are required to identify and report transactions of a suspicious nature to the financial intelligence unit in the respective country. For example, a bank must verify a customer's identity and, if necessary, monitor transactions for suspicious activity. This is often termed as "know your customer". This means knowing the identity of the customer and understanding the kinds of transactions in which the customer is likely to engage. By knowing one's customers, financial institutions can often identify unusual or suspicious behaviour, termed anomalies, which may be an indication of money laundering.

Bank employees, such as tellers and customer account representatives, are trained in anti-money laundering and are instructed to report activities that they deem suspicious. Additionally, anti-money laundering software filters customer data, classifies it according to level of suspicion, and inspects it for anomalies. Such anomalies include any sudden and substantial increase in funds, a large withdrawal, or moving money to a bank secrecy jurisdiction. Smaller transactions that meet certain criteria may also be flagged as suspicious. For example, structuring can lead to flagged transactions. The software also flags names on government "blacklists" and transactions that involve countries hostile to the host nation. Once the software has mined data and flagged suspect transactions, it alerts bank management, who must then determine whether to file a report with the government.

Value of Enforcement Costs and Associated Privacy Concerns

The financial services industry has become more vocal about the rising costs of anti-money laundering regulation and the limited benefits that they claim it brings. One commentator wrote that "[w]ithout facts, [anti-money laundering] legislation has been driven on rhetoric, driving by ill-guided activism responding to the need to be "seen to be doing something" rather than by an objective understanding of its effects on predicate crime. The social panic approach is justified by the language used—we talk of the battle against terrorism or the war on drugs". *The Economist* magazine has become increasingly vocal in its criticism of such regulation, particularly with reference to countering terrorist financing, referring to it as a "costly failure", although it concedes that other efforts (like reducing identity and credit card fraud) may still be effective at combating money laundering.

There is no precise measurement of the costs of regulation balanced against the harms associated with money laundering, and given the evaluation problems involved in assessing such an issue, it is unlikely that the effectiveness of terror finance and money laundering laws could be determined with any degree of accuracy. *The Economist*estimated the annual costs of anti-money laundering efforts in Europe and North America at US$5 billion in 2003, an increase from US$700 million in 2000. Government-linked economists have noted the significant negative effects of money laundering on economic development, including undermining domestic capital formation, depressing growth, and diverting capital away from development. Because of the intrinsic uncertainties of the amount of money laundered, changes in the amount of money laundered, and the cost of anti-money laundering systems, it is almost impossible to tell which anti-money laundering systems work and which are more or less cost effective.

Besides economic costs to implement anti-money-laundering laws improper attention to data-protection practices may entail disproportionate costs to individual privacy rights. In June 2011, the data-protection advisory committee to the European Union, issued a report on data protection issues related to the prevention of money laundering and terrorist financing, which identified numerous transgressions against the established legal framework on privacy and data protection. The report made recommendations how to address money laundering and terrorist financing in ways that safeguard personal privacy rights and data-protection laws. In the United States, groups such as the American Civil Liberties Union have expressed concern that money laundering rules require banks to report on their own customers, essentially conscripting private businesses "into agents of the surveillance state".

Many countries are obligated by various international instruments and standards, such as the 1988 United Nations Convention Against Illicit Traffic in Narcotic Drugs and Psychotropic Substances, the 2000 Convention against Transnational Organized Crime, the 2003 United Nations Convention against Corruption, and the recommendations of the 1989 Financial Action Task Force on Money Laundering to enact and enforce money laundering laws in an effort to stop narcotics trafficking, international organised crime, and corruption. Mexico, which has faced a significant increase in violent crime, established anti-money laundering controls in 2013 to curb the underlying crime issue.

Global Organizations Working Against Money Laundering

Formed in 1989 by the G7 countries, the FATF is an intergovernmental body whose purpose is to develop and promote an international response to combat money laundering. The FATF Secretariat is housed at the headquarters of the OECD in Paris. In October 2001, FATF expanded its mission to include combating the financing of terrorism. FATF is a policy-making body that brings together legal, financial, and law enforcement experts to achieve national legislation and regulatory AML and CFT reforms. As of 2014 its membership consists of 36 countries and territories and two regional organizations. FATF works in collaboration with a number of international bodies and organizations. These entities have observer status with FATF, which does not entitle them to vote, but permits them full participation in plenary sessions and working groups.

FATF has developed 40 recommendations on money laundering and 9 special recommendations regarding terrorist financing. FATF assesses each member country against these recommendations in published reports. Countries seen as not being sufficiently compliant with such recommendations are subjected to financial sanctions.

FATF's three primary functions with regard to money laundering are:

1. Monitoring members' progress in implementing anti-money laundering measures.
2. Reviewing and reporting on laundering trends, techniques, and countermeasures.
3. Promoting the adoption and implementation of FATF anti-money laundering standards globally.

The FATF currently comprises 34 member jurisdictions and 2 regional organisations, representing most major financial centres in all parts of the globe:

- Argentina
- Australia
- Austria
- Belgium
- Brazil
- Canada
- China
- Denmark
- European Commission
- Finland
- France
- Germany
- Greece
- Gulf Cooperation Council
- Hong Kong
- Iceland
- India
- Ireland
- Italy
- Japan
- Luxembourg
- Mexico
- Netherlands
- New Zealand
- Norway
- Portugal
- Russia
- Singapore
- South Africa
- South Korea
- Spain

- Sweden
- Switzerland
- Turkey
- United Kingdom
- United States

The United Nations Office on Drugs and Crime maintains the *International Money Laundering Information Network*, a web site that provides information and software for anti-money laundering data collection and analysis. The World Bank has a web site that provides policy advice and best practices to governments and the private sector on anti-money laundering issues.

LAWS AND ENFORCEMENT BY REGION

Many jurisdictions adopt a list of specific predicate crimes for money laundering prosecutions, while others criminalize the proceeds of any serious crimes.

AFGHANISTAN

The Financial Transactions and Reports Analysis Center of Afghanistan (FinTRACA) was established as a Financial Intelligence Unit (FIU) under the Anti Money Laundering and Proceeds of Crime Law passed by decree late in 2004. The main purpose of this law is to protect the integrity of the Afghan financial system and to gain compliance with international treaties and conventions. The Financial Intelligence Unit is a semi-independent body that is administratively housed within the Central Bank of Afghanistan (Da Afghanistan Bank). The main objective of FinTRACA is to deny the use of the Afghan financial system to those who obtained funds as the result of illegal activity, and to those who would use it to support terrorist activities.

To meet its objectives, the FinTRACA collects and analyzes information from a variety of sources. These sources include entities with legal obligations to submit reports to the FinTRACA when a suspicious activity is detected, as well as reports of cash transactions above a threshold amount specified by regulation. Also, FinTRACA has access to all related Afghan government information and databases. When the analysis of this information supports the supposition of illegal use of the financial system, the FinTRACA works closely with law enforcement to investigate and prosecute the illegal activity. FinTRACA also cooperates internationally in support of its own analyses and investigations and to support the analyses and investigations of foreign counterparts, to the extent allowed by law. Other functions include training of those entities with legal obligations to report information, development of laws and regulations to support national-level AML objectives, and international and regional cooperation in the development of AML typologies and countermeasures.

AUSTRALIA

AUSTRAC (Australian Transaction Reports and Analysis Centre) is Australia's anti-money laundering and counter-terrorism financing regulator and specialist financial intelligence unit.

The Anti-Money Laundering and Counter-Terrorism Financing Act 2006 (Cth) (AML/CTF Act) is the principal legislative instrument, although there are also offence provisions contained in Division 400 of the Criminal Code Act 1995 (Cth). Upon its introduction, it was intended that the AML/CTF Act would be further amended by a second tranche of reforms extending to designated non-financial businesses and professions (DNFBPs) including, inter alia, lawyers, accountants, jewellers and real estate agents; however, those further reforms have yet to be progressed.

AUSTRAC works collaboratively with Australian industries and businesses in their compliance with anti-money laundering and counter-terrorism financing legislation. Financial institutions in Australia are required to track significant cash transactions (greater than A$10,000.00 or equivalent in physical cash value) that can be used to finance terrorist activities in and outside Australia's borders and report them to AUSTRAC.

BANGLADESH

In Bangladesh, this issue has been dealt with by the Prevention of Money Laundering Act, 2002 (Act No. VII of 2002). In terms of section 2, "Money Laundering means (a) Properties acquired or earned directly or indirectly through illegal means; (b) Illegal transfer, conversion, concealment of location or assistance in the above act of the properties acquired or earned directly of indirectly through legal or illegal means". In this Act, "properties" means movable or immovable properties of any nature and description.

To prevent these Illegal uses of money, the Bangladesh government has introduced the Money Laundering Prevention Act. The Act was last amended in the year 2009 and all the financial institutes are following this act. Till today there are 26 circulars issued by Bangladesh Bank under this act. To prevent money laundering, a banker must do the following:

- While opening a new account, the account opening form should be duly filled up by all the information of the customer.
- The KYC must be properly filled.
- The Transaction Profile (TP) is mandatory for a client to understand his/her transactions. If needed, the TP must be updated at the client's consent.
- All other necessary papers should be properly collected along with the National ID card.
- If any suspicious transaction is noticed, the Branch Anti Money Laundering Compliance Officer (BAMLCO) must be notified and

accordingly the Suspicious Transaction Report (STR) must be filled out.

- The cash department should be aware of the transactions. It must be noted if suddenly a big amount of money is deposited in any account. Proper documents are required if any client does this type of transaction.
- Structuring, over/ under invoicing is another way to do money laundering. The foreign exchange department should look into this matter cautiously.
- If any account has a transaction over 1 million rupees in a single day, it must be reported in a cash transaction report (CTR).
- All bank officials must go through all the 26 circulars and use them.

CANADA

In 1991, the Proceeds of Crime (Money Laundering) Act was brought into force in Canada to give legal effect to the former FATF Forty Recommendations by establishing record keeping and client identification requirements in the financial sector to facilitate the investigation and prosecution of money laundering offences under the Criminal Code of Canada and the Controlled Drugs and Substances Act.

In 2000, the Proceeds of Crime (Money Laundering) Act was amended to expand the scope of its application and to establish a financial intelligence unit with national control over money laundering, namely FINTRAC.

In December 2001, the scope of the Proceeds of Crime (Money Laundering) Act was again expanded by amendments enacted under the Anti-Terrorism Act with the objective of deterring terrorist activity by cutting off sources and channels of funding used by terrorists in response to 9/11. The Proceeds of Crime (Money Laundering) Act was renamed the Proceeds of Crime (Money Laundering) and Terrorist Financing Act.

In December 2006, the Proceeds of Crime (Money Laundering) and Terrorist Financing Act was further amended, in part, in response to pressure from the FATF for Canada to tighten its money laundering and financing of terrorism legislation. The amendments expanded the client identification, record-keeping and reporting requirements for certain organizations and included new obligations to report attempted suspicious transactions and outgoing and incoming international electronic fund transfers, undertake risk assessments and implement written compliance procedures in respect of those risks.

The amendments also enabled greater money laundering and terrorist financing intelligence-sharing among enforcement agencies.

In Canada, casinos, money service businesses, notaries, accountants, banks, securities brokers, life insurance agencies, real estate salespeople and dealers in precious metals and stones are subject to the reporting and record keeping obligations under the Proceeds of Crime (Money Laundering) and Terrorist Financing Act.

EUROPEAN UNION

The EU directive 2005/60/EC "on the prevention of the use of the financial system for the purpose of money laundering and terrorist financing" tries to prevent such crime by requiring banks, real estate agents and many more companies to investigate and report usage of cash in excess of €15,000. The earlier EU directives 91/308/EEC and 2001/97/EC also relate to money laundering. The European Union is currently negotiating a New 4th Anti-Money Laundering Directive that will change the nature of anti-money laundering compliance across the European Union. The current draft Directive has some laudable features and improvements over the previous Directive, not least the intention to move to a risk based and evidence based approach to identifying and managing money laundering and counter terrorist finance risks rather than a tick-box approach to compliance. However, the draft Directive is also causing concern from experts within the financial services and gambling industries due to its failure to co-ordinate cross-border issues for electronic businesses, the risk that it will be disproportionately burdensome and costly for European businesses, it will damage innovation in new business areas such as the regulated e-money and payment services sectors (*e.g.* prepaid cards, e-wallets and money remittance) and will perversely increase the use of cash where there are less controls and there is less monitoring information available to the relevant authorities and law enforcement agencies. The 4th Directive is currently going through the European Parliament and is intended to be finalised in 2014.

INDIA

In 2002, the Parliament of India passed an act called the Prevention of Money Laundering Act, 2002. The main objectives of this act are to prevent money-laundering as well as to provide for confiscation of property either derived from or involved in, money-laundering.

Section 12 (1) describes the obligations that banks, other financial institutions, and intermediaries have to

(a) Maintain records that detail the nature and value of transactions, whether such transactions comprise a single transaction or a series of connected transactions, and where these transactions take place within a month.

(b) Furnish information on transactions referred to in clause (a) to the Director within the time prescribed, including records of the identity of all its clients.

Section 12 (2) prescribes that the records referred to in sub-section (1) as mentioned above, must be maintained for ten years after the transactions finished. It is handled by the Indian Income Tax Department. The provisions of the Act are frequently reviewed and various amendments have been passed from time to time. The recent activity in money laundering in India is through political parties, corporate companies and the shares market. It is investigated by the Enforcement Directorate and Indian Income Tax Department. According to Government of India, out of the total tax arrears of ₹2480 billion (US$40 billion) about 1300 billion (US$21 billion) pertains to money laundering and securities scam cases.

Bank accountants must record all transactions over ₹. 1 million. Bank accountants must maintain this records for 10 years. Banks also must make cash transaction reports (CTRs) and suspicious transaction reports over ₹. 1 million within 7 days of doubt. They must submit the report to the Enforcement Directorate and income tax department.

UNITED KINGDOM

Money laundering and terrorist funding legislation in the UK is governed by four Acts of primary legislation:-

- Terrorism Act 2000
- Anti-terrorism, Crime and Security Act 2001
- Proceeds of Crime Act 2002
- Serious Organised Crime and Police Act 2005
- Money Laundering Regulations 2007

Money Laundering Regulations are designed to protect the UK financial system. If a business is covered by these regulations then controls are put in place to prevent it being used for money laundering.

The Proceeds of Crime Act 2002 contains the primary UK anti-money laundering legislation, including provisions requiring businesses within the "regulated sector" (banking, investment, money transmission, certain professions, etc.) to report to the authorities suspicions of money laundering by customers or others.

Money laundering is broadly defined in the UK. In effect any handling or involvement with any proceeds of any crime (or monies or assets representing the proceeds of crime) can be a money laundering offence. An offender's possession of the proceeds of his own crime falls within the UK definition of money laundering. The definition also covers activities within the traditional definition of money laundering, as a process that conceals or disguises the proceeds of crime to make them appear legitimate.

Unlike certain other jurisdictions (notably the US and much of Europe), UK money laundering offences are not limited to the proceeds of serious crimes, nor are there any monetary limits. Financial transactions need no money laundering design or purpose for UK laws to consider them a money laundering offence. A money laundering offence under UK legislation need not even involve money, since the money laundering legislation covers assets of any description.

In consequence, any person who commits an acquisitive crime (*i.e.*, one that produces some benefit in the form of money or an asset of any description) in the UK inevitably also commits a money laundering offence under UK legislation.

This applies also to a person who, by criminal conduct, evades a liability (such as a taxation liability)—which lawyers call "obtaining a pecuniary advantage"—as he is deemed thereby to obtain a sum of money equal in value to the liability evaded. The principal money laundering offences carry a maximum penalty of 14 years imprisonment.

Secondary regulation is provided by the Money Laundering Regulations 2003, which was replaced by the Money Laundering Regulations 2007. They are directly based on the EU directives 91/308/EEC, 2001/97/EC and 2005/60/EC. One consequence of the Act is that solicitors, accountants, tax advisers, and insolvency practitioners who suspect (as a consequence of information received in the course of their work) that their clients (or others) have engaged in tax evasion or other criminal conduct that produced a benefit, now must report their suspicions to the authorities (since these entail suspicions of money laundering). In most circumstances it would be an offence, "tipping-off", for the reporter to inform the subject of his report that a report has been made. These provisions do not however require disclosure to the authorities of information received by certain professionals in privileged circumstances or where the information is subject to legal professional privilege. Others that are subject to these regulations include financial institutions, credit institutions, estate agents (which includes chartered surveyors), trust and company service providers, high value dealers (who accept cash equivalent to □15,000 or more for goods sold), and casinos.

Professional guidance (which is submitted to and approved by the UK Treasury) is provided by industry groups including the Joint Money Laundering Steering Group, the Law Society. and the Consultative Committee of Accountancy Bodies (CCAB). However there is no obligation on banking institutions to routinely report monetary deposits or transfers above a specified value. Instead reports must be made of all suspicious deposits or transfers, irrespective of their value.

The reporting obligations include reporting suspicious gains from conduct in other countries that would be criminal if it took place in the UK. Exceptions were later added for certain activities legal where they took place, such as bullfighting in Spain.

More than 200,000 reports of suspected money laundering are submitted annually to authorities in the UK (there were 240,582 reports in the year ended 30 September 2010. This was an increase from the 228,834 reports submitted in the previous year). Most of these reports are submitted by banks and similar financial institutions (there were 186,897 reports from the banking sector in the year ended 30 September 2010).

Although 5,108 different organisations submitted suspicious activity reports to the authorities in the year ended 30 September 2010 just four organisations submitted approximately half of all reports, and the top 20 reporting organisations accounted for three-quarters of all reports.

The offence of failing to report a suspicion of money laundering by another person carries a maximum penalty of 5 years imprisonment.

Bureaux de Change

All UK *Bureaux de change* are registered with Her Majesty's Revenue and Customs, which issues a trading licence for each location. Bureaux de change and money transmitters, such as Western Union outlets, in the UK fall within the "regulated sector" and are required to comply with the Money Laundering Regulations 2007. Checks can be carried out by HMRC on all Money Service Businesses.

UNITED STATES

The approach in the United States to stopping money laundering is usually broken into two areas: preventive (regulatory) measures and criminal measures.

Preventive

In an attempt to prevent dirty money from entering the U.S. financial system in the first place, the United States Congress passed a series of laws, starting in 1970, collectively known as the Bank Secrecy Act (BSA). These laws, contained in sections 5311 through 5332 of Title 31 of the United States Code, require financial institutions, which under the current definition include a broad array of entities, including banks, credit card companies, life insurers, money service businesses and broker-dealers in securities, to report certain transactions to the United States Department of the Treasury. Cash transactions in excess of a certain amount must be reported on a currency transaction report (CTR), identifying the individual making the transaction as well as the source of the cash. The law originally required all transactions of US$5,000 or more to be reported, but due to excessively high levels of reporting the threshold was raised to US$10,000.

The U.S. is one of the few countries in the world to require reporting of all cash transactions over a certain limit, although certain businesses can be exempt from the requirement. Additionally, financial institutions must report transaction on a Suspicious Activity Report (SAR) that they deem "suspicious", defined as a knowing or suspecting that the funds come from illegal activity or disguise funds from illegal activity, that it is structured to evade BSA requirements or appears to serve no known business or apparent lawful purpose; or that the institution is being used to facilitate criminal activity. Attempts by customers to circumvent the BSA, generally by structuring cash deposits to amounts lower than US$10,000 by breaking them up and depositing them on different days or at different locations also violates the law. The financial database created by these reports is administered by the U.S.'s Financial Intelligence Unit (FIU), called the Financial Crimes Enforcement Network (FinCEN), located in Vienna, Virginia. The reports are made available to U.S. criminal investigators, as well as other FIU's around the globe, and FinCEN conducts computer assisted analyses of these reports to determine trends and refer investigations.

The BSA requires financial institutions to engage in customer due diligence, which is sometimes known in the parlance as know your customer. This includes obtaining satisfactory identification to give assurance that the account is in the customer's true name, and having an understanding of the expected nature and source of the money that flows through the customer's accounts. Other classes of customers, such as those with private banking accounts and those of foreign government officials, are subjected to enhanced due diligence because the law deems that those types of accounts are a higher risk for money laundering. All accounts are subject to ongoing monitoring, in which internal bank software scrutinizes transactions and flags for manual inspection those that fall outside certain parameters. If a manual inspection reveals that the transaction is suspicious, the institution should file a Suspicious Activity Report.

The regulators of the industries involved are responsible to ensure that the financial institutions comply with the BSA. For example, the Federal Reserve and the Office of the Comptroller of the Currency regularly inspect banks, and may impose civil fines or refer matters for criminal prosecution for non-compliance. A number of banks have been fined and prosecuted for failure to comply with the BSA. Most famously, Riggs Bank, in Washington D.C., was prosecuted and functionally driven out of business as a result of its failure to apply proper money laundering controls, particularly as it related to foreign political figures.

In addition to the BSA, the U.S. imposes controls on the movement of currency across its borders, requiring individuals to report the transportation of cash in excess of US$10,000 on a form called Report of International Transportation of Currency or Monetary Instruments (known as a CMIR). Likewise, businesses, such as automobile dealerships, that receive cash in excess of US$10,000 must file a Form 8300 with the Internal Revenue Service, identifying the source of the cash.

On 1 September 2010, the Financial Crimes Enforcement Network issued an advisory on "informal value transfer systems" referencing *United States v. Banki*.

Criminal Sanctions

Money laundering has been criminalized in the United States since the Money Laundering Control Act of 1986. The law, contained at section 1956 of Title 18 of the United States Code, prohibits individuals from engaging in a financial transaction with proceeds that were generated from certain specific crimes, known as "specified unlawful activities" (SUAs). The law requires that an individual specifically intend in making the transaction to conceal the source, ownership or control of the funds.

There is no minimum threshold of money, and no requirement that the transaction succeeded in actually disguising the money. A "financial transaction" has been broadly defined, and need not involve a financial institution, or even a business. Merely passing money from one person to another, with the intent to disguise the source, ownership, location or control of the money, has been deemed a financial transaction under the law.

The possession of money without either a financial transaction or an intent to conceal is not a crime in the United States. Besides money laundering, the law contained in section 1957 of Title 18 of the United States Code, prohibits spending more than US$10,000 derived from an SUA, regardless of whether the individual wishes to disguise it. It carries a lesser penalty than money laundering, and unlike the money laundering statute, requires that the money pass through a financial institution.

According to the records compiled by the United States Sentencing Commission, in 2009, the United States Department of Justice typically convicted a little over 81,000 people; of this, approximately 800 are convicted of money laundering as the primary or most serious charge. The Anti-Drug Abuse Act of 1988 expanded the definition of financial institution to include businesses such as car dealers and real estate closing personnel and required them to file reports on large currency transaction. It required verification of identity of those who purchase monetary instruments over $3,000. The Annunzio-Wylie Anti-Money Laundering Act of 1992 strengthened sanctions for BSA violations, required so called "Suspicious Activity Reports" and eliminated previously used "Criminal Referral Forms", required verification and recordkeeping for wire transfers and established the Bank Secrecy Act Advisory Group (BSAAG).

The Money Laundering Suppression Act from 1994 required banking agencies to review and enhance training, develop anti-money laundering examination procedures, review and enhance procedures for referring cases to law enforcement agencies, streamlined theCurrency transaction report exemption process, required each Money services business (MSB) to be registered by an owner or controlling person, required every MSB to maintain a list of businesses authorized to act as agents in connection with the financial services offered by the MSB, made operating an unregistered MSB a federal crime, and recommended that states adopt uniform laws applicable to MSBs. The Money Laundering and Financial Crimes Strategy Act of 1998 required banking agencies to develop anti-money laundering training for examiners, required the Department of the Treasury and other agencies to develop a "National Money Laundering Strategy", created the "High Intensity Money Laundering and Related Financial Crime Area" (HIFCA) Task Forces to concentrate law enforcement efforts at the federal, state and local levels in zones where money laundering is prevalent.

HIFCA zones may be defined geographically or can be created to address money laundering in an industry sector, a financial institution, or group of financial institutions. The Intelligence Reform and Terrorism Prevention Act of 2004 amended the Bank Secrecy Act to require the Secretary of the Treasury to prescribe regulations requiring certain financial institutions to report cross-border electronic transmittals of funds, if the Secretary determines that reporting is "reasonably necessary" in "anti-money laundering /combatting financing of terrorists (Anti-Money Laundering/Combating the Financing of Terrorism AML/CFT).

ELECTRONIC MONEY

In theory, electronic money should provide as easy a method of transferring value without revealing identity as untracked banknotes, especially wire transfers involving anonymity-protecting numbered bank accounts. In practice, however, the record-keeping capabilities of Internet service providers and other network resource maintainers tend to frustrate that intuition. While some cryptocurrencies under recent development have aimed to provide for more possibility of transaction anonymity for various reasons, the degree to which they succeed—and, in consequence, the degree to which they offer benefits for money laundering efforts—is controversial.

In 2013, Jean-Loup Richet, a research fellow at ESSEC ISIS, surveyed a new techniques that cybercriminals were using in a report written for the United Nations Office on Drugs and Crime. A common approach was to use a digital currency exchanger service which converted dollars into a digital currency called Liberty Reserve and could be sent and received anonymously. The receiver could convert the Liberty Reserve currency back into cash for a small fee. In May 2013, the US authorities shut down Liberty Reserve charging its founder and various others with money laundering. Another increasingly common way of laundering money is to use online gaming. In a growing number of online games such as Second Life or World of Warcraft, it is possible to convert money into virtual goods, services or virtual cash that can later be converted back into money.

NOTABLE CASES

- Bank of Credit and Commerce International: Unknown amount, estimated in billions, of criminal proceeds, including drug trafficking money, laundered during the mid-1980s.
- Bank of New York: US$7 billion of Russian capital flight laundered through accounts controlled by bank executives, late 1990s.
- Ferdinand Marcos: Unknown amount, estimated at US$10 billion of government assets laundered through banks and financial institutions

in the United States, Liechtenstein, Austria, Panama, Netherlands Antilles, Cayman Islands, Vanuatu, Hong Kong, Singapore, Monaco, the Bahamas, the Vatican and Switzerland.

- In December 2012, HSBC: paid a record $1.9 Billion fines for money-laundering hundreds of millions of dollars for drug traffickers, terrorists and sanctioned governments such as Iran. The money-laundering occurred throughout the 2000s.
- In May 2013, Liberty Reserve was seized by United States federal authorities for laundering $6 billion.
- Institute for the Works of Religion: Italian authorities investigated suspected money laundering transactions amounting to US$218 million made by the IOR to several Italian banks.
- Nauru: US$70 billion of Russian capital flight laundered through unregulated Nauru offshore shell banks, late 1990s
- Sani Abacha: US$2–5 billion of government assets laundered through banks in the UK, Luxembourg, Jersey (Channel Islands), and Switzerland, by the president of Nigeria.
- Standard Chartered: paid $330 million in fines for money-laundering hundreds of billions of dollars for Iran. The money-laundering took place in the 2000s and occurred for "nearly a decade to hide 60,000 transactions worth $250 billion".
- In June 2014, BNP Paribas pleaded guilty to falsifying business records and conspiracy, having violated U.S. sanctions against Cuba, Iran, and Sudan. It agreed to pay an $8.9 billion fine, the largest ever for violating U.S. sanctions.

Reverse money laundering []

Reverse money laundering is a process that disguises a legitimate source of funds that are to be used for illegal purposes. For example, in an affidavit filed 24 March 2014 in United States District Court, Northern California, San Francisco Division, FBI special agent Emmanuel V. Pascau alleged that several people associated with the Chee Kung Tong organization, and California State Senator Leland Yee, engaged in reverse money laundering activities.

INTERNATIONAL MONETARY FUND

The International Monetary Fund (IMF) is an international organization that was initiated in 1944 at the Bretton Woods Conference and formally created in 1945 by 29 member countries. The IMF's stated goal was to assist in the reconstruction of the world's international payment system post–World War II. Countries contribute funds to a pool through a quota system from which countries with payment imbalances temporarily can borrow money and other resources. As of the *14th General Review of Quotas* in late 2010 the fund stood at SDR476.8bn, or about US$755.7bn at then-current exchange rates. Through this fund, and other activities such as surveillance of its members' economies and the demand for self-correcting policies, the IMF works to improve the economies of its member countries.

The IMF is a self-described "organization of 188 countries, working to foster global monetary cooperation, secure financial stability, facilitate international trade, promote high employment and sustainable economic growth, and reduce poverty around the world."The organization's objectives are stated in the Articles of Agreement and can be summarised as: to promote international economic co-operation, international trade, employment, and exchange-rate stability, including by making financial resources available to member countries to meet balance of payments needs. Its headquarters are in Washington, D.C., United States.

FUNCTIONS

The IMF works to foster global growth and economic stability. It provides policy advice and financing to members in economic difficulties and also works with developing nationsto help them achieve macroeconomic stability and reduce poverty. The rationale for this is that private international capital markets function imperfectly and many countries have limited access to financial markets. Such market imperfections, together with balance of payments financing, provide the justification for official financing, without which many countries could only correct large external payment imbalances through measures with adverse effects on both national and international economic prosperity. The IMF can provide other sources of financing to countries in need that would not be available in the absence of an economic stabilization programme supported by the Fund.

Upon initial IMF formation, its two primary functions were: to oversee the fixed exchange rate arrangements between countries, thus helping national governments manage their exchange rates and allowing these governments to prioritise economic growth, and to provide short-term capital to aid balance of payments. This assistance was meant to prevent the spread of international economic crises. The Fund was also intended to help mend the pieces of the international economy post the Great Depression and World War II.

The IMF's role was fundamentally altered after the floating exchange rates post 1971. It shifted to examining the economic policies of countries with IMF loan agreements to determine if a shortage of capital was due to economic fluctuations or economic policy. The IMF also researched what types of government policy would ensure economic recovery. The new challenge is to promote and implement policy that reduces the frequency of crises among the emerging market countries, especially the middle-income countries that are open to massive capital outflows. Rather than maintaining a position of oversight of only exchange rates, their function became one of "surveillance" of the overall macroeconomic performance of its member countries. Their role became a lot more active because the IMF now manages economic policy instead of just exchange rates. In addition, the IMF negotiates conditions on lending and loans under their policy of conditionality, which was established in the 1950s. Low-income countries can borrow onconcessional terms, which means there is a period of time with no interest rates, through the Extended Credit Facility (ECF), the Standby Credit Facility (SCF) and the Rapid Credit Facility (RCF). Nonconcessional loans, which include interest rates, are provided mainly through Stand-By Arrangements (SBA), the Flexible Credit Line (FCL), the Precautionary and Liquidity Line (PLL), and the Extended Fund Facility. The IMF provides emergency assistance via the newly introduced Rapid Financing Instrument (RFI) to all its members facing urgent balance of payments needs.

SURVEILLANCE OF THE GLOBAL ECONOMY

The IMF is mandated to oversee the international monetary and financial system and monitor the economic and financial policies of its 188 member countries. This activity is known as surveillance and facilitates international co-operation. Since the demise of the Bretton Woods system of fixed exchange rates in the early 1970s, surveillance has evolved largely by way of changes in procedures rather than through the adoption of new obligations. The responsibilities of the Fund changed from those of guardian to those of overseer of members' policies.

The Fund typically analyses the appropriateness of each member country's economic and financial policies for achieving orderly economic growth, and assesses the consequences of these policies for other countries and for the global economy.

In 1995 the International Monetary Fund began work on data dissemination standards with the view of guiding IMF member countries to disseminate their economic and financial data to the public.

The International Monetary and Financial Committee (IMFC) endorsed the guidelines for the dissemination standards and they were split into two tiers: The General Data Dissemination System (GDDS) and theSpecial Data Dissemination Standard (SDDS).

The International Monetary Fund executive board approved the SDDS and GDDS in 1996 and 1997 respectively, and subsequent amendments were published in a revised *Guide to the General Data Dissemination System*. The system is aimed primarily at statisticians and aims to improve many aspects of statistical systems in a country. It is also part of the World Bank Millennium Development Goals and Poverty Reduction Strategic Papers.

The primary objective of the GDDS is to encourage IMF member countries to build a framework to improve data quality and increase statistical capacity building. Upon building a framework, a country can evaluate statistical needs, set priorities in improving the timeliness, transparency, reliability and accessibility of financial and economic data. Some countries initially used the GDDS, but later upgraded to SDDS.

Some entities that are not themselves IMF members also contribute statistical data to the systems:

- Palestinian Authority – GDDS
- Hong Kong – SDDS
- Macau – GDDS
- EU institutions:
- the European Central Bank for the Eurozone – SDDS
- Eurostat for the whole EU – SDDS, thus providing data from Cyprus (not using any DDSystem on its own) and Malta (using only GDDS on its own)

Conditionality of Loans

IMF conditionality is a set of policies or conditions that the IMF requires in exchange for financial resources. The IMF does require collateral from countries for loans but also requires the government seeking assistance to correct its macroeconomic imbalances in the form of policy reform. If the conditions are not met, the funds are withheld.Conditionality is perhaps the most controversial aspect of IMF policies. The concept of conditionality was introduced in an Executive Board decision in 1952 and later incorporated in the Articles of Agreement. Conditionality is associated with economic theory as well as an enforcement mechanism for repayment. Stemming primarily from the work of Jacques Polak in the Fund's research department, the theoretical underpinning of conditionality was the "monetary approach to the balance of payments."

Structural Adjustment

Some of the conditions for structural adjustment can include:

- Cutting expenditures, also known as austerity.
- Focusing economic output on direct export and resource extraction,
- Devaluation of currencies,
- Trade liberalisation, or lifting import and export restrictions,
- Increasing the stability of investment (by supplementing foreign direct investment with the opening of domestic stock markets),
- Balancing budgets and not overspending,
- Removing price controls and state subsidies,
- Privatization, or divestiture of all or part of state-owned enterprises,
- Enhancing the rights of foreign investors vis-a-vis national laws,
- Improving governance and fighting corruption.

These conditions have also been sometimes labelled as the Washington Consensus.

Benefits

These loan conditions ensure that the borrowing country will be able to repay the Fund and that the country won't attempt to solve their balance of payment problems in a way that would negatively impact the international economy. The incentive problem of moral hazard, which is the actions of economic agents maximising their own utility to the detriment of others when they do not bear the full consequences of their actions, is mitigated through conditions rather than providing collateral; countries in need of IMF loans do not generally possess internationally valuable collateral anyway.

Conditionality also reassures the IMF that the funds lent to them will be used for the purposes defined by the Articles of Agreement and provides safeguards that country will be able to rectify its macroeconomic and structural imbalances. In the judgement of the Fund, the adoption by the member of certain corrective measures or policies will allow it to repay the Fund, thereby ensuring that the same resources will be available to support other members.

As of 2004, borrowing countries have had a very good track record for repaying credit extended under the Fund's regular lending facilities with full interest over the duration of the loan. This indicates that Fund lending does not impose a burden on creditor countries, as lending countries receive market-rate interest on most of their quota subscription, plus any of their own-currency subscriptions that are loaned out by the Fund, plus all of the reserve assets that they provide the Fund.

HISTORY

The International Monetary Fund was originally laid out as a part of the Bretton Woods system exchange agreement in 1944. During the earlier Great Depression, countries sharply raised barriers to foreign trade in an attempt to improve their failing economies. This led to the devaluation of national currencies and a decline in world trade.

This breakdown in international monetary co-operation created a need for oversight. The representatives of 45 governments met at theBretton Woods Conference in the Mount Washington Hotel in the area of Bretton Woods, New Hampshire in the United States, to discuss framework for post-World War II international economic co-operation. The participating countries were concerned with the rebuilding of Europe and the global economic system after the war.

There were two views on the role the IMF should assume as a global economic institution. British economist John Maynard Keynesimagined that the IMF would be a cooperative fund upon which member states could draw to maintain economic activity and employment through periodic crises. This view suggested an IMF that helped governments and to act as the US government had during the New Dealin response to World War II.

American delegate Harry Dexter White foresaw an IMF that functioned more like a bank, making sure that borrowing states could repay their debts on time. Most of White's plan was incorporated into the final acts adopted at Bretton Woods.

The International Monetary Fund formally came into existence on 27 December 1945, when the first 29 countries ratified its Articles of Agreement. By the end of 1946 the Fund had grown to 39 members. On 1 March 1947, the IMF began its financial operations,and on 8 May France became the first country to borrow from it.

The IMF was one of the key organisations of the international economic system; its design allowed the system to balance the rebuilding of international capitalism with the maximisation of national economic sovereignty and human welfare, also known as embedded liberalism. The IMF's influence in the global economy steadily increased as it accumulated more members. The increase reflected in particular the attainment of political independence by many African countries and more recently the 1991 dissolution of the Soviet Unionbecause most countries in the Soviet sphere of influence did not join the IMF.

The Bretton Woods system prevailed until 1971, when the US government suspended the convertibility of the US$ (and dollar reserves held by other governments) into gold. This is known as the Nixon Shock.

Since 2000

In May 2010, the IMF participated, in 3:11 proportion, in the first Greek bailout that totalled □110bn. This bailout was notable for several reasons: the funds were funnelled directly to the (largely European) private bondholders, which endured no haircuts to the chagrin of the Swiss, Brazilian, Indian, Russian, and Argentinian Directors; the Greek authorities (at the time, George Papandreou andGiorgos Papakonstantinou) themselves ruled out a haircut of the private bondholders; the Greek private sector was happy to curtail the 13th and 14th month civil service pay scheme, because the Greek government was otherwise impotent.

A second bailout package of more than □100bn was agreed over the course of a few months from October 2011, during which time Papandreou was forced from office. The so-called Troika, of which the IMF is part, are joint managers of this programme, which was approved by the Executive Directors of the IMF on 15 March 2012 for SDR23.8bn, and which saw private bondholders take a haircut of upwards of 50 per cent. In the interval between May 2010 and February 2012 the private banks of Holland, France and Germany managed to reduce their exposure to Greek debt from a total of □122bn to a total of □66bn.

As of January 2012, the largest borrowers from the IMF in order were Greece, Portugal, Ireland, Romania and Ukraine.

On 25 March 2013, a □10bn international bailout of Cyprus was agreed by the Troika, at the cost to the Cypriots of its agreement: to close the country's second-largest bank; to impose a one-time bank deposit levy on all uninsured deposits there. No insured deposit of □100k or less were to be affected under the terms of a novel bail-inschcmc.

The topic of sovereign debt restructuring was taken up by the IMF in April 2013 for the first time since 2005, in a report entitled "Sovereign Debt Restructuring-Recent Developments And Implications For The Fund's Legal And Policy Framework". The paper, which was discussed by the board on 20 May,summarised the recent experiences in Greece, St Kitts and Nevis, Belize and Jamaica. An explanatory interview with Deputy Director Hugh Bredenkamp was published a few days later, as was a deconstruction by Matina Stevis of the Wall Street Journal.

In the October 2013 Financial Monitor publication, the IMF suggested that a capital levy capable of reducing Euro-area government debt ratios to "end-2007 levels" would require a very high tax rate; about 10 percent.

The Fiscal Affairs department of the IMF, headed by Dr. Sanjeev Gupta, produced in January 2014 a report entitled "Fiscal Policy and Income Inequality" which stated that "Some taxes levied on wealth, especially on immovable property, are also an option for economies seeking more progressive taxation.... Property taxes are equitable and efficient, but underutilized in many economies.... There is considerable scope to exploit this tax more fully, both as a revenue source and as a redistributive instrument."

At the end of March 2014, the IMF secured an $18bn bailout fund for the provisional government of the Ukraine in the aftermath of the 2014 Ukrainian revolution.

The topic of the US executive board veto was discussed again by some junior members in April 2014. The countries were fed up with the failure to ratify a four-year old agreement to restructure the lender. Singaporean Finance Minister and IMF steering committee chairman Tharman Shanmugaratnam said it could cause "disruptive change" in the global economy: "We are more likely over time to see a weakening of multilateralism, the emergence of regionalism, bilateralism and other ways of dealing with global problems," and that would make the world a "less safe" place.

MEMBER COUNTRIES

Since the IMF is affiliated with the UN and falls under its umbrella, the 188 corporate members of the IMF include187 members of the UN and the Republic of Kosovo. The corporate members appoint *ex-officio* voting members, who are listed below. All members of the IMF are also International Bank for Reconstruction and Development (IBRD) members and vice versa.

Former members are Cuba (which left in 1964) and the Republic of China, which was ejected from the UN in 1980 after losing the support of then US President Jimmy Carter and was replaced by the People's Republic of China.However, "Taiwan Province of China" is still listed in the official IMF indices.

Apart from Cuba, the other UN states that do not belong to the IMF are Andorra, Liechtenstein, Monaco, Nauru andNorth Korea.

The former Czechoslovakia was expelled in 1954 for "failing to provide required data" and was readmitted in 1990, after the Velvet Revolution. Poland withdrew in 1950—allegedly pressured by the Soviet Union—but returned in 1986.

Qualifications

Any country may apply to be a part of the IMF. Post-IMF formation, in the early postwar period, rules for IMF membership were left relatively loose. Members needed to make periodic membership payments towards their quota, to refrain from currency restrictions unless granted IMF permission, to abide by the Code of Conduct in the IMF Articles of Agreement, and to provide national economic information. However, stricter rules were imposed on governments that applied to the IMF for funding.

The countries that joined the IMF between 1945 and 1971 agreed to keep their exchange rates secured at rates that could be adjusted only to correct a "fundamental disequilibrium" in the balance of payments, and only with the IMF's agreement.

Some members have a very difficult relationship with the IMF and even when they are still members they do not allow themselves to be monitored. Argentina for example refuses to participate in an Article IV Consultation with the IMF.

Benefits

Member countries of the IMF have access to information on the economic policies of all member countries, the opportunity to influence other members' economic policies, technical assistance in banking, fiscal affairs, and exchange matters, financial support in times of payment difficulties, and increased opportunities for trade and investment.

LEADERSHIP

Board of Governors

The Board of Governors consists of one governor and one alternate governor for each member country. Each member country appoints its two governors. The Board normally meets once a year and is responsible for electing or appointing executive directors to the Executive Board. While the Board of Governors is officially responsible for approving quota increases, Special Drawing Right allocations, the admittance of new members, compulsory withdrawal of members, and amendments to the Articles of Agreement and By-Laws, in practice it has delegated most of its powers to the IMF's Executive Board.

The Board of Governors is advised by the International Monetary and Financial Committee and the Development Committee. The International

Monetary and Financial Committee has 24 members and monitors developments in global liquidity and the transfer of resources to developing countries. The Development Committee has 25 members and advises on critical development issues and on financial resources required to promote economic development in developing countries. They also advise on trade and global environmental issues.

Executive Board

24 Executive Directors make up Executive Board. The Executive Directors represent all 188 member-countries in a geographically-based roster. Countries with large economies have their own Executive Director, but most countries are grouped in constituencies representing four or more countries.

Following the *2008 Amendment on Voice and Participation* which came into effect in March 2011, eight countries each appoint an Executive Director: the United States, Japan, Germany, France, the United Kingdom, China, the Russian Federation, and Saudi Arabia. The remaining 16 Directors represent constituencies consisting of 4 to 22 countries. The Executive Director representing the largest constituency of 22 countries accounts for 1.55 per cent of the vote. This Board usually meets several times each week. The Board membership and constituency is scheduled for periodic review every eight years.

Managing Director

The IMF is led by a managing director, who is head of the staff and serves as Chairman of the Executive Board. The managing director is assisted by a First Deputy managing director and three other Deputy Managing Directors. Historically the IMF's managing director has been European and the president of the World Bank has been from the United States. However, this standard is increasingly being questioned and competition for these two posts may soon open up to include other qualified candidates from any part of the world.

Previous managing director Dominique Strauss-Kahn was arrested in connection with charges of sexually assaulting a New York hotel room attendant. Strauss-Kahn subsequently resigned his position on 18 May. On 28 June 2011 Christine Lagardewas confirmed as managing director of the IMF for a five-year term starting on 5 July 2011. In 2012, Lagarde was paid a salary of US$467,940, and this is automatically increased every year according to inflation. In addition to that, the director receives an allowance of US$83,760, and additional expenses for entertainment. This income is tax-free.

VOTING POWER

Voting power in the IMF is based on a quota system. Each member has a number of basic votes (each member's number of basic votes equals 5.502 per cent of the total votes), plus one additional vote for each Special Drawing Right

(SDR) of 100,000 of a member country's quota. The Special Drawing Right is the unit of account of the IMF and represents a claim to currency.

Effects of the Quota System

The IMF's quota system was created to raise funds for loans. Each IMF member country is assigned a quota, or contribution, that reflects the country's relative size in the global economy. Each member's quota also determines its relative voting power. Thus, financial contributions from member governments are linked to voting power in the organisation.

This system follows the logic of a shareholder-controlled organisation: wealthy countries have more say in the making and revision of rules. Since decision making at the IMF reflects each member's relative economic position in the world, wealthier countries that provide more money to the fund have more influence in the IMF than poorer members that contribute less; nonetheless, the IMF focuses on redistribution.

Developing Countries

Quotas are normally reviewed every five years and can be increased when deemed necessary by the Board of Governors. Currently, reforming the representation of developing countries within the IMF has been suggested. These countries' economies represent a large portion of the global economic system but this is not reflected in the IMF's decision making process through the nature of the quota system. Joseph Stiglitz argues "There is a need to provide more effective voice and representation for developing countries, which now represent a much larger portion of world economic activity since 1944, when the IMF was created." In 2008, a number of quota reforms were passed including shifting 6 per cent of quota shares to dynamic emerging markets and developing countries.

United States Influence

A second criticism is that the United States' transition to neo liberalism and global capitalism also led to a change in the identity and functions of international institutions like the IMF. Because of the high involvement and voting power of the United States, the global economic ideology could effectively be transformed to match the US's. This is consistent with the IMF's function change during the 1970s after the Nixon Shock ended the Bretton Woods system. Another criticism is that allies of the United States are able to receive bigger loans with fewer conditions.

Overcoming Borrower/creditor Divide

The IMF's membership is divided along income lines: certain countries provide the financial resources while others use these resources. Both developed country "creditors" anddeveloping country "borrowers" are members of the IMF. The developed countries provide the financial resources but rarely enter into IMF loan agreements; they are the creditors. Conversely, the developing countries use the lending services but contribute little to the pool of money available to lend because their quotas are smaller; they are the borrowers. Thus, tension is created around governance issues because these two groups, creditors and borrowers, have fundamentally different interests in terms of the conditions of these loans.

The criticism is that the system of voting power distribution through a quota system institutionalises borrower subordination and creditor dominance. The resulting division of the Fund's membership into borrowers and non-borrowers has increased the controversy around conditionality because the borrowing members are interested in making loan access easier while the creditor members want to maintain reassurance that the loans will be repaid.

USE

A recent source reveals that the average overall use of IMF credit per decade increased, in real terms, by 21 per cent between the 1970s and 1980s, and increased again by just over 22 per cent percent from the 1980s to the 1991–2005 period. Another study has suggested that since 1950 the continent of Africa alone has received $300 billion from the IMF, the World Bank and affiliate institutions

A study done by Bumba Mukherjee found that developing democratic countries benefit more from IMF programmes than developing autocratic countries because policy-making, and the process of deciding where loaned money is used, is more transparent within a democracy. One study done by Randall Stone found that although earlier studies found little impact of IMF programmes on balance of payments, more recent studies using more sophisticated methods and larger samples "usually found IMF programmes improved the balance of payments."

Exceptional Access Framework - Sovereign Debt

The Exceptional Access Framework was created in 2003 when John B. Taylor was Under Secretary of the U.S. Treasury for International Affairs. The new Framework became fully operational in February 2003 and it was applied in the subsequent decisions on Argentina and Brazil. Its purpose was to place some sensible rules and limits on the way the IMF makes loans to support governments with debt problem—especially in emerging markets—and thereby move away from the bailout mentality that came out of the 1990s. Such a reform was essential for ending the terrible crisis atmosphere that then existed in emerging markets.

The reform was closely related to, and put in place nearly simultaneously with, the actions of several emerging market countries to place collective action clauses in their bond contracts.

In 2010, the framework was abandoned so the IMF could make loans to Greece in an unsustainable and political situation.

The topic of sovereign debt restructuring was taken up by IMF staff in April 2013 for the first time since 2005, in a report entitled "Sovereign Debt Restructuring-Recent Developments and Implications for The Fund's Legal and Policy Framework". The paper, which was discussed by the board on 20 May,summarised the recent experiences in Greece, St Kitts and Nevis, Belize and Jamaica. An explanatory interview with Deputy Director Hugh Bredenkamp was published a few days later, as was a deconstruction by Matina Stevis of the Wall Street Journal.

The staff was directed to formulate an updated policy, which was accomplished on 22 May 2014 with a report entitled "The Fund's Lending Framework and Sovereign Debt-Preliminary Considerations", and taken up by the Executive Board on 13 June. The staff proposed that "in circumstances where a (Sovereign) member has lost market access and debt is considered sustainable... the IMF would be able to provide Exceptional Access on the basis of a debt operation that involves an extension of maturities," which was labelled a "reprofiling operation". These reprofiling operations would "generally be less costly to the debtor and creditors—and thus to the system overall—relative to either an upfront debt reduction operation or a bail-out that is followed by debt reduction... (and) would be envisaged only when both (a) a member has lost market access and (b) debt is assessed to be sustainable, but not with high probability... Creditors will only agree if they understand that such an amendment is necessary to avoid a worse outcome: namely, a default and/or an operation involving debt reduction... Collective action clauses, which now exist in most—but not all—bonds, would be relied upon to address collective action problems."

IMF AND GLOBALIZATION

Globalization encompasses three institutions: global financial markets and transnational companies, national governments linked to each other in economic and military alliances led by the US, and rising "global governments" such as World Trade Organization (WTO), IMF, and World Bank. Charles Derber argues in his book *People Before Profit,*"These interacting institutions create a new global power system where sovereignty is globalized, taking power and constitutional authority away from nations and giving it to global markets and international bodies." Titus Alexander argues that this system institutionalises global inequality between western countries and the Majority World in a form of global apartheid, in which the IMF is a key pillar.

The establishment of globalised economic institutions has been both a symptom of and a stimulus for globalization. The development of the World Bank, the IMF regional development banks such as the European Bank for Reconstruction and Development (EBRD), and, more recently, multilateral trade institutions such as the WTO indicates the trend away from the dominance of the state as the exclusive unit of analysis in international affairs. Globalization has thus been transformative in terms of a reconceptualising ofstate sovereignty.

Following US President Bill Clinton's administration's aggressive financial deregulation campaign in the 1990s, globalisation leaders overturned long-standing restrictions by governments that limited foreign ownership of their banks, deregulated currency exchange, and eliminated restrictions on how quickly money could be withdrawn by foreign investors.

CRITICISMS

Overseas Development Institute (ODI) research undertaken in 1980 pointed to five main criticisms of the IMF which support the analysis that it is a pillar of what activist Titus Alexander calls global apartheid. Firstly, developed countries were seen to have a more dominant role and control over less developed countries (LDCs) primarily due to the Western bias towards a capitalist form of the world economy with professional staff being Western trained and believing in the efficacy of market-oriented policies.

Secondly, the Fund worked on the incorrect assumption that all payments disequilibria were caused domestically. The Group of 24 (G-24), on behalf of LDC members, and theUnited Nations Conference on Trade and Development (UNCTAD) complained that the Fund did not distinguish sufficiently between disequilibria with predominantly external as opposed to internal causes.

This criticism was voiced in the aftermath of the 1973 oil crisis. Then LDCs found themselves with payments deficits due to adverse changes in their terms of trade, with the Fund prescribing stabilisation programmes similar to those suggested for deficits caused by government over-spending. Faced with long-term, externally generated disequilibria, the Group of 24 argued that LDCs should be allowed more time to adjust their economies and that the policies needed to achieve such adjustment are different from demand-management programmes devised primarily with internally generated disequilibria in mind.

The third criticism was that the effects of Fund policies were anti-developmental. The deflationary effects of IMF programmes quickly led to losses of output and employment in economies where incomes were low and unemployment was high. Moreover, it was sometimes claimed that the burden of the deflationary effects was borne disproportionately by the poor.

Fourthly is the accusation that harsh policy conditions were self-defeating where a vicious circle developed when members refused loans due to harsh conditionality, making their economy worse and eventually taking loans as a drastic medicine.

Lastly is the point that the Fund's policies lack a clear economic rationale. Its policy foundations were theoretical and unclear due to differing opinions and departmental rivalries whilst dealing with countries with widely varying economic circumstances.

ODI conclusions were that the Fund's very nature of promoting market-oriented economic approach attracted unavoidable criticism, as LDC governments were likely to object when in a tight corner. Yet, on the other hand, the Fund could provide a 'scapegoat service' where governments could take loans as a last resort, whilst blaming international bankers for any economic downfall. The ODI conceded that the fund was to some extent insensitive to political aspirations of LDCs, while its policy conditions were inflexible.

Argentina, which had been considered by the IMF to be a model country in its compliance to policy proposals by the Bretton Woods institutions, experienced a catastrophic economic crisis in 2001, which some believe to have been caused by IMF-induced budget restrictions—which undercut the government's ability to sustain national infrastructure even in crucial areas such as health, education, and security—and privatisation of strategically vital national resources. Others attribute the crisis to Argentina's misdesigned fiscal federalism, which caused subnational spending to increase rapidly. The crisis added to widespread hatred of this institution in Argentina and other South American countries, with many blaming the IMF for the region's economic problems. The current—as of early 2006—trend towards moderate left-wing governments in the region and a growing concern with the development of a regional economic policy largely independent of big business pressures has been ascribed to this crisis.

In an interview, the former Romanian Prime Minister Cãlin Popescu-Tãriceanu claimed that "Since 2005, IMF is constantly making mistakes when it appreciates the country's economic performances." Former Tanzanian President Julius Nyerere famously questioned, "Who elected the IMF to be the ministry of finance for every country in the world?" and therefore described it as the *International Ministry of Finance.*

He also claimed that many of debt-ridden African states were losing their sovereignty to the IMF and the World Bank by agreeing to their support measures.

Conditionality of Loans

The IMF has been criticised for being 'out of touch' with local economic conditions, cultures, and environments in the countries they are requiring policy reform. The economic advice the IMF gives might not always take into consideration the difference between what spending means on paper and how it is felt by citizens.

For example, some people believe that Jeffrey Sachs' work shows that "the Fund's usual prescription is 'budgetary belt tightening to countries who are much too poor to own belts'". It has been said that the IMF's role as a generalist institution specialising in macroeconomic issues needs reform.

Conditionality has also been criticised because a country can pledge collateral of "acceptable assets" to obtain waivers on certain conditions. However, that assumes that all countries have the capability and choice to provide acceptable collateral.

One view is that conditionality undermines domestic political institutions. The recipient governments are sacrificing policy autonomy in exchange for funds, which can lead to public resentment of the local leadership for accepting and enforcing the IMF conditions. Political instability can result from more leadership turnover as political leaders are replaced in electoral backlashes. IMF conditions are often criticised for their bias against economic growth and reduce government services, thus increasing unemployment.

Another criticism is that IMF programmes are only designed to address poor governance, excessive government spending, excessive government intervention in markets, and too much state ownership. This assumes that this narrow range of issues represents the only possible problems; everything is standardised and differing contexts are ignored.A country may also be compelled to accept conditions it would not normally accept had they not been in a financial crisis in need of assistance.

On top of that, regardless of what methodologies and data sets used, it comes to same conclusion of exacerbating income inequality. With Gini coefficient, it became clear that countries with IMF programmes face increased income inequality.

It is claimed that conditionalities retard social stability and hence inhibit the stated goals of the IMF, while Structural Adjustment Programmes lead to an increase in poverty in recipient countries. The IMF sometimes advocates "austerity programmes," cutting public spending and increasing taxes even when the economy is weak, to bring budgets closer to a balance, thus reducing budget deficits. Countries are often advised to lower their corporate tax rate. In *Globalization and Its Discontents*, Joseph E. Stiglitz, former chief economist and senior vice-president at the World Bank, criticises these policies. He argues that by converting to a more monetarist approach, the purpose of the fund is no longer valid, as it was designed to provide funds for countries to carry out Keynesian reflations, and that the IMF "was not participating in a conspiracy, but it was reflecting the interests and ideology of the Western financial community."

International politics plays an important role in decision making in the IMF. The power each member state has is often proportional to its economic clout and contribution to IMF finances. The United States, the initial founding member of IMF, has the greatest number of votes and therefore has the largest influence on IMF policy. Domestic politics often come into play, with politicians in developing countries using conditional lending to gain leverage over the opposing side of the population in order to influence policy.

Reform

The IMF is only one of many international organisations and it is a generalist institution for macroeconomic issues only; its core areas of concern in developing countries are very narrow. One proposed reform is a movement towards close partnership with other specialist agencies to better productivity. The IMF has little to no communication with other international organisations such as UN specialist agencies like UNICEF, the Food and Agriculture Organization (FAO), and the United Nations Development Programme (UNDP).

Jeffrey Sachs argues in *The End of Poverty* that "international institutions like the International Monetary Fund (IMF) and the World Bank have the brightest economists and the lead in advising poor countries on how to break out of poverty, but the problem is development economics". Development economics needs the reform, not the IMF. He also notes that IMF loan conditions need to be partnered with other reforms such as trade reform in developed nations, debt cancellation, and increased financial assistance for investments in basic infrastructure to be effective. IMF loan conditions cannot stand alone and produce change; they need to be partnered with other reforms or other conditions as applicable.

Reforms to give more powers to emerging economies were agreed by the G20 in 2010, however as of April 2014 the U.S. Congress has not agreed to these reforms, making eventual agreement uncertain.

Support of Military Dictatorships

The role of the Bretton Woods institutions has been controversial since the late Cold War period, due to claims that the IMF policy makers supported military dictatorshipsfriendly to American and European corporations and other anti-communist regimes. Critics also claim that the IMF is generally apathetic or hostile to their views of human rights, and labour rights. The controversy has helped spark the Anti-globalization movement.

Arguments in favour of the IMF say that economic stability is a precursor to democracy; however, critics highlight various examples in which democratised countries fell after receiving IMF loans.

Impact on Access to Food

A number of civil society organisations have criticised the IMF's policies for their impact on people's access to food, particularly in developing countries. In October 2008, former US president Bill Clinton presented a speech to the United Nations World Food Day, which criticised the World Bank and IMF for their policies on food and agriculture:

We need the World Bank, the IMF, all the big foundations, and all the governments to admit that, for 30 years, we all blew it, including me when I was president. We were wrong to believe that food was like some other product in international trade, and we all have to go back to a more responsible and sustainable form of agriculture.

—Former U.S. president Bill Clinton, *Speech at United Nations World Food Day, October 16, 2008*

Impact on Public Health

In 2009 a study by analysts from Cambridge and Yale universities published on the open-access Public Library of Science concluded that strict conditions on the international loans by the IMF resulted in thousands of deaths in Eastern Europe by tuberculosis as public health care had to be weakened. In the 21 countries to which the IMF had given loans, tuberculosis deaths rose by 16.6 per cent.

In 2009, a book by Rick Rowden titled *The Deadly Ideas of neo-liberalism: How the IMF has Undermined Public Health and the Fight Against AIDS*, claimed that the IMF's monetarist approach towards prioritising price stability (low inflation) and fiscal restraint (low budget deficits) was unnecessarily restrictive and has prevented developing countries from being able to scale up long-term public investment as a percent of GDP in the underlying public health infrastructure. The book claimed the consequences have been chronically underfunded public health systems, leading to dilapidated health infrastructure, inadequate numbers of health personnel, and demoralising working conditions that have fuelled the "push factors" driving the brain drain of nurses migrating from poor countries to rich ones, all of which has undermined public health systems and the fight against HIV/AIDS in developing countries.

Impact on Environment

IMF policies have been repeatedly criticised for making it difficult for indebted countries to avoid ecosystem-damaging projects that generate cash flow, in particular oil, coal, and forest-destroying lumber and agriculture projects. Ecuador for example had to defy IMF advice repeatedly to pursue the protection of its rain forests, though paradoxically this need was cited in IMF argument to support that country. The IMF acknowledged this paradox in a March 2010 staff position report which proposed the IMF Green Fund, a mechanism to issue special drawing rights directly to pay for climate harm prevention and potentially other ecological protection as pursued generally by other environmental finance.

While the response to these moves was generally positive possibly because ecological protection and energy and infrastructure transformation are more politically neutral than pressures to change social policy. Some experts voiced concern that the IMF was not representative, and that the IMF proposals to generate only US$200 billion a year by 2020 with the SDRs as seed funds, did not go far enough to undo the general incentive to pursue destructive projects inherent in the world commodity trading and banking systems—criticisms often levelled at the World Trade Organization and large global banking institutions.

In the context of the May 2010 European banking crisis, some observers also noted that Spain and California, two troubled economies within Europe and the United States respectively, and also Germany, the primary and politically most fragile supporter of a euro currency bailout would benefit from IMF recognition of their leadership in green technology, and directly from Green Fund–generated demand for their exports, which might also improve their credit standing with international bankers.

PROPOSED ALTERNATIVES

In March 2011 the Ministers of Economy and Finance of the African Union proposed to establish an African Monetary Fund.

At the 6th BRICS summit in July 2014 the BRICS nations (Brazil, Russia, India, China, and South Africa) announced the signing of a Treaty for the establishment of the BRICS Contingent Reserve Arrangement (CRA) with an initial size of US$100 billion. The Agreement is a framework for the provision of liquidity through currency swaps in response to actual or potential short-term balance of payments pressures.

IN THE MEDIA

Life and Debt, a documentary film, deals with the IMF's policies' influence on Jamaica and its economy from a critical point of view. *Debtocracy*, a 2011 independent Greek documentary film, also criticises the IMF and its tactics for providing financial help to indebted nations.

6

Global Warming and Climate Change in Moder World

GLOBAL WARMING

Measurements of temperature taken by instruments all over the world, on land and at sea have revealed that during the 20th century the Earth's surface and lowest part of the atmosphere warmed up on average by about 0.6°C. During this period, man-made emissions of greenhouse gases, including carbon dioxide, methane and nitrous oxide have increased, largely as a result of the burning of fossil fuels for energy and transportation, and land use changes including deforestation for agriculture. In the last 20 years, concern has grown that these two phenomena are, at least in part, associated with each other.

That is to say, global warming is now considered most probably to be due to the increases in greenhouse gas emissions and concurrent increases in atmospheric greenhouse gas concentrations, which have enhanced the Earth's natural greenhouse effect. Whilst other natural causes of climate change can cause global climate to change over similar periods of time, computer models demonstrate that in all probability there is a real discernible human influence on the global climate.

If the climate changes as current computer models have projected, global average surface temperature could be anywhere from 1.4 to 5.8°C higher by the end of the 21st century than in 1990. To put this temperature change into context, the increase in global average surface temperature which brought the Earth out of the last major ice age 14,000 years ago was of the order of 4 to 5°C. Such a rapid change in climate will probably be too great to allow many ecosystems to suitably adapt, and the rate of species extinction will most likely increase.

In addition to impacts on wildlife and species biodiversity, human agriculture, forestry, water resources and health will all be affected. Such impacts will be related to changes in precipitation (rainfall and snowfall), sea level, and the frequency and intensity of extreme weather events, resulting from global warming. It is expected that the societies currently experiencing existing social, economic and climatic stresses will be both worst affected and least able to adapt. These will include many in the developing world, low-lying islands and coastal regions, and the urban poor.

The Framework Convention on Climate Change and the Kyoto Protocol represent the first steps taken by the international community to protect the Earth's climate from dangerous man-made interference. Currently, nations have agreed to reduce greenhouse gas emissions by an average of about 5 per cent from 1990 levels by the period 2008 to 2012. The UK, through its Climate Change Programme, has committed itself to a 12.5 per cent cut in greenhouse gas emissions. Additional commitments for further greenhouse gas emission reduction will need to be negotiated during the early part of the 21st century, if levels of greenhouse gas concentrations in the atmosphere are to be stabilised at reasonable levels. Existing and future targets can be achieved by embracing the concept of sustainable development - development today that does not compromise the development needs of future generations. In practical terms, this means using resources, particularly fossil-fuel-derived energy, more efficiently, re-using and recycling products where possible, and developing renewable forms of energy which are inexhaustible and do not pollute the atmosphere.

Global warming begins when sunlight reaches Earth. The clouds, atmospheric particles, reflective ground surfaces and ocean surface then reflected about 30 per cent of it back into space, while the remaining is absorbed by oceans, lands and air. This in turn heats the planet's surface and atmosphere, making life possible. As Earth warmed up, this solar energy is radiated by thermal radiation or infrared heat, travelling directly out to space, thus cooling the Earth. However, some of the outgoing radiation is re-absorbed by carbon dioxide, water vapour and other gases in the atmosphere and is radiated back to Earth's surface; these gases are known as greenhouse gases due to their heat-trapping capacity. This re-absorption process is naturally good; the Earth's average surface temperature would be very cold if not for the greenhouse gases.

The problem begins when the concentration of greenhouse gases in the atmosphere were artificially raised by humankind at an ever-increasing rate since the past 250 years. As of 2004, over 8 billion tons of carbon dioxide was pumped out per year; natural carbon sinks such as forests and the ocean absorbed some of this, while the rest accumulated in the atmosphere. Millions of pounds of methane are produced in landfills and agricultural decomposition of biomass and animal manure. Nitrous oxide is released into the atmosphere by nitrogen-based fertilizers and other soil management practices. Once released, these greenhouse gases stay in the atmosphere for decades or longer. According to the Intergovernmental Panel on Climate Change (IPCC), carbon dioxide and methane levels have increased by 35 and 148 per cent since the 1750 industrial revolution. Paleoclimate readings taken from ice cores and fossil records dating back to 650 000 years show that both gases are at their highest levels. Thermal radiation is obstructed further by the increased concentrations of greenhouse gases, resulting in what is known as enhanced global warming.

Recent observations of global warming have solidified the theory that it is indeed an enhanced greenhouse effect that is causing the world to warm. The planet has experienced the largest increase in surface temperature over the last century. Between 1906 and 2006, the Earth's average surface temperature rose between 0.6 to 0.9 degrees Celsius; the last 50 years saw the temperature increase rate almost doubling. Sea levels have shown a rise of about 0.17 metres during the twentieth century. The extent of Arctic sea ice has steadily shrunk by 2.7 per cent per decade since 1978, just as world's glaciers steadily receded.

As the world continues to consume ever more fossil fuel energy, greenhouse gas concentrations will continue to rise, and with them Earth's temperature. The IPCC estimates that based on plausible emission scenarios, average surface temperatures could increase between 2°C and 6°C by the end of the 21st century. Continued warming at current rates poses serious consequences. Low-lying coastal regions, with dense population, are especially vulnerable to climate shifts, with the poorer countries and small island nations having the hardest time adapting. It has been projected that by 2080, 13 to 88 million people around the world would lose their home to floods.

20 th Century Climate Change

There is now considerable evidence that indicates a relationship between the man-made enhancement of the Earth's natural greenhouse effect through greenhouse gas pollution of the atmosphere and the global warming that has been observed.

Measurements of surface temperature recorded around the world during the last 150 years indicate that global temperatures are now higher than in any decade over this period. During the 20th century a global average surface temperature increase of about 0.6°C years has taken place, although the warming trend has not been smooth and has taken place rather differently between the Northern and Southern Hemispheres. With this in mind, it is important to recognise that global average surface temperature, as a measure of the global climate, represents an over-simplification. Winter temperatures and night-time minimums for example, may have risen more than summer temperatures and daytime maximums.

With higher global temperatures one would expect an increase in rainfall and other forms of precipitation, because of the greater amount of moisture available within the atmosphere. Striking changes in precipitation have occurred on regional scales, most notably the drought in the African Sahel between the 1960s and 1980s. Nevertheless, the accuracy of many precipitation records should be treated with caution. Precipitation is more difficult to monitor than temperature due to its greater geographical variability.

Variations in land- and sea-ice coverage and the melting or growth of glaciers occur in response to changes in temperature, sunshine, precipitation, and for sea-ice changes in wind. Since 1966 Northern Hemisphere snow cover maps have been produced by the United States using satellite imagery. Consistent with the surface and tropospheric temperature measurements is the decrease (by about 10 per cent) in snow cover and extent since the late 1960s. There has been a widespread retreat of mountain glaciers in non-polar regions during the 20th century. Variations in sea-ice extent have also been reported, with spring and summer sea-ice extent in the Northern Hemisphere decreasing by between 10 an 15 per cent since the 1950s. Considerable interest is now focusing on Antarctica, where regional warming, as predicted by climate models, has been more rapid than global warming as a whole. In recent years the summertime disintegration of the Larsen Sea Ice Shelf adjacent the Antarctic continent has been occurring on an unprecedented scale. In view of the rapidity at which it is taking place, such an event has been viewed as a possible signal of global warming.

Increased global cloudiness, as for increased global evaporation and precipitation, would be an expected consequence of higher global temperatures. It is likely that there has been a 2 per cent increase in cloud cover over mid - to high latitude land areas during the 20th century. In most areas the trends relate well to the observed decrease in daily temperature range (since cloudier nights tend to be warmer and cloudier days cooler).

21ST CENTURY CLIMATE CHANGE

Prediction of climate change over the next 100 to 150 years is based solely on climate model simulations run on computers. The vast majority of modelling has concentrated on the effects of continued man-made pollution of the atmosphere by greenhouse gases, and to a lesser extent, atmospheric aerosols. The main concern at present is to determine how much the Earth will warm in the near future.

Significant results from some of the best climate models available indicate that a global average warming of 0.3°C per decade can be expected to occur during the 21st century, assuming that mankind fails to control current emissions of greenhouse gases, although it could be as high as 0.6°C. In addition regional variations in the patterns of temperature and precipitation change will occur, with greater warming likely in the polar regions. Currently, models suggest that if the atmospheric concentration of carbon dioxide, the main greenhouse gas, is doubled from pre-industrial levels, the Earth will warm by between 1.5 and 4.5°C sometime over the next 200 years or so. The large margin of error in future prediction of temperature emphasises that modelling the climate is inherently a difficult business. Part of the problem stems from trying to guess what climate feedbacks might occur that may enhance the initial warming due to an enhanced greenhouse effect. Melting ice in the polar regions for example could accelerate warming because exposed ground absorbs more energy from the Sun than snow and ice, which reflect about 80 to 90 per cent.

Whilst uncertainties concerning the actual response of the global climate to man-made greenhouse gas emissions exist, most scientists agree that the global warming trend of the 20th century will continue into the 21st century. The projected rate of warming is faster than at any time during recent Earth history. If nations fail to respond, the world may experience numerous adverse impacts as a result of global warming in the decades ahead.

Aerosols

Atmospheric aerosols are very fine particles suspended in air. They are formed by the dispersal of material at the Earth's surface (primary aerosols), or by reaction of gases in the atmosphere (secondary aerosols). They include sulphates and nitrates from the oxidation respectively of sulphur dioxide and nitric oxide during the burning of fossil fuels, organic materials from the oxidation of volatile organic compounds (VOCs), soot from fires, and mineral dust from wind-blown processes. Natural aerosols, which also include sea salt and volcanic dust, are probably 4 to 5 times larger than man-made ones on a global scale, but regional variations in man-made pollution may change this ratio significantly in certain areas, particularly in the industrialised Northern Hemisphere. Although making up only 1 part in a billion of the mass of the atmosphere, they have the potential to significantly influence the amount of sunlight reaching the Earth's surface, and therefore climate. Removal of most aerosols is mainly achieved by rainfall (wet deposition) and by direct uptake at the surface (dry deposition). Explosive volcanic eruptions however, can inject large quantities of dust and gaseous material, such as sulphur dioxide, high into the atmosphere (the stratosphere). Here, sulphur dioxide is rapidly converted into sulphuric acid aerosols. Whereas pollution of the lower atmosphere is removed within days by the effects of rainfall and gravity, stratospheric pollution may remain there for several years, gradually spreading to cover much of the globe.

Like greenhouse gases, aerosols influence the climate. Atmospheric aerosols influence the transfer of energy in the atmosphere in two ways: directly through the scattering of sunlight; and indirectly through modifying the optical properties and lifetimes of clouds. The scattering of sunlight by aerosols is clearly demonstrated in the aftermath of a major volcanic eruption, when exceptionally colourful sunsets may be witnessed. The volcanic pollution results in a substantial reduction in the direct solar beam, largely through scattering by the highly reflective sulphuric acid aerosols. Overall, there is a net reduction of 5 to 10 per cent in energy received at the Earth's surface. An individual eruption may cause a global cooling of up to 0.3°C, with the effects lasting 1 to 2 years.

Estimation of the impact aerosols have on longer-term global climate change however, is more complex and hence more uncertain than that due to the well-mixed greenhouse gases. This is largely because the geographical distribution of aerosols is highly variable and strongly related to their sources.

The best estimates of global cooling attributable to man-made aerosols are based on computer models. These show that the global cooling effect of man-made aerosols could offset the warming effect of increased greenhouse gas concentrations by as much as 30 per cent. The variable distribution of aerosols however, makes calculation of a global average difficult. Nevertheless, it is likely that aerosols may slow the rate of projected global warming during the 21st century.

AGRICULTURE

Climate is the most significant factor in determining plant growth and productivity. Without intervention to reduce emissions of greenhouse gases, global average surface temperature is projected to increase by about 0.2°C per decade during the 21st century. This rapid change in climate will have major implications for agriculture around the world. Crop growth is often limited by temperature. Temperatures during the 21st century are expected to increase more in the higher latitudes where shifts in vegetation will be greater. In Britain an increase in temperature of 1.5°C by 2050 is the equivalent of a decrease in altitude of approximately 200m.

This is the same as a shift southward in latitude of 200-300 km. Such an increase in temperature would allow widespread maize cultivation across southern England to take place. In other regions however, a rise in temperature may not be so beneficial. Small increases in temperature would extend the range of temperature-limited pests. The European Corn Borer for example, a major pest of grain maize, may shift between 165 and 500 km northwards with a rise of 1°C.

Moisture and water availability will be affected by a temperature increase, regardless of any change in rainfall. Higher temperatures increase the evaporation rate, thus reducing the level of moisture available for plant growth, although other climatic elements are involved. A warming of 1°C, with no change in precipitation, may decrease yields of wheat and maize in the core cropping regions such as the US by about 5 per cent. A very large decrease in moisture availability in the dryer regions of the world would be of great concern to the subsistence farmers that farm these lands. Reduced moisture availability would only exacerbate the existing problems of infertile soils, soil erosion and poor crop yields. In the extreme case, a reduction in moisture could lead to desertification.

Sea levels have been projected to rise by anywhere up to a metre by 2100, although considerable uncertainty is attached to this. The greatest threat to low-lying agricultural regions from sea level rise is that of inundation and flooding. Southeast Asia would have the greatest threat of inundation because of the deltaic nature of the land. Furthermore, the pollution of surface and groundwater with salty seawater is another potential problem facing farmers situated in low-lying regions. The costs of agricultural production would increase, resulting in higher food prices for the consumer. Although climate changes may have some detrimental impacts on agricultural production around the world, the increase in atmospheric carbon dioxide concentrations could be beneficial.

Plants grow as a result of photosynthesis - the mechanism whereby the plant converts carbon dioxide from the atmosphere into food. With higher levels of carbon dioxide stimulating the rate of photosynthesis, the growth rate and productivity of plants could be expected to increase. This would be beneficial for global food stocks. Most crops grown in cool, temperate regions respond positively to an increased concentration of carbon dioxide, including some of the current major food staples such as wheat, rice and soybean. Some studies have shown that growth rate in these crops may increase up to 50 per cent if carbon dioxide in the atmosphere is doubled. Crops grown in the tropical regions of the world, including sorghum, maize, sugar cane and millet, which together account for about one fifth of the world's food production, do not respond as well to increases in carbon dioxide.

In order to maintain agricultural output to meet the demand for a growing world population, farmers will have to adjust and adapt as and when necessary to the possible changes imposed by changing climate. Higher temperatures would increase the demand for irrigation of agricultural land.

Unfortunately, in many arid and semi-arid regions of the world the demand for water already exceeds supply. Increased spread of pests and disease may also place additional demands on the need for fertilizers, pesticides and herbicides which are costly. The ability to adapt to the effects of climate change will vary greatly between countries and regions.

Economic and technological constraints will limit the rate of adaptability, with poorer economies lagging behind. Consequently, without intervention the effects of climate change in the 21st century look set to further widen the gulf between developed and developing nations.

Evidence for Global Warming: Degradation of Earth's Atmosphere; Temperature Rise; Glacial Melting and Sealevel Rise; Ozone Holes; Vegetation Response

"Global change". "Greenhouse effect". "Global warming". The media are full of statements, concerns, guesses, and speculation about these phenomena, as scientists and policy-makers around the world struggle to address recent scientific observations that indicate human activities impact our environment. And yet, each of these is a "natural" phenomenon, as are many others. Hurricanes, droughts, and monsoons all occur without any control by humans, to initiate, forestall or moderate them.

Most readers of this Tutorial already know that global warming is litreally a "hot" topic. For those still with relative unfamiliarity, we recommend this Wikpedia review: effects of global warming.

Effects of Ozone Depletion and Global Warming

(UV-B) radiation causes skin cancer, cataracts and immune suppression in both animals and humans. UV-B also damages plants including hardwood forests, and phytoplankton (an alga is a type of phytoplankton which is the building block of the oceanic food chain).

EFFECT ON INFECTIOUS DISEASES

Most infectious diseases are transmitted by insects and rodents. Transmitters of disease are called vectors. For example, mosquitoes transmit malaria, dengue and viral encephalitis (inflammation of the brain). Like other animals and plants, vectors are accustomed to certain climate conditions. If the climate becomes warmer, the mosquito will try to fly to new places where it can survive and expose more people to the disease. Changes in sea surface temperature and sea level can lead to higher incidence of water-borne infectious and toxin-related illnesses such as malaria (severe chills and fever), cholera (intestinal disease), dengue (characterized by severe pains in the joints and back), and leishmaniasis (skin ulcers).

Human susceptibility to infections can be further compounded by malnutrition. UV-B radiation from ozone depletion damages both plants and animals. UV-B harms amphibian eggs, midge larvae and trout. Crops that are damaged will reduce food availability. UV-B also can damage mammalian immune systems which makes humans and other animals more susceptible to infectious diseases. Approximately 92 million people are expected to become refugees from global warming and climate change by 2100, not including any added from population growth.

EFFECTS ON EARTH'S FOOD CHAIN

Ozone depletion and global warming have harmful effects on plants and animals. If allowed to continue, our food chain will be seriously disrupted. For example, phytoplantkton are tiny floating algae in the ocean which are the base of the marine food chain.

In Antarctica, there has been upwards of 50 percent ozone depletion. This means that an unusually high amount of UV-B radiation has reached the Earth's surface in the Antarctic region. UV-B harms the productivity of phytoplankton, thereby reducing the available food for animals that feed on phytoplankton. Krill eat phytoplankton and penguins eat krill.

From a climate change perspective, phytoplankton normally absorbs a lot of carbon from the air. As phytoplankton dies from UV-B radiation, this carbon is no longer absorbed. This means that more carbon will be left in the atmosphere, contributing to more global warming. More global warming can increase ozone depletion, which kills more phytoplankton, and the process repeats itself.

"Total Environmental Impact" of Refrigerants

Six parameters define the "total environmental impact" of refrigerants on our environment.

- Ozone Depletion Potential (ODP)
- Global Warming Potential (GWP)
- Atmospheric Life
- Energy Use
- Equipment Emission Rate
- Refrigerant Charge

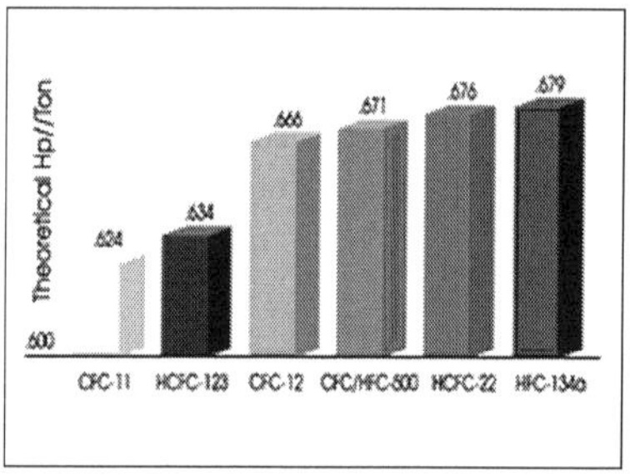

Fig. Efficiency comparison for various refrigerants

Approximately 70 percent of the world's electricity is generated by the burning of fossil fuels. For every additional kWh used, there are more greenhouse gas emissions generated by electric utility power plants. This is the indirect effect of global warming refrigerants. The environmental impact of even small changes in chiller energy use has an impact.

There is a need to use refrigerants that minimize both ODP and GWP to address global environmental concerns. If the efficiency of every centrifugal chiller in the world were increased by only 0.08 kW/ton, power plant-generated greenhouse gas emissions would be reduced by literally billions of pounds. This is an amount equal to removing nearly two million cars from the road each year, or to planting nearly a half billion trees every year.

ACTION PLAN FOR ORGANIZATIONS USING REFRIGERANTS

Most refrigerants used in air conditioning and refrigeration contribute to global warming in addition to ozone depletion. Even the new non-ozone depleting alternative refrigerants add to the global warming problem. Businesses and organizations using refrigerants are encouraged to take action now to do what's right for both their organization and for the environment. Persons responsible for HVAC and/or environmental concerns in their company or organization need to take strong, immediate actions to reduce ozone depletion and global warming.

Minimize emissions of ozone depleting (ODP) and direct global warming (GWP) refrigerants used by your organization. The most effective way to start reducing emissions is to implement a Refrigerant Management Plan and insure that your organization is complying with EPA's Section 608 Refrigerant Recycling Regulations. Refrigerants should be handled as a controlled substance.

A defined leak management programme, including leak monitoring and leak repair policies is essential. Provide Refrigerant Management and Regulations Compliance Training to your responsible employees. Organization's using refrigerants should review and implement industry best practices in refrigerant management to minimize emissions at every stage of refrigerant handling. Implement a process to keep current with regulatory changes to insure going compliance requirements are met. Reduce energy consumption of HVAC systems using refrigerants to reduce indirect global warming emissions. Conduct a building tune-up to reduce your heating, cooling, and electrical loads, and thus your overall energy consumption.

Replace older HVAC systems containing high ozone depleting and/or global warming refrigerants with newer, more efficient systems. Frequently, HVAC systems are oversized. Thus, you may want to consider right-sizing your existing system with a smaller, more energy-efficient one that matches the newly reduced loads. The operating costs of a high efficiency system may offer an attractive pay back of your investment. Evaluate HVAC systems on a total cost of ownership basis, rather than first cost.

OZONE DEPLETION

Ozone depletion describes two distinct, but related observations: a slow, steady decline of about 4 per cent per decade in the total volume of ozone in Earth's stratosphere (ozone layer) since the late 1970s, and a much larger, but seasonal, decrease in stratospheric ozone over Earth's polar regions during the same period. The latter phenomenon is commonly referred to as the ozone hole. In addition to this well-known stratospheric ozone depletion, there are also tropospheric ozone depletion events, which occur near the surface in Polar Regions during spring.

The detailed mechanism by which the polar ozone holes form is different from that for the mid-latitude thinning, but the most important process in both trends is catalytic destruction of ozone by atomic chlorine and bromine. The main source of these halogen atoms in the stratosphere is photodissociation of chlorofluorocarbon (CFC) compounds, commonly called freons, and of bromofluorocarbon compounds known as halons. These compounds are transported into the stratosphere after being emitted at the surface. Both ozone depletion mechanisms strengthened as emissions of CFCs and halons increased.

CFCs and other contributory substances are commonly referred to as ozone-depleting substances (ODS). Since the ozone layer prevents most harmful UVB wavelengths (270–315 nm) of ultraviolet light (UV light) from passing through the Earth's atmosphere, observed and projected decreases in ozone have generated worldwide concern leading to adoption of the Montreal Protocol banning the production of CFCs and halons as well as related ozone depleting chemicals such as carbon tetrachloride and trichloroethane. It is suspected that a variety of biological consequences such as increases in skin cancer, damage to plants, and reduction of plankton populations in the ocean's photic zone may result from the increased UV exposure due to ozone depletion. Three forms (or allotropes) of oxygen are involved in the ozone-oxygen cycle: oxygen atoms (O or atomic oxygen), oxygen gas (O_2 or diatomic oxygen), and ozone gas (O_3 or triatomic oxygen).

Ozone is formed in the stratosphere when oxygen molecules photodissociate after absorbing an ultraviolet photon whose wavelength is shorter than 240 nm.

This produces two oxygen atoms. The atomic oxygen then combines with O_2 to create O_3. Ozone molecules absorb UV light between 310 and 200 nm, following which ozone splits into a molecule of O_2 and an oxygen atom. The oxygen atom then joins up with an oxygen molecule to regenerate ozone. This is a continuing process which terminates when an oxygen atom "recombines" with an ozone molecule to make two O_2 molecules: $O + O_3 ! 2 O_2$

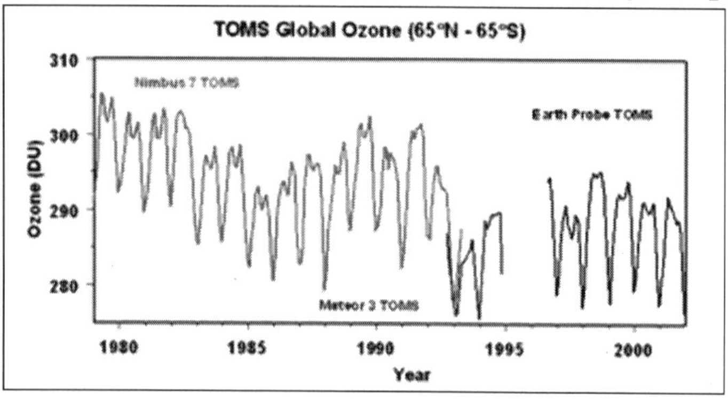

Fig. Global monthly average total ozone amount.

The overall amount of ozone in the stratosphere is determined by a balance between photochemical production and recombination. Ozone can be destroyed by a number of free radical catalysts, the most important of which are the hydroxyl radical (OH·), the nitric oxide radical (NO·) and atomic chlorine (Cl·) and bromine (Br·). All of these have both natural and anthropogenic (manmade) sources; at the present time, most of the OH· and NO· in the stratosphere is of natural origin, but human activity has dramatically increased the levels of chlorine and bromine.

These elements are found in certain stable organic compounds, especially chlorofluorocarbons (CFCs), which may find their way to the stratosphere without being destroyed in the troposphere due to their low reactivity. Once in the stratosphere, the Cl and Br atoms are liberated from the parent compounds by the action of ultraviolet light, *e.g.* ('h' is Planck's constant, 'í' is frequency of electromagnetic radiation)

$$CFCl_3 + hv \rightarrow CFCl_2 + Cl$$

The Cl and Br atoms can then destroy ozone molecules through a variety of catalytic cycles. In the simplest example of such a cycle, a chlorine atom reacts with an ozone molecule, taking an oxygen atom with it (forming ClO) and leaving a normal oxygen molecule. The chlorine monoxide (*i.e.*, the ClO) can react with a second molecule of ozone (*i.e.*, O_3) to yield another chlorine atom and two molecules of oxygen. The chemical shorthand for these gas-phase reactions is:

$$Cl + O_3 \rightarrow ClO + O_2$$

$$ClO + O_3 \rightarrow Cl + 2\,O_2$$

The overall effect is a decrease in the amount of ozone. More complicated mechanisms have been discovered that lead to ozone destruction in the lower stratosphere as well. A single chlorine atom would keep on destroying ozone (thus a catalyst) for up to two years (the time scale for transport back down to the troposphere) were it not for reactions that remove them from this cycle by forming reservoir species such as hydrogen chloride (HCl) and chlorine nitrate ($ClONO_2$). On a per atom basis, bromine is even more efficient than chlorine at destroying ozone, but there is much less bromine in the atmosphere at present.

As a result, both chlorine and bromine contribute significantly to the overall ozone depletion. Laboratory studies have shown that fluorine and iodine atoms participate in analogous catalytic cycles. However, in the Earth's stratosphere, fluorine atoms react rapidly with water and methane to form strongly-bound HF, while organic molecules which contain iodine react so rapidly in the lower atmosphere that they do not reach the stratosphere in significant quantities. Furthermore, a single chlorine atom is able to react with 100,000 ozone molecules. This fact plus the amount of chlorine released into the atmosphere by chlorofluorocarbons (CFCs) yearly demonstrates how dangerous CFCs are to the environment.

QUANTITATIVE UNDERSTANDING OF THE CHEMICAL OZONE LOSS PROCESS

New research on the breakdown of a key molecule in these ozone-depleting chemicals, dichlorine peroxide (Cl_2O_2), calls into question the completeness of present atmospheric models of polar ozone depletion. Specifically, chemists at NASA's Jet Propulsion Laboratory in Pasadena, California, found in 2007 that the temperatures, and the spectrum and intensity of radiation present in the stratosphere created conditions insufficient to allow the rate of chemical-breakdown required to release chlorine radicals in the volume necessary to explain observed rates of ozone depletion. Instead, laboratory tests, designed to be the most accurate reflection of stratospheric conditions to date, showed the decay of the crucial molecule almost a magnitude lower than previously thought.

OBSERVATIONS ON OZONE LAYER DEPLETION

The most pronounced decrease in ozone has been in the lower stratosphere. However, the ozone hole is most usually measured not in terms of ozone concentrations at these levels (which are typically of a few parts per million) but by reduction in the total *column ozone*, above a point on the Earth's surface, which is normally expressed in Dobson units, abbreviated as "DU". Marked decreases in column ozone in the Antarctic spring and early summer compared to the early 1970s and before have been observed using instruments such as the Total Ozone Mapping Spectrometer (TOMS).

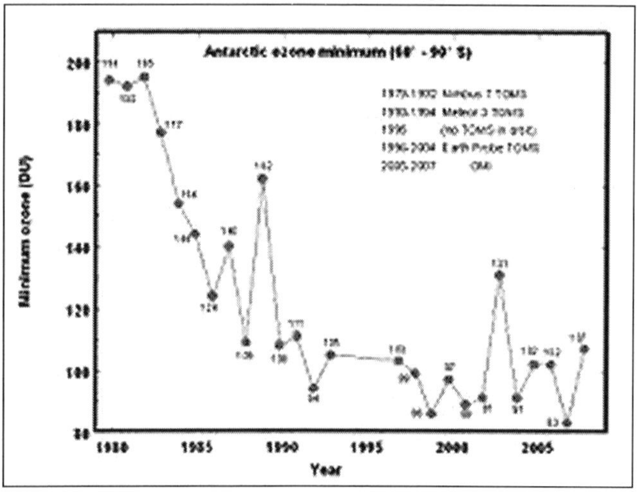

Fig. Lowest value of ozone measured by TOMS each year in the ozone hole.

Reductions of up to 70 per cent in the ozone column observed in the austral (southern hemispheric) spring over Antarctica and first reported in 1985 (Farman et al. 1985) are continuing.

Through the 1990s, total column ozone in September and October have continued to be 40–50 per cent lower than pre-ozone-hole values. In the Arctic the amount lost is more variable year-to-year than in the Antarctic. The greatest declines, up to 30 per cent, are in the winter and spring, when the stratosphere is colder.

Reactions that take place on polar stratospheric clouds (PSCs) play an important role in enhancing ozone depletion. PSCs form more readily in the extreme cold of Antarctic stratosphere. This is why ozone holes first formed, and are deeper, over Antarctica. Early models failed to take PSCs into account and predicted a gradual global depletion, which is why the sudden Antarctic ozone hole was such a surprise to many scientists.

In middle latitudes it is preferable to speak of ozone depletion rather than holes. Declines are about 3 per cent below pre-1980 values for 35–60°N and about 6 per cent for 35–60°S. In the tropics, there are no significant trends. Ozone depletion also explains much of the observed reduction in stratospheric and upper tropospheric temperatures. The source of the warmth of the stratosphere is the absorption of UV radiation by ozone, hence reduced ozone leads to cooling.

Some stratospheric cooling is also predicted from increases in greenhouse gases such as CO_2; however the ozone-induced cooling appears to be dominant. Predictions of ozone levels remain difficult. The World Meteorological Organization Global Ozone Research and Monitoring Project - Report No. 44 comes out strongly in favour for the Montreal Protocol, but notes that a UNEP 1994 Assessment overestimated ozone loss for the 1994–1997 period.

CLIMATE CHANGE SCIENCE

To better understand the science assessed in this Fourth Assessment Report, it is helpful to review the long historical perspective that has led to the current state of climate change knowledge. This stage starts by describing the fundamental nature of earth science. It then describes the history of climate change science using a wide-ranging subset of examples, and ends with a history of the IPCC. There is no counterpart in previous IPCC assessment reports for an introductory stage providing historical context for the remainder of the report. Here, a restricted set of topics has been selected to show key accomplishments and challenges in climate change science. The topics have been chosen for their significance to the IPCC task of assessing information relevant for understanding the risks of human-induced climate change, and also to show the complex and uneven pace of scientific progress. The time frame under consideration stops with the publication of the Third Assessment Report. Developments subsequent to the TAR are described in the other stages of this report, and we refer to these stages throughout this first stage.

THE NATURE OF EARTH SCIENCE

Science may be stimulated by argument and debate, but it generally advances through formulating hypotheses clearly and testing them objectively. This testing is the key to science. In fact, one philosopher of science insisted that to be genuinely scientific, a statement must be susceptible to testing that could potentially show it to be false. In practice, contemporary scientists usually submit their research findings to the scrutiny of their peers, which includes disclosing the methods that they use, so their results can be checked through replication by other scientists. The insights and research results of individual scientists, even scientists of unquestioned genius, are thus confirmed or rejected in the peer-reviewed literature by the combined efforts of many other scientists. It is not the belief or opinion of the scientists that is important, but rather the results of this testing. However, that one opposing scientist would have needed proof in the form of testable results.

Thus science is inherently self-correcting; incorrect or incomplete scientific concepts ultimately do not survive repeated testing against observations of nature. Scientific theories are ways of explaining phenomena and providing insights that can be evaluated by comparison with physical reality. Each successful prediction adds to the weight of evidence supporting the theory, and any unsuccessful prediction demonstrates that the underlying theory is imperfect and requires improvement or abandonment. Sometimes, only certain kinds of questions tend to be asked about a scientific phenomenon until contradictions build to a point where a sudden change of paradigm takes place. At that point, an entire field can be rapidly reconstructed under the new paradigm.

Despite occasional major paradigm shifts, the majority of scientific insights, even unexpected insights, tend to emerge incrementally as a result of repeated attempts to test hypotheses as thoroughly as possible. Therefore, because almost every new advance is based on the research and understanding that has gone before, science is cumulative, with useful features retained and non-useful features abandoned. Active research scientists, throughout their careers, typically spend large fractions of their working time studying in depth what other scientists have done. Superficial or amateurish acquaintance with the current state of a scientific research topic is an obstacle to a scientist's progress. Working scientists know that a day in the library can save a year in the laboratory. Even Sir Isaac Newton wrote that if he had 'seen further it is by standing on the shoulders of giants'. Intellectual honesty and professional ethics call for scientists to acknowledge the work of predecessors and colleagues.

The attributes of science briefly described here can be used in assessing competing assertions about climate change. Can the statement under consideration, in principle, be proven false? Has it been rigorously tested? Did it appear in the peer-reviewed literature? Did it build on the existing research record where appropriate? If the answer to any of these questions is no, then less credence should be given to the assertion until it is tested and independently verified. The IPCC assesses the scientific literature to create a report based on the best available science. It must be acknowledged, however, that the IPCC also contributes to science by identifying the key uncertainties and by stimulating and coordinating targeted research to answer important climate change questions.

A characteristic of Earth sciences is that Earth scientists are unable to perform controlled experiments on the planet as a whole and then observe the results. In this sense, Earth science is similar to the disciplines of astronomy and cosmology that cannot conduct experiments on galaxies or the cosmos. This is an important consideration, because it is precisely such whole-Earth, system-scale experiments, incorporating the full complexity of interacting processes and feedbacks, that might ideally be required to fully verify or falsify climate change hypotheses. Nevertheless, countless empirical tests of numerous different hypotheses have built up a massive body of Earth science knowledge. This repeated testing has refined the understanding of numerous aspects of the climate system, from deep oceanic circulation to stratospheric chemistry. Sometimes a combination of observations and models can be used to test planetary-scale hypotheses. For example, the global cooling and drying of the atmosphere observed after the eruption of Mt. Pinatubo provided key tests of particular aspects of global climate models.

THE HUMAN FINGERPRINT ON GREENHOUSE GASES

The high-accuracy measurements of atmospheric CO2 concentration, initiated by Charles David Keeling in 1958, constitute the master time series documenting the changing composition of the atmosphere. These data have iconic status in climate change science as evidence of the effect of human activities on the chemical composition of the global atmosphere. Keeling's measurements on Mauna Loa in Hawaii provide a true measure of the global carbon cycle, an effectively continuous record of the burning of fossil fuel. They also maintain an accuracy and precision that allow scientists to separate fossil fuel emissions from those due to the natural annual cycle of the biosphere, demonstrating a long-term change in the seasonal exchange of CO2 between the atmosphere, biosphere and ocean. Later observations of parallel trends in the atmospheric abundances of the 13CO2 isotope and molecular oxygen uniquely identified this rise in CO2 with fossil fuel burning.

To place the increase in CO2 abundance since the late 1950s in perspective, and to compare the magnitude of the anthropogenic increase with natural cycles in the past, a longerterm record of CO2 and other natural greenhouse gases is needed. These data came from analysis of the composition of air enclosed in bubbles in ice cores from Greenland and Antarctica. The initial measurements demonstrated that CO2 abundances were significantly lower during the last ice age than over the last 10 kyr of the Holocene. From 10 kyr before present up to the year 1750, CO2 abundances stayed within the range 280 ± 20 ppm. During the industrial era, CO2 abundance rose roughly exponentially to 367 ppm in 1999 and to 379 ppm in 2005.

Direct atmospheric measurements since 1970 have also detected the increasing atmospheric abundances of two other major greenhouse gases, methane and nitrous oxide. Methane abundances were initially increasing at a rate of about 1 per cent yr–1 but then slowed to an average increase of 0.4 per cent yr–1 over the 1990s with the possible stabilisation of CH4 abundance. The increase in N2O abundance is smaller, about 0.25 per cent yr–1, and more difficult to detect. To go back in time, measurements were made from firn air trapped in snowpack dating back over 200 years, and these data show an accelerating rise in both CH4 and N2O into the 20th century. When ice core measurements extended the CH4 abundance back 1 kyr, they showed a stable, relatively constant abundance of 700 ppb until the 19th century when a steady increase brought CH4 abundances to 1,745 ppb in 1998 and 1,774 ppb in 2005. This peak abundance is much higher than the range of 400 to 700 ppb seen over the last half-million years of glacial-interglacial cycles, and the increase can be readily explained by anthropogenic emissions. For N2O the results are similar: the relative increase over the industrial era is smaller, yet the 1998 abundance of 314 ppb, rising to 319 ppb in 2005 is also well above the 180- to-260 ppb range of glacial-interglacial cycles

Several synthetic halocarbons are greenhouse gases with large global warming potentials. The chemical industry has been producing these gases and they have been leaking into the atmosphere since about 1930. Lovelock first measured CFC-11 in the atmosphere, noting that it could serve as an artificial tracer, with its north-south gradient reflecting the latitudinal distribution of anthropogenic emissions.

Atmospheric abundances of all the synthetic halocarbons were increasing until the 1990s, when the abundance of halocarbons phased out under the Montreal Protocol began to fall. In the case of synthetic halocarbons, ice core research has shown that these compounds did not exist in ancient air and thus confirms their industrial human origin.

At the time of the TAR scientists could say that the abundances of all the well-mixed greenhouse gases during the 1990s were greater than at any time during the last half-million years and this record now extends back nearly one million years. Given this daunting picture of increasing greenhouse gas abundances in the atmosphere, it is noteworthy that, for simpler challenges but still on a hemispheric or even global scale, humans have shown the ability to undo what they have done. Sulphate pollution in Greenland was reversed in the 1980s with the control of acid rain in North America and Europe and CFC abundances are declining globally because of their phase-out undertaken to protect the ozone layer.

GLOBAL SURFACE TEMPERATURE

Shortly after the invention of the thermometer in the early 1600s, efforts began to quantify and record the weather. The first meteorological network was formed in northern Italy in 1653 and reports of temperature observations were published in the earliest scientific journals. By the latter part of the 19th century, systematic observations of the weather were being made in almost all inhabited areas of the world. Formal international coordination of meteorological observations from ships commenced in 1853.

Inspired by the document Suggestions on a Uniform System of Meteorological Observations, the International Meteorological Organization was formed in 1873. Its successor, the World Meteorological Organization, still works to promote and exchange standardised meteorological observations. Yet even with uniform observations, there are still four major obstacles to turning instrumental observations into accurate global time series:

- access to the data in usable form;
- quality control to remove or edit erroneous data points;

- homogeneity assessments and adjustments where necessary to ensure the fidelity of the data; and
- area-averaging in the presence of substantial gaps.

UNDERSTANDING CLIMATE PROCESSES

THE EARTH'S GREENHOUSE EFFECT

The realisation that Earth's climate might be sensitive to the atmospheric concentrations of gases that create a greenhouse effect is more than a century old. Fleming and Weart provided an overview of the emerging science. In terms of the energy balance of the climate system, Edme Mariotte noted in 1681 that although the Sun's light and heat easily pass through glass and other transparent materials, heat from other sources does not. The ability to generate an artificial warming of the Earth's surface was demonstrated in simple greenhouse experiments such as Horace Benedict de Saussure's experiments in the 1760s using a 'heliothermometer' to provide an early analogy to the greenhouse effect. It was a conceptual leap to recognise that the air itself could also trap thermal radiation. In 1824, Joseph Fourier, citing Saussure, argued 'the temperature [of the Earth] can be augmented by the interposition of the atmosphere, because heat in the state of light finds less resistance in penetrating the air, than in repassing into the air when converted into non-luminous heat'. In 1836, Pouillit followed up on Fourier's ideas and argued 'the atmospheric stratum...exercises a greater absorption upon the terrestrial than on the solar rays'. There was still no understanding of exactly what substance in the atmosphere was responsible for this absorption.

In 1859, John Tyndall identified through laboratory experiments the absorption of thermal radiation by complex molecules. He noted that changes in the amount of any of the radiatively active constituents of the atmosphere such as water or CO2 could have produced 'all the mutations of climate which the researches of geologists reveal'. In 1895, Svante Arrhenius followed with a climate prediction based on greenhouse gases, suggesting that a 40 per cent increase or decrease in the atmospheric abundance of the trace gas CO2 might trigger the glacial advances and retreats. One hundred years later, it would be found that CO2 did indeed vary by this amount between glacial and interglacial periods. However, it now appears that the initial climatic change preceded the change in CO2 but was enhanced by it.

G. S. Callendar solved a set of equations linking greenhouse gases and climate change. He found that a doubling of atmospheric CO2 concentration resulted in an increase in the mean global temperature of 2°C, with considerably more warming at the poles, and linked increasing fossil fuel combustion with a rise in CO2 and its greenhouse effects: 'As man is now changing the composition of the atmosphere at a rate which must be very exceptional on the geological time scale, it is natural to seek for the probable effects of such a change. From the best laboratory observations it appears that the principal result of increasing atmospheric carbon dioxide... would be a gradual increase in the mean temperature of the colder regions of the Earth.' In 1947, Ahlmann reported a 1.3°C warming in the North Atlantic sector of the Arctic since the 19th century and mistakenly believed this climate variation could be explained entirely by greenhouse gas warming. Similar model predictions were echoed by Plass in 1956: 'If at the end of this century, measurements show that the carbon dioxide content of the atmosphere has risen appreciably and at the same time the temperature has continued to rise throughout the world, it will be firmly established that carbon dioxide is an important factor in causing climatic change'. In trying to understand the carbon cycle, and specifically how fossil fuel emissions would change atmospheric CO2, the interdisciplinary field of carbon cycle science began. One of the first problems addressed was the atmosphere-ocean exchange of CO2.

Revelle and Suess explained why part of the emitted CO2 was observed to accumulate in the atmosphere rather than being completely absorbed by the oceans. While CO2 can be mixed rapidly into the upper layers of the ocean, the time to mix with the deep ocean is many centuries. By the time of the TAR, the interaction of climate change with the oceanic circulation and biogeochemistry was projected to reduce the fraction of anthropogenic CO2 emissions taken up by the oceans in the future, leaving a greater fraction in the atmosphere.

In the 1950s, the greenhouse gases of concern remained CO2 and H2O, the same two identified by Tyndall a century earlier. It was not until the 1970s that other greenhouse gases – CH4, N2O and CFCs – were widely recognised. By the 1970s, the importance of aerosol-cloud effects in reflecting sunlight was known and atmospheric aerosols were being proposed as climate-forcing constituents. Charlson and others built a consensus that sulphate aerosols were, by themselves, cooling the Earth's surface by directly reflecting sunlight. Moreover, the increases in sulphate aerosols were anthropogenic and linked with the main source of CO2, burning of fossil fuels. Thus, the current picture of the atmospheric constituents driving climate change contains a much more diverse mix of greenhouse agents.

PAST CLIMATE OBSERVATIONS, ASTRONOMICAL THEORY AND ABRUPT CLIMATE CHANGES

Throughout the 19th and 20th centuries, a wide range of geomorphology and palaeontology studies has provided new insight into the Earth's past climates, covering periods of hundreds of millions of years. The Palaeozoic Era, beginning 600 Ma, displayed evidence of both warmer and colder climatic conditions than the present; the Tertiary Period was generally warmer; and the Quaternary Period showed oscillations between glacial and interglacial conditions. Louis Agassiz developed the hypothesis that Europe had experienced past glacial ages, and there has since been a growing awareness that long-term climate observations can advance the understanding of the physical mechanisms affecting climate change. The scientific study of one such mechanism – modifications in the geographical and temporal patterns of solar energy reaching the Earth's surface due to changes in the Earth's orbital parameters – has a long history. The pioneering contributions of Milankovitch to this astronomical theory of climate change are widely known, and the historical review of Imbrie and Imbrie calls attention to much earlier contributions, such as those of James Croll, originating in 1864.

The pace of palaeoclimatic research has accelerated over recent decades. Quantitative and well-dated records of climate fluctuations over the last 100 kyr have brought a more comprehensive view of how climate changes occur, as well as the means to test elements of the astronomical theory. By the 1950s, studies of deep-sea cores suggested that the ocean temperatures may have been different during glacial times. Ewing and Donn proposed that changes in ocean circulation actually could initiate an ice age. In the 1960s, the works of Emiliani and Shackleton showed the potential of isotopic measurements in deepsea sediments to help explain Quaternary changes. In the 1970s, it became possible to analyse a deep-sea core time series of more than 700 kyr, thereby using the last reversal of the Earth's magnetic field to establish a dated chronology. This deep-sea observational record clearly showed the same periodicities found in the astronomical forcing, immediately providing strong support to Milankovitch's theory.

Ice cores provide key information about past climates, including surface temperatures and atmospheric chemical composition. The bubbles sealed in the ice are the only available samples of these past atmospheres. The first deep ice cores from Vostok in Antarctica provided additional evidence of the role of astronomical forcing.

They also revealed a highly correlated evolution of temperature changes and atmospheric composition, which was subsequently confirmed over the past 400 kyr and now extends to almost 1 Myr. This discovery drove research to understand the causal links between greenhouse gases and climate change. The same data that confirmed the astronomical theory also revealed its limits: a linear response of the climate system to astronomical forcing could not explain entirely the observed fluctuations of rapid ice-age terminations preceded by longer cycles of glaciations.

The importance of other sources of climate variability was heightened by the discovery of abrupt climate changes. In this context, 'abrupt' designates regional events of large amplitude, typically a few degrees celsius, which occurred within several decades – much shorter than the thousand-year time scales that characterise changes in astronomical forcing. Abrupt temperature changes were first revealed by the analysis of deep ice cores from Greenland. Oeschger et al. recognised that the abrupt changes during the termination of the last ice age correlated with cooling in Gerzensee and suggested that regime shifts in the Atlantic Ocean circulation were causing these widespread changes. The synthesis of palaeoclimatic observations by Broecker and Denton invigorated the community over the next decade. By the end of the 1990s, it became clear that the abrupt climate changes during the last ice age, particularly in the North Atlantic regions as found in the Greenland ice cores, were numerous, indeed abrupt and of large amplitude. They are now referred to as Dansgaard-Oeschger events. A similar variability is seen in the North Atlantic Ocean, with north-south oscillations of the polar front and associated changes in ocean temperature and salinity. With no obvious external forcing, these changes are thought to be manifestations of the internal variability of the climate system.

The importance of internal variability and processes was reinforced in the early 1990s with analysis of records with high temporal resolution. New ice cores new ocean cores from regions with high sedimentation rates, as well as lacustrine sediments and cave stalagmites produced additional evidence for unforced climate changes, and revealed a large number of abrupt changes in many regions throughout the last glacial cycle.

Long sediment cores from the deep ocean were used to reconstruct the thermohaline circulation connecting deep and surface waters and to demonstrate the participation of the ocean in these abrupt climate changes during glacial periods.

By the end of the 1990s, palaeoclimate proxies for a range of climate observations had expanded greatly. The analysis of deep corals provided indicators for nutrient content and mass exchange from the surface to deep water, showing abrupt variations characterised by synchronous changes in surface and deep-water properties.

Precise measurements of the CH4 abundances in polar ice cores showed that they changed in concert with the Dansgaard-Oeschger events and thus allowed for synchronisation of the dating across ice cores. The characteristics of the antarctic temperature variations and their relation to the Dansgaard-Oeschger events in Greenland were consistent with the simple concept of a bipolar seesaw caused by changes in the thermohaline circulation of the Atlantic Ocean. This work underlined the role of the ocean in transmitting the signals of abrupt climate change.

Abrupt changes are often regional, for example, severe droughts lasting for many years have changed civilizations, and have occurred during the last 10 kyr of stable warm climate.

This result has altered the notion of a stable climate during warm epochs, as previously suggested by the polar ice cores. The emerging picture of an unstable oceanatmosphere system has opened the debate of whether human interference through greenhouse gases and aerosols could trigger such events. Palaeoclimate reconstructions cited in the FAR were based on various data, including pollen records, insect and animal remains, oxygen isotopes and other geological data from lake varves, loess, ocean sediments, ice cores and glacier termini. These records provided estimates of climate variability on time scales up to millions of years. A climate proxy is a local quantitative record that is interpreted as a climate variable using a transfer function that is based on physical principles and recently observed correlations between the two records.

The combination of instrumental and proxy data began in the 1960s with the investigation of the influence of climate on the proxy data, including tree rings, corals and ice cores. Phenological and historical data are also a valuable source of climatic reconstruction for the period before instrumental records became available.

Such documentary data also need calibration against instrumental data to extend and reconstruct the instrumental record. With the development of multi-proxy reconstructions, the climate data were extended not only from local to global, but also from instrumental data to patterns of climate variability. Most of these reconstructions were at single sites and only loose efforts had been made to consolidate records.

Mann et al. made a notable advance in the use of proxy data by ensuring that the dating of different records lined up. Thus, the true spatial patterns of temperature variability and change could be derived, and estimates of NH average surface temperatures were obtained. The Working Group I WGI FAR noted that past climates could provide analogues. Fifteen years of research since that assessment has identified a range of variations and instabilities in the climate system that occurred during the last 2 Myr of glacial-interglacial cycles and in the super-warm period of 50 Ma. These past climates do not appear to be analogues of the immediate future, yet they do reveal a wide range of climate processes that need to be understood when projecting 21stcentury climate change.

SOLAR VARIABILITY AND THE TOTAL SOLAR IRRADIANCE

Measurement of the absolute value of total solar irradiance is difficult from the Earth's surface because of the need to correct for the influence of the atmosphere. Langley attempted to minimise the atmospheric effects by taking measurements from high on Mt. Whitney in California, and to estimate the correction for atmospheric effects by taking measurements at several times of day, for example, with the solar radiation having passed through different atmospheric pathlengths. Between 1902 and 1957, Charles Abbot and a number of other scientists around the globe made thousands of measurements of TSI from mountain sites. Values ranged from 1,322 to 1,465 W m–2, which encompasses the current estimate of 1,365 W m–2. Foukal et al. deduced from Abbot's daily observations that higher values of TSI were associated with more solar faculae.

In 1978, the Nimbus-7 satellite was launched with a cavity radiometer and provided evidence of variations in TSI. Additional observations were made with an active cavity radiometer on the Solar Maximum Mission, launched in 1980. Both of these missions showed that the passage of sunspots and faculae across the Sun's disk influenced TSI.

At the maximum of the 11-year solar activity cycle, the TSI is larger by about 0.1 per cent than at the minimum. The observation that TSI is highest when sunspots are at their maximum is the opposite of Langley's hypothesis. As early as 1910, Abbot believed that he had detected a downward trend in TSI that coincided with a general cooling of climate.

The solar cycle variation in irradiance corresponds to an 11-year cycle in radiative forcing which varies by about 0.2 W m–2. There is increasingly reliable evidence of its influence on atmospheric temperatures and circulations, particularly in the higher atmosphere. Calculations with three-dimensional models suggest that the changes in solar radiation could cause surface temperature changes of the order of a few tenths of a degree celsius. For the time before satellite measurements became available, the solar radiation variations can be inferred from cosmogenic isotopes and from the sunspot number.

Naked-eye observations of sunspots date back to ancient times, but it was only after the invention of the telescope in 1607 that it became possible to routinely monitor the number, size and position of these 'stains' on the surface of the Sun. Throughout the 17th and 18th centuries, numerous observers noted the variable concentrations and ephemeral nature of sunspots, but very few sightings were reported between 1672 and 1699. This period of low solar activity, now known as the Maunder Minimum, occurred during the climate period now commonly referred to as the Little Ice Age. There is no exact agreement as to which dates mark the beginning and end of the Little Ice Age, but from about 1350 to about 1850 is one reasonable estimate. During the latter part of the 18th century, Wilhelm Herschel noted the presence not only of sunspots but of bright patches, now referred to as faculae, and of granulations on the solar surface.

He believed that when these indicators of activity were more numerous, solar emissions of light and heat were greater and could affect the weather on Earth. Heinrich Schwabe published his discovery of a '10-year cycle' in sunspot numbers. Samuel Langley compared the brightness of sunspots with that of the surrounding photosphere. He concluded that they would block the emission of radiation and estimated that at sunspot cycle maximum the Sun would be about 0.1 per cent less bright than at the minimum of the cycle, and that the Earth would be 0.1°C to 0.3°C cooler.

These satellite data have been used in combination with the historically recorded sunspot number, records of cosmogenic isotopes, and the characteristics of other Sun-like stars to estimate the solar radiation over the last 1,000 years. These data sets indicated quasi-periodic changes in solar radiation of 0.24 to 0.30 per cent on the centennial time scale. These values have recently been re-assessed.

The TAR states that the changes in solar irradiance are not the major cause of the temperature changes in the second half of the 20th century unless those changes can induce unknown large feedbacks in the climate system. The effects of galactic cosmic rays on the atmosphere and those due to shifts in the solar spectrum towards the ultraviolet range, at times of high solar activity, are largely unknown.

The latter may produce changes in tropospheric circulation via changes in static stability resulting from the interaction of the increased UV radiation with stratospheric ozone. More research to investigate the effects of solar behaviour on climate is needed before the magnitude of solar effects on climate can be stated with certainty.

7

Issues of Climate Change

AZOLLA EVENT

The Azolla event occurred in the middle Eocene period, around 49 million years ago, when blooms of the freshwater fern Azolla are thought to have happened in the Arctic Ocean. As they sank to the stagnant sea floor, they were incorporated into the sediment; the resulting draw down of carbon dioxide has been speculated to have helped transform the planet from a "greenhouse Earth" state, hot enough for turtles and palm trees to prosper at the poles, to the icehouse Earth it has been since.

GEOLOGICAL EVIDENCE OF THE EVENT

In sedimentary layers throughout the Arctic basin, a unit reaching at least 8 m in thickness is discernible. This unit consists of alternating layers; siliceous clastic layers representing the background sedimentation of planktonic organisms, usual to marine sediments, switch with millimetre-thick laminations comprising fossilised Azolla matter. This organic matter can also be detected in the form of a gamma radiation spike, that has been noted throughout the Arctic basin, making the event a useful aid in lining up cores drilled at different locations. Palynological controls and calibration with the high-resolution geomagnetic reversal record allows the duration of the event to be estimated at 800,000 years. The event coincides precisely with a catastrophic decline in carbon dioxide levels, which fell from 3500 ppm in the early Eocene to 650 ppm during this event.

AZOLLA

Azolla has been deemed a "super-plant" as it can draw down as much as a tonne of nitrogen per acre per year; this is matched by 6 tonnes per acre of carbon drawdown. Its ability to use atmospheric nitrogen for growth means that the main limit to its growth is usually the availability of phosphorus: carbon, nitrogen and sulphur being three of the key elements of proteins, and phosphorus being required for DNA, RNA and in energy metabolism. The plant can grow at great speed in favourable conditions – modest warmth and 20 hours of sunlight, both of which were in evidence at the poles during the early Eocene – and can double its biomass over two to three days in such a climate.

CONDITIONS ENCOURAGING THE EVENT

During the early Eocene, the continental configuration was such that the Arctic sea was almost entirely cut off from the wider oceans. This meant that mixing — provided today by deep water currents such as the Gulf Stream — did not occur, leading to a stratified water column resembling today's Black Sea. High temperatures and winds led to high evaporation, increasing the density of the ocean, and — through an increase in rainfall — high discharge from rivers which fed the basin. This low-density freshwater formed a nepheloid layer, floating on the surface of the dense sea. Even a few centimetres of fresh water would be enough to allow the colonization of Azolla; further, this river water would be rich in minerals such as phosphorus, which it would accumulate from mud and rocks it interacted with as it crossed the continents. To further aid the growth of the plant, concentrations of carbon and accessible nitrogen in the atmosphere are known to have been high at this time. Blooms alone are not enough to have any geological impact; to permanently draw down CO_2 and cause climate change, the carbon must be sequestered, by the plants being buried and eventually fossilised. The anoxic bottom of the Arctic basin, a result of the stratified water column, permitted just this: the anoxic environment inhibits the activity of decomposing organisms and allows the plants to sit unrotted until they are buried by sediment and incorporated into the fossil record.

GLOBAL EFFECTS

With 800,000 years of Azolla bloom episodes and a 4,000,000 km^2 basin to cover, even by very conservative estimates more than enough carbon could be sequestered by plant burial to account for the observed 80 per cent drop in CO_2 by this one phenomenon alone. This drop initiated a global temperature decline which continued for millions of years; the Arctic cooled from an average sea-surface temperature of 13 °C to today's “9 °C, and the rest of the globe underwent a similar change. For perhaps the first time in its history, the planet had ice caps at both of its poles. A geologically rapid decrease in temperature between 49 and 47 million years ago, around the Azolla event, is evident: dropstones — which are taken as evidence for the presence of glaciers — are common in Arctic sediments thereafter. This is set against a backdrop of gradual, long-term cooling: It is not until 15 million years ago that evidence for widespread polar freezing is common.

ALTERNATIVE EXPLANATIONS

While a verdant Arctic Ocean is a viable working model, sceptical scientists point out that it would be possible for Azolla colonies in deltas or freshwater lagoons to be swept into the Arctic Ocean by strong currents, removing the necessity for a freshwater layer.

BALI COMMUNIQUÉ

On 30 November 2007, the business leaders of 150 global companies published a communiqué to world leaders calling for a comprehensive, legally binding United Nations framework to tackle climate change.

The initiative represents an unprecedented coming together of the international business community and includes some of the biggest companies and brands from around the world, including the United States, Europe, Australia and China.

It has been led by The Prince of Wales's UK and EU Corporate Leaders Groups on Climate Change, which are developed and run by the University of Cambridge Programme for Industry.

It was hoped that the Bali Communiqué will have a significant impact on the UN climate negotiations starting on December 3, 2007 in Bali, Indonesia.

The Bali Communiqué calls for:

- a comprehensive, legally binding United Nations framework to tackle climate change
- emission reduction targets to be guided primarily by science
- those countries that have already industrialised to make the greatest effort
- world leaders to seize the window of opportunity and agree on a work plan of negotiations to ensure an agreement can come into force after 2012

THE BALI COMMUNIQUÉ

This communiqué comes from the business leaders of over 150 global companies. It is being issued in advance of the United Nations Climate Change Conference 2007, taking place from December 3 to 14 in Bali, Indonesia.

The scientific evidence is now overwhelming. Climate change presents very serious global social, environmental and economic risks and it demands an urgent global response.

As business leaders, it is our belief that the benefits of strong, early action on climate change outweigh the costs of not acting:

The economic and geopolitical costs of unabated climate change could be very severe and globally disruptive. All countries and economies will be affected, but it will be the poorest countries that will suffer earliest and the most.

The costs of action to reduce greenhouse gas emissions in order to avoid the worst impacts of climate change are manageable, especially if guided by a common international vision. Each year we delay action to control global emissions increases the risk of unavoidable consequences that will likely necessitate even steeper reductions in the future, causing potentially greater economic, environmental and social disruption. The shift to a low-carbon economy will create significant business opportunities. New markets for low-carbon technologies and products, worth billions of dollars, will be created if the world acts on the scale required. In summary, we believe that tackling climate change is the pro-growth strategy. Ignoring it will ultimately undermine economic growth.

It is our view that a sufficiently ambitious, international and comprehensive legally binding United Nations agreement to reduce greenhouse gas emissions will provide business with the certainty it needs to scale up global investment in low-carbon technologies. We believe that an enhanced and extended carbon market needs to be part of this framework as it offers the necessary flexibility, allows for a cost-effective transition and provides financial support to developing countries.

In order to avoid dangerous climate change, the overall targets for emissions reduction must be guided primarily by science. Even an immediate peaking in global emissions would require a subsequent reduction of at least 50 per cent by 2050, just as to the Fourth Assessment Report of the Intergovernmental Panel of Climate Change, and the later the peak in emissions, the greater the required reduction. All countries will need to play their part but we recognise that the greatest effort must be made by those countries that have already industrialised.

At the United Nations Climate Change Conference in December in Bali, Indonesia, countries will have an opportunity to agree a work-plan of comprehensive negotiations to ensure such an agreement can be signed in Copenhagen in 2009, to come into force after 2012.

We urge world leaders to seize this window of opportunity.

- In return, we pledge to engage positively with governments to help develop the policies and measures that are needed internationally and nationally for the business sector to contribute effectively to building a low carbon economy.

BALI ROAD MAP

After the 2007 United Nations Climate Change Conference on the island Bali in Indonesia in December, 2007 the participating nations adopted the Bali Road Map as a two-year process to finalizing a binding agreement in 2009 in Copenhagen. The conference encompassed meetings of several bodies, including the 13th Conference of the Parties to the United Nations Framework Convention on Climate Change and the 3rd Meeting of the Parties to the Kyoto Protocol.

The Bali Road Map includes the Bali Action Plan that was adopted by Decision 1/CP.13 of the COP-13. It also includes the Ad Hoc Working Group on Further Commitments for Annex I Parties under the Kyoto Protocol negotiations and their 2009 deadline, the launch of the Adaptation Fund as well as decisions on technology transfer and on reducing emissions from deforestation.

BALI ACTION PLAN

Pillars

The Conference of Parties decided to launch a comprehensive process to enable the implementation of the Convention through long-term cooperative action, now, up to and beyond 2012, by addressing:

- A shared vision for long-term cooperative action, including a long-term global goal for emission reductions.
- Enhanced national/international action on mitigation of climate change.
- Enhanced action on adaptation.
- Enhanced action on technology development and transfer to support action on mitigation and adaptation.
- Enhanced action on the provision of financial resources and investment to support action on mitigation and adaptation and technology cooperation.

Cutting emissions

The nations acknowledge that evidence for global warming is unequivocal, and that humans must reduce emissions to reduce the risks of "severe climate change impacts" and emhasized the urgency to address climate change. There was a strong consensus for updated changes for both developed and developing countries.

Although there were not specific numbers agreed upon in order to cut emissions, the Decision recognized that there was a need for "deep cuts in global emissions" and that "developed country emissions must fall 10-40 per cent by 2020".

Mitigation

Enhanced action on mitigation of climate change includes, inter alia:

- Nationally appropriate mitigation commitments or actions by all developed countries.
- Nationally appropriate mitigation actions by developing countries.
- Cooperative sectorial approaches and sector-specific actions.
- Ways to strengthen the catalytic role of the convention.

Forests

The nations pledge "policy approaches and positive incentives" on issues relating to reducing emissions from deforestation and forest degradation in developing countries; and enhancement of forest carbon stock in developing countries This paragraph is referred to as "REDD-plus".

Adaptation

The nations opt for enhanced co-operation to "support urgent implementation" of measures to protect poorer countries against climate change, including NAPAs. impacts.

Technology

In technology development and transfer, the nations will consider how to facilitate the transfer of clean and renewable energy technologies from industrialised nations to the developing countries.This includes, inter alia:

- Removal of obstacles to, an provision of financial and other incentives for, scaling up the development and transfer of technology to developing country Parties in order to promote access to affordable environmentally sound technologies.
- Ways to accelerate the deployment, diffussion and transfer of such technologies.
- Cooperation on research and development of current, new and innovative technology, including win-win solutions.
- The effectiveness of mechanism and tools for technology cooperation in specific sectors.

Finance

Provision of financial resources and investment includes:

- Improved access to predictable and sustainable financial resources and the provision of new and additional resources, including official and concessional funding for developing country Parties.
- Positive incentives for dcP for national mitigation strategies and adaptation action.
- Innovative means of funding for dcP that are particularly vulnerable to the adverse impacts of climate change in meeting the costs of adaptation.
- Incentivisation of adaptation actions on the basis of sustainable development policies.
- Mobilization of funding and investment, including facilitation of climate-friendly investment choices.
- Financial and technical support for capacity-building in the assessment of costs of adaptation in developing countries, to aid in determining their financial needs.

AD HOC WORKING GROUPS

The Conference decided establish a subsidiary bodies under the Convention to conduct the process, the Ad Hoc Working Group on Long-term Cooperative Action and the Ad Hoc Working Group on Further Commitments for Annex I

Parties under the Kyoto Protocol, that were to complete their work in 2009 and present the outcome to the COP15/MOP 5. The Group must develop its working programme in its first session in a coherent and integrated manner.

The AWG-LCA and AWG-KP presented draft conclusions to COP15 and CMP5, which contained many unresolved issues. These working groups are now due to report to COP16 and CMP6 in Mexico.

TIMESCALES

Four major UNFCCC meetings to implement the Bali Road Map were planned for 2008, with the first to be held in either March or April and the second in June, with the third in either August or September followed by a major meeting in Poznan, Poland in December 2008. The negotiations process was scheduled to conclude at the United Nations Climate Change Conference 2009 in Copenhagen, Denmark.

BALTICCLIMATE

BalticClimate is the acronym for the project "Baltic Challenges and Chances for local and regional development generated by Climate Change". It was approved in October 2008 in the first Call of the "Baltic Sea Region Programme 2007-2013", a programme financed from the European Regional Development Fund, the European Neighbourhood and Partnership Instrument, the Norwegian national funding as well as by own contributions by the project partner institutions. The lead partner of BalticClimate is the Academy for Spatial Research and Planning Germany.

Within the project lifetime of November 2008 until April 2012 BalticClimate is implemented by 23 official project partner institutions and 16 associated organisations from 8 countries of the Programme area. The project focuses on supporting regions, municipalities as well as cities in the Baltic Sea Region to pro-actively deal with the issue of climate change.

BIO-ENERGY WITH CARBON CAPTURE AND STORAGE

Bio-energy with carbon capture and storage is a greenhouse gas mitigation technology which produces negative carbon emissions by combining biomass use with geologic carbon capture and storage. It was pointed out in the IPCC Fourth Assessment Report by the Intergovernmental Panel on Climate Change as a key technology for reaching low carbon dioxide atmospheric concentration targets.

The negative emissions that can be produced by BECCS has been estimated by the Royal Society to be equivalent to a 50 to 150 ppm decrease in global atmospheric carbon dioxide concentrations and just as to the International Energy Agency, the BLUE map climate change mitigation scenario calls for more than 2 gigatonnes of negative emissions with BECCS in 2050.

The concept of BECCS is drawn from the integration of biomass processing industries or biomass fuelled power plants with carbon capture and storage. BECCS is a form of carbon dioxide removal, along with technologies such as biochar, carbon dioxide air capture and biomass burial.

NEGATIVE EMISSION

The main appeal of BECCS is in its ability to result in negative emissions of CO_2. The capture of carbon dioxide from bioenergy sources effectively removes CO_2 from the atmosphere.

Bio-energy is derived from biomass which is a renewable energy source and serves as a carbon sink during its growth. During industrial processes, the biomass combusted or processed re-releases the CO_2 into the atmosphere. The process thus results in a net zero emission of CO_2, though this may be positively or negatively altered depending on the carbon emissions associated with biomass growth, transport and processing. Carbon capture and storage technology serves to intercept the release of CO_2 into the atmosphere and redirect it into geological storage locations. CO_2 with a biomass origin is not only released from biomass fuelled power plants, but also during the production of pulp used to make document and in the production of biofuels such as biogas and bioethanol. The BECCS technology can also be employed on such industrial processes.

It is argued that through the BECCS technology, carbon dioxide is trapped in geologic formations for very long periods of time, whereas for example a tree only stores its carbon during its lifetime. In its report on the CCS technology, IPCC projects that more than 99 per cent of carbon dioxide which is stored through geologic sequestration is likely to stay in place for more than 1000 years. Compared to other types of carbon sinks such as the ocean, trees and soil, the BECCS technology is likely to provide a better permanence.

GEOENGINEERING

The ability of stratospheric sulfur aerosols to create this global dimming effect has made them a possible candidate for use in geoengineering projects to limit the effect and impact of climate change due to rising levels of greenhouse gases. Delivery of precursor gases such as H_2S and SO_2 by artillery, aircraft and balloons has been proposed.

Understanding of this proposed technique is partly based on the fact that it is the adaptation of an existing atmospheric process. The technique is therefore potentially better understood than are comparable geoengineering schemes. It is also partly based on the speed of action of any such solution deployed, in contrast to carbon sequestration projects such as carbon dioxide air capture which would take longer to work. However, gaps in understanding of these processes exist, for example the effect on stratospheric climate and on rainfall patterns, and further research is needed.

This technique has been studied more extensively than most other geoengineering techniques, and is suggested by commentators including Tom Wigley.

SHIP TRACKS

Ship tracks are clouds that form around the exhaust released by ships into the still ocean air. Water molecules collect around the tiny particles from exhaust to form a cloud seed. More and more water accumulates on the seed until a visible cloud is formed. In the case of ship tracks, the cloud seeds are stretched over a long narrow path where the wind has blown the ship's exhaust, so the resulting clouds resemble long strings over the ocean.

In 1965, the first "anomalous cloud lines" were observed in images from the TIROS VII satellite. It was hypothesized that the most likely cause was from the exhaust from ships. Many studies since have confirmed the cause, and they are now referred to as ship tracks. Scientists soon realized that the climatic impacts from aerosols could have a large effect on climate through the indirect effect, and that ship tracks provided an excellent laboratory for their studies.

Scientists who study how human-produced aerosols affect cloud formation observe ship tracks because in most urban areas, they are unable to discern exactly how pollutants contribute to forming clouds because the atmosphere over the land is too tumultuous. In contrast, ships release their exhaust into the relatively clean and still marine air, where the scientists have an easier time of measuring the effects of fossil fuel emissions on cloud formation.

In general, the air above the oceans suffers from less turbulence and convection than the air above land. The lower atmosphere is especially calm over the eastern Pacific in the summertime due to a layer of hot air that settles in 500 to 700 meters above that region of the ocean. This effect creates a temperature inversion, placing a cap on the cooler air below, trapping pollutants and water vapor. While the inversion is responsible for the smog that reduces air quality in Los Angeles, it also allows for the formation of long lasting ship tracks. The particles billowing from ships' smokestacks enter the air above the eastern Pacific and create long, thin clouds that remain there for days.

It is theorised that sulfur dioxide released from ships' smokestacks could be forming sulfate aerosol particles in the atmosphere, which cause the clouds to be more reflective, carry more water and possibly stop precipitating. This is regarded as proof that humans have been creating and modifying clouds for generations through the combustion of fossil fuels.

Although ship tracks can sometimes be visible, researchers usually scan the near-infrared light coming off the clouds. At this wavelength many ship tracks appear as bright lines that can be distinguished from the surrounding, uncontaminated clouds. On average, polluted clouds reflect more sunlight than their unaffected counterparts. When compared to normal clouds, the number of water droplets per volume of air in ship tracks are more than doubled, the radius of the drops is decreased by roughly six percent and the total volume of liquid water per volume of air is increased twofold. In other words, this excessive cloud seeding from the ship causes the clouds to retain more water.

Normally, rain forms when cloud drops coagulate and reach a size where gravity can pull them to the ground. Yet, in ship tracks, the cloud seeding made the drops so small that they could no longer easily merge together to reach the size needed to escape. Since no drizzle comes out of the seeded clouds, the liquid water just keeps building in the cloud. This makes the cloud brighter and more reflective to incoming sunlight, especially in the near-infrared part of the spectrum.

ATTRIBUTION OF RECENT CLIMATE CHANGE

Attribution of recent climate change is the effort to scientifically ascertain mechanisms responsible for recent changes observed in the Earth's climate. The effort has focused on changes observed during the period of instrumental temperature record, when records are most reliable; particularly on the last 50 years, when human activity has grown fastest and observations of the troposphere have become available. The dominant mechanisms to which recent climate change has been attributed all result from human activity. They are:

- increasing atmospheric concentrations of greenhouse gases
- global changes to land surface, such as deforestation
- increasing atmospheric concentrations of aerosols.

Attribution of recent change to anthropogenic forcing is based on the following facts:

- The observed change is not consistent with natural variability.
- Known natural forcings would, if anything, be negative over this period.
- Known anthropogenic forcings are consistent with the observed response.
- The pattern of the observed change is consistent with the anthropogenic forcing.

Recent reports from the Intergovernmental Panel on Climate Change have concluded that:

- "Most of the observed increase in globally averaged temperatures since the mid-20th century is very likely due to the observed increase in anthropogenic greenhouse gas concentrations."; It is extremely unlikely that the global pattern of warming during the past half century can be explained without external forcing and very unlikely that it is due to known natural external causes alone. The warming occurred in both the ocean and the atmosphere and took place at a time when natural external forcing factors would likely have produced cooling.
- "From new estimates of the combined anthropogenic forcing due to greenhouse gases, aerosols, and land surface changes, it is extremely

likely that human activities have exerted a substantial net warming influence on climate since 1750."

- "It is virtually certain that anthropogenic aerosols produce a net negative radiative forcing with a greater magnitude in the Northern Hemisphere than in the Southern Hemisphere.

The panel defines "very likely," "extremely likely," and "virtually certain" as indicating probabilities greater than 90 per cent, 95 per cent, and 99 per cent, respectively.

KEY ATTRIBUTIONS

Greenhouse Gases

Scientific consensus has identified carbon dioxide as the dominant greenhouse gas forcing. Methane and nitrous oxide are also major forcing contributors to the greenhouse effect. The Kyoto Protocol lists these together with hydrofluorocarbons, perfluorocarbons, and sulphur hexafluoride, which are entirely artificial gases which also contribute to radiative forcing in the atmosphere. The chart at right attributes anthropogenic greenhouse gas emissions to eight main economic sectors, of which the largest contributors are power stations, industrial processes, transportation fuels, and agricultural by-products.

Land use

Climate change is attributed to land use for two main reasons. While 66 per cent of anthropogenic CO_2 emissions over the last 250 years have resulted from burning fossil fuels, 33 per cent have resulted from changes in land use, primarily deforestation.

Deforestation both reduces the amount of carbon dioxide absorbed by deforested regions and releases greenhouse gases directly, together with aerosols, through biomass burning that frequently accompanies it. A second reason that climate change has been attributed to land use is that the terrestrial albedo is often altered by use, which leads to radiative forcing. This effect is more significant locally than globally.

Livestock and Land use

Worldwide, livestock production occupies 70 per cent of all land used for agriculture, or 30 per cent of the ice-free land surface of the Earth. More than 18 per cent of anthropogenic greenhouse gas emissions are attributed to livestock and livestock-related activities such as deforestation and increasingly fuel-intensive farming practices. Specific attributions to the livestock sector include:

- 9 per cent of global anthropogenic carbon dioxide emissions
- 35–40 per cent of global anthropogenic methane emissions

- 64 per cent of global anthropogenic nitrous oxide emissions, chiefly due to fertilizer use.

Aerosols

With virtual certainty, scientific consensus has attributed various forms of climate change, chiefly cooling effects, to aerosols, which are small particles or droplets suspended in the atmosphere. Key sources to which anthropogenic aerosols are attributed include:

- biomass burning such as slash and burn deforestation. Aerosols produced are primarily black carbon.
- industrial air pollution, which produces soot and airborne sulfates, nitrates, and ammonium
- dust produced by land use effects such as desertification

ATTRIBUTION OF 20TH CENTURY CLIMATE CHANGE

Over the past 150 years human activities have released increasing quantities of greenhouse gases into the atmosphere. This has led to increases in mean global temperature, or global warming. Other human effects are relevant—for example, sulphate aerosols are believed to lead to cooling—and natural factors also contribute. The historical temperature record of the last century, the Earth's near-surface air temperature has risen around 0.74 ± 0.18 °Celsius.

A historically important question in climate change research has regarded the relative importance of human activity and non-anthropogenic causes during the period of instrumental record. In the 1995 Second Assessment Report the IPCC made the widely quoted statement that "The balance of evidence suggests a discernible human influence on global climate". The phrase "balance of evidence" suggested the common-law standard of proof required in civil as opposed to criminal courts: not as high as "beyond reasonable doubt". In 2001 the Third Assessment Report refined this, saying "There is new and stronger evidence that most of the warming observed over the last 50 years is attributable to human activities". The 2007 fourth assessment report strengthened this finding:

- "Anthropogenic warming of the climate system is widespread and can be detected in temperature observations taken at the surface, in the free atmosphere and in the oceans. Evidence of the effect of external influences, both anthropogenic and natural, on the climate system has continued to accumulate since the TAR."

Over the past five decades there has been a global warming of approximately 0.65 °C at the Earth's surface. Among the possible factors that could produce changes in global mean temperature are internal variability of the climate system, external forcing, an increase in concentration of greenhouse gases, or any combination of these. Current studies indicate that the increase in greenhouse gases, most notably CO_2, is mostly responsible for the observed warming. Evidence for this conclusion includes:

- Estimates of internal variability from climate models, and reconstructions of past temperatures, indicate that the warming is unlikely to be entirely natural.
- Climate models forced by natural factors and increased greenhouse gases and aerosols reproduce the observed global temperature changes; those forced by natural factors alone do not.
- "Fingerprint" methods indicate that the pattern of change is closer to that expected from greenhouse gas-forced change than from natural change.
- The plateau in warming from the 1940s to 1960s can be attributed largely to sulphate aerosol cooling.

DETECTION VS. ATTRIBUTION

Detection and attribution of climate signals, as well as its common-sense meaning, has a more precise definition within the climate change literature, as expressed by the IPCC.

Detection of a signal requires demonstrating that an observed change is statistically significantly different from that which can be explained by natural internal variability.

Attribution requires demonstrating that a signal is:

- unlikely to be due entirely to internal variability;
- consistent with the estimated responses to the given combination of anthropogenic and natural forcing
- not consistent with alternative, physically plausible explanations of recent climate change that exclude important elements of the given combination of forcings.

Detection does not imply attribution, and is easier to show than attribution. Unequivocal attribution would require controlled experiments with multiple copies of the climate system, which is not possible. Therefore, attribution can only be done within some margin of error. For example, the IPCC's Fourth Assessment Report says "it is extremely likely that human activities have exerted a substantial net warming influence on climate since 1750," where "extremely likely" indicates a probability greater than 95 per cent.

Following the publication of the Third Assessment Report in 2001, "detection and attribution" of climate change has remained an active area of research. Some important results include:

- A review of detection and attribution studies by the International Ad Hoc Detection and Attribution Group found that "natural drivers such as solar variability and volcanic activity are at most partially responsible for the large-scale temperature changes observed over the past century, and that a large fraction of the warming over the last 50 yr can be attributed to greenhouse gas increases. Thus, the recent research supports and strengthens the IPCC Third Assessment Report conclusion that 'most of the global warming over the past 50 years is likely due to the increase in greenhouse gases.'"

- Multiple independent reconstructions of the temperature record of the past 1000 years confirm that the late 20th century is probably the warmest period in that time
- Two documents in the journal Science in August 2005 resolve the problem, evident at the time of the TAR, of tropospheric temperature trends. The UAH version of the record contained errors, and there is evidence of spurious cooling trends in the radiosonde record, particularly in the tropics.
- Barnett and colleagues say that the observed warming of the oceans "cannot be explained by natural internal climate variability or solar and volcanic forcing, but is well simulated by two anthropogenically forced climate models," concluding that "it is of human origin, a conclusion robust to observational sampling and model differences"

Bibliography

Puran Chandra: *Determinants of World Politics*, Akansha Pub, 2004.

T.K. Balakrishanan: *Globalisation of World Politics* , Mohit Publications, 2012.

Hartmut Elsenhans and Amrjit S. Narang, Rajendra K. Jain: *The European Union in World Politics*, Radiant Pub, 2006.

Rameshwar Prasad: *The Impact of Air Power : National Security and World Politics*, Cyber Tech Pub, 2012.

Giulio M. Gallarotti: *The Power Curse : Influence and Illusion in World Politics*, Viva Books, 2011.

Sujatha Ramcharit, Kanishka: *United Nations and World Politics*, Viva Books, 2011.

Deepika Jha: *Women in World Politics*, Pearl Books, 2010.

Puran Chandra: *World Politics : Theories and Approaches*, Akansha, 2004.

M.K. Singh: *World Politics : Theory and Practice*, Sumit Enterprises, 2010.

Eva Pfoestl: *Between Ethics and Politics*: *Gandhi Today*, Routledge India, 2013.

Ghanshyam Shah: *Caste and Democratic Politics in India*, Orient Blackswan Publications, Delhi, 2004.

Ghanshyam Shah: *Caste and Democratic Politics in India*, Permanent Black Publications, Delhi, 2002.

Gyanendra Nath Aryal and Binaya Adhikari: *An Introduction to Nepal and Contemporary Nepalese Politics*, Awareness Forum for Development, 2008.

Harish Sharma: *Communal Angle in Indian Politics*, Rawat Publications, Delhi, 2000.

Ian Bryant Wells: *Ambassador of Hindu-Muslim Unity*: *Jinnah's Early Politics*, Permanent Black Publications, Delhi, 2005.

Jacques Pouchepadass: *Champaran and Gandhi*: *Planters, Peasants and Gandhian Politics*, Oxford University Press, 1999.

Jagannath P. Panda: *China's Path to Power: Party, Military and the Politics of State Transition*, Pentagon Publications, Delhi, 2010.

Jagdish Kumar: *Communal Politics In the Punjab*, Unistar Books, Chandigarh, 2010.

Jagpal Singh: *Capitalism and Dependence: Agrarian Politics in Western Uttar Pradesh 1951-1991*, Manohar Publications, Delhi, 1992.

James Leigh and Predrag Vukovic: *Beyond Oil Bust: Investigating Oil Economics Society and Geopolitics*, Atlantic Publications, Delhi, 2011.

Jari Kupiainen, Erkki Sevanen and John A. Stotesbury: *Cultural Identity in Transition: Contemporary Conditions, Practices and Politics of a Global Phenomenon*, Atlantic Publications, Delhi, 2004.

Jaya Arunachalam and U. Kalpagam: *Development and Empowerment: Rural Women in India*, Rawat Publications, Delhi, 2006.

Joyce L. Rahim and Enayetur Rahim: *Bengal Politics: Documents of the Raj, Vol. I.*, Univ. Press, 1996.

Judith Bara and Mark Pennington: *Comparative Politics*, Sage Publications, Delhi, 2009.

Jyotsana Sharma: *Backward Caste Politics: A Study in Socio-Political Mobility*, Satyam Publications, Delhi, 2006.

K. Vidyasagar: *Communist Politics in India: Struggle for Survival*, Academic Excellence Publications, Delhi, 2005.

K.M. Ashraf: *An Overview of Indian Muslim Politics*, Manak Publications, Delhi, 2001.

Index